To. Dear Alan.

Wishing You a Very Happy Xmas.

Fondest love.

Cookie - George.

Xmas. 1974.

THE ILA-SPEAKING PEOPLES OF
NORTHERN RHODESIA

KAKUA, A BAMBALA CHIEF.
(See Vol. I. p. 77.)

THE
ILA-SPEAKING PEOPLES
OF
NORTHERN RHODESIA

BY

EDWIN W. SMITH
HONORARY CHAPLAIN TO THE FORCES
FELLOW OF THE ROYAL ANTHROPOLOGICAL INSTITUTE
AUTHOR OF "A HANDBOOK OF THE ILA LANGUAGE," ETC.
CHIEF TRANSLATOR OF THE NEW TESTAMENT IN ILA

AND

ANDREW MURRAY DALE
MAGISTRATE IN THE BRITISH SOUTH AFRICA COMPANY'S ADMINISTRATION

Θεστορίδη, θνητοῖσιν ἀνωίστων πολέων περ
οὐδὲν ἀφραστότερον πέλεται νόου ἀνθρώποισιν.
HOMER.

IN TWO VOLUMES
VOL. II

UNIVERSITY BOOKS   New Hyde Park, New York

CONTENTS

PART IV

CHAPTER XX

CHAPTER XXI

CHAPTER XXII

CHAPTER XXIII

PART V

CHAPTER XXIV

CONTENTS

ILLUSTRATIONS

PART III—(*continued*)

CHAPTER XVIII

*

FROM BIRTH TO PUBERTY

1. PREGNANCY

To have children, and many of them, is one of the great ambitions of our natives. Any man will tell you that to leave children, especially sons, when he departs from this earth is one of the greatest desires of his heart. He who fails in this respect is regarded by others, and he regards himself, as something less than a man. When he dies they cut off his little finger and little toe, and enclose a piece of charcoal in his fist, before burying him. Their reason for doing this is obscure. They suppose that it will either prevent his being reborn, or if it fails to that extent, at least they will be able to recognise him by the absence of those members should he return to earth. To avoid this indignity it is incumbent upon every man to try every possible means to have children. Thinking that the fault is in his wife, if she fails to bear children after trying a course of treatment by the doctors skilled in that branch of medicine, he will either divorce her or marry other women. If still no offspring come he will be told that the fault is his own, and he also will seek drugs. If no favourable result follows he has to reconcile himself to disappointment and to the jokes, if not contempt, of his fellowmen and wives. A barren woman is also despised. They will say of her, "*Wakatuluka izhadilo*" (" She had her womb pierced," *i.e.* by too frequent illicit intercourse). Sometimes, when there is no result, the people of the husband and wife meet and offer a prayer to Leza ; saying, " Give this child of ours a child."

Sons are preferred to daughters, because through sons the family is continued, *i.e.* a man cannot be reborn on earth through his daughter, only through his son. The children, sons and daughters, take the mother's clan name, but it is not her people, it is the father's people, that are born in her sons. Girls are regarded as riches only, *i.e.* as so many cattle to the credit of the clan's account.

In the ordinary course of things a woman is expected to conceive very soon after marriage. If she goes three months without doing so, her people will seek medicine *owa kwimita* (" for conception "), and the doctor gives her a potion to drink each day.

A woman accepts the sign of the cessation of the menses. She may not, if it is her first child, inform her husband of the fact. Nor may the husband ask his wife if such is the case. She goes home and tells her mother; the mother tells the woman's father, who first sends to the husband asking for a spear or hoe or shell. By this the husband recognises what is in the wind, and gladly sends what is asked for. Then they tell him. The woman may tell her husband in subsequent pregnancies, but he is not allowed to mention the fact to others. The news is not told outside the family, except to the doctor, through fear that somebody by ill-practices may cause a miscarriage. Should any one break the custom by asking a woman if she is pregnant, and should a miscarriage follow, or the child die, that person has committed a great fault and has to pay damages. They say he or she has *milọmo mibiabe* (" evil lips "), and has bewitched the child. If any one asks the husband, he will deny his wife's condition; even if it be evident to all he will profess ignorance. Nor may people mention the fact in conversation before the husband or any relation of the woman.

The woman is taken to the doctor who is told of her condition. He prepares a charm which is put around her waist and gives her a small pot in which medicine has been placed. He then gives her various instructions as to her conduct during the time of pregnancy, warning her especially against those things and actions that are taboo.

The woman is taboo : her condition makes her a source

of danger to the community. Especially is she liable to injure the new life developing within her womb. The husband, from his close connection with her, is also taboo. Strict rules are therefore laid down to avoid any evil consequences that may come from these dangerous persons; above all, nothing must be done to prejudice the well-being of the unborn child.

The injunction as to silence which we have already noted is for the good of the child. Other *mitondo* ("taboos") are as follows. There are things she may not eat. Above all, blood is bad for her and bad for the child; if she eats it she will suffer severely at her confinement and the child may die. She must therefore abstain from eating the flesh of animals, lest there be any blood left in it. The exception made is the flesh of hippopotamus, though why, it is hard to say, for the hippopotamus has plenty of blood. The barbel fish when fresh is taboo to her for the same reason, but may be eaten dried.

There are some foods that are *tonda* to the husband as well. Neither husband nor wife may eat flesh of hartebeest, the reason given being that that animal gives birth to its young blind; and if they eat of it their child will be born blind.

Neither of them, again, may eat *makwelekwele, i.e.* the flesh of an animal that has been torn and pulled about by birds. The reason given is that *avhwe wazhoka mwifu bubona mbu bakwelakwela bazune* ("when the child is about to come out it will return into the womb, just as the birds pull about the meat").

They must not eat the goose, lest the child should have a long neck like a goose.

The wildebeest is said to occupy a long time in parturition; and the flesh of it is taboo to husband and wife lest by eating it they should cause a protracted confinement to the woman.

Food cooked the day before and left over (called *chidyo ch'ona* or *chidyo cha mulala*) is forbidden lest the confinement be lengthy.

The woman may not sleep in the daytime lest her child should be dull and sleepy-headed.

She must be careful not to cross the spoor of a bushbuck, nor if she can avoid it must it cross hers ; in either case the result to the child will be fatal. This taboo applies also to a nursing mother.

She must avoid looking upon unpleasant objects for fear of damaging her child. For instance, Mrs. Smith was examining once a hawk that had just been shot, when two women approached. One of them had no sooner caught sight of the dead hawk than she pushed the other (who was pregnant) away, saying, " Don't look ! Don't look ! " and the woman ran away.

It is *tonda* to both husband and wife to go and take a look into a house and then withdraw without entering. It is *tonda* for any one to do the same at the woman's door. The reason is that it may lead the child also to *sumba*, *i.e.* to act in a similar way when it comes to be born. And for either of them to go in and out of the hut as if not knowing their own minds, is also *tonda*, lest the child should act similarly in birth.

Intercourse between husband and wife is not *tonda* during the early months of pregnancy. Indeed it is regarded as conducive to the child's welfare. During the last month or so, however, all this must cease lest the child be killed. As they say, "*Ulamutulula a lubwebwe*" ("He would pierce the child's fontanelle ").

The woman is forbidden to have connection with other men, and any man who assaulted her would be liable to heavy damages. She may not sit on others' beds or stools, nor sit with *bakwakwe* (" her relations-in-law "), nor with her lover, nor may she sport with men. She is *tonda*. She on her part might do them mischief, and they might blight the unborn child.

The husband *watonda ku mwinakwe* ("is taboo on account of his wife "). He, in her interest and in that of the child, may not have intercourse with other women, except his other wives if he is a polygamist, may not sit on other people's stools nor lie on their beds.

·   Of a hunter it is said, " *Mwinakwe wemita wakeka kuyaya banyama kambo ka mamba* " (" He stops killing game because of the wars "). Whether it means that by going hunting

he will bring an injury upon the wife or the child, or whether
the pregnancy of the woman means he will have no luck,
is not clear to us ; but he finds a way out of the difficulty
whichever it may be. *Wachita busongo* they say ("He
acts wisely"). He goes out as usual and on reaching a
place where the roads divide (*a masanga a nzhila*) he calls
out, "*Na mwinangu udimishi mukaintu n'ashale a munzhi
akudima budio ; na mulombwana atuende, tukaweze*" ("If
my wife be pregnant of a woman let her (*i.e.* the child)
stay at the village and hoe, if it be a man let us (*i.e.* he
and the boy) go on the hunt"). Having said this he goes
on and kills game : but if he does not say it he may not,
or will not kill: as they say, "*Pele atachita bobo udi mukaintu
wemita tayaya munyama, pe*" ("But if he did not act thus he
who has a pregnant wife would not kill an animal").

*Mulier pregnans vaginam distendere manibus conatur,
quas suco aloarum inunguit. Os vaginae eo usque expandere
iubetur dum pugnus suus facile inseri possit.* She must
also take care not to allow the cold to reach her, and to
this end must always wear a piece of cloth or other covering
between the legs. Unless this is done the child may die.

In the fifth month the woman goes home and is given
medicine. She is given an *insungu* ("medicine receptacle")
and a basket to cover it. A three-pronged stick (*chango*)
of the *mufumu* tree is planted at the head of her bed and
the *insungu* placed in the fork. Into the *insungu* is placed
the medicine mixed with light beer (*ibwantu*), or, in the
absence of light beer, with water. This *insungu* must
never be left uncovered, but as soon as some of the medicine
has been taken out of it the basket must be replaced over
it. This medicine is *tonda* ; it must on no account be given
to others, and is to be drunk by the husband and wife only.
Should any one steal and drink it, *uladitaya, i.e.* he commits
buditazhi against the owners. The two continue to drink
this medicine until the child is born ; its purpose is to give
them both strength. The man is said to drink because
shilwazhi sha mulumi shilakasha mukaintu kutumbuka
("diseases in the husband would prevent the woman from
giving birth").

Other medicine is given to people outside, the purpose

being thus stated : *ati bakatole shilwazhi akatumbuke kabotu* (" so that they may take away the diseases in order that the woman may give birth properly ").

There is thus, in the thoughts of the people, a sympathetic connection between father, mother, even the neighbours, and the unborn child, so that to secure the child's well-being they must all be free from sickness.

The *insungu* in which their medicines have been kept is also in sympathetic connection with the child. After the child is born the mother or father returns the *insungu* to those who gave it to them, and makes them a present of a hoe or some beads. The *insungu* is then carefully preserved inviolate : it may not be used for any such base purpose as drawing water, *ilatonda* (" it is taboo "). *Yafwa ati ulafwa mwana, yafwa mukaintu ulaba namatezi, kambo kako ilazobolwa insungu ukwabo* (" If it dies (*i.e.* is broken) it means that the child will die ; if it is broken the woman will become a Namantezi, *i.e.* a woman whose children all die, and for that reason it is preserved at her home ").

Abortion is regarded with horror ; the woman is in a state of uncleanness and is a distinct danger to the community. She is therefore isolated and treated in the manner shown in the following account :

" If a woman becomes pregnant but plays the harlot by having converse with other men, then she aborts. When she has aborted they build her a shelter out west, and there she has to remain all the time of her uncleanness. After a time, they prepare medicine for her, putting it into a basin, that she may wash with it every day. Her food she has to cook in potsherds. When it is over, her mother seeks medicine for the return to the village, and all the people wash in that medicine. When she enters the village she gives the medicine to all that are in the village and they drink it, which means that the abortion (*kasowe*) shall not stick to them. And the woman when she enters her house, she and her husband may not come together before she has been with other men. On her return from the other men, then they come together as man and wife. This is the affair of a woman who has aborted."

2. BIRTH

The people do not seem to have accurate ideas as to the time of gestation. One of our most intelligent informants, himself a married man, put it at twelve months; some women we have known to make it ten months. This is perhaps hardly to be wondered at when we remember the uncertain way in which they reckon time.

It is taboo for a woman to give birth in a hut; were she to do so and the child be born dead, she would suffer heavy penalties: her husband might, unless they were redeemed by her clansmen, enslave her and her children. All grain and medicines in the hut would have been contaminated, and hence would be destroyed.

When the woman feels that her time is drawing near she goes to her home. The birth takes place either in a shelter some distance from the house, or on the verandah of the house, a space being enclosed with mats for the purpose. Other women come to help. There are those who have the reputation of being skilled in midwifery, and a woman who is known to have medicine for use in some irregularity may be specially called in should occasion arise. Owing to their hardy manner of living, their freedom from constricting garments, and the smallness of the children's heads, the birth is usually unattended with serious complications, and the woman quickly resumes her usual life in the community. To those accustomed to the usages of civilisation it comes as a shock to see a woman rise up and carry her child, half-an-hour old, back to the house from a shelter in the forest. But deaths do occur. Such a complication as a transverse presentation often proves fatal. They claim to have medicine to administer to the patient; and there are midwives who will, after bathing their hands in certain medicines, endeavour to turn the child, but often without success. There is a complication called *Kavhwi kakosoka* (" the breaking of the *Kavhwi* "), which is said to be fatal, but we are not sufficiently acquainted with anatomy to say what the *Kavhwi* is.

As men are not allowed to be present on such occasions, we cannot describe at first-hand the procedure at a birth;

but we have the advantage of notes prepared for us by two ladies who have attended and watched cases.

When a woman is about to become a mother and the first pains of confinement are felt, she is given an infusion made from the roots of the castor-oil plant. This she drinks from time to time until the child is born. During the first pains she may lie down if she gets tired, but she is not allowed to lie for long and has to get into a sitting position now and again. When the last pains arrive she sits all the time and is not allowed to lie down on any account, as doing so might kill the child. Generally two women attend her. During the first pains one woman supports her back while the other holds her knees, which are drawn up close to the body. When the strong pains come on, the woman who is supporting the knees puts her feet close together and presses the patient's buttocks, and the woman who was supporting the back comes in front and puts a strong long piece of cloth round the loins of the patient and holds the two ends. *Quotienscunque dolor acrior incessit, mulier ea quae ex adverso consedit, pedibus suis parturientis poplites premit, simul maximo pedis pollice anum eius occludens; velut interdum fit, anulum ad id factum impositumque adprimens. Haec ideo faciunt ne quid excrementi parturiens remittat; quod si accidit, parturientem destitui mos non vetat.* The woman with the two ends of the cloth in her hands pulls with all her strength. This goes on until the child is born. If the woman gets impatient or expresses a wish to stand or lie down, or groans or complains, she is spoken to very roughly, told she will be thrashed, accused of wanting to kill her child, and generally treated like a naughty, disobedient youngster. When the child is born, the cord (*ludila*) is tied once and then cut. As they are doing this the women sing a little song; the first words coming from the woman or women sitting by, and the last, as a refrain, from the woman actually cutting.

Uteend'anji! Nyama!   ("Do not travel elsewhere!   Meat!")

If the afterbirth does not come away at once, the patient is given a medicine to drink, made from the roots of the *mukonono* tree. The root is roasted on the embers, then put in water. If this is not efficacious, two leaves of the same tree are taken and inserted in the woman. The hands are then put in, the placenta grasped and pulled out.

We have the following account from Mrs. Price. It describes what happened at the birth of Lissie's child at Nanzela, July 1913 :

"When I arrived the child was already born and was lying on its left side on the mud floor of the hut, but the afterbirth had not yet come away. The mother was sitting on a bit of rag on the floor with her head against Matsediso. Marta several times put three fingers into the mother's throat to make her heave, the idea seeming to be that this would help the afterbirth to come away. Afterwards Lissie knelt (the afterbirth being then halfway out) leaning on her hands, and the afterbirth came away. She was then given hot water, in which bark of some tree had been boiled, to drink. This was for the *ifu* ('womb'). Then Matsediso gave her a kind of warm watery gruel to drink. The child was lying on the ground all this time with the cord still attached. The woman sat a while talking, the mother sitting up all the time, naked with the exception of a bit of twisted calico around her abdomen. This she had asked for as her *ifu* hurt her. The women sat a while and seemed to be looking for something with which to cut the cord. Marta went out and found an old penknife and also a piece of old dirty rag about six inches long. This they twisted to tie the cord with. Each seemed afraid to perform the operation : first Marta and then Galassi essaying to do it. Galassi then took out of the wall where the earth had broken away a thick reed, and broke off a piece about three inches long and laid it under the cord ; then she took the knife, drew it across once, and as she did so all together sang in monotone. They cut across four times before it was through, singing all the time. Another woman took the child on her knee. Marta took a calabash, smashed the top and made the broad part into a bath. Into this they put hot water, and the woman who held the child dipped a hand into it and washed the blood from the child. Then Lissie washed her breasts in the same water. Then the woman holding the child, still sitting, jerked it towards the east, and then towards the west, head foremost each time, and as she did so all the women in the hut lululooed and clapped very loudly. Then all shouted ' *Ezeulu* ' (' Up '), and as she shot the child up all shouted praises to the wife of Petrose who had borne a child. Then all thanked her : *Ndalumba chinichini usunu mb'uwazhala mwana* (' I give much thanks to-day that you have given birth to a child '). Marta got a stick and scraped the earth from a rat-hole in the hut to about 9 inches deep. Lissie edged off the rag on which she had been sitting on to bare earth and Marta scraped it into the hole with a stick. Then Lissie took hold of the afterbirth with the right hand (the hole was towards the left) and dropped it into the hole. Immediately the woman holding the child cried out, ' *Ndapenga, ndapenga, weh !* ' (' I am troubled, I am troubled, oh dear ! '). Whispering among the women, then Lissie carefully laid hold of the afterbirth and straightened it out, half turning it over. Then Marta covered it with earth. Then a skin of an animal was spread out, one end over the place where the afterbirth was buried ; Marta's clothes were made into a bundle for a pillow, the child was put down beside the mother and both blankets thrown over them. The child was not put to the breast."

The afterbirth is buried in the hut. There would seem, from several phrases in the above account, to be some mysteries attached to the afterbirth ; but we have not been able to investigate them. The caul also, if there is one, is buried in the hut.

After the confinement, the woman goes back into her house and stays there for some time, six days at least.

All the time of her pregnancy there have been dangers surrounding her ; hence the precautions we have described. And now the child is born, care is taken to fend off from it perils of a mystical kind. After the birth and for several days the child is given a concoction made of the leaves of the castor-oil plant as a preventive against the malign influence of pregnant women. And a string, made of palm-leaf, is suspended on poles in front of the hut to give warning, especially to those same women. This is *kukobaika ingozhi* (" to fend off by means of string "). A pregnant woman must on no account come to the hut lest the child *ulafwa luvhumwe na imamba* ("should die of *luvhumwe* or wars"). *Luvhumwe* is the condition of something split or parted asunder. If a pregnant woman passes through a calabash garden, the calabashes will all drop off their stalks or split; if she passes a tree laden with fruit, the fruit will fall to the ground; if she passes near a litter of pups their heads will split and they will die; if she passes a hen sitting on a nest of eggs, they will all crack. This is *kufwa luvhumwe*: in the same way, were she to enter a hut where there is a baby its skull would part asunder.

The mother is not absolutely secluded from the world during the days of retirement. After the birth, her husband may go and see her and offer his congratulations, taking presents of beads or hoes to his parents-in-law. And her male relations may enter the hut, clap their hands to her, and give her bracelets or leglets by way of congratulation.

A person who has had sexual intercourse the night previous may not enter; he or she is called a *Shimalo*.

When the woman emerges from her seclusion, the father ties a string of beads on the child's wrists and legs, and takes and nurses it in his arms. By so doing he acknowledges the child to be his. And the relations come to congratulate the parents; but every one who approaches the child is more or less under suspicion. Unless they give the child a small present they are not allowed to take it in their arms, lest they should *tensha* it, *i.e.* hinder its growth.

On coming out from her hut, the woman takes an *insungu* and places it by the door. Those who pass in or out must jump over it, *batole shilwazhi shivhwe ku mwana* ("that they may take away the diseases, so that they may leave the child"). When the day gets warm they carry the *insungu* outside; and the mother pouring some of the contents into her hand, first makes the child drink some of it and then sprinkles some *a lubwebwe, a mozo* ("on the fontanelle, on the heart"). Then she washes it all over. This done, the *insungu* is taken back into the hut. This is done every day until the child becomes a *mupumpula*, *i.e.* about three years old. The medicine is named *Isamba-bacheche* (" the babies' washer ").

A woman who has recently given birth is called a *Mutumbu* (*kutumbuka,* "to give birth"). Artificial feeding is of course a thing unknown to the Ba-ila. The nursing period lasts two or three years. Very early the mother's milk is supplemented by porridge. The child is running about long before it is weaned. The weaning must take place at a new moon. If there is any difficulty in the matter, the mother rubs a little nicotine from her pipe on the nipples.

The *Mutumbu* has to avoid many things; they are *tonda* to her, lest harm should come to the child she is nursing. Among these things we find the following:

It is *tonda* for her to come out of her house very early in the morning. The reason given is that she may step on the footprints of the nocturnal animal *shibandilwabana,* which, as we saw in Chapter X., is very maleficent to children. By her waiting indoors until there are many people moving about, it is hoped that the baneful influence attending the footprints may be obliterated.

She is forbidden to eat *inshima ya kubwenga,* lest she should have the milk in her breasts dry up.

It is *tonda* for her to drink cold water; should she drink, either she or the child will die—perhaps both.

It is *tonda* for her to sit on the beds of married people. Should she do so, the child will *manuka mu chamba, ulafwa,* (" will get sick in the chest and die ").

It is *tonda* for her to strip; for should she do so and any one should happen to see her, the child would waste away.

Above all, the woman is *tonda* to all men, her husband included. The reason for this is that she might conceive, and the drain upon her system would be bad alike for the child living and the child unborn. Should she break this taboo and conceive, she would be despised by other women. Such cases do happen and then the women often secure abortion by taking medicines.

Not until the milk is dried up in her breasts may her husband resume cohabitation with her.

Others say that the taboo extends to the time when the child's teeth are grown. If she has intercourse before then, they say, " *Mwana wamusotoka. Atafwamba kuleta musamo wafwa* " (" She has jumped over the child ; it will waste away, and unless they quickly doctor it, it will die ").

3. CHILD LIFE

Ba-ila children are most delightful little creatures : so weirdly solemn at times and then changing so rapidly into romping, laughing little rascals. Even to those whom the

Photo E. W. Smith.

FOUR BA-ILA CHILDREN.

adults fail to attract, but rather inspire with feelings of disgust or contempt, the sight of the little children rolling about in their play brings a warming of the heart.

The saddest thing about the child life is the considerable mortality. It is only the hardiest that can survive the way they are treated. If love were synonymous with intelligent care of the children then indeed there would not be so many die, but the mothers are woefully ignorant of sanitary rules. On a hot day a woman goes to her field with her baby slung on her back in a skin ; she works while the baby dozes with only its head visible above the skin. When it wakes up and cries the mother finds a shady place, takes the baby out dripping with perspiration, and proceeds to nurse it. A cool wind is blowing and the child lies naked with no protection. Then they wonder that the child catches cold and is carried off by pneumonia. Again, the women have no idea of cleaning out a baby's mouth : you rarely find one with a clean mouth. It drinks at all times ; when-

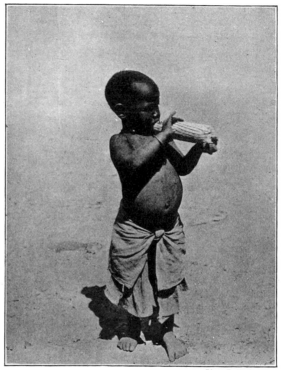

Photo E. W. Smith.

ENJOYING HER BREAKFAST.

ever it cries it is put to the breast. Indigestion inevitably results. Another deleterious practice is to cover the head of the child with a fatty mess, and undoubtedly the pressure on the brain is often disastrous. Nor is the beer given to the young babies a good thing for them.

These are only examples of the disregard of hygienic principles. We find it impossible to calculate the proportion of dead to living children. It is reckoned *tonda* to question

a woman as to the number of her children, and we have
therefore failed to estimate the extent of infant mortality ;
but we know it to be very great. As we have seen in another
chapter, some children are destroyed at or shortly after
birth, but the numbers so disposed of, even in the older
times, were small compared to those who died of sickness.
Mrs. Smith, who has had the longest experience of any
lady among the Ba-ila, thinks that fully seventy per cent
of the children die.

In the tsetse-fly districts the number is even larger,
owing to the absence of milk. We have even heard the
figure ninety per cent given. It is not at all uncommon
to find young women who have borne four or five children,
not one of whom is living. Nothing, we may say here, has
so commended the Christian religion to the Ba-ila as the
fine healthy families reared by the converts.

We shall describe in a later chapter the games of the
children. Their life is not all play. The young girls are
early made to help their mothers in looking after the baby
and other domestic duties. They are taught to carry
burdens upon their head, such as pots of water and bundles
of firewood, and this practice undoubtedly is one cause of
the splendid figure and upright carriage a girl develops.
The boys too have their duties : while still young they are
set to herd goats or sheep and later the calves. It is a proud
day for the lad when he goes out with young men to herd
the cattle. The boys, too, do much of the milking.

There is a system something like that of fagging in
English public schools. Under this the boys have to do a
great many services for their elder brothers and their friends.
Indeed we sometimes think that the Ba-ila never work so
hard as when they are boys. Of the men we may say, as
a Spanish Ambassador once said of the Irish : " *La gente
is muy olgazana, enemiga de trabagar* " (" The people are
lazy and do not like work "). They seem to think that
they did enough while they were boys, and are now glad
to make their juniors do as they themselves had to do.
At the same time, Ba-ila childhood is not burdensome but
happy. While they are made to work there are not so
many restrictions upon them as obtained in our own

boyhood. There are no worries about clothes and keeping clean ; and there is no school to creep unwillingly to in

Photo E. W. Smith.

GIRLS CARRYING WATER.

the morning.[1] Indeed it would be better for the people if children were treated with rather less lenity. Children are largely exempt from punishment. A mother rarely beats

[1] At least this is true where there are no mission schools in the neighbourhood : as yet, there are all too few of them.

her child. If a girl refuses to stamp grain the mother eats alone without offering any to her. Similarly, if she refuses to fetch water she must go thirsty. If in drawing water she breaks a calabash, the mother quietly sends her a longer distance with a new and perhaps larger one. But parental discipline extends no further.

"*Lemeka kana ako kakulemeke*," says the proverb ("Honour a child and it will honour you"), and it is interpreted to mean that you must not be severe with them, however naughty. Children are precious in their eyes, and they are constantly haunted by the idea that the child may make up its mind to return to the spirit world whence it came, if it is not treated properly.

Ba-ila children, like children perhaps all the world over, are intimidated by means of awesome bogeys. "*Utakudila, ulakuluma Pompo*," one may hear a mother say to a child ("Do not cry, or Pompo will bite you!"). Shezhimwe—Pumpa—Shilombamudilo—Momba—there is quite an array of these fearsome creatures.

We may mention here some of the taboos imposed upon children. There are some things that are regarded as dangerous for them to eat. Boys and girls may not eat fat, for it is said *adïa mafuta alabavhwa ku bulombwana o ku bukaintu* ("the fat will pour out at the genital organs"). Eggs are forbidden on the plea that they will stop up the passages of the genitalia. For the same reason *mukamu*, bread made of sorghum grains, is *tonda*, and also *katongola*, a kind of ground-nut. They may not eat the unground grains of corn, lest they should sprout and block the passages. *Bufufu*—meal made by splitting the grain in a certain way—is also taboo; should they eat it they would split at the genitals, just as the grain is split to make *bufufu*. The fish called *Inkungwe, Mazanzhi*, and *Shimulele* are also *tonda* because of their softness: should a girl eat them her children when she grows up would be soft like them, and a boy would be afflicted with softness in the pudenda. Girls may not eat the root called Miseza, for it is said *n'adipena wakadya miseza mushimbi ulakupuluka mashino* "*Ubi vagina distendi coepta erit (id quod infra descriptum est) pudendi labiae destringentur*" (see p. 20). It is also said that they would *puka mu shibelo* ("have the skin of their thighs peel off"). Young girls are forbidden to touch the *miandu* drums used in connection with the initiation ceremonies. Children must never say, "*Ndasata chibunu*" ("I have a pain in my loins"); if they do, their elders may die.

4. INITIATION

The boys and girls thus develop until the time when they think, and their elders think, they should become men and women. The passage from childhood to adolescence lies through the initiation ceremonies, three of which fall to be described here: *Kudivhunga, Kuzaluka*, and *Kushinga*. The first is practised by the Nanzela people; the second by the Ba-ila proper; the third by both. In the nature of things, we have been unable to witness much that we now describe, but have done our best to get information from reliable sources. A girl before initiation is *mushimbi* (plural, *bashimbi*); afterwards she is called *kamwale* (plural, *bakamwale*).

(a) Kudivhunga

Some time during the wet season the young girls (*bashimbi*) in a village get together and make up their minds that it is time for them to be initiated into womanhood. So they go out and look for a *munto* bush, around which they scuffle a clear space. That night they sleep at home but at dawn arise, unfasten their scanty clothing, and throw it on the roof of their parents' hut. They go off naked to the *munto* bush and lie around it, curling themselves up (*badivhunga*), whence the name of the proceedings. In the morning their mothers discover the clothes on the roofs and know that their girls have entered upon their initiation. They go off to find them and on coming upon them start lululooing. It is a glad day to them. They dress the girls in new clothes, and dance from the morning till the afternoon. As the sun is declining they pick up the girls, put them on their shoulders, and carry them back to the village. There they are all put into one hut, where they have to stay.

They also choose out a young boy, called *shakamwale*
(" master of the
maidens "), who is
put into the same
hut and has to be
treated with respect
by the girls.   Food
is taken to them, but
before eating they
must close their eyes
while the *shakamwale*
eats first. In the day-
time a shady place is
sought for them in
the fields among the
grain, and there they
sit with their *shaka-
mwale*. He keeps on
the look-out ; if he
sees any one ap-
proaching he gives
warning and the girls
must cover their
heads.   To be un-
covered in the pres-
ence of an outsider
would result in their
wasting away.   Any
one thus discovering
the girls will plague
them : a man will
give them a beating
with a stick ; a
woman will pinch
them on the thighs ;
but they must en-
dure the pain without

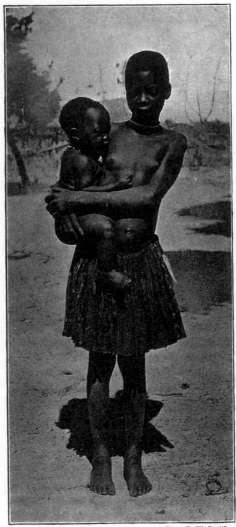

Photo E. W. Smith.

A YOUNG NURSE.

either speaking or crying.   It is *tonda* to utter a sound ; if
they did people would exclaim, " What sort of a *kamwale*
will this be who speaks to people ! "   During the day they

are occupied in weaving mats and baskets   When darkness falls they steal back to their hut, all covering their heads. In the hut they may not sleep on a bed, but on the ground, or under the bed.

After a time the parents and relations of the girls bring fowls and meat and other things as a preparation for a dance : this is called *kuhololwa*.   They invite the dancers of the *Kashimbo* dance and the players of the *mwandu* drums to assist them, and the dance is kept up through the night.   These assistants are rewarded (*balatailwa*) with beads, tobacco, and spears.   Another month passes away and they dance again.

All the time the girls are in the initiation hut they are being instructed ; that is to say, they teach each other what they know, and an old woman is called in as their *mubudi* (" instructress ").   There where they sit in the veld they put themselves through several operations which they think will prepare them for marriage.   *Baladichita misamo ku bukaintu, baladipena o kudieleka chinkodi chepopwe, na mufuma owa chikampe cha musekese, ati babone sena mulombwana akabatwale ulayana musena :* " *Genitalibus medicinas applicant, rimam pudendi distendentes, metientesque vel spica farris quod vocatur Indiani, vel arboris fetu quam musekese vocant, id sciscitantes num, si nubant, viro aditum sat largum praebiturae sint.*"   They do this for ten or twenty days, " when they find they have grown and become women," as our informant says.   The old woman with them gives them many instructions as to their conduct when married.   She holds one by the ear, to secure proper attention, and says : " A man has to be reverenced and well looked after in the house ;   your parents-in-law also."   The girl is not supposed to speak, but to nod her head to signify her assent.

A third month passes and now the girls' relations brew great quantities of beer and lay in a stock of other things for a feast.   They levy contributions on all the girls' clansmen, so that they may worthily feast the dancers.   When the brew is ready the feast is held.   The girls are anointed with fat, dressed, and decorated.   After the people have danced the girls come out.   Before doing so they are given

their final lessons and among other things are told always
to reverence the *munto* bush, under which they curled themselves up ; and also the *shakamwale* boy—respecting him
and obeying him in all things.

Coming out of the hut thus attired in their best, they
are the centre of admiration ; the news goes through the
country that the daughters of So-and-so have passed
through the initiation, and are now women.

When in seclusion in the house the girls are made to
play the *Indavu* (*kupwa indavu*). They sit round with a
number of pieces of broken pot and play as in the game of
" Five stones." They also play the *mantimbwa* and sing
songs, such as this :

> *Namunkulungu tobele musamo,*
> *Muntembwe ndo, muntembwe ngu musamo.*
> (" *Namunkulungu* is not the medicine,
> *Muntembwe,* my dear, *muntembwe* is the medicine ").

(b) Kuzaluka

The principal difference between the Balumbu custom
described above and that of the Ba-ila proper is in the time
of the ceremony. At Nanzela it takes place before the
first menstruation, and girls believe that if they do not go
through it they never will menstruate. On the other hand,
the Ba-ila defer their ceremony until the first menstruation
has taken place. A secondary difference, following on this,
is that at Nanzela the girls enter in company ; while among
the Ba-ila each girl goes through the rite of initiation alone.

Among the Ba-ila, when a girl first menstruates, she
must keep quiet about it. If she were to mention it the
women would say : " *Mwaniche chilatonda checho. Mukoa
ako ulamana kufwa* " (" Child, that is taboo ; all your clan
will die "). The women discover it by examining the
girl's clothes ; then they say to her, " You have menstruated " ; and they take hold of her and dance. It is
a great occasion to them. The mother, it is said, weeps on
hearing the news ; probably because it means that she will
soon lose her daughter. But in another respect she is glad,
because now her child has grown up. All the girl's clansmen share in the rejoicing, saying, " *Mwanesu wakomena* "

("Our child has grown up"). They take the *Mwandu* and
dance. Before the dance is commenced the girl's father
formally presents the men with a hoe and asks them to
dance for his daughter. The girl is now secluded in a hut.
To amuse herself she is told to play the *indavu*, as described
below. A round hole is dug by the mother of the girl close
to the bed; this is called the *Mulao*. Broken pieces of
pottery are placed around the edge of the hole; the girl
takes one of these pieces, throws it into the air, and while

Photo E. W. Smith.

A GIRL PLAYING THE *MANTIMBWA.*

it is in the air she knocks one of the other pieces into the
mulao, catching the piece she has thrown up as it comes
down. If she knocks in two pieces, the women who are
standing by, teach her. This is her occupation during the
seclusion; *ngu mudimo wakwe* ("it is her work"). She
also plays the *mantimbwa*. She sits on the ground with a
pot between her legs, with knees drawn up. The *mantimbwa*
consists of two bows; the end of one is placed on one
shoulder, the end of the second on the other; the other
ends of the bows resting on a basket covering the pot.
The bows are kept in position by a stick which passes over
the middle of the bow under the string and held under the

knees. She plays the instrument with her fingers   The *mantimbwa* is brought to the initiate by her betrothed husband.   At the same time, he brings a *mwana wa chisamo* ("a wooden doll"), which he has decorated with strings of beads. The *mantimbwa,* and, some say, the doll, must be made of *munkulungu* wood, though why nobody can tell.   The betrothed husband is accompanied by a woman bearing the name that he will give the girl after marriage ; together they are admitted into the initiation hut, but may not see the girl.   These two after presenting the things they have brought must sit down and have a game of *indavu* together, taking every care that the *impwisho*, the stones thrown up, do not fall on the ground ;

Photo E. W. Smith.

A BA-ILA DOLL.

for should that happen the man would have to pay a fine.

This seclusion lasts two or three months.   The girl may not be seen by any man during this period.   She is carried out well covered up to answer the calls of nature and does not leave the hut for any other purpose.

Sometimes when paying a visit to a village, you may see several figures, with covered heads, come creeping

stealthily out of the grass towards the huts, one of them
bearing a burden on her back. It is the initiate and her
attendants.

We were once invited to enter a hut in which one of
these girls was being initiated, but there was very little to
see. The girl herself we were unable to catch a glimpse of,
as she was under the bed in the inner chamber, which was
in utter darkness. It is there she has to spend most of
her time. As our eyes became accustomed to the gloom of
the outer room we could distinguish the forms of several
women. One, the girl's maternal aunt, was sitting near
the door leading into the inner chamber. She had between
her legs a large earthenware pot, covered with a piece of
dressed skin ; in one hand she was grasping loosely a reed
standing upright on the skin ; the other hand she dipped
into water and drew up and down along the reed : the
vibration caused a deep harsh sound. This is the *mwandu*,
the instrument consecrate to the initiation ceremonies.
Two girls were sitting on the ground near by, with a pot
between them ; each had a long hollow reed, with one
end resting on the rim of the pot ; down the other end
they blew, making a noise. If you ask the meaning of these
things, the reply is that they are to amuse the girl lying
there in the darkness.

When staying in a village you may see a party of women
dressed up and going from *mukobo* to *mukobo* dancing.
They enter the cattle-kraal, and, standing in a circle outside
the inner fence in front of the principal hut, they dance.
The wives of the headman join in, singing and dancing for
a few minutes, and the party goes on its way. This is a
little diversion in honour of the girl passing through the
rites.

Some time early in the period the young man comes
again with his friends, and they join with the villagers in
dancing the *Chululu*. An ox is killed and consumed, together
with much beer. This feast lasts one night.

Towards the end of the period the impatient man
begins to worry the girl's relations to get the initiation
completed. " I want my wife to come from under the bed,"
he says. They put him off as long as possible, and at last

consent that on a certain day she shall emerge. Great preparations are now made for the *Chisungu*, as the final feast is named. Before the girl may leave the hut, however, she has to be given final instructions as to her future conduct as a wife. Here is an account we have received of the teaching given : " They seek out an old woman to teach the girl, and give her things, a hoe, or ten strings of beads. Then she begins to instruct her, saying, ' So-and-so, you are to be married. Remember that a man is to be obeyed, and his food cooked. And when people come to pay a visit, do not hide your face, but receive them warmly and hospitably. When you have people in the house, treat them kindly. And if your mothers-in-law send you on an errand be quick in starting ; they are to be honoured ; food is to be ground for them, water drawn for them, and they are always to be answered respectfully. And in your house, things are to be done nicely ; the pots are to be kept clean and in good condition, and the house is to be swept within. And your husband is to be obeyed implicitly and not answered angrily. When you are married, do not act childishly ; you are to provide food. Oh woman, cook well and do not spoil the food ; you are to be perfect in cooking. The husband too must be cleansed and washed[1], after his pubic hair has been plucked out. And so on and so on, for a day or two before the close of the seclusion. The girl is also anointed with butter, dressed in a new *lechwe* skin, and ornamented with beads. etc., to enhance her beauty

On the day appointed, the young man and his friends arrive at the village, and all the other guests assemble. On entering the courtyard the young man, or his companions, plant a spear upright in the ground, and are given in return a present named *Chikwatamasumo*, which may take the form of an ox or something else of value. The *Chisungu* is kept up for two or three nights and days, and is the occasion for much unbridled licence.

The cattle killed, or given, during these ceremonies have special names. The first one killed is provided by the father and is named *chululu* ; the second one, provided by the father

---

[1] This term, kusansumuna, signifies a custom that requires the wife, after coitus, to wipe off from her husband's body every drop of semen, however small it may be.

when the beer is brewed, is *ing'ombe ya kusotoka* ("the jumping-over ox ") ; at the same time he kills one called *ankalisho*. The ox, provided by the father, exchanged for tobacco and given to the friends of the husband, is called *ing'ombe ya banamusela*. The *ing'ombe ya mukako* is given to the girl's mother : the *ing'ombe ya muchizhi* is given to whoever cooked for the girl in her retirement. These last two are provided by the husband's people. Another calf is given by the father to the husband and called *wakusangana tuntu tutonda* (" for to abolish the taboo things ").

Some time during the proceedings the girl's clansmen bring an ox and stuff things down its throat, or close up its mouth and nostrils with clay, in order to kill it without a sound. Should it succeed in making a sound it means bad luck or death to the father. When the ox is dead the clansmen leave and the girl comes out and jumps twice over the ox ; or if she is unable to jump the father takes her on his shoulder and jumps over with her. This is evidently a symbolic act. It signifies that the girl has now passed over from childhood to womanhood.

After the *Chisungu*, among the Ba-ila, the marriage follows immediately. It involves the taking of the girl away from her home to her future husband's (for marriage is patrilocal), often to a village some distance away. She must be carried, however far it may be ; the bridegroom may not help in the carrying, nor may he see her on the road : that is taboo. We have often seen these processions : perhaps on a very hot day have seen one of a company of men struggling along, with the perspiration rolling down him, under the burden of a well-favoured damsel. This carrying may be regarded as the first marriage rite and what follows we must leave for the next chapter.

Menstruation Taboos

Here we may describe some of the taboos imposed upon the woman during the time of the menses. To menstruate is *kusea* and the woman is called *Namusea*. She is spoken of euphemistically as being *kumbadi* (" in retreat "), and *uina matashi* (" having no hands ").

She is a dangerous woman, and must be separated as far as possible from contact with her fellows.

She may not enter a hut in which people are sitting who have " eaten medicine " ; if she must enter, they have first to come out.   It is taboo for her to eat in company. Were she to eat in company with a man he would lose his virility.   If he went from that place into the veld and started to run, he would have something burst within his chest and would die.   Should she venture to sleep on her husband's bed, she would incur his righteous indignation and be made to pay damages : it would be reckoned *buditazhi* by some. She may not sit near people, lest there should be mutual injury.   For if the shadow of any man whatsoever falls upon the wife, the belief prevails that his outward flow (effluence) will always persist, with the result that she will shortly die from this taint.   She must have nothing to do with the common fire, but must light one for her own use.   She must not handle other people's pots, nor eat out of their basins, nor drink out of their cups, nor smoke their pipes.   She may not cook food for anybody, nor draw water for another.   If she sleeps in her hut, it must be on the floor.   She may not enter a village other than her own.   She may not wear nice clothes.   For five days is she *tonda* ;   then she washes and may rejoin her fellows.

It is evident from this that there is something about the woman that is dangerous ;   moreover, her condition lays her open to receive malign effluence from others.

That she is dangerous is shown also in the procedure with regard to a person called an *Imbala*.   He is a man that is wasting away.   Nothing seems to stop the emaciation. Then they say there is a *musangushi* (" ghost ") taking away his flesh.   They put him into a hut and young girls enter and kindle a new fire for him.   No menstruating woman must enter, for she is particularly dangerous to him.

But the mysterious radiation from her, that ordinarily is so baneful, may be made use of.   It is believed that if tsetse fly invade a district they can be driven away by the menstruating women going and sitting where they are and allowing themselves to be bitten.   One of our friends was told by natives that a certain fly-infested road was now free because so many women had passed along it.

(c) The Boys' Initiation: Kushinga

The boys go to their elders and say: " Take us to the cattle outpost and let us *shinga, i.e.* be initiated." So next day they take them there and they sleep. In the morning they milk the cows. Then all the herdsmen take sticks, lumps of dry dung, and stones, and line up outside the cattle-kraal, the cattle having already come out. The boys have then to dart out one by one and run the gauntlet of the

Photo E. W. Smith.

A GROUP OF BA-ILA BOYS IN FRONT OF AN ANT-HILL.

men, who beat them with the sticks and pelt them with the lumps and stones. The goal which the boys must reach is the bull of the herd, and until they succeed in striking the bull they continue to be beaten. Once a boy has touched the bull he is free. The boys then take the cattle to pasture. They return in the evening. They may not dress nor sleep on a bed.

When the unsatisfying evening meal, consisting of some very sour milk, is over, the men devote an hour or two to disciplining the boys: the Ila word is *kukoma*. Whatever they are told to do, they must respond with alacrity or they are thrashed unmercifully. " Fight!" say the men, and the boys must take sticks and belabour each other, or grapple and wrestle. Any one not entering heartily into it is abused as a coward by the men and beaten. " *Zhana !* " say the men, and the boys leave the fighting and dance. Names of various dances are shouted and they must instantly change their steps accordingly, or the stick descends upon them. " Dance as your mothers dance. . . . Dance as your fathers dance. . . . Dance the *mwandu* as your mothers dance . . ." and so on. Then other orders. " Grind corn as your mothers grind," and the boys have to flop down on their knees, and go through the action of grinding corn between two stones. They have to be quick about it too. Other things follow. The boys are initiated into the use of the genital organs and are required to imitate coitus with each other, and are also bidden to masturbate. The men exhaust their rich vocabularies of abuse upon the boys—all the *matuski* they can think of. They may not show the slightest resentment at any of this treatment, or it will be the worse for them.

Next morning, early at dawn, they are sent to the water to bathe. It is bitterly cold and they creep shivering back to the kraal ; but if they attempt to warm themselves at a fire they are driven away, and have to crouch naked and get warm as best they can. No bread is given them to eat, but only very sour milk, *mabishi alula*. For two days this is done. On the third day they take out the cattle to herd ; when the sun reaches that point which is called *Akabonzhabeembezhi* (" when the herdboys are tired "), *i.e.* about 3 P.M., they bring back the cattle near to the kraal, and then run off home, naked as they are. Reaching the village they sit outside and call aloud for something to wear, and when this is brought them they enter.

Like the girls, the boys have their private operations to perform to fit them for marriage, the chief business of life. We give here a literal translation of an account of these dictated to us by an intelligent native :

" They also (*i.e.* the boys) sit in like manner and look for medicines at the village ; medicines for *difuka* and for drinking, and for the first semen, and for to make them strong, and for enlarging, and for blowing into themselves.

To *fuka* himself, he takes a certain bush [1] and on making incisions into it a juicy substance flows out; this he rubs on the scrotum morning and evening. He goes to the meeting of the roads and leaves the medicine, burying it in the ground and covering it with a piece of pot; then people jump over it, saying, 'May this boy soon know his testicles.' The medicine for strengthening is drunk; he does not know the plant it comes from, but is simply given it by the elders. The medicine of the first semen (*shitompo*) is to be drunk, it is the root of the mubanga tree. He cooks it three times; at the fourth he puts in white meal of the first grinding and cooks it with an axe; when he has done cooking he eats some of the porridge, and the rest he puts into his small calabash; at dawn he drinks; only he climbs up on his bed and drinks standing, before the flies have come to sit upon his body. The medicine for enlarging is the same Mufufuma, the roots. He digs a small hole at the threshold and buries there the medicine root. Early in the morning he duly digs out this root and rubs it a number of times in ashes. Then he spreads it all over his penis, he evidently thus hopes that the member will grow and swell like the root itself. From this same root a poison is prepared. It is crushed and reduced to a powdery form. Then through a tiny reed it is blown into the orifice of the member. By this means it is assumed that any malignant element is eliminated from the member. After a time when he has finished these medicines, he seeks that of the first pubic hairs (*koza ka chisokwe*), dry small sticks of the Mupazopazo tree; he digs a little hole and plants over it a small platform; then he makes fire by friction; when the fire has burnt down he has to take the ash of the fire which he made and rub it on the pubic bone to pluck out the first hairs there. He does this till it is quite clean. He does not leave even one little bit of a hair, because if he were to leave one it would break off, and he would become lame, swell at the knees, and be without strength. Having done this, he runs off to the river to bathe. And, again, there where he plucked out the hair, he will not pass again, lest the hair should return to him which he plucked out there.

" Also they take away the fraenum. They tie tightly

[1] The Mufufuma, see Vol. I. p. 254.

the hair of a wildebeest, and after a whole day and night it cuts through."

The initiation proceedings, then, are to serve two purposes : first, to harden the boys and teach them to endure pain without complaint ; second, to prepare them for their manly functions.   There is a third thing which cannot be passed over lightly, namely, the better kind of instruction the boys receive from their elders during the time.   We cannot vouch for the universality of this instruction among the people ; it may take different forms, be less or more in different districts ; but such as we have learnt from men of the teaching they received we transcribe here.   It will be seen that moral teaching of a high character is mixed up with other things not so admirable.

We have three accounts of the teaching, and will give them just as they were communicated to us.[1]

The first man said : " I was taught not to curse my elders, nor the initiator who is called *mulumi* (' husband ') ; to be humble before my *mulumi* and listen to all he told me, not transgressing one of his commands, for they were to me as the words of God ; to go where I am sent and go willingly ; always to take of the spoils of my hunting to my *mulumi*, even were it far away I must go ; always to be ready to assist him in his work ; not to be afraid of approaching his wife,[2] and if ever I found another man with her to thrash him, or if unable to do that at least to inform her husband of the fact ; but I was not to eat in her presence unless I had given her a bracelet."

The second man said : " He told me : ' Now you are grown, honour your elders.   If you find anything on the path, or meat, give it to any of your companions who are older than you ; it is not good for them to ask you for it. While you are still young you must not stand near your elders who are discussing affairs.   If your friend is a thief and he asks you to go and look at things not your own you must refuse.'   I was told wisdom as to sleeping at my *mulumi's*.   (*Ndakashimwinwa busongo bwa kuteba ku*

---

[1] See W. Chapman, *A Pathfinder in Central Africa*, pp. 334 sq.

[2] The initiate sleeps with the wife of his *mulumi* about five nights, and may always cohabit with her if invited, even until and after he is married.

mulumi angu.)   He said : 'Beware of other people's things, even if it be a child's ; people will curse me because I have not taught you wisdom if you do not respect all the things of other people.   Honour all the people of the community, especially your chief.   If you are travelling with an elder in the road help him with the things he is carrying, so that people may praise you for being good and kind.   Let there be no conceit (*kandokando*) no rudeness (*chisapi*).   If your

Photo E. W. Smith.

BOYS CARRYING FIREWOOD.

elder sends you for firewood you must bring him some. If he sends you on a journey you must not refuse but fetch him what he desires.   If you are travelling with an elder you must fetch water for him, if he sends you you must answer, "I will go, I am still a child."   When you return he will tell your father what a good boy you are.   Honour all others as you honour your *mulumi*.   If you do this you will live well, if you do not honour the elders you will not live well.'"

The third man said : "This is what I was taught :

'You must not speak evil things to your elders. If they strike you it is no fault in them. If they curse you, you must not curse them in return, but simply enquire : " For what reason do you curse me ? " If you meet a woman you must not strike her, nor ask her to give you tobacco. If a woman meets you, you must not cause her to stand or the neighbours will ask you, " For what reason do you cause this woman to delay ? " If a woman wants to discuss affairs with you intimately (*kudisha makani*), you must not agree ; if she persists you may even beat her. If she comes into your house, you shall cry : " There is a woman here ! " And on the morrow they will enquire of her : " Why do you follow after this child of ours ? You must not get him into evil habits." Again, if a woman comes to you saying, " Give me tobacco, my man," you must say to her, " Tobacco ! Where shall I find it ? " The woman will say, " Here is a little piece of tobacco, I will give you a smoke." Then you shall reply, " I do not desire tobacco that has medicine in it." She will go on to say, " You can love me," but you must reply, " I refuse you, why do you cling to me ? " She will reply, " Why, man, do you not want ' to eat ' anything ? It may be you are only a child. Are you not yet grown ? " Then you must say, " I do not want you." She will go on, " Are you a fool or an idiot ? Why, man, let us divide the tobacco." You must say : " I have no pipe with which to smoke. There are among the people those who desire to smoke. I am sickened and weary of being importuned. I curse you." She will reply : " You ought to marry me. Simply marry me ! " You must refuse her by saying : " I have no desire to marry you." Then she will say, " Well ! this child ! How was he begotten ? He does not love these 'affairs.' This man soon brings out his anger ! Well ! Whenever did a man beget a child who gave birth to another who curses a poor woman ? " Then after a time she will say, " Man, come now, discuss this matter, you are stubborn and very angry." Then finally you shall say to her : " I curse you because you weary me by following after me. This woman clings to me in an evil way. These things tire me. I will now disclose this thing to her husband, and say to him, ' This woman came to my house, but I refused her.' Then her lord will say, ' Yon woman clings to men in an evil way. I have thrashed her, but she does not repent,' and turning to her, he will say, ' You walk in an evil way. Your eyes are constantly towards men. The person that gave birth to you gave birth to an evil person.' '' They will help you. You are a man. This thing will go on and on and never end.' ''

These proceedings completed, the boys, like the girls, are dressed and decorated with beads, *impande* shells, and anklets. The boy is now at liberty to begin growing an *impumbe*. *Wakubuka* ('' he has become a young man,'' a *mukubushi*).

CHAPTER XIX

*

THE RELATIONS OF THE SEXES

THERE is much that is unpleasant in this part of our subject
—much that we would fain pass over in silence. But if
we are to be faithful to our purpose to give a true picture
of the Ba-ila, we must not dwell upon what R. L. Stevenson
called "the prim, obliterated, polite surface of life,"
but must lay bare "the broad, bawdy, and orgiastic—or
maenadic—foundations." To write of the Ba-ila and omit
all reference to sex would be like writing of the sky and
leaving out the sun ; for sex is the most pervasive element
of their life. It is the atmosphere into which the children
are brought. Their early years are largely a preparation
for the sexual function ; during the years of maturity it is
their most ardent pursuit, and old age is spent in vain and
disappointing endeavours to continue it. Sex overtowers
all else. In the magistrate's court, cases arising out of sex
are ninety per cent of the whole number. It is the rock
against which break all efforts to improve the young and
influence the old. We were speaking to a chief once about
sending his sons to school, and his reply was, "I want them
to go, but they are adolescent (*badikwete mabolo, i.e. Iam
testiculos habent*), and won't leave the women to go to school."
They were lads of twelve to fourteen years of age. At the
other end of life the commonest request made to us by the
old men is for aphrodisiacs.

We desire to look at even these things from their point
of view. Our object is not to hold them up to reprobation,
but simply to describe and understand. To them, the union
of the sexes is on the same plane as eating and drinking,

35

to be indulged in without stint on every possible occasion.
There are limits even to eating and drinking; you may
not take a pot of beer out of my hut without permission,
nor strip the maize from my field; if you do, I shall take
you to court. Of course a glutton may be subject to ridicule
or even to scorn, but as long as the food he eats is his own,
what right has any one to interfere? In precisely the
same way may men or women indulge their sexual instincts;
only they must respect the proprietary rights of others.
The sexual quality of a woman is somebody's property;
while she is immature that quality is absent and she is
not regarded except prospectively; but once that quality
develops, it enters into the possession of her husband, and
his right cannot be infringed with impunity. He may
give his right to a friend, just as he may give him a meal;
but if the friend presumes and takes either without permission he may be fined. It is a matter of property, not
of moral reprobation. The anger of a man may be raised
by some one interfering with his wife; he would feel just
as angry if the man drove cattle into his gardens; and in
either case is easily placated by payment of a fine.

1. Before Marriage

It will be sufficient to say that boys and girls are under
no restraint. Whatever they may do is looked upon merely
as " play" (*kusobana*). Adults rather encourage than
otherwise these precocious acts, for they regard them as a
preparation and training for what is man's and woman's
chief business in life. We have seen how the initiation
ceremonies are largely a preparation for this, and how
boys and girls employ various devices to hasten the time
when they shall be able to fulfil their ambitions. More
and more as the period of adolescence approaches are their
minds centred upon the one thing. Whatever they may do
during these early years, no blame is assignable.

The game named *mantombwa* is a kind of children's
harvest festival. There are different forms of it: this is
how it is played in Bwila. One day at harvest time the
young girls (*bashimbi*) get together, and having come to an

agreement on the matter go and tell the chief. He bids
them wait while he procures a house for them from one of
his people. Having taken possession of the house and
swept it, they then pair off : as they say, *batwalana, umwi
umwi watwala mushimbi nina* (" they marry each other,
every one marrying her fellow "). They beg food from the
villagers, and having cooked it, " man " and " wife " eat
together in the house. They sleep together ; and at sunset
they begin to sing :

> *Bana-mantombwa tababoni izuba nku dibidila,*
> *Bamukwelakwela bamutola ambo*
> *Suntwe akamudye.*

Which, being freely translated, means : " The *mantombwa*
players are not to see the sunset ; if any one ventures out
they take her to the west that the hyena may eat her."
Then at dawn they sing again :

> *Kumbo ukwa Mukonga twakeyana inzake ;*
> *Tu busongo, twaandwa, ye !*
> *Chilumino muchele ;*
> *Chiyulamudiango, tuyudile,*
> *Tulakusadila wa lukombo.*

These songs are not easily translated on account of the
strange words used ; this one may be rendered thus : " In
the west, at Mukonga's place, we found a building ; We the
wise ones are frozen with cold : Here's a dish and some salt
in it. O ! opener of the door, open for us, And we will
choose you something for your stomach." So they play
and sing, until they weary of the game. Then they break
up, by running off one morning to the water to bathe.
If any boys see them bathing, they beat them saying :
" *Kamukatupa inkungo sha mapopwe a mantombwa* " (" Give
us a bundle of the maize of the *mantombwa* "). Then they
return to their homes.

Played thus the game is innocent enough. But in some
localities it is different. The young girls go out of the
village and build play-huts of grass, and take up their abode
there, being assisted in their preparations by the boys.
They beg plenty of food—the new grain, new ground-nuts,
and milk. The night before the play begins they all collect

at one of the huts in the village—perhaps the chief's—
where they sleep. Next morning at cockcrow they rise
and begin to sing : " *Tuyudile, tuyudile, tuyudile* " (" Open
the door for us, open, open "). It is *tonda* for any female
to open the door : a man must do it, or a boy. Then they
take the food they have collected and scamper off to the
play-huts. There they set about putting things in order
and cook the food. During the morning the boys put in
an appearance, and eat with the girls. Having eaten their
fill, one of the boys says : " *Atuone* " (" Let us sleep ").
Then the boys and girls pair off and go to bed in the huts.
Later in the day they rise, and as the sun is setting they
go back to their homes. This may be kept up for a few
days or even for a month. During all this time the boy
and girl are as man and wife. It is indeed a game counter-
feiting the life of their elders.

All these things are included under the general title of
chikunku, meaning " childishness " and the things that are
done by children in the state of immaturity.

We have been assured by leading men in the tribe that
it is *tonda* for an adult man to have connection with
immature girls ; but in the same breath they admit that
such things are done. We fancy they are done very largely.
We have seen young girls, of seven or eight years of age,
suffering from primary chancres, not on the genital organs,
but on the inner sides of the thighs. This can only mean
one thing. Penetration being impossible, the connection
has been external ; what they call *kuchompa*. Should
this be discovered, the man does not get into trouble ; the
girl is simply rebuked by her elders and told not to allow
it to happen again.

Owing to these things, it is doubtful whether any girls
who could be called chaste are discoverable over ten years
of age. Such a thing as a grown virgin is not known. In
seeking for the word to add to our vocabulary we asked
many old men, but for long in vain. In seeking information
from Mungalo we had this conversation :

" My friend, what do you call a woman who repels
men ? "

" A *namauwa*."

" What do you call a woman who has borne one child ? "

" A *nakasomona*."

" What would you call a woman who has grown up without ever knowing a man ? "

" You mean such and such a woman ? "

" Yes."

" Well, I should call her a *mudimbushi* " (" a fool ").

Of course it happens sometimes that a girl becomes pregnant ; and what follows depends somewhat upon whether she has passed through the initiation ceremonies or not, that is, whether or no she is recognised as a woman.

If the girl has not been through the ceremony, they say, " *Waimita imfunshi* " (" She has conceived a monstrosity "), and the man, if discovered, is fined one or two head of cattle, not because he has deflowered the girl, but because of that " monstrosity," which, however, is not allowed to live but is killed as soon as born. The girl too is punished, not for unchastity but because of that uncanny thing. We knew a case at Lubwe of a slave girl who was found pregnant before having menstruated ; she was taken and put into a rude shelter away in the forest in order that she might be killed by wild beasts. The native teacher from the Mission rescued her, much to the indignation of the people, who foretold all manner of calamities upon him. He persisted however ; the child was born and lived. When it was two years old the people, and her master in particular, clamoured for her return to the village, but she refused to go, and the teacher to give her up. Should she go back, she said, and were to be married, her next child would be killed in order that she might be purified from the contagion of the " monstrosity."

If the girl has been initiated, the man will have to reckon with her affianced husband, who will claim damages from him. The " husband " may, however, claim to be released and to have his presents returned. In that case, they may try to persuade the seducer to marry the girl ; if he agrees and pays the *chiko*, all is well. If he refuses, they will insist upon his bringing things from time to time to the young mother in order *kukuzha mwana* (" to help rear the child "). But he has no right in the child ; whoever marries the girl is regarded as the father. By her loss of chastity she suffers no degradation in prospects ; her fiancé may marry her, but even if he does not, somebody else will. Nor will he object to the child, but rather be pleased, because he has already got a start with a family.

In a case like this, action is taken by relations of the girl other than the father. In our eyes, the father is the one to take proceedings, but to Ba-ila ideas it is strictly *tonda* for him to do anything ; if his wife had been assaulted he would be allowed, if not required, by public opinion to take steps ; but if he did it on behalf of his child, people would say, " He makes his child his wife " ; in fine, he would be vilified as an incestuous person.

Of course, in cases of inconvenient pregnancy, resort is often had to abortifacients.

Of an unmarried mother it is said, " *Mwana wakazhala wakatanda ; ifu ledia ndia mwisokwe* " (" The child has given birth before marriage, the stomach is of the veld ").

We recall the words of Professor William James : " No one need be told how dependent all human social elevation is upon the prevalence of chastity. Hardly any factor measures more than this the difference between civilisation and barbarism. Psychologically interpreted chastity means nothing more than the fact that present solicitations of sense are overpowered by suggestions of aesthetic and moral fitness which the circumstances awaken in the cerebrum ; and that upon the inhibitory or permissive influence of these alone, action directly depends." The unchastity of the Ba-ila is due to the fact that these inhibitory influences are weak or do not exist, and that the permissive influences are powerful. Where the passions are strong, solicitations frequent, opportunities abundant, moral restraints feeble, and tribal discipline weak, such a state of things as here exists, while it earns the reprobation of the strict moralist, cannot be wondered at. The unchastity has had, and still has, dire results upon the people. But their determinations are swayed by reference to immediate ends and without regard to consequences to themselves and the tribe. They see no wrong in it, and there is no public opinion to serve as an inhibitive conscience.

2. RESTRICTIONS UPON INTERCOURSE

Yet it must be said here, the Ba-ila fall short of actual promiscuity in their sexual relations ; and the above remarks are to be qualified by reference to certain inhibitive influences. There is, first, the intense horror with which incest is regarded. We have not heard a word that is equivalent to "incest" ; but there can be no doubt as to their abhorrence of it. In one respect their idea of incest is wider, in another it is narrower, than ours. Wider, because as we have seen, our prohibited degrees are enlarged to take in all the members of the clan, who are regarded as relations. All sexual intercourse, regular or irregular, is taboo between those who stand in the relation of *bakwesu*,[1] *banokwesu, bakwe besu, batatesu*. These regulations are carried out with some amount of strictness. Those who are taboo are always taboo ; there are no saturnalian carnivals where the restrictions are removed ; even in licentious dances, such as the *chisungu*, they may not take each other as partners. Their bounds to legal intercourse are narrower than ours in that ortho-cousins [2] are prohibited from marry- ing and from illicit intercourse. It is done occasionally, it is true, but only by those of whom the Ba-ila say *baina insoni*, (" they have no shame "). We see here an eking out of the totemic taboo ; for these cousins, even if not clansmen, are under a taboo. Two brothers will marry from different clans, and their children will take their mothers' totems, and so may be of different clans from each other, but the rule holds good. A man must not cohabit with his brother's wives, nor with his wife's sisters, while brother or wife is alive ; but a man may inherit his brother's widow, and a second wife is usually taken from the deceased's sisters, if there are any.

For relations to cohabit is *kukozha babwa o banyama* (" to be like dogs and animals "). One who should cohabit with his sister, except in the case mentioned on p. 261, Vol. I. would be put to death as a warlock.

The following tale was told us as relating the first instance of an incestuous relation :

---

[1] But see Vol. I. p. 319.
[2] Some cross-cousins are allowed to marry. See Vol. I. p. 318.

" When the people had gone out of the village, a certain man called his daughter into the house. As soon as the child came, she said : ' What do you call me for, father ? ' The father said nothing, but just caught hold of her, and the child was ashamed. The man had no feeling of shame, he made his daughter to be like his wife. Then the child said : ' What's the meaning of this ? ' The father answered nothing. As soon as the people returned, the child said, ' Father, do to me as you did to-day.' Thereupon the father chaffed her, and the child said : ' Father, do to me as you did to-day.' She caught hold of her father, saying : ' Let us do as we did to-day.' Thereupon the people were amazed and said : ' You have made your child to be as your wife.' To this day if a man acts thus he resembles that man who slept with his daughter as a wife."

Another tale may be quoted here :

" A certain man had two children, son and daughter. Their father and mother both died, so they went to another district. On the way they slept together. But a bird seeing them, began to sing, saying :

Chobe, Chobe, wezo ngu mwend'aze nguni ?	C. C. who is it you travel with ?
Chobe, Chobe, ngu mukwesu, kazune.	C. C. it is my sister, oh bird.
Chobe, Chobe, nadi mukwenu ni mwalala.	C. C. how is she your sister lying with you ?
Chobe, Chobe, wambonena kwi, kazune ?	C. C. whence did you see me, oh bird ?
Mu chisamo chikonkomene.	Out of the crooked stick.

" ' My mother ! ' said the boy, ' how that bird lies. I will hit it with a stick.' Then when they arrived at the village, the bird also arrived and began to sing, saying :

Chobe, Chobe, wezo ngu mwend'aze nguni ?	C. C. who is it you travel with ?
Chobe, Chobe, ngu mukwesu, kazune.	C. C. it is my sister, oh bird.
Nadi mukwenu ni mwalala.	How is she your sister when you sleep together ?
Wambonena kwi kazune ?	Whence did you see me, oh bird ?
Mu chisamo chikonkomene.	Out of the crooked stick.

" ' My ! that bird lies ! ' said the boy. ' My ! I will

hit it with a stick ! ' Then the people said, ' Hear what the bird is saying. These people have been sleeping together, brother and sister.' So they put them into a house and burnt them."

The facts with regard to incest among the Ba-ila do not bear out Westermarck's theory as to its origin. He maintains that there is an innate aversion to sexual intercourse between persons living very closely together from early youth, and that as such persons are in most cases related this feeling displays itself chiefly as a horror of intercourse between near kin. We may easily credit the statement that boys and girls in civilisation, unrelated, living under the same roof from childhood, are more likely to grow up as comrades than to become lovers, but we cannot credit it among the Ba-ila. As a matter of fact people in a village are not " in most cases related." We can hardly imagine a state of life where the young people can see more of each other than in the intensely open life of a Ba-ila village ; yet there is no aversion to intercourse between them ; and marriage between such does take place, and is welcomed by the elders, provided, of course, that the family and clan taboos are respected. And to show that it is not mere contiguity that accounts for the horror of incest, we have only to remind ourselves of the fact that a man would readily marry a girl he knew and had lived next door to from childhood if she were not of his clan ; while he would not marry a woman from a hundred miles off who belonged to his clan.

Besides the restrictions we have been dealing with, there are a number of particular occasions when sexual intercourse is prohibited to men and women.

1. Menstruous women are to be strictly avoided. If a woman tells the man of her condition and he persists his is the crime ; if she conceals it, she *ditaya*'s him.

2. A woman whose full term of pregnancy is approaching is also to be respected.

3. While a woman is nursing a child she must have no intercourse with any man.

4. When she weans the child, she is still under this law, so long as any milk is in her breasts.

5. If the child dies while a suckling, she must also wait till her breasts are dry. Should any man sleep with her while there is milk in her breasts, he would be liable to the sickness called *mabishi, i.e.* " sour milk."

6. If either man or woman is sick, intercourse is avoided, lest the sickness should be worsened by " jumping over it " (*kusotoka bulwazhi*). The Ba-ila are not so particular about this as their neighbours at Nanzela ; they will abstain only in cases of serious illness.

7. If either is suffering from open sores (not necessarily syphilitic) on the body, they abstain. But we have known a young man marry a girl whose legs and arms were covered with festering sores.

8. A woman while making beer must abstain, or the beer would refuse to ferment.

9. A woman just before sowing her fields will abstain, lest the seed should not sprout.

10. The people who thresh out the grain also have to abstain the night before they commence the work.

11. Also those who store the grain away in the bins.

12. A man starting on a journey must keep away from his wife and all women the night before, or he will meet with bad luck on the road, and the purpose of his journey will be frustrated. Thus, if he is going to trade, he will make only bad bargains.

13. Also men going to fish, or to set traps, or to dig game-pits must not visit their wives or other women the night before. Some men will not do it before going to hunt, lest, as they say, they should be hurt on the way or be mauled by a wild beast. Others, on the contrary, regard intercourse as giving them good luck during the hunt. The *bashilwando* must abstain all the time they are fishing.

14. Men engaged in smelting iron must abstain from all commerce with women.

15. Above all, men going to war must absolutely have nothing to do with women from the time that preparations are begun and the doctors have started to doctor the army. Breach of this would mean certain death in the fight ; and likely enough bring disaster to the army.

3. SEXUAL ATTRACTION

Before going further, we may well ask, what is it particularly that attracts Ba-ila men and women to each other?

In a woman there are many things that appeal to a man. He likes to see bright eyes, and long eyelashes; small ears and lips that close evenly. He likes to see a head without a lot of depressions in it; they are called *makozhi*, or *mangungunya*—the latter a rude term. The head that attracts him is shaven clean, with an even surface (*mutwi uueme*), and not straight up and down behind! He does not pay much attention to the girl's breasts, for though he admires the contour, he knows that they will soon fall and be unsightly; but he likes an abdomen rounded and not big. If the girl has a navel hernia (*lukombo*) an inch or so long, it is an additional attraction because out of the common. He likes red thighs (*shibelo shisubila*) and calves that are fat and firm and able to fill out many leglets. He likes to see an erect carriage and a graceful walk. But there are other things he wants in a wife: above all, she must be good at agricultural work and a good cook. She must not simply be able to cook but must serve the food in a charming manner; and be attentive to his visitors. He likes to see her well dressed, with a skin-petticoat that fits her, and pretty *mishini* on her head.

Many of these things are also attractive in a woman's eyes. She likes her lover to have bright eyes and long eyebrows. She admires a head-dress that is built and kept straight, and well ornamented with feathers and *twala*.

In addition, the woman admires a large penis. They talk very frequently and quite frankly about the organ, and the groom often commends or depreciates his member in the bride's presence. In the same way, men who have the means of knowing soon communicate private knowledge to their friends, and a woman's reputation for beauty is largely in their hands. Women like men to be men; strong, brave, and skilled in hunting and fighting.

4. BETROTHAL

What are the steps taken by the young people themselves, or by others on their behalf, to bring about a marriage ? There is no one set rule.

1. There are cases of genuine love matches, where two young people are mutually attracted, the marriage is not one arranged for them by others. The aspirant to their daughter's hand has, of course, to satisfy the parents and guardians in the matter of the *chiko*. There is no doubt that there are such love matches.

2. More commonly the parents or guardians arrange the marriage. We will quote here an account of a betrothal of this kind taken down by us in the original :

" They do this : when the son is grown, she who bore the boy begins to discuss with her husband, saying : ' The child has grown, he ought to be married to somebody.' Thereupon they arrange the matter, and next morning the boy's mother and sister go walking round the villages where they have seen marriageable girls. On arrival at a village, and after exchanging salutations, they say : ' We are looking for a pot.' The people of the village know by this that they are looking for a wife. They may answer, ' There is no pot here ; all the pots are finished.' They answer, ' And if it be only a little pot ? ' They say, ' There is none.' So they leave that village and go to another. There also after being greeted they tell them the same thing, saying, ' We are looking for a pot.' If there are any who are agreeable, they answer, ' For whom are you seeking a pot ? ' The mother of the boy says, ' It is for my own child that I am seeking a pot.' They reply, ' There is a pot, but it is not fit for work.' They answer, saying, ' We shall improve it.' They say, ' Come back again,' — which means that the relations of the child wish to talk the matter over quietly. Again they tell them, ' Sleep thrice, and on the fourth day you may come back.' They go back and spend three days ; on the fourth they return. On their arrival the relations say, ' Bring the *muyumusho*.' The wife-seekers return, and go to bring the *muyumusho*, five or four hoes ; when they produce them they say,

' Return and come back here to-morrow.'   So they go back."

Here, under the well-understood fiction of seeking a pot, the girl is sought for, and the preliminary arrangements are made for the marriage. The *muyumusho* is not reckoned part of the *chiko*, but is a sort of retainer, or sign of betrothal. The two young people are now known as man and wife, and the marriage may take place a few days after, or as soon as the *chiko* has been arranged. The saying with which this account ends, " Come back to-morrow," means they are to return for the marriage to be completed.

3. Another form of betrothal is termed *bubadikile* : a word derived from the verb *kubadikila*, which means, " to cause somebody to carry on his (or her) back for somebody else." It signifies that a man becomes betrothed to a young girl, perhaps to a baby, and contributes to her support until she is ready to be married. He causes, or helps, the mother to rear the child for him. What takes place is shown in the following account :

" It may be one like my daughter Namunza (*i.e.* about four) : a man loves her (or wants her) and says : ' That's my wife.' As for me, I suppose that he is joking ; then one day I see a blanket which he has sent, saying, ' Take this to my wife.' Again on another day, if he finds meat he sends it, saying, ' Take this to my wife.' Why, then that man must be respected, and when he arrives and says, ' You are seen, father,' and salutes by clapping his hands, you also clap your hands for him. Another day he will send a potful of fat and it arrives ; he will go on doing this all the time. Mayhap there is no good fortune, and while the child is still growing, the man to whom she is betrothed dies. Well, then you weep, and the child becomes a widow. If she be not shaven, at least she has all her hair cut off, and is called a widow. When the mourning is over, he who eats the name of the deceased follows just into their betrothal. He goes there and they do not forbid him, for he also is a son-in-law (*mukwe*) ; he does just the same, sending things just as the other did. Afterwards when the child is grown up they talk about the selfsame *chiko*. He

also gives the *chiko*, the amount stated.   Whether they
decide upon ten or four cattle he will give it, and will marry
her."

In this way it sometimes happens that a very young
girl is betrothed to a man greatly her senior, perhaps a
hoary old polygamist, or at least one old enough to be her
grandfather.   The girls cannot be expected to welcome such
a state of affairs ; in fact, to our knowledge, many of them
strenuously rebel, even to the extent of running away.
But if one runs away, she is chased and brought back forcibly to her husband.   It is by no means a matter of mere
coquetry ; we have known many cases where the young
girls were forced into a relationship that they abhorred.
Very often before the marriage takes place she has conceived
an affection for a lad of her own age.   We have known
instances where in such an event the old man has been
induced for a consideration to relinquish his claim ; but,
generally speaking, the girl has to obey.   Once married, she
may find herself fairly happy, as she may be the favoured
wife, and especially as custom allows her to console herself
with more youthful lovers.

The things given by the man to the girl's parents are
called the *chibonesho* (" the sign ") ; the purpose being not
only to assist in the child's upkeep but also as a token to
all that the child is bespoken.

Before she becomes properly his wife, the man has
certain rights over her.   When she is about ten she is taken
to his hut and they cohabit.   She may carry out the custom
to be mentioned later (*kunyonkola mazha*), but all the time
she remains at his home she may not speak to him.   If he
orders her, say, to fetch water, she must obey in silence.
When she first menstruates, she goes to her home to pass
through the initiation ceremony, and then the marriage
proper takes place.

5. THE CHIKO

The goods given by, or on behalf of, the bridegroom to
the clansmen and parents of the bride are called the *chiko*.
To give such things is *kukwa*.   It would be incorrect to
translate this term " dowry," for, according to the dictionary,

a dowry is the portion a woman brings to her husband. It is also misleading to call the *chiko* a bride-price. To us it may seem to be a matter of buying and selling, but the Ba-ila would repudiate any such idea. They use quite different words for the two kinds of transaction. To buy is *kuula*; and the word is used not only of ordinary merchandise but of slaves. A slave is *muntu muule* (" a bought person "), but the term is never used of a wife. The woman is not bought. Her husband does not acquire such proprietary rights in her as he does in a slave that he purchases. The *chiko* is more properly regarded as a compensation to the girl's clan, a return to parents and guardians for the expense they have incurred in her rearing, the seal of a contract by which she is to become the mother of the man's children, and a guarantee of good treatment. We therefore avoid using the terms dowry and bride-price, and keep to the native term, *chiko*.

Whether a slave is proud of the price paid for him, as an indication of his worth; and whether a ten-pound slave looks down upon a five-pound slave are matters we do not know; but certainly a woman among the Ba-ila has a certain pride in the amount of *chiko* given by her husband, because it is an indication of her worth in his eyes. The *chiko* is an acknowledgment that the marriage is an honourable one, and even Ba-ila women have some feeling on that score.

A case in point was once brought into court. A as a child was married by B, who gave for her an ox-skin and two calabashes of fat. Later on, when she was visiting her own home, another man, C, fell in love with her and married her. B naturally complained of this to the girl's parents, and they endeavoured to console him by saying that perhaps he might get her later. The girl soon tired of this interim husband and went back to B, saying she left C because he was poor, and did not know how to work like others; she also said she would not stay with a man who had given nothing for her. Womanlike, she had plenty of reasons, and the true one, as usual, was the last.

The amount of the *chiko* depends upon the position of the girl and the wealth of the suitor and his backers.

Here are the items in some of the settlements we have known :

(1) One blanket, three goats, one hoe, one basket of salt. (2) Two oxen, one cow. (3) Two *impande* shells, one blanket, five shillings' worth of print, and some beads. (4) Four cows and three oxen. (5) One cow, one ox, one blanket, ten shillings in cash, and one *impande* shell. (6) Nine hoes, two blankets, six yards of calico. (7) (*Basala*) Six sheep, one goat, two loaves of tobacco, and one ox. (8) (*Basala*) Two cows, one ox, one *impande*, and five strings of beads.

For a chief's daughter as much as thirty head of cattle may have to be given. It is said that at Nanzela formerly the chiefs would not allow of a big *chiko* ; two or three hoes were to be sufficient. We have known of as little as three strings of beads being given there. But in later years they have taken to imitating the Ba-ila proper in demanding substantial amounts. Generally speaking, we may reckon the *chiko* as four or five head of cattle, say from £12 to £15.

The amount having been arranged, the bridegroom or his representatives, as we saw in a previous chapter, seek help among their family and clan. The man's chief helps and he himself does what he can. The help is readily given and the *chiko* paid over, not necessarily in a lump, but often in instalments as it is forthcoming. As the *chiko* is contributed by the bridegroom's clansmen mostly on the one hand, so, on the other, it is distributed mostly among the bride's clansmen ; the parents, especially the father, getting little of it. The one who gets the lion's share is the *Shimalelo*, the guardian of the girl. The mother always has her portion called *mukako* (" of the belt "). If the *chiko* is given in hoes there may be ten, and a further five, *mamba osanwe a mukako wa baina* (" five hoes of the mother's belt ") ; or if it be ten head of cattle, *musune wa mukako* (" an ox of the belt "). Another portion is called *lushila*, given to defray the expenses of doing up the girl's hair with *chishila* (" ochre ") : this is perhaps not part of the actual *chiko*, but like the *muyumusho* more a sign of appropriation given before the settlements are made. An occasion like this becomes a kind of clearing-house for all disputes and claims ; and infinite adjustment is required before the whole business is completed.

It is regarded as wrong ever to dispose of the offspring of the cattle received as *chiko*. The calves as born may go to clansmen who could not be given their portion at first.

Rescission of the *chiko* is claimable by the parties who give it on the following grounds : virulent or contagious disease ; laziness ; neglect to provide husband with food by hoeing or by cooking ; inability to bear children. Persistent adultery is a ground rarely put forward. Should the woman be incapacitated by accident, the husband would claim another wife. And in the same way, if she dies her people must provide a woman to take her place.

If for any reason the man is dissatisfied with his wife and wishes the *chiko* returned ; or if the relations of the wife have reason to be dissatisfied with him and refuse to give up anything ; or if the woman runs away to join another man : then endless disputes arise occasioning litigation.

We may quote the following cases to illustrate the kind of litigation that arises. They throw light upon the life of the Ba-ila in certain aspects.

(1) In one case the girl was a slave and her parents went to the man and offered her as his wife. She had had two husbands previously. Her release was obtained and he married her. After a time he got sick with syphilis, and as her mother was also ill he sent her home to visit. He went to see her several times ; but when he wanted her back the mother put him off by saying that she was working in the fields. Then he heard they had married her to another man. He was disgusted with this, and instead of trying to regain her he put in a claim for the return of the *chiko* he had given.

(2) A married the daughter of B ; then later B took her away and gave her to C. When A put in a claim against him C gave him a woman D in settlement. On his way home A called at B's, who seized D on the pretext that she had thrown ash on him—a serious offence. He afterwards promised to send D back to A, but as she did not come A went for her, and they threatened to kill him.

For four years he continued to try to get the woman, but in vain. He lost both women and also the *chiko* he had given for the first.

(3) A took B as his wife when she was a child, and she stayed at his brother's. When the latter died, C took both her and another girl as inheritance. Then D married her, giving *chiko* to C, and promised to compensate any one who claimed her. Then A paid an ox to C for B and got possession of her; A also gave a boy and some tobacco to her father. When D sought to get her, A admitted that D was the lawful husband and claimed five cows to release her. In the event B was returned to D.

(4) M married a girl N in childhood, and when she grew up she went back to her home as the parents were not satisfied with the *chiko*. M said he would continue to work and add to the amount. Meanwhile O came along, fell in love with N, and his father went to her parents, who agreed to the marriage, saying that M had given only a bit of tobacco and some beads, and if he claimed for them they would settle with him. Then M put in his claim, saying that he had lived with her two years. N's father then said that M had left the girl for some time, and when she had gone to the initiation he refused to come to the dance, thus repudiating her. So O kept her.

(5) This is a good instance of the extraordinary way in which these claims become entangled.

A man named Lushika died (he was Namudionto's brother's son) and Shisumba took the name. One of the wives did not like him and went off to Kabulamwanda and married Nalubi (Husband No. 2). Then later Sichianji saw her at Mala and married her (Husband No. 3). He promised to pay two cows for her, but as he failed to do so her parents took her away. Then she went to Lubwe, and Namudionto said, "There's my brother's son's wife; I will take her." He paid two cows, one blanket, and an ox to the parents (Husband No. 4). Now the complications arose. When Namudionto's nephew married, Namudionto had given three cows towards the *chiko*, and when Namudionto's brother died, Namudionto's nephew, Lushika, took a cow as his share of the inheritance. Namudionto had two sons ; the younger, Molo, lived with him, and the other, Shaba, lived with the Sichianji mentioned above. When Molo wanted to join his brother, Namudionto stopped his wife and Sichianji stopped another wife that he had got. Sichianji also took a cow from Chilondo, telling him to go and claim the woman from Namudionto ; that is, he transferred his claim in her to this man Chilondo. Thereupon Chilondo claimed the wife or a cow from Namudionto. The cow Sichianji took from Chilondo belonged to Namudionto, so Namudionto claimed a cow back from Sichianji.

(6) R married S when she was young and gave a shell and five hoes for her. Before R married her, she had been promised to T, who had given a cow, ten baskets of salt, and two hoes. Then another man, U, gave T a cow for his rights, and when R took her U claimed a cow from him and he refused to pay. The girl rejected her original suitors and said she loved U.

(7) A died of smallpox ten years before this case came up. B took his name and married C. Then C got into trouble through a woman taking medicine because her children all died after birth, and the woman's people took C as a slave in consequence. A man, D, redeemed her with a cow and an ox and took her to wife, to the annoyance of B, who had not been told of the trouble. B then made a claim against D. C lived with D for years and then ran back to B. B then claimed from D for C's children, and D claimed against B for the return of C.

(8) X took the girl Y as his share of an inheritance. Then Z married Y, giving X as *chiko* a person and an ox. Then Z died and X brought an ox to mourn with at the funeral and asked for a big present in return. Z's son gave him the girl Y. Then X asked for more and was given another person, and as Y did not wish to stay with him she gave a slave to release herself. However, X took away the woman, and then Z's son brought a claim against him for the return of his wife, and got her.

(9) F married G and then H took her away. She ran away from H, and another man, I, seized her and took her to his hut. Her husband was away working at the time,

and on his return he claimed against I. In his defence I declared that H had given her to him in payment of a fault. The woman said that of the three men she wanted F; and she was sent back to him as the result of the case.

(10) X wanting a wife went to the parents of B's wife and they gave him B's daughter, *i.e.* their granddaughter. X gave five cows as *chiko* and they handed B a small ox and a small cow as his share. Then the girl died and according to Ila custom the sister should have taken her place. As there was no other daughter, X claimed for the return of the *chiko*. The parents had to find him another wife to settle the case.

(11) This case was over a woman who had died three years before. As a girl she (we call her A) was promised to B and he gave her to C. C paid *chiko* of an ox to her father. Then B made a claim against C for the return of his wife, and C gave him ten baskets of salt, two blankets, and two strings of beads, which went to the father. Then B took A and C seized a cow from the father. The woman was two years with C and one with B. Now five years after, the girl having died in the meantime, the father brought a case against C for the cow.

(12) The following is an instance of how a man may be held accountable to his parents-in-law for the death of his wife. A married B's daughter. She fell sick and he asked for medicine and got it from the parents. After her death B claimed and got ten cows from A because his daughter had died of an unknown disease.

These cases are quoted as specimens of what is continually occurring, and they show clearly how fragile the marriage bond is among the Ba-ila. Women are bandied about from man to man; and of their own accord leave one husband for another. It is no unusual thing for a young woman scarcely out of her teens to have had four or five husbands, all still living.

6. Marriage Ceremonies

Following immediately, in most cases, after the Initiation rites, come the marriage ceremonies, which we will first describe in the natives' own words:

" So when all is done (*i.e.* the Initiation) they take the girl to where she is to be married. And they tell the men who are at the village, ' When you hear us shout, catch hold of the man (*i.e.* the bridegroom).' When they arrive before the village they shout, and those in the village catch the bridegroom and carry him to his home. They put the man into his house. As soon as it is dark they take the woman to his house and they sleep. After the marriage is consummated, the bridegroom rises, takes strings of beads equal in total length to the measurement of the bride from head to foot, and hangs them on the bedpost. He also puts a hoe on the fireplace. At early dawn the wife rises and begins to pluck off the hair from her husband's pubis and from his jaws, until the entire area is smooth. At cockcrow the old woman enters and inspects the naked pair. With her fingers she feels the man's pubis and his jaws. Then if she finds everything smooth, she cries out in a loud voice. 'This girl has obeyed my orders.' The old woman takes the beads from the bedpost and the hoe from the fireplace—they are her reward—and after sweeping the house, goes her way. In the morning the man's people cook bread and relish and take the newly married couple there. When they arrive they place bread between them (as they sit face to face) with the relish. The woman breaks off a morsel, dips it into the relish, and gives it to the man ; and the man also breaks, dips, and gives a piece to the woman. When he has done this, he gives her a name, saying : ' It is So-and-so.' The woman refuses it. Says he : ' So-and-so.' The woman refuses it. Again he says : ' Well perhaps So-and-so.' The woman nods her head, which is to say that she agrees.

" Now this bread is given to all the people, old and young, that they may eat and join in ' the-eating-of-bread ' (*madyanshima*). So they eat and sleep ; next day they sleep ; on the third day come the woman's sisters and all her relations ; they come to *fwenezha*. And the man begs things from all the community ; one gives him beads, another a fish-spear, another a spear, a hoe, an axe, anything. He puts them in his house. When the visitors arrive they bring a basket of meal and he puts into it a hoe. When he has done this well, they who *fwenezha* go into his house

and he gives one a fish-spear, another beads, another a
spear, and another an axe. When they have all got something they return home.

" Next day the woman goes to her home ; she goes to
throw away the *masansa* ; she goes to spend two nights, on
the third she returns. So ends the account of a marriage."

We may supplement this account by another.

" Now in the evening they come to fetch her and on
arrival they hide near by. Then they go. They (the men)
catch the bridegroom and say : ' You are to marry to-day.'
Then when the women give their shrill cry and he hears it
he loses heart (lit. his heart comes out) and leaving them
he runs away to hide. Then they bring the son of his uncle
to sleep with the woman to ' eat her the marriage ' (*kumudya
bwinga*). When he has done this, next morning they fetch
the bridegroom that he may give the name. Then they
cook bread ; having done this, they make them eat together.
Then they tell the man : ' Give the name.' He gives her
a name, saying : ' It is So-and-so.' If the woman likes it
she agrees, if she doesn't like it she refuses by shaking her
head ; she may not speak to indicate her refusal. Again
he gives her another name and then she agrees.

" After spending three days with her husband the
woman goes to her home to throw away the *masansa* ;
the man takes a spear and accompanies her. When he
arrives before the village of his parents-in-law, he throws
the spear in front of the woman ; she picks it up and takes
it into the village. The man returns home. The woman
enters the village of her people and sits. They begin to say
to her : ' You have got up ! ' She answers : ' I have got
up.' Then they ask her : ' Is your husband good ? ' ' Yes,
he is good.' They sleep and next morning they give their
child meal and she takes it to the house of her parents-in-
law ; and on arrival she hands it to her husband's people,
because she hasn't yet begun to do their own cooking.
Then after two days her namesake comes to see her and
takes a hoe ; on arrival she gives the woman the hoe and
returns. And the husband goes begging things to *fwenezha*
withal and to feed them from his relations and comrades
and brothers-in-law They all give him things. He returns

and sleeps. Next day they arrive to *fwenezha*; they enter
the house and sit and have bread cooked for them and eat.
When they have done eating they are given beads and
spears. All have something. Then in the basket they put
a hoe and then return home and stay. After a time the
people of the man collect grain and make beer of the-
cooking-for-themselves (*kudiikila*) and they mould the fire
cones (*mafua*). They who mould them are the people of
the woman. They drink beer, and sing, and the people of
the woman instruct their child, saying: 'You are grown
to-day. Cook for yourselves; a man is to be given food
when alone. When he has done eating with many people
and you enter the house, give the-food-put-by (*mafubikila*),
which you have hidden, whether it be beer or bread, give
it him and he will eat.' And they also instruct the man:
' That child of others is to have fruit gathered for her and
be anointed with fat and clothed with rugs. That is good
husbandship, and if you do not anoint her they will take
her away from you.' Then when they have done telling
them these things there remains the entering of his mother-
in-law's house and the parents-in-law make beer. Then
when he enters the house they also will give him a hoe.
When they begin drinking beer the mother-in-law hands
him a hoe. That is partly doing away with the taboo,
and all that remains is to shout and say: ' You are seen,
O father of So-and-so.' "

From these accounts we may gather that the following
elements enter into the constitution of a marriage: 1. The
teaching of the girl and of the man; 2. The hiding away
of the bridegroom; 3. The *kudya bwinga*; 4. *Kunyonkola
mazha*; 5. The *madyanshima*; 6. Giving the new name:
kuudika; 7. *Kufwenezha*; 8. *Kusowa masansa*; 9. Throwing
the spear;   10. *Kudiikila*; 11. Entering the mother-in-
law's house.

Some of these are explicable as *Rites de passage*:
ceremonies accompanying and symbolising the passing out
from an old stage of life into a new one, and there is a
recognition that this transition is accompanied by some
danger arising out of entering into the unknown. The
instruction given to the young people as described here

and in connection with the Initiation, seems to be in the nature of a separation rite : they are no longer children, but are about to enter into new relations and need to be prepared for their duties. Much of this teaching is admirably practical in character. The hiding away of the bridegroom is also separative : it is to be explained not as mere bashfulness on his part but as due to dread of the unknown. It is thus that the people explain it themselves. Probably the counterpart of this action of the boy is the custom of *kudya bwinga* : both are due to the desire to escape from some mysterious miasma arising from the union of the sexes. A young boy, chosen for the purpose, spends the first night with the bride. Between them friendly relations continue to exist afterwards, and they address each other as *mwashangu*. It is as if something physical and tangible existed which needs to be removed by the boy in order that the marriage may be consummated with impunity. It is difficult to reconcile this with the fact of pre-nuptial unchastity. It cannot be the passage from maidenhood, as we understand it, that must be accomplished that night, for the simple reason that there is little or no likelihood of the woman being a virgin when she comes to the marriage bed. It may possibly be a custom surviving from times when pre-nuptial intercourse was more strictly prohibited. Or it may have its origin in that play-acting that is so characteristic of these savage races[1] ; they pretend that a thing is not that really is, in order to mislead the mysterious powers that rule their life. The bride is not a virgin : anything inherent in her that would damage her husband has really long since been removed by other men ; true, we may suppose them to say, but let us act as if it were not so, so that if there be any penalty we may avoid it. After the marriage, the bride goes back to her people for two or three days, for the purpose, as they say, *kusowa masansa* ("to throw away the *masansa*"). What that is we cannot explain : it seems to be allied to the *lusasa* to be explained in another connection ; and to be something that results from sexual intercourse. If that is so, then

---

[1] " In ritual, fiction is frequently as good as fact."—Dr. Farnell, *Cults of the Greek States*, vol. iv. p. 188.

something in the woman has already been conveyed to the boy ; now what was in the man has been conveyed to the woman and she gets rid of it by visiting her home.

These, we say, may be regarded as separation rites ; others are much more definitely aggregation rites. The young people are assimilated by certain things ; and their families are also brought into closer relationship through them ; the bridegroom is especially brought into relationship with his wife's family. The first of these ceremonies is *kunyonkola mazha*. It is the custom of the Ba-ila to remove all hair growing on the pubes ; both boys and girls pluck it out on its appearance, and continue to do so afterwards. The reason given is that they may be clean. It is impossible to tell whether they mean physically or ceremonially clean : the one idea merges into the other and the word used, *kusalala*, expresses both, though more often the latter. The woman does for the man what he has been accustomed to do for himself ; she will continue to do it during their married life. We may therefore see in this a symbol of the wife's subordination to her husband. In the next ceremony, that of *madyanshima*, on the other hand, we see a recognition of the equality of the two : they eat together, in a way that reminds us of the Roman custom of *confarreatio*. Eating together means union in close friendship between equals. The next custom, of giving a new name, shows very clearly that the woman has passed into a new stage of existence ; to get a new name is to be reborn, remade ; she is no longer the girl she was, but something else. She shows her reluctance to pass into this by refusing the first names proposed.

The husband and his wife are now one ; but there are the relations to consider. According to the Ila proverb, " *Shimukwelansanzhi inkwaya weletelela* " (" He who pulls a branch brings the leaves with it "), if you marry a woman you marry her family too. Not only have you given the *chiko*, but now after the marriage is consummated her people come to get what they can out of you, *kufwenezha* ; it is their way of recognising you as their relation. The " throwing of the spear " when the woman returns to her home is not explicable. But the *kudiikila* is readily understood. Up to this time the two young people have not commenced housekeeping on their own account. But now the bride's people mould the *mafua*—the conical lumps of baked clay used to support the fire ; and the bride henceforth is to be mistress of her own ménage. One more ceremony remains. Between the man and his wife's family, especially her mother, a very strict taboo exists, which if it were kept in its entirety would prevent any social intercourse. So at the final feast she hands her son-in-law a hoe, taking the initiative in approaching him, and henceforth he is free of her house under restrictions. As our informant quoted above has it, *kwamana kutonda chinichini* ("that is partly doing away with the taboo"). Now they salute the bridegroom not by his own name but as " *Baushe nini* " ("the father of So-and-so "). So ends the ceremonial. This last part of it may not be carried out until after the birth of the first child.

The Marriage of a Widower and of a Widow

What happens in the case of a widower is shown in the following account :

" If the woman dies they weep very much and spend five days before seizing the heiress. Next day (*i.e.* the sixth) they shave the widower's head and give him a hoe on which he treads, and also the *chishonsho*. So he begins to inherit ; in the evening they seize the heiress. Then they put out the fire which is in the house, and only leave that which is outside. They put a sherd on the fire and it gets red-hot. They put the woman into the house ; when he arrives he sits and cuts away the strings around her loins, throwing them on the ground, so that she is left naked. *Inde lumbis tantum mulieris vir mentulam admovet* (*wachompa*) and the woman coughs so that they hear who are sitting at the door. When she coughs they bring that red-hot sherd, putting it on some grass and quickly carrying it so The grass catches fire. Then those two lying on the bed move apart, and the people light a fire from that of the sherd ; that fire is thus a new one and the woman becomes new. So they sleep. Next morning they anoint

her with fat and take her outside. Then the man's relations
clap their hands and begin to charge her, saying : ' Look
after us well just as the deceased looked after us.' And
others say to the man : ' You also, you must gather fruit
for her just as you gathered it for the deceased.' Again,
that woman, if she does not like him, returns to the house
of him who brought her up. If he be a vagabond she leaves
him. Or if he who married her first is a vagabond she leaves
him and stays where she ate the name."

A little explanation will clear up several obscure things
in this narrative. The widower on the death of his wife
is taboo ; he may not go visiting until the vacant hut is
again occupied. There 'is hanging about him something
contagious : something left over from his marital relationship with his deceased wife. This is called *lusasa*, or by
others *chibinde*. We have heard this explained as being the
spirit (*muzhimo*) of the deceased which attaches itself to
him and his clothes ; but it would appear to be physical
rather than psychical, for it can be got rid of by transferring
it to somebody else.

A friend of his deceased wife comes to his hut and
by having intercourse with her he gets rid of the miasma,
and so is ready to marry again. The people to whom he
gave *chiko* for his first wife have to provide a substitute ;
before they do this the procedure of *kudya chishonsho* must
be gone through. The relations of the wife and the widower
exchange presents ; first of all they present him with a
hoe, on which, for some esoteric reason, he places his foot.
In the evening the woman's people put her into a hut,
out of which all fire is carefully removed. Then the man
enters, and removes her garments and the belt or strings
around her waist. It ought to be said that this woman
has perhaps been married before and is now taken away from
her husband for the purpose of " eating the name " of the
deceased. As such she is unclean, the contagion of her
former marriage is still about her ; by throwing off her
garments, and especially the belt, the new husband throws
away the contagion. Then follows the action named
above. On hearing the signal given by the cough, the people
enter, bearing a brand of grass, lighted from a red-hot

sherd, and a new fire is kindled in the hut. As it is significantly stated, the fire is new and the woman also becomes new.

In the case of a widow, she also is taboo, and may not carry on her usual occupations, nor marry again, until the *lusasa* (or *chibinde*) is removed. This is done, some say, by a boy coming into the house and cutting the belt (*kukosola mukaba* is the name of the operation). Others say a relation of the deceased husband has intercourse with her; and this also is *kukosola mukaba*, even though the belt may not be actually cut. If neither of the things happens, the woman goes about seeking a man to take away the contagion from her.

The widow for three days after her husband's death is not allowed to prepare food for herself lest she should injure the vessels by infecting them with her contagion. A woman is appointed to give her food and is later given a new hoe by the widow. When the relations of the deceased meet to appoint the heir who shall take the widow, she has a say in the matter; and there is a special word (*kutangaza*) which describes the woman's way of refusing first one and then another until she gets the man she wants. After the cleansing process just described has been carried out, she is put into a hut with the new husband and the new fire is lighted and the other things done as narrated above of the widower. After the mourning and before taking the new husband she is freshly shaved, and given *chishonsho*, a cow or ox; if this should be omitted the heirs of the deceased's property would be regarded as having committed *buditazhi* against her. The woman who shaves the widow must also be rewarded by the heir.

A *namantezi* is a woman whose children all die. The name is also applied to a man whose wives die in childbirth. It is believed that should the first die in childbirth, the second and third will do the same, but the fourth will survive. Why, with such a belief, women will consent to be the second and third wives we do not know, unless it is an instance of the fatalism so strongly marked in the Ba-ila.

Marriage of a Chief's Daughter, and of a Chief

Among the Ba-ila proper there is no difference in procedure in the case of a chief's marriage or the marriage of his daughters. But at Nanzela there is this custom. When a chief's daughter is grown up she tells her people that she wishes to marry a certain man whom she names. Owing to her position she has the right of choosing her own partner. They send a messenger to pour over the chosen man a potful of fat, which must be, wholly or in part, that of a hyena. This is the equivalent of making the man a slave. By marrying the chief's daughter he becomes a *mukwetunga, i.e.* the son-in-law of the ruling family, and the position is practically one of serfdom : as they say, " *Bukwetunga mbuzhike* " (" Son - in - lawship - to - a - chief is slavery "). The man's friends are quite insensible of the honour bestowed upon him ; indeed the messenger runs the risk of severe maltreatment at their hands. But once the fat is thrown over the man he can only escape his destiny by payment of a heavy ransom. If none is forthcoming, he is taken to the headmen and they instruct him in the duties of *bukwetunga,* impressing particularly upon his mind the necessity of continence as far as other women are concerned. If he is at all obstreperous he may be soused in the river until he is half-dead. That takes the devil out of him. In his new position he is avoided by the women. *Si qua mulier cum illo coire audeat, statim eam arripiunt pudendique labias maiores recidunt.* No such law of faithfulness is imposed upon the chief's daughter ; she, without blame, has the run of the men.

Similarly, if a chief so admires a woman that he wishes to marry her, he sends some women to throw a pot of fat over her. They go stealthily, and having achieved their object run off in fear of the consequences. The woman is brought and she is instructed in her duties and especially warned against unfaithfulness. If she is obstinate or recalcitrant, she also may be half-drowned to subdue her spirit. If she is lascivious and goes to other men, they will, or rather would under the old regime, be killed. Of such a man they say : " *Wakaya ku mibanga, wadiyazha mwini* " (" He went to forbidden things and so destroyed himself ").

7. POLYGYNY

Whether the preponderance of females over males is due to such general causes as the hot climate, the plenteous food-supply, or the practice of exogamy, certainly it seems a fact that there is an excess of female births among the Ba-ila, and while the proportions may be increased owing to the higher mortality of the males, the census shows a surplus of fully 10 per cent of adult women over men. This means, of course, that in a system of strict monogamy ten women out of every hundred would remain unmarried. But celibacy is regarded by the Ba-ila as highly unnatural, and the ambition of all the men is to marry as early and to have as many wives as possible. As a matter of fact, monogamous marriages are in the majority; for there are two conditions of polygyny which cannot always, with the best of wills, be met; namely, first the women and secondly the *chiko*. Owing to the small excess of women only ten men out of every hundred should be able to get more than one wife, and these extra wives, in the nature of the case, would fall to the men who could best afford to give *chiko* for them. And when some men have up to twenty wives it is evident that many have to do without any. There is always a number of men without wives. On the other hand, there are always many unmarried women. Most of these are slaves and may be said to live in a state of concubinage. A slave is often given to wife, but frequently the master, while not marrying her himself, is unwilling to forgo her services as labourer and concubine, though he may give her temporarily to a man without a wife.

Having mentioned this point, we may reproduce here what we were told by a man who himself had married a slave. " It is best," said he, " not to marry a slave. If you marry her, clothing her and giving *chiko* for her, the owner still has rights over her and will have intercourse with her secretly. And no fault is attached to him; it is his right because he had to travel far perhaps to purchase her. And if you have a quarrel with him, he will simply take her away altogether. Another reason for not marrying a slave is that she will not hoe well in her own fields but

only in her master's. Better to marry a free woman and
then her people will help you to hoe your fields. Again, if
you marry a slave and you die, her master takes her and
the children and they become slaves."

It seems superfluous to enquire into the reason for the
polygynous propensities of the Ba-ila. The natural desires
of men, who, it must be remembered, are by custom debarred
from their wives for lengthy periods, find allies in economic
considerations, for the more wives the more likelihood of
the husband having plenty to eat and the better his status
among his fellows. The idea also prevails, in direct contradiction to what we should say is the truth, that a multiplicity
of wives means so many more children, and children are
always an object of desire. Other reasons given by the
men are that they may have a wife to lend to a friend or
visitor, and that their wives may be able to provide visitors
with plenty to eat.

It is well pointed out by Westermarck that " polygyny
implies a violation of woman's feelings." Ba-ila women
can be most furiously jealous ; and the only things that
reconcile them to sharing their husbands with other women
are the fact that many hands make light work and the
reflected dignity that comes of being the wife, albeit an
inferior one, of a wealthy man.

Polygyny is called *madi* ; a polygynist is *shimadi* ; to
marry more than one wife is *kuadika bakazhi* ; and to be
married to a polygynist is *kuadikwa*.

Some interesting glimpses into such a state of life are
afforded by the following native account :

" If she has no fault, a man will tell his wife, ' I am
going to marry another.' If on account of jealousy the
wife does not like it, she will refuse to allow it. Then perhaps
the husband gives her things and propitiates her and she
agrees. So he does this : he seeks to wife a woman, or an
initiated girl, or a young girl. And the people of the girl,
if they do not wish her to become the wife of a polygynist,
refuse, and say : ' We have no child to be a polygynist's
wife.' Perhaps after a time they will agree. The man's
chief wife (*nabukando*) goes seeking a wife for him to the
mother of the man her husband, and they say : ' Won't

you be constantly fighting ? ' The woman says : ' It depends
upon our natures, perhaps we shall fight.' Then they agree
who have the girl sought in marriage and she is married
by that man. When they marry thus, he will build two
houses side by side, or one in another enclosure, for fear
they should fight if they were side by side. Then as to the
duties of that man to the two wives : if he gather firewood
for the chief wife, it must be in greater quantity than for
the lesser wife. If he clothes one with a goatskin, he must
also clothe the other in a goatskin. If he draws water he
will carry two calabashes, and if one is full he must fill
the other to the brim so that the wives may not fight.
Because if he does not do so, they will often be a-fighting.
One will say, ' I am not loved,' and then they will fight.
With food the same. If at one house she cooks bread,
and he eats and finishes it, there also at the other house he
must go and finish it. If he does not, those women will
fight ; one says, ' As for me, my bread he didn't finish it,
whereas he did finish yours.' If he sleeps four nights in
one house, he must also sleep four in the other. He will
sit and talk a while at the one house in the evening and then
go to the other to sleep. That is how he does, and perhaps
they won't fight ; if he does not do so they will constantly
be fighting. Again, if the spears at one house number four,
at the other they must also number four. And axes the
same : at one house an axe and at the other an axe : blankets
and stools the same. When the husband changes about, he
does not take a pipe to the other house, nor a spear of this
house, nor an axe, nor a rug, nor tobacco ; he must go
and find them at the other house to which he goes. He
who acts thus is the one to manage polygyny ; he will
keep married to those wives always. Whereas if he does
not act thus, he cannot manage polygyny. One of them
will run away and go to her home, and there at her home
they may refuse to let her return, saying, ' We have no
child to be treated ficklely and made into a servant. She
also is a daughter just as the other one you married.' So
they will restrain her ; if they keep her thus he gets back
the *chiko*. If he is clever he will say when they return the
chiko : ' I throw away the woman : when I am dead the

cattle will belong to many.' His relations will miss him, and when they haven't him they will insist upon an equivalent for the cattle. That is why he will refuse the *chiko* and allow the woman to stay at her place.'' The idea is that by abandoning the cattle, when he dies his people will benefit ; the woman's people will have to find a wife for his heir or other relations, and be unable to claim any more *chiko*.

From this it is very evident that the life of a polygynist is not always a rosy one ; if he wishes to preserve domestic peace he has to exercise considerable tact. While he must be careful to show no marked favour to one wife at the expense of another, there is a recognised scale of dignity in the family. The *nabukando* (chief wife), *e.g.*, may, if the man is rich in cattle, have thirty cows allotted to her household to milk, the second wife fifteen, and the third ten. While they fight among themselves they will in case of necessity unite against the husband. Cases are not unknown where the husband is chastised by his wives when they consider themselves slighted collectively by his attentions to other women. A friend of ours once witnessed such a scene in a village. The four wives of a man were giving him a thrashing and talking something like this : '' Why did you marry us ? You spend your strength on other women and we have no children. Are we not women also ? If we cannot have children by you, what is the use of you ? We will all leave you.'' On the other hand, many polygynists are very devoted to their wives and live happily. We know of one such man, who, in his anxiety to satisfy his eleven wives, sought a strong aphrodisiac from a missionary that would enable him to visit them all each night.

8. LUBAMBO

In addition to the forms of marriage already described, there is a kind of Cicisbeism named *Lubambo*, which is really a species of polyandry. This is a recognised institution and one of those things that the Ba-ila very strongly hold to and very much resent any deprecation of. It differs from an ordinary system of paramours, in that there is a public ceremony, so that everybody knows of it, even the woman's husband. He cannot throw stones at his wife because he does the same. We have seen this public ceremony. One year we were present at the great annual gathering in honour of Shimunenga at Mala. There were hundreds of people present, all dressed in their best, singing and dancing around the grove sacred to the *muzhimo*. Then there was a lull, and we saw a procession of men approaching; all of them in the extremity of Ba-ila finery. One of them was leading a young ox. The drums now resumed; and another procession came forward, of women dressed finely. In the centre was one woman, conspicuous by her extra fine appearance: freshly shaven and anointed, and wearing polished bangles and a new *lechwe* skin. The two parties met, and the man formally presented the woman with the ox and received a spear in return. Then they separated, and singing and dancing were resumed by the whole multitude. What it meant was that these two had already agreed in private and now signified the fact publicly that they were lovers. At a feast, they, leaving their spouses, become partners and drink and sleep together. During the feasting no young man without such a lover is allowed entrance into the hut, but is driven away with ridicule. The next day, if the man is wealthy he may present the woman with a second ox, and she may give him a blanket. This is not a temporary arrangement simply for the feast, but continues as long as they desire, the man and woman paying each other visits at intervals. No Mwila male or female lacks these lovers.

The system is called *Lubambo* ("an arranged thing"), from *kubamba*, to arrange. The paramour is called *Umambakwe*.

Husbands naturally exhibit great complacency in regard to this custom. To their minds it is the best policy, for they benefit by it. Occasionally they show resentment when the wife shows undue affection for her paramour. In one case we know of, a husband brought a claim against his wife's lover because she so often visited him that he thought she meant to leave him altogether. Once after she had been away visiting for a long period, she returned home and immediately announced her intention of going to her lover. This very naturally made the husband very angry. He said he would not have grumbled if she had stayed with him a day and then gone to her lover ; what he objected to was not only the indecent haste but also the manner in which she took to her lover the cloth that he gave her for clothing. So he brought a case against the lover to recover his wife.

It must be noted that men and women are restricted in the choice of paramours : the same restrictions apply to *lubambo* as apply to marriage. The lover must also recognise the occasions when intercourse between man and wife is forbidden. It is, for instance, a serious offence for a man to visit his paramour while she is nursing a child : not because of any damage done to the woman, but simply because the child may suffer. Should he break this rule the husband would claim substantial damages

9. KUSENA

In addition to the above there are less permanent forms of recognised sexual partnership. *Kusena* means to hand a wife temporarily to another man ; *kusenana* means to exchange wives. *Kusena* is a courtesy extended to a friend or honoured visitor. The woman is given a present, *chipo*, but this does not devolve any right upon the giver. Should he venture to enter the woman's hut on another occasion, without the husband's invitation, he would render himself liable to a fine for adultery.

Kusenana is a mutual arrangement, for a brief or long period, by which each of two men gives the other the privilege of entering his wife's hut. Innumerable disputes arise out of this ; as when one thinks the other takes undue advantage.

For example, Jongo and Namaunga made such an arrangement ; the former used the other's wife several times, and Namaunga used Jongo's once. Jongo gave the woman a small ox, but the husband returned it saying that he wanted a big one. That was tantamount to breaking the agreement and claiming damages for adultery, and Jongo felt aggrieved.

Jongo paid the ox demanded in addition to the small one, and bided his time. Then when Namaunga visited the other woman, Jongo made him pay two cows.

While the arrangement is usually between married men, a man will sometimes lend his wife to a bachelor friend on the understanding that when he marries he will fulfil his share of the bargain. But it happens that sometimes the younger man does not feel inclined to do so, and then the other claims damages. Or it may be that the older man wishes to enjoy his privilege while refusing to allow the other a continuance of his. Such a case arose between two men, A and B, who were friends. Before A married, B used to allow him access to his wife. Then A married and B refused A his privilege while maintaining his own. This made A angry and he watched for his opportunity which came when some one told him that B had a sickness. He promptly claimed against B for making his wife sick.

In all such cases children are recognised as the husband's. Sometimes a claim is brought against the man for causing the woman's pregnancy. In one case, after the agreement had been made and the man had given the woman a shell and a hoe as a present, the husband died leaving his wife pregnant. Then the husband's brother claimed against the man for making the woman pregnant. The man agreed to pay two oxen, a blanket, and a shell; but the brother returned them and claimed a cow.

The infertility of a marriage is a source of such disappoint-ment to both parties that neither can rest content with the other. The account given below explains what may happen in such an event; and it will be seen that the custom of *kusena* may be practised when the husband is impotent. First he proves that the cause of the infertility is in himself, and then hands his wife to a friend, bind-ing himself by an oath before the heads of the village not to charge him with adultery. Any children resulting from this will of course be acknowledged by the husband as his.

"A woman who doesn't give birth is a harlot, many have pierced her womb and she will not bear children again. Even if she is handsome she will be divorced. If you do not divorce her, where are you going to find a child ? Then therefore if you are not an adulterer, you prove yourself by having intercourse with another woman, saying, ' Let us see whether I cannot give her a stomach.' If she conceives, those who laughed at you will be confounded. Having thus proved that the sterility is in the wife, you divorce her. Or if you love her too much to divorce her, you build another house for a second wife who will bear children. Again, when a man marries a woman, they put them into a hut, that they may sleep together. Then when he does so, and he cannot manage to function, the next morning the woman rises early and goes to her mother-in-law's hut and sits down. And the man's people cook very early a little bread for the naming. They call the man, and he comes, and sits. When he breaks off a small morsel and gives it to the wife and she refuses to accept it, they know that their son is impotent, he has no strength. Then they speak to the woman : ' Just agree to the name.' Then he names her. And they say, ' All right, let us see how he is.' So at evening when they sleep together, and the same thing happens, in the morning they ask the woman, ' Can he do it ? ' She denies, and says, ' No, your son cannot. He is only a woman, what he ate was pap only, he is not a man who can beget children.' Then the woman rebels, and goes back to stay at her home. They then say to him, ' You must give your wife to another ' So he gives her to another man whom he loves, and brings her, saying, ' Let us go to the house.' Then she gets up and he brings her. On arrival he calls that friend of his and takes him to the elders that they may judge. Says he : ' This friend of mine I bring to the elders here so that they may hear our business.' Then he says : ' This is the one that I lend (lit. give) my wife to, if they converse I will not bring a fault against him. Before the sun sets, let me die the death if I bring a fault against him.' So all salute and the woman is afterwards justified by bearing a child ; she cannot be expected to remain with him who is only a bit of pap."

10. ADULTERY

Besides these forms of recognised sexual relations, there is a very considerable amount of illicit intercourse that comes under the heading of Adultery. As we have already seen, it is attended by no moral disapprobation, but is looked upon as a breach of proprietary rights and reckoned as *buditazhi*. In former days the offence was often punished by cutting off the man's hands, as if he were a thief. That was only sometimes; mostly then, and always now, the offence is met by the payment of a cow. The offender, unless he ransoms himself by paying a fine, is enslaved. Among the Batema there have been instances of a husband spearing the offender caught in the act, but we have never known such a thing among the Ba-ila; they are usually content with a cow.

If the woman is the wife of a chief, the damages may be increased to three cows. If the adultery be committed with a pregnant or nursing woman the offence is a very serious one, because of the harm done to the child. In a certain case the child was still-born and the woman suffered greatly. The husband claimed six cows from the adulterer. Should the woman die the case is still more serious: it is then a matter of *lwembe* ("blood money"). Twenty cows will hardly expiate his crime. He has, as they say, *kudia mutwi wa muntu* ("to pay for the head of a person").

A feature of adultery cases is that very often they are not brought to court until a considerable time has elapsed. The woman keeps quiet, and then one day in an outburst of confidence, or perhaps when having an altercation with her husband, she tells him. He does not bear any resentment to her, but goes and claims damages from the adulterer.

Sometimes a man makes a claim against another who "played" with his wife when they were still children. If he had not been betrothed to her in her childhood, he has no right to any damages, but he may succeed in bullying the man into parting with a beast or something. If the girl had been betrothed to him when the thing happened, he would be justified by custom in making the claim.

In claims for adultery it is not necessary at all to prove

that actual connection took place. Indeed the interfering with a woman's garment would be grounds for a claim. Cases have been known where a woman has been touched accidentally and a claim was made against the man for adultery.

Finally, we must notice that it is a common custom for women, after agreement with their husbands, to go and prostitute themselves. They call this *kuweza lubono munganda* (" to hunt wealth in the house "). The woman returns with her report, and the husband straightway claims damages. The proceeds belong to him, the woman having to be content with the *chipo* given her by the man, but after she has earned several cows for him, he may give her one, but she has no right to it. It happens sometimes that when a wife is divorced she puts in a claim against her husband for her share of these proceeds. Custom does not substantiate her claim, but if she is backed by an influential, strong man in the shape of a new husband she, or he, may succeed in forcing him to pay. A woman will say on such an occasion that she makes the demand because she hunted that game herself.

To illustrate the kind of thing that takes place, we may recall a famous case that was brought to the court at Namwala. In 1905 a man named Kalosa came to Mr. Dale to complain that his wife had run away ; as it transpired that he had thrashed her, Mr. Dale refused to intervene. Shortly afterwards a man named Shalampondo told Mr. Dale that he wished to marry this woman ; and was advised not to do so until she was properly divorced. He waited three weeks, and then, being much in love, he married the woman. As was to be expected, Kalosa's representative immediately claimed the woman ; the case came into court and damages were given against Shalampondo. Then the woman was divorced and Shalampondo married her properly. He kept her four or five years and then Kakobela, Kalosa's chief, tried to get her back, but failed because the *chiko* having been returned they had no more right to her. Kakobela declared his fixed intention to get her by hook or crook, no matter what the magistrate might say. Three months later the woman ran away from

Shalampondo to Kakobela, and when a case was brought declared that she preferred the latter. Then another case came on to get back the *chiko* that Shalampondo had given. When the case was over, the woman put in a claim against Shalampondo for the proceeds of her prostitution while his wife ; as this was contrary to native law it was dismissed. But in such cases the success of the claimant depends less upon legality than upon his own influential position and his capacity for bullying. And Kakobela being a strong man would achieve his purpose.

11. RAPE

This is a common occurrence, though it does not often come before the European magistrate. Damages are given up to ten cows.

One of the worst offences known to the Ba-ila is to assault a woman in her sleep. This applies, not only to an unmarried, but also to a married woman assaulted thus by her husband. A woman has been known to leave her husband for this cause. Of such a man the people say, " *Watwala mukaintu, wamuteba madiabona, waditaya. Nkambo kakando* " (" He married a woman, and had intercourse with her in her sleep, and so committed *buditazhi*. It is a great fault ").

12. PERVERSIONS

Instances of sexual inversion are known, but whether congenital or acquired it is impossible to say. We have known of only one man who dressed always as a woman, did woman's work such as plaiting baskets, and lived and slept among, but not with, the women. This man was a *mwaami* (" a prophet ").

The practice of pederasty, which is not very rare, is condemned, particularly as they are afraid that the one who submits may conceive. The penalty imposed on the lover, as decreed by law, is the payment of three or four oxen.

We have heard of the use, among women, of a priapus, that is, a phallus made of hide or wood.

Masturbation is quite prevalent.

Certain forms of sexual relations with animals are not unknown.

Cunnilingus is considered an extreme crime. The guilty persons are required to forfeit ten or twelve oxen. In a court case, a wife once charged her divorced husband with this crime. She asserted that the act had made her sterile and that he had committed it during her sleep: this was the worst crime of all.

A woman guilty of fellatio may, according to the law, be bound into slavery.

NOTE.—Captain Dale, writing from Rhodesia in November 1917, tells me that the Government is endeavouring to stop some of the evil customs we have described.   No marriage with girls under puberty is to be permitted, though betrothal is allowed.   All marriages have now to be reported to the District Official and the girl is to declare her willingness.   Something is also being done against the Lubambo custom.

To correct an impression that might be conveyed by this chapter, I add a note written by Captain Dale : "There are so many unhappy unions, and so many instances of infidelity come under the official's notice, that he is apt to conclude they are all of a like character.   I believe this to be a mistake; there are many instances of sincere affection and many happy unions of long standing; a number of instances, too, where, when death has severed the tie, the survivor has proved inconsolable and sought relief and oblivion in suicide."   With this I agree.—E. W. S.

PART IV

CHAPTER XX

*

DYNAMISM

1. THE THEORY

WE now enter upon a part of our subject the interest and importance of which are only equalled by its difficulty. Behind all the actions and customs of the people lies their conception of the unseen. A casual observation of the Ba-ila might lead one to the conclusion that they are a materialistic people, but in fact they are very largely concerned with what is invisible and mysterious. Indeed we may say that they are more concerned with the invisible than with the visible. To understand their life we must strive to understand the things which lie behind. To attain this understanding is very difficult, largely because of the haziness in their own minds. For any one to expect reasoned precise statements from them is to be disappointed. They are content with resting in the beliefs inculcated in childhood without exercising their minds as to their logicality. It may be there are ideas current among them that have been derived from different sources. As we have seen, the Ba-ila are very largely a mixed people; and we can easily imagine women introduced from other tribes teaching their children the ideas they have brought with them from their native places. In this way, probably, different beliefs have been thrown into the cauldron and the result is a hotchpotch. These ideas all, to change the figure, get into circulation and the people accept them without question as to their origin and without comparison. Hence one must be prepared to find incongruous elements in their beliefs.

Professor W. James in his *Varieties of Religious Experience* says : " The religious phenomenon studied as an inner fact and apart from ecclesiastical and theological complications has shown itself to consist everywhere, and at all its stages, in the consciousness which individuals have of an intercourse between themselves and higher powers with which they feel themselves to be related."

That the Ba-ila have such a consciousness of higher powers cannot be questioned by any one with even a superficial knowledge of them. They not only believe in their existence but are quite sure that they have intercourse with them. That is to say, they are religious.

But in explicating their ideas on these subjects we have to begin on a lower level than this. Besides these higher powers—the Mizhimo and Leza—the Ba-ila, as we have already repeatedly seen in previous chapters, have a consciousness of hidden mysterious forces that we should call impersonal. Whether or not there has been a historical development of belief, there is certainly what to our minds is a logical development in their ideas, a development from the impersonal to the personal, from charm to prayer, from *musamo* to *mizhimo*, from *mizhimo* to Leza. In other words, we can distinguish traces of development from dynamism to something approaching monotheism.

In the earlier chapters of this book we have used the words magic, magical as convenient expressions for the mysterious elements in life ; but we prefer not to use the words in this connection. And that for two reasons. They are ambiguous in meaning, and they appear to convey the sense of something inferior, illicit, bad. Nor for similar reasons do we use that other term so commonly employed in descriptions of African races : Fetishism. We prefer the word Dynamism, because the beliefs and practices we wish to include under it have not necessarily any evil intention, and because it expresses simply what we believe to be the nature of their belief and practice—the belief in, and the practices associated with the belief in hidden, mysterious, super-sensible, pervading energy, powers, potencies, forces. We may call them what we please ; there is no need to be more definite than the Ba-ila are themselves; the more vague the name we give to the dunamis the nearer we shall come to the Ba-ila conception. We may call it X, or use the word Od : the name does not matter, as long as we recognise the existence and nature of the belief itself.

In previous chapters we have recognised a certain dualism in the practices of the Ba-ila; such as that expressed in their terms *Tonda* and *Buditazhi*. In regard to homicide, for example, we found that in some cases the offender is punished by the community, and in others is left to the vengeance of mysterious powers. There is, on the one hand, the action of persons, living or dead; on the other hand there is the X vaguely connoted by such terms as *tonda, malweza, chikuto, lusasa, musamo, matushi*. This dualism is a marked feature of their life and runs through all their conceptions of the unseen; on the one hand there are the *mizhimo* and Leza : both to be regarded, as we shall see, as personal; on the other hand, the Od, which is impersonal, though often it is vaguely personal.

We use the terms with hesitancy. It is very difficult indeed to decide as to what extent the Ba-ila recognise personality in the world. In their marvellous grammatical classification of words, the Ba-ila put in a class by themselves, substantives with the singular prefix *mu-*, and the plural prefix *ba-* ; to this class belong personal names : *muntu, bantu*, are definitely " person, persons." Another class has the prefixes *chi-, shi-*, and comprises things. *Chintu* is a thing. The root *ntu* would seem to indicate existence : the prefix *mu-*, personality ; and *chi-*, " thing-ship." So far all is clear. But there is another class, with the prefixes *mu-, mi-*, to which belong the names of trees and, among others, the words *musamo, misamo* (" medicines "), *muzhimo, mizhimo*, the divinities, which seem to belong to an intermediate concept : neither personal nor impersonal. They have the personal singular prefix, *mu-*, but *mi-* in the plural. Another feature of the classification is that the names of animals, though not in many cases carrying the *mu-* prefix, belong to the *mu- ba-* class, forming the plural with *ba-*. This might seem to predicate personality in the animals. But what their idea of personality is we do not know. Some of the animals, as we shall see presently, are in many respects classed as persons, others are not. We can only leave the question in this vague state : there are persons—reckoning personality as we reckon it ; there are impersonal things ; and there are things on the hazy borderland between personality and impersonality.

Are we to reckon this Dynamism as religion or not ? If the concept of a personal God is essential to religion, then it is not. Whether the X can be described as a " higher power " is difficult to say : it is higher in the sense of being super-sensible, mightier than men ; and higher in that it is treated with reverence and submission ; but we could not, with any regard for the accepted meaning of the word, call it a god. If intense faith in the efficacy of the ritual and in the powers recognised in the ritual ; and if a strong, and, on the whole, a wholesome influence on conduct, are constituent elements of religion, then Dynamism is certainly a religion. Perhaps it may best be regarded as a proleptic stage in the growth of religious ideas.

If we are to bring Dynamism into relation to the Ancestor-worship and Leza-cult to be described in subsequent chapters, we must revert to the already mentioned dualism. On the one hand, on a horizontal line, we have the X ; on a parallel line, the belief in personality, which, prolonged into the unseen world, brings us to the ghosts. The X powers are extended into the cosmical sphere ; and somehow in a paradoxical way the two lines there meet : the X powers come to partake of the personal characteristics of the ghost : and the result is a personal, or quasi-personal, Being uniting the potency of the X with the personality of men and ghosts. In some such diagrammatic fashion we may venture to describe the undoubted connection. The lines, however, are not to be drawn clear and distinct, but shaded into each other—the shading representing all the vague undefinable gradations between personality and impersonality.

It seems that the X pervades all things. Usually it is quiescent. In itself it is neither good nor bad ; it is amoral, neutral ; but it can be tapped by people and turned to use—to evil use or good according to the intention of the person who uses it. The *banganga, basonzhi*, and *balozhi* are those who have the secret of manipulation. The *banganga* can draw out the forces contained in various plants and other things and put them to beneficent purposes, as in curing the sick and making amulets and talismans; or to maleficent purposes, as when they provide the warlock with death-dealing drugs. The *basonzhi* can tap the forces, and by their means look into the future and discover things unknown; they are uniformly beneficent in intention. On the other hand, the *balozhi* draw on these mysterious energies to plague and destroy their fellow-men.

The only thing in civilisation which we can compare with this conception is electricity. We are to imagine all things charged with something as mysterious and pervasive as electricity. Like electricity, it can be utilised for legitimate ends: but it is a perilous thing to mishandle. For any rash or ignorant person to come into contact with a live wire is, as we know, dangerous. And, we suppose, a person could be so charged with electricity that he would be a danger to any one touching him. So in the minds of the Ba-ila is it with this immanent energy.

The forces are dangerous things to interfere with. They are therefore *tonda* (taboo). For an ordinary person, under ordinary circumstances, and without an antidote, to interfere with them is forbidden; it is dangerous to himself and the community. By saying certain things, doing certain actions, eating certain foods, he may liberate these energies with fatal consequences to himself and his neighbours. Persons in certain conditions, and things put to certain uses, come into intimate contact with these forces and are therefore *tonda*. It is as if at certain times the separating medium becomes attenuate, the insulating rubber, so to speak, gets worn off the live wire, and people come into close contact with the forces.

That the neutral force may be turned to good or bad use explains many curious things in the practices of the Ba-ila. Incest is one of the things that bring men into violent connection with it, and is therefore taboo. The incestuous person is expressly called a *mulozhi* (" a warlock "), a trafficker with forbidden powers. But incest under certain conditions, *i.e.* when a man is wishful of special good fortune, is not only permitted but enjoined. So with words. Phallic songs that on ordinary occasions are *tonda*, must be used on the occasion of a funeral, during smelting operations, and on other occasions when the forces are intimately in evidence. In normal times the abnormal is taboo, but in abnormal times the abnormal things are done to restore the normal condition of affairs.

These our generalisations are based, not upon direct information derived from the natives, but upon their customs. We need not repeat what we have already described at some length of their practice of medicine. It would seem that almost any object can be used as a *musamo*. True, there are specific drugs for specific diseases, but it seems that a doctor can discover in anything he chooses a remedy for some complaint, or a charm for some purpose. It is not he who imparts the potency to the object, but he discovers it to be a peculiar manifestation of the all pervading force. And the drugs work not only upon diseases of the body, but also directly upon a man's feelings and disposition. It is not necessary by any means that they should be brought into close contact with him, by wearing or swallowing ; they can act over a distance. Moreover, they can separate by their mysterious action some part of his constitution—his " life "—from the rest, and can change him into another form, both before and after death. Indeed, they can affect ghosts ; and also the elements—changing the direction of rain-clouds, keeping off lightning, and producing rain. Many are the tales told of the way people have gained happiness and prosperity in life through the action of the *misamo*. Here is one example. " There was a very old man who was driven away by his children and went crawling into the forest. There some boys found him and began to jeer and mock the poor old fellow—all but one, who bade them desist, and who brought him some water and food. When the boys were departing the old man called the kind lad back and told him to sit down by his side. He began to cough, and spat the sputum into a small pot ; he then scraped his skin, and the scrapings he added to the sputum. He mixed it all up and told the boy

to drink it. The boy was rather disgusted and couldn't
make out what the old man was up to, but he obeyed.
The old man then said to him : ' That was *musamo,* very
powerful in effect. By giving it to you, I am giving you
bwami (chieftainship), and wealth and long life and good
fortune in hunting. Nothing shall be able to hinder you.'
And so it came to pass. The boy grew up fortunate, wealthy,
renowned, and died at a ripe old age." There would seem to
be no limit to the range of the possibilities of the medicines.
We are reminded of Virgil's lines :

> *has herbas atque haec Ponto mihi lecta venena*
> *ipse dedit Moeris (nascuntur plurima Ponto)*
> *his ego saepe lupum fieri et se condere silvis*
> *Moerim, saepe animas imis excire sepulcris*
> *atque satas alio vidi traducere messis.*
>
> (*Eclogue,* viii. 95.)

And it is not an animistic belief. These things are not
supposed to be possessed of a " soul." When the lover,
the trader, the warrior, the diviner addresses the *musamo*
he is not as a rule conscious of any ghost or spirit in it
(we have noted exceptions to this), he speaks to the
medicine itself. Yet it seems there is an approxima-
tion to animistic conceptions in the importance attached
to the name. Without the name the medicine would
not be what it is with it. One might almost say that
the name bears something of the same relation to the
thing as " soul" to " body." We have even instances
where the people have spoken of the *izhina* (" name ")
entering a person and causing sickness.

We may give here some additional information with
regard to manifestations of this power.

There is a bush called Kamwaya (" the scatterer "),
which may not be used as firewood, nor its poles taken for
building purposes. It has the quality of dispersing things :
hence the name. If you were rash enough to burn it, your
friendship with another person would be dispersed and you
would fight him that day ; and if you were to build a pole
of it into your house it would part asunder. The ancients,
we are informed, found this out. They built a fence partly

of Kamwaya around the village, and afterwards could not understand why one by one their people left them. One of the elders had it revealed to him that it was on account of the Kamwaya ; so all the poles of that tree were pulled up and others put in their places. After a short time strangers began coming to ask permission to build at the village, so the community was restored to its former strength. Then they spread the news abroad, saying, " *Tadizasha, tadizotwa, dilamwaya munzhi* " (" Don't build with it or warm yourselves at its heat, it will scatter the village "). From that day to this *diatonda* (" the tree is taboo ").

But under certain circumstances the power within it can be made to serve a useful purpose. When there has been more rain than is required and the clouds are still gathering, if you take this bush and wave it about you will scatter the clouds, and rain will not fall. And you can make a medicine out of its roots to get rid of that horrible disease called *kafungo*.

Another tree not to be used as firewood is the Mabanga. As we shall see, the corpses of certain people are burnt, and Mabanga is used for the purpose because it burns fiercely, so much so that it can destroy not only the body but the spirit. Because of this power in it, its use is taboo under ordinary circumstances. But, as we saw in Chapter IX., because of its power it is used in smelting iron.

Certain animals and birds are peculiarly manifestations of the X ; they are called *mupuka* (" a monster "), or *muntu* (" a man "), or *mulozhi* (" a witch ") ; some are said to be *malweza* (*i.e.* bad omens, unlucky).

We have already mentioned some of them.

The Chinao cat (see Vol. I. p. 239) is particularly unlucky to children.   It is called *ushibandilwabana* (" He that may not be named to or by children "). If a child is ill in a way that makes it resemble the cat (*kusata kuchinkozha cha munyama wezo*—" to be sick in the likeness of that animal "), its eyes starting out of its head, its fists clenched, its body shaking all over, then they know that the Chinao has affected it ; somebody has brought a skin of the cat into touch with the child, or named the cat in its presence, or the cat has passed by near the child. But a kind of

homeopathic prophylactic can be made from the animal—
that is, it provides its own antidote. Many children for this
purpose have, sewn into the carrying-skin, small medicine-
receptacles made of pieces of the Chinao pelt ; or the mother
wears a Chinao skin. The pelt of the cat is taboo to a person
as a garment—*i.e.* he may not enter a village wearing it,
unless the children have been in this way made proof
against the Chinao's influence. Once protected they can
handle the skin with impunity, and any one can wear it.

The *chikambwe* (blue jay) is another *malweza*. It is
said to fly with a scream up into the sky and to fall lifeless.
Should any one in charge of a child notice this bird, he
would distract the child's attention, lest it should see it and
be influenced by it. It can so affect a child that it too will
die a sudden death. But the power in *chikambwe* can be
made use of, not to cause but to prevent untimely death ;
its feathers are converted into *musamo* for that purpose.

Some animals and birds are termed *bantu* (" persons "),
and *balozhi* (" warlocks "). In them there is a quasi-
personal quality. They are said to have *shingvhule* (*i.e.*
" shadow-souls ") just as men have ; but, unlike men, they
are not reincarnated after death.

We have described the ceremonies following the death
of an elephant. When a man kills an eland he must also
go through certain rites to avert the retaliating power in
the animal. After killing an eland the hunter chews leaves
of a Mukono or Munto bush, together with a piece of
kaumbuswa (ant-heap), holding meanwhile a lump of the
latter under his foot. Some of the chewed leaves he rubs
on his forehead and some on the eland's forehead. Having
done this he throws at the eland's head the piece of ant-
heap that was under his foot. He also cuts and splits a
stick and jumps through the cleft, as the killer of a man
does. He then goes off to the village to get people to help
him in carrying home the meat. On their arrival at the
eland he sits apart while they open the carcass. He must
not join them at first, but once it is opened he may help
them to skin and cut up the animal. Were these rites
omitted, the eland would trouble him—would come at night
and horn him, or in any case cause his death. But the

power in the eland can be put to use. Medicine put into
its horn derives therefrom a more potent efficacy.

The owl (*shishishini*) is another *mulozhi*. If you see it
sitting on your roof in the dusk, and it wakes up and cries,
there will be a death in your home. You are then to throw
a firebrand (*chishishi*) at it to drive it away and take off
the spell. You must not throw a stone at it lest the owl
should micturate upon it and it should dissolve—and you
with it !

The plantain-eater (*induba*), whose red feathers, thought
to be dyed with human blood, are worn as a trophy by
warriors and others, is also reckoned as a *muntu*. As far as
reputation goes, killing an *induba* is the same as killing a
man ; even if you find it lying dead you are entitled to
" put up " the feathers.[1]

The *nakansakwe* (" secretary bird ") is another *mulozhi*.
Ulatonda, it is taboo, because of the mysterious force
manifest in it. It is said that once three people were going
along a road and saw one of these birds ahead. Being
alarmed, they asked each other, " What bird is that ? "
As they were speaking the bird jumped over the path.
One of the three went forward and passed the place where
it had jumped ; the others returned to the village. When
they told why they had turned back, one of the elders
said, " You have done well. That bird is *nakansakwe* ;
he is *tonda* when he jumps the road." The man who
ventured ahead was never seen again ; he disappeared.
So the news went abroad. *Waluchimba nakansakwe* ;
mozo wakwe washia (" Abandon your journey because of
nakansakwe ; his heart is black "). But he can be turned
to use : one of his feathers is a powerful medicine to give
good fortune.

It is to be noticed that it is especially strange, unusual
things, uncommon sights, new-fangled habits, strange foods
and ways of doing things, that are regarded as manifestations
of the hidden powers. It is here that we find the root of
the conservatism of the Ba-ila and their hatred of new

---

[1] This, by the way, is an artifice practised sometimes by a murderer.
When asked by curious people why he wears the feathers, he replies that
he found an *induba* lying dead.

ways. When, *e.g.*, bananas were first introduced by us at Kasenga, we offered some of the fruit to Mungalo. He turned from it with expressions of great horror. " No ! No ! I have never seen that before ! It is *tonda* ! "

There is a certain animal named Chivubavuba, said to live in water. Whether fabulous or no, we cannot say; we have never seen one. If it lives, it is rarely seen, and therefore it is among the things that are *tonda*. The Shilufukwe (the mole) is not rare, but it is rarely seen on the surface in the daytime ; and therefore it is *tonda* to see it out of its burrow. If you saw it, it would grin and one of your friends would die in consequence. To see it in the burrow means nothing.

We have said enough, perhaps, to illustrate what we believe to be the basis of the Ba-ila conception of the world. If we are vague in our descriptions it is because the thing itself is vague. The Ba-ila have never formulated their belief ; it is not so clear, *e.g.*, as their conception of the ghost. We have found no name for the power. The nearest, we think, is *bwanga*, which etymologically would mean " the tying-up, the contents," or better, " content—that which is contained in things." It is used commonly of the medicines.

Vague as it is, this conception is one we can understand, and understand better now than we could have understood it twenty years ago. Is not Science to-day telling us of the energy stored up in the very paving-stones of our streets ? Have we not gained some insight into mysterious metapsychical forces ? Have not bacteriological researches opened up to us a new world of agencies ? We can understand that some experience of the powers of drugs would confirm, if it did not originate, their belief. And we have met with things only explicable on the supposition that they are not ignorant of psychic phenomena. This latter is a subject we hope will be further investigated by more competent observers. We can only express our conviction that these things are known to them.

But there is no formulation of the belief by themselves. It is rather the result of an emotional response to their environment—a world which, to them as to us, is a thing of mystery.

It cannot be wondered at that they should regard any traffic with these hidden powers with horror, traffic, *i.e.*, of an illegitimate sort. They are dreaded in any case, but for a person deliberately to invoke their aid for the purpose of harming and killing his fellows is the most monstrous of all crimes in their eyes. Such people are *balozhi* (witches, warlocks, sorcerers). We have now to give an account of them.

2. WITCHCRAFT

It is impossible to say how many people used to meet with their deaths through suspicion of witchcraft, but the number was probably very great. Under European government it is a crime either to practise or to accuse of practising it. One might have thought that this action of the authorities would have been welcomed by the people ; but as a matter of fact it is a standing grievance that the white man no longer allows them to deal with witches as they used to do. A leading chief said to us one day, " You white men are destroying the community. The *balozhi* are exultant and doing just as they please, because they know we can no longer kill them as we used to do." He then went on to describe what had recently happened in a neighbouring community. A warlock had committed adultery with the chief's wife, caused her to swell up and die. Four wives of the chief had met with the same fate. For his witchcraft he had been driven out of the community, but if he had met with his deserts he would have been burnt.

If it seems strange to any of our readers that what appears to them as a cruel superstition should be thus upheld by the leaders of the people, let them at least recognise the sincerity of the belief. If we believed as they do we should act as they do, or would like to do. Suppose a foreign conqueror made a law in England forbidding any accusation of murder as well as abolishing capital punishment, should not we regard it as the very limit of wickedness ? And witchcraft is murder to the Ba-ila.

We will first transcribe an account dictated to us by an intelligent native of the doings of the *balozhi*.

" A warlock, when he hears of a person's death, goes to

' press ' the deceased. He raises him up as an evil spirit
and takes it away to his own house. This is what he does
with it : if he sees one whom he does not like he sends the
evil spirit to kill that person. When it arrives where that
person is, it appears and he sees it, and, seeing it, dies. It
seems that he sees a person he knows to be dead, and being
greatly startled he dies. Before dying he makes it known,
saying, ' I have seen so-and-so who is dead.' Thereupon,
if they don't hurry and doctor him, he dies. It means,
that that evil spirit was sent by a sorcerer. Others are
sent to the grain-fields, being told to go and bring ears of
corn from so-and-so's field. So the evil spirits go and take
the ears to that sorcerer. He works and works upon them,
so that when the owner of the field comes to harvest he
may gather a large quantity, but it does not increase (*i.e.*
the heap in his granary), because it is made mysteriously
to disappear. And so it is said, ' His grain is fleeting grain
on account of the spirits, that's why it does not last, does
not stay.' Again, if a man has a lot of grain left over from
last year, and all the time it does not come to an end, it
means that he has something that goes on and on,[1] that's
why it does not end. What takes place is, that as soon as
it begins to end the spirit adds to it, puts more there : that
is witchcraft.

" Again, spirits are sent to clansmen. If that warlock
has a clansman who is very rich, he sends evil spirits that
they may kill his children. So they are bereft of their
children ; two die perhaps in one month. If then the
children are all killed, he begins at the wives, saying, ' Go
and kill such-and-such a wife.' So the spirits kill them.
Or if he has got two they kill one of them. If he sees that
is done, he then sends the spirits to the man's people,
saying, ' Go and kill them.' So they kill all his slaves.
If he be a chief, his chieftainship vanishes and he becomes
the poor owner of a single hut, he who had built a great
village. Or he becomes a vagabond, and it is said of him,

[1] *Kafunduluzho* (a thing that does not come to an end). The verb is
kufunda (" to regrow ") ; *Maila alafunduluka*, (" the maila keeps on
coming "). The word would be applied to the widow of Zarephath's barrel
of meal which wasted not and to the cruse of oil which failed not.
(1 Kings xvii. 16.)

'That man was a chief. He was invaded by witchcraft; people bewitched him.'

" This is *inzuikizhi* (witch medicine). The warlock sends a snake, saying, ' Go and bite so-and-so.' So it does; the snake goes and bites him and he dies. They doctor and doctor him, but he does not recover, the wound from the snake does not heal. Presently it kills him. They say it is witch medicine, which means, it was sent from the hand of a person, *i.e.* from a sorcerer. Others send lions, saying, ' Bite so-and-so.' They go and bite him. They who know the medicine for lions, doctor and doctor him, but he gets worse and dies. It is to say, the lion is from the hands of a man. Others work upon the very food—food that is eaten, whether bread or meat or fish or boiled maize, or strong beer or light beer, or anything else, anything that is eaten. It is sent in just the same way, the warlock saying, ' Kill so-and-so.' So he eats that food as he always eats, and it introduces sorcery into his body, and he gets sick perhaps in the stomach, and he says, ' I am dead in the stomach! I am dead in the stomach!' They who know stomach medicine doctor and doctor him, but he does not recover, he dies. They say it is *inzuikizhi*. As for bewitching, they bewitch in this way. He who does it leaves his place at night, and at the village opens the gateway, and though there may be dogs they do not bark. On arrival at the door of the person whom he is going to bewitch he dances in the night, he pulls out grass above the door, and dances with the bunches in his hands, he stamps about, dancing. Tired of dancing, he begins to measure out funeral fire-places all over the village of the person he is bewitching. This is what he does, saying to himself, ' You people light a fire here!. And you, so-and-so, light here! You women light here! And you men light here! And you dancers light here!' So in time he completes the circle of the village, measuring out the fire-places, where they are to light the fires for cooking. Presently he against whom he danced begins to sicken and then dies. They light the fires just as he had measured them out in the village; yes, they do just like that.

" The shadow that is seen, they say it is the person.

When a person dies the corpse remains alone and the shadow goes to God. It is sorcerers who say they will take the shadow while he is still living and the body will remain by itself. The sorcerer takes the shadow and goes to work on it with medicine, and having done that, why, the man dies. When he dies, he does not become reborn on earth : so they say he is a *mudimbe* (' a pressed-one '), he has utterly perished."

As a further illustration of the working of witchcraft, we give the following account, dictated by a native, of the doings of a woman named Namiyobo. She was trying to get the chieftainship at Nanzela for herself, and so, in the belief of the people, bewitched the chief. The point of this narrative is not whether the accusation was true, but the manner in which she and others are related to have acted.

" Now there the old woman went to the doctors that they might give her medicine ; and the doctor administered medicine to her and said, ' He will die, he will not cultivate his fields this year.' Then she gave him a gun and some sovereigns, that doctor of hers. Then as they were leaving, the doctor told her, ' Take some ash from his fire-place.' Indeed they took some ash and put it with the medicine, and so doctored it. Having done this, they put a curse upon him, saying, ' You, oh medicine, we eat you, so that when we arrive at our home Namanza may die. And, see, he must not die here ; let him die at his home.' And truly they took some ground from his footprints. On their arrival they (her attendants) passed through the village ; she herself passed by through the veld. Then they began to discuss the matter of the chieftainship. And she with false lips (lit. greasy lips) made it good for herself, saying, ' I am only an old woman, I will have only the power of *Kachinka* (*i.e.* an inferior position) and Namanza shall have that of *Shambala*.' But Namanza refused, saying, ' No, not so.'

" Before long he went to Kazangala, and on arrival there he sent people to bring him some milk. Then arose Kayoba and Mwanamboloma and took the milk. On arrival they found him quite well. He was very grateful, but they had done to him so that he should die at his home and not return. Thereupon he began to sicken, and before many days Namanza was dead.

" Then arose a great tumult.

" ' Who has bewitched him ? ' Some said, ' It is Kazhiampande ; if it is not he who bewitched him, who is it ? Is it not that youngster who long ago destroyed the chiefs ? ' They had falsely accused Pobola long ago of bewitching somebody. But the Creator had refused, and also his divinities saw to him that Pobola should not die. Nevertheless they disputed.

" ' Who is it ? ' Then they said, ' It is Nakabanga, the son of Kanchemba.' And then again there was a great row. And Nakabanga resented it, saying, ' Why do you, Mutabakomo, and your wife falsely accuse me ? '[1] Then they denied, saying, ' We simply put the fault on others, saying that perhaps it is Kazhiampande the younger, whom they named before.' Others said, ' No, this is not the one you named, it is the other.' So then Nakabanga went to his relations, and on arrival called them all, saying, ' Come, they are accusing me of witchcraft.' So all the ba-Mala came together, and on their arrival they asked, ' Who is it that accused our child ? ' Mutabakomo and his people said, ' We don't know, ask him himself.' Nakabanga answered ' Kazhiampande is the warlock, ask them ; if he is not afraid we will buy *mwazhi*.' So Mutabakomo bought it, and when they arrived they seized a dog, and made it drink, beginning thus to charge it, ' O *mwazhi*, if it was we who said that Kazhiampande was a witch, this very day, oh do you die ; if it was not we, you must not die.' Really the dog lived, and when it recovered the ba-Mala stood condemned. So they left it, saying, ' Let us wait for the chief,' *i.e.* the magistrate."

We have to make a clear distinction between the *munganga* and the *mulozhi* : the former is the doctor, skilled in all kinds of *misamo* (" medicines ") ; the latter is a warlock or witch, a dealer in black magic, a trafficker in forbidden forces, always with a bad purpose. They come

---

[1] This seems obscure. There were two men of the name of Kazhiampande, one Pobola and the other Nakabanga. The latter thought he was being accused, whereas really it was the former.

into association when the *mulozhi* secures from the *munganga* the powerful drugs with which he or she works. Further, a *munganga* may be a *mulozhi*, but that is not part of his profession. *Bunganga*, the quality, practices of the doctor, is quite distinct from *bulozhi*, the quality, practices of the witch.

A person, moved by hatred or jealousy, may send to a doctor to secure witchcraft medicine. It is such powerful stuff that it needs very delicate handling. We know of a case where the medicine was so strong that it killed the messenger who had been sent to fetch it! We have known people assembled in court during a witchcraft trial to make a bolt for the door when the presiding magistrate proposed to open up and examine the contents of the packages of medicine.

The warlock secures his medicine, and in virtue of it can exercise his black art. As we have seen, there are several ways in which he can set to work.

First, by "pressing" (*kudimba*) a man's spirit. The man may be alive at the time, but the witch abstracts his "soul," and what is left is only the empty shell, and of course that soon withers, and the man dies; or, the warlock waits until the actual death and then impresses the disembodied spirit into his service. This spirit is called a *Chizwa*, *Shikazwa*, *Kazwa*, all forms of the same name; or *Kayobela* (a chirping spirit); or *Kapeo*. The names vary, but the demon is much the same. The essential thing is that it is in the possession of the warlock and is subservient to his will. He may send it to appear to any one; the person sees the spirit, and in terror falls sick and dies. Or he may send it to fetch the grain out of another person's field. The owner does not notice the theft, for to all appearance the grain is still there. But it is only phantasmal; the essence has been abstracted. It has no body, and when he harvests it the store does not get any bigger. It has been taken away long ago by the warlock's familiar. Not only does his enemies' grain disappear, but his own is increased by this means; he grows rich through the activities of his demons.

The technical term for the effluence from the warlock is

inzuikizhi. The root of the word is *zua* : *kuzua*, or *kuzuwa*, means to push over, thrust out ; and the word means literally, " that by means of which you thrust out in the direction of somebody." It may take several forms. It may be an animal or a snake, either a real one or a phantom. It may be the witch himself in the shape of a hyena or lion or snake. While the rest of the village is sound asleep the warlock may arise, transform himself into a hyena, and attack his enemy.

Or the *inzuikizhi* may take another form. Our informant speaks of food which is " worked upon." The verb here used is *kuindauka* (to turn over and over, reshape, transform). The reference is not to the poisoning of food in the ordinary sense of the word, though we do not deny that some witches may be mere poisoners. The meaning is this. The warlock takes food in his hands, says some incantation over it, and sends forth a phantom of the food, which appears in the man's dish as if it were his own food, but which in reality is full of a deadly essence that, entering his body, will kill him. So when the account speaks of a chief being killed through his milk, it does not necessarily mean that it was poisoned ; but in some way the milk was " worked upon " by the witch, either by actual contact or by *actio in distans*. Or the witch may secure something that has been more or less in contact with the person : some earth from his footprints, ash from his fire, hair or nail-parings, and by working on these he is able to kill the owner.

The essential point is that the action of the warlock takes place telergetically, *i.e.* over a distance.

Sometimes he approaches nearer his victim, but still remains out of actual touch with him. It is a weird picture, drawn by our informant, of the warlock rising at night and making his way unseen and unheard, so that even the dogs do not bark at him, to the door of his enemy's hut. He casts a spell upon the person. He dances with the grass in his hands, repeating over and over in his mind the words that are to send the person to his doom. He plans out the person's funeral. At funerals a number of fires are built in a village for the accommodation of the visitors ; and the warlock marks the places where these fires are to be lit. He could not more plainly indicate his evil intention. He is not only predicting, but actually causing, the person's death.

The dire effects of this belief in witchcraft have often been pointed out, and we need not enlarge upon them. It is inimical to industry and economy. A person who should labour hard to increase his crops above those of his fellows, or who should be sparing and not waste his grain, would expose himself to a charge of witchcraft. Some spiteful person is sure to start whispering, " Yes, we know what that means ! If we had *tuyobela* in our huts we could have plenty of grain also ! " Once set going, such suspicions soon spread and grow, and the person is lucky if he does not have to swallow the *mwazhi*, or have it swallowed for him by proxy by some unfortunate dog. So a man dare not be too prosperous, and the ambition, if he feels it, to rise above his fellows is very rudely checked. An accusation of witchcraft is a very useful weapon in the hands of an enemy. People who make themselves in any way obnoxious to their neighbours can very easily be despatched. Some-times whole families are wiped out. When a death occurs, as is vividly portrayed by one of our informants, there is suspicion and tumult, and innocent people are seized upon and made to pass the ordeal. It is horrible to think of the hundreds and thousands of people who have been hurried to a violent death through such means.

How much is there in it ? Is there anything at all ? It may seem strange to any one who regards witchcraft as " the culminant example of human ignorance and folly " that we should ask such questions. But at the risk of ridicule we will profess that we believe there is really some-thing behind the intense conviction of the Ba-ila. We readily allow there are many cases where there is not a shadow of any rational ground for suspicion ; perhaps most cases are like that. Yet if there be not a modicum of truth in the thing we cannot account satisfactorily to ourselves for the intense belief in it.

Auto-suggestion plays a considerable part—that much is certain. We remember a man—a big stalwart fellow, who never appeared to us of a cowardly nature—being greatly concerned because after returning home he found a string of beads, with a small black mass attached, hanging in his hut. Nobody could tell who had put it there. It seemed to have sprung up out of the earth. The strangeness of it preyed on the man's mind. He had of course from childhood been accustomed to hearing about warlocks and their doings, and had never for a moment doubted their power. Now what was to him the awful truth took possession of his mind : somebody had put this in his hut to bewitch him. He was changed at once from a bright, laughing, cheerful being into a miserable creature. You could see him getting ill, and we believe that if we had not taken him in hand he would have died. He was, by auto-suggestion, killing himself. It must be remembered that the minds of these people are very suggestible. Again and again have we noticed people giving up all hope because they believed they would die of the sickness that had seized them. They made no effort, but simply resigned themselves to their fate. It is in such soil that witchcraft flourishes.

And if they can suggest themselves into death, it is easy to see that they can receive suggestions to the same effect from others. We cannot support our belief by any range of illustrative facts, but we are inclined to see in suggestion the ground for much of the witchcraft. Mr. F. V. Worthington, who has had a very wide experience of natives, related to us two instances that had come under his personal knowledge. In one of these an old man sitting in a hut was much tormented by some boys jeering at him outside. At last he rushed out, seized one of them, gripped him by the leg, and said, " You are lame ! " And the boy was lame. When Mr. Worthington saw him he had been lame ever since. This is a very good example of the power of suggestion.

But even if this accounts for some of the cases of witchcraft it cannot account for all. As we have seen, the essential part of witchcraft is that it is done from a distance without any mediating instrument that can be sensed. They believe in telepathy and telesthesia and telergy. The first of these is perhaps accepted by most

people in these days; and we have only to go a step
further and grant that one mind can affect another over a
distance and we have all that is necessary to support belief
in witchcraft. Or if we cannot go so far, simply by
acknowledging as a fact that there is telepathic communion
of mind with mind, we grant what is necessary: for
if I can convey to another mind suggestions of sickness
and death that is quite sufficient. The suggestion from
without will set up auto-suggestion, and the man will
persuade himself that he is going to die, and he will die.

It would seem, therefore, that our modern psychology
is bringing us back to where the Ba-ila stand in this
respect—an illustration of the dictum: " The intuitions
of the savage are the reasoned convictions of modern
science." The difference is that the Ba-ila would not
recognise the occult power as latent in the mind; they
would say it is derived from the *musamo*, the expression
and vehicle of the all-pervading force.

CHAPTER XXI

*

THE DOCTRINE OF SOULS

IN trying to discover what the Ba-ila believe about the psychical structure of man it will be best to take a somewhat roundabout course and lead up to the conclusion through a study of the funerary and other practices.

1. DEATH AND FUNERARY CUSTOMS

These people, like all others, have meditated about death, and like so many others have come to the conclusion that death is not in the original constitution of things. Unlike other peoples, they do not say that every death is unnatural and caused by witchcraft, for, as we have seen, they ascribe sickness and death to other and some natural causes. But they look back to the beginning of things and speak of a time when death was not. Sir James Frazer says there are four types of myth explaining the origin of death.[1] The first of these, the type of the Two Messengers, is common to the Ba-ila with many other Bantu tribes. Their story is as follows :

God (Leza) sent Chameleon, saying : " Go and tell men that they shall die and pass away for ever." He started on his journey but travelled very slowly, and rested often on the way. Then God saw that he delayed and sent Hare, saying : " Tell them that they shall die and return." On his arrival Hare announced to the people : " You shall die and return." But Chameleon contradicted him, saying : " No, that is not what God sent us to say. He sent us,

---

[1] *The Belief in Immortality* (London, 1913), vol. i. p. 60.

saying : ' They shall die and pass away for ever.' '' But Hare would not have it so : " That is not the message. He said : ' They shall return.' '' Thereupon Hare returned to God in anger and said : " Yon person whom you sent, he has told them : ' You shall pass away for ever.' '' And God answered : " All right, let it be as he has told them."

We have heard another version of this myth : God sent Hare and sending him said : " Go and take a message of death to men. You go also, Chameleon, and take a message of life." The Hare arrived first and announced : " Men shall die and pass away for ever." After he had delivered this message Chameleon arrived. Said he : " Men shall die and shall return." But it was too late.

In the first version Hare brings a promise of life ; Chameleon of death ; in the second Hare arrives first with a message of death and Chameleon follows, too late, with a promise of life.

Notwithstanding the contradiction, the meaning is plain : death was not in the original constitution of things, but came afterwards.

This myth is common to the Bantu tribes, but the Ba-ila have another, to the same effect, which seems to be peculiar to them.

In the beginning, it is said, a man descended from above accompanied by his mother, his wife, his mother-in-law, cattle, goats, and dogs. The women herded the cattle but used to quarrel about it. One would say : " It's your turn to-day," and another would reply : " No, it's yours." Consequently the cattle frequently got lost. One evening the cattle had not returned and it was too late to find them. They went next morning into the forest to look for them, and found that they had turned into buffaloes. That was the first misfortune. After a time, another misfortune arrived : the mother of the man's wife died. Then the woman said to her husband : " Let us go and bring back my mother, she must not be allowed to leave us like this." The man answered : " Oh, it's all right, she will turn up of her own accord." After a time the man's dog died, and he said to his wife : " Let us go and bring back my dog." But the woman refused, saying : " You want to go and fetch your dog, but my mother went away and has not returned and you wouldn't go and fetch her." Then the man's mother died. And he said to his wife, " Let us go and fetch my mother." But the woman refused, saying : " No, when my mother died you wouldn't go after her, and now I refuse to go after yours." And that is why that ever since people die and do not come back ; it was because of the doings of those first people who lived.

We have heard another version of this myth among the Bambala. The place of the man is taken by Leza (God), of whom it is said that he had a wife, mother, a mother-in-law, and five children, three sons and two daughters. His mother died, but when he told his wife that she must return to life, she said : " No, let her die, she has eaten all my beans in the field." Leza agreed to this. After five months, Leza's mother-in-law died, and his wife said : " Let her return ! " But he said : " She return ! And my mother already rotten ! " The wife said : " Do you refuse, husband ? " He replied : " Yes, I do refuse, for when my mother died you refused." So the woman said : " Let her die, then. This is *lufu lukando*, the great death." And that is how death began ; it was owing to the *butavhu* (" greed ") of Leza's wife. And Leza told those whom he had sent down to earth : " I also shall die. And when my heir begins to weep, I shall descend to you and burn houses.[1] And I give you medicine which you must quickly give to the people who are burnt in the houses. Because here above my relation is dead, I shall kill you on earth." So he sent down diseases, and also medicines. Said he : " I give you both : when a person is sick doctor him. If I will that he live, he will live ; if I will that he die, he will die." And having given them death, he also gave them *musamo wa luzhalo* (" birth medicine ") so that the race should not die out. So it is that when a person with no children weeps and says : " If only I had children to leave behind me ! " they say : " Leza it is that refuses that you should bear children."

---

[1] The reference of course is to rain and lightning. The idea appears to be that at the end of a rainy season Leza dies, and next season his heir takes his place and weeps for him.

With reference to these statements about men passing away and not returning, we must explain that they do not mean that at death a person is utterly extinct. It is the resurrection of the body that is denied. The person himself lives on, as we shall see.

While any notion of a general bodily resurrection appears very ridiculous to them, we have had vague tales told us of people who have actually returned in the flesh. They do so in virtue of some very rare and enormously powerful medicine called *musamo wa lwende*. Having taken it, a man warns his people not to weep after his death. They erect a platform in the veld and place the body upon it without ceremony. Three days afterwards the man is supposed to get up and set out for the east. As he comes to each kraal, the people, believing him to be alive, give him food. Afterwards when he has resumed his journey they hear that he was dead. He travels east until he comes to a land called Chundu, where he marries and settles down again, but if one from his former home comes and sees him alive he immediately dies in earnest. One of our most intelligent informants told us that he had seen one of these men. Another said that in his village there was once a *mulozhi* who on two occasions was killed outright, but not buried, and in virtue of drugs came to life and lived in the veld, where he was seen by people going to water.

Another idea to be mentioned is that a man does not die except at the return of the hour in which he was born. As they express it : "*Muntu tafwi ansha chishika chindi nch'akazhalwa*" (" A person does not die except when the hour arrives of his birth ").

If a Mwila falls sick away from home, his chief desire is to return home to his village. His idea is that should the disease prove fatal he must be buried among his own people, be properly mourned for by them, and his ghost join the ghosts of his fathers. If at all possible he will struggle home ; but unless he is at the point of death his companions will not carry him, as it is reckoned very unlucky ever to carry a living person in an improvised stretcher. We have known instances of men being carried home to die but only because recovery was known to be impossible.

Often when camping near a village at night we have been awakened by a loud, shrill, agonising cry ; it is the sound raised by the watcher at a deathbed and soon arouses the village. Messengers are sent out to inform friends and preparations are soon made for the funeral, which takes place a few hours later.

What takes place may be seen from the following notes written by one of us after watching the burial of a friend who had died elsewhere and was brought home to be buried :

" Went down to the village at 9.30 A.M. and presently saw the procession coming up from the river ; the corpse was carried suspended in a skin from a pole. They put it in the shade and opened the skin so that the corpse lay on it upon the ground. They then sat up the corpse and tucked in the knees, with the hands folded over the chest. Two men held it in that position and arranged the *impande* on the head. They then laid the corpse down to take its measurement. Then Shikatakala (a chief) went with some men towards the centre of the cattle kraal and pointed out where they were to dig. Impossible to watch the scene unmoved. An old one-eyed woman, the deceased's wife, walked about with a spear (its point stuck into a mealie cob) in one hand and a calabash churn and a fly-whisk in the other. She kept approaching the corpse, crying : ' *Ndezila ike !* ' (' I come alone ! '). Other women were running about calling, but I could not distinguish what they said. Meanwhile the corpse was being prepared, anointed with butter, decorated with strings of large white beads around the neck and waist. The piece of cloth I gave as my *chidizho* was put round the neck and over the chest. A second *impande* was put on the head. The head was shaved. Mungalo told me that if a man's head were not shaved his fellow-ghosts would not receive him. Finally the corpse was put into the pre-natal position and wrapped in a skin. But just before this there was a touching scene. People made way for the wife and children. The wife lay down and embraced the corpse, calling out something I could not catch. The children followed ; first three stalwart sons and then several girls, all crouching at the side, with tears streaming down their faces and crying: '*Tata! Tata!*' ('Father! Father!'). The grave was now ready, in depth about five feet six inches. One digger was standing in the grave and when the corpse was brought to the graveside there was some confusion; several men were loudly called to enter the grave but declined. At last one entered. The two stood side by side, received the corpse and gradually lowered it. The grave was oval in shape, lying west and east, head to the west. The corpse was placed on a skin, lying on its left side, and under the head a carved stool. Then they brought things: some maize, ground-nuts, a small calabash of milk or beer (I couldn't see which), a lump of tobacco and a pipe; also a packet of beads I had given. (By the way, when I asked Shikatakala whether the things had come I had sent for, he replied: '*Ndamupa kale*'—' I have already given them to *him*'). One by one these things were put into the grave and placed under a fold of the skin. All the time one son knelt by the graveside and called as each thing was put in, '*Tata*, here is tobacco which we give you to smoke,' etc. This done, the men standing around retired and one old woman, kneeling by the graveside, gently swept with her arm a quantity of soil into the grave; others followed, kneeling on three sides (we stood on the fourth). When they had put some in they desisted while the diggers, still standing in the grave, firmly pressed the soil down with their feet. This went on till the grave was almost full, the women keeping up a mournful chant all the time. When the grave was so full that the soil under their feet was level with the ground, a curious thing was done. A woman brought an old yoke-skey found lying in the kraal (dropped, I suppose, by my waggon) and presented the tip of it to the nose of each man in turn; they sniffed at it and then left the grave. On asking the meaning of this, I was told that it was to enable the men to leave the grave well. Can't make this out. The grave now being levelled, some of the women ran and threw themselves headlong upon it (it's a wonder they don't hurt themselves), others sat at the foot and kept up a song: a solo with chorus.

To my surprise it was a song praising Shikatakala and saying that he has as many cattle as Lewanika. Couldn't see why they should sing such a song at that time. Women then began running from the end of the kraal and throwing themselves on the grave. Meanwhile the men were sitting in the shade smoking. As I came away the men were about to do their part. In fact before the actual burial they were at it. Two would stand at one side of the kraal, with spears raised and quivering, shouting out their names, and then set off racing across the kraal at top speed. On reaching the other side they stood and made as if spearing a prostrate foe. Shikatakala told me that the *ing'ombe sha mavhwika* ('the wrapping-up cattle') were not killed on this occasion as it was a poor man who hadn't an ox; to-morrow they will kill and eat what is brought by mourners."

There are some features in the funerals among the Nanzela people slightly different from the typical Ba-ila funeral described above.

The shape of the grave is different. At Nanzela it is excavated on one side at the bottom and the corpse is placed in this cavity. When the grave is filled, before the diggers step off from it, water is brought and all who have handled the corpse wash their hands over the grave. This is to cleanse them from the defilement they have contracted. The custom of pressing the piece of stick to the lips of the diggers, as described above, has undoubtedly the same meaning. The stick is previously rubbed in the ashes of the fire and afterwards thrown away. They say this is *basalale munkumu* ("that they may be pure as to the forehead"). Should this ceremony be omitted they would *shimbalwa* ("be unfortunate").

The duration of a mourning (*idilwe*) varies in proportion to the importance of the deceased. A child who dies before its teeth are cut is buried outside the hut and no mourning takes place. Only its mother weeps for it. At the other extreme an important chief's obsequies may extend over a month.

A funeral is a great occasion. We fancy sometimes that

Photo E. W. Smith.

A Scene at a Funeral.

some men spend their lives in going to funerals. One's workmen seem to be always wanting to go, and are quite clever in tracing their relationship with the deceased in

Photo E. W. Smith.

THREE MOURNERS AT A FUNERAL.

order to have a good excuse for going. The reasons for this practice of flocking to a funeral are many. Family feeling is strong, and it is considered a great fault if a man does not weep for a relation ; this extends not only to blood relations but to all members of the clan, to allied clansmen, and to friends. If a person absented himself he might very easily be charged with having bewitched the deceased. Without question the mourning in many instances is sincere ; indeed many show a lot of emotion. We recall what we saw at the funeral of Chongo, one of the Kasenga headmen. Mungaila, the chief, and a relation of the deceased, was coated from head to foot with white ash and wore the scantiest bit of cloth around his loins. With a broken stick in one hand and a wildebeest tail, containing *musamo*,

Photo E. W. Smith.

CUTTING UP AN OX AT A FUNERAL.

in the other he was going about alone. As he stood, with his long thin shanks and wizened body, gesticulating with the tail and shouting, as if expostulating with death, he presented a most pathetic figure. Every now and then he would flop down and wallow in the dust, throwing ash from the *mukwashi* over himself. When after a time he came over to speak to us, the old man was quite exhausted. Three old women, the picture of grief, were sitting together, with their arms around each other. On the grave four of the deceased's wives were lying as if lifeless. A son, a lad of fourteen or so, was lying on an ash-heap, his body shaking with sobs. These were real mourners. In the case of others it is a very perfunctory affair. Men take their spears and run across the kraal a few times in a listless fashion and think they have done quite enough to show their respect for the deceased. It may be that many are attracted to the funeral by the meat that is provided for the mourners. It is almost their only chance of getting a taste of beef.

Funerals are occasions for much feasting. Every one in a position to do so brings a *chidizho* (literally, " a thing to weep with ")—an ox, a pot of beer, some grain, goats, or some beads or print or something else. In addition, cattle belonging to the deceased are killed. We have known as many as a hundred beasts killed in this way at a funeral. Every man's ambition is to set aside a number of fine large oxen to be killed at his funeral, and these he will not part with for love or money. They are named the *masunto*, and are killed on the second day of the mourning. As many as five are killed immediately ; they are called *ing'ombe sha mavhwika* (" the wrapping-up cattle "), because the skins are used to lay at the bottom of the grave and to wrap round the corpse. If, as in the case described above, a man has no cattle, his friends may contribute these wrappings and also cattle for the feast. The flesh of the ox whose skin is laid on the floor of the grave is not eaten by the mourners but is given to the dogs.[1] As already related (see Vol. I. p. 305), every one who brings a

[1] Writing to me in Nov. 1917, Captain Dale describes the funeral of Kakobela, one of the most prominent of the Ba-ila chiefs. " I promised to send an ox. and Kakobela, before he died, said he would wait for it *below*, and ordered that no one was to kill until it came or he would be displeased ; only his own oxen might be killed first. The first day ten were killed, four being left to the dogs, next day ten, and the next ten ; then all the people from the districts began to kill. The fifth day his own people began to kill—those on the left side of the village ; the next day all from the other side, and then his people from outlying kraals. The corpse was put on three dry skins, and wrapped in a blanket. Then shells (*impande*) were put all over him—on the head, under the armpits, and on the back, then beads ; bracelets for which there was no room on him were put in a basket, together with tobacco (for he would be in great trouble without it), pipes, mealies for seed, also Kaffer corn, millet, *mabele*, ground-nuts. He was then covered with four blankets given by his children and fresh ones for him were put in a box. Fat was put all over him and his pipe put into his mouth. Then finally the people addressed him : ' *Lubeta lwako luambe, utalutola lubeta anshi, pe, kuyaya chishi chako* ' (' Speak out your complaints now (if you have them), do not take them with you below to destroy your community '). As there was no answer he was taken to be satisfied, and the funeral proceeded."—E. W .S.

chidizho has the right to receive an equivalent or more from the deceased's estate.

A word as to the killing of these animals. It is done in a cruel manner, for the beasts are not slain outright, but speared in an unvital spot and allowed to bleed to death. We have, on some occasions, been allowed to put an end to their sufferings with a rifle bullet. They are mostly torn to pieces in a few minutes without being flayed.

The mourners at a funeral seem to have three objects : to make themselves look as unhappy as possible, to make as much noise as they can, and to eat and drink to the utmost. The men smear themselves with clay and ashes, the women also plaster themselves over and neglect their appearance entirely. We have never noticed any self-mutilation at these ceremonies, but whether it be the natural consequence of grief or some vague idea of pleasing the spirit of the deceased, certainly they look most haggard and miserable. Yet this does not apply to all : we have seen many people at a funeral looking very happy.

By way of making a noise drums are kept sounding day and night, and there are singing and dancing as well. At the funeral of old Sezongo, at Nanzela, this went on for a month with hardly an hour's cessation ; while one party feasted another would sing and drum and dance night and day.

The writer of the notes above expresses his surprise at the nature of the funeral songs. One would expect, perhaps, songs reflecting on the sadness of life and death, the shortness of the one and the inevitableness of the other ; or at least praising the virtues of the deceased. But the songs we have heard have been either extolling the living chief or phallic—mostly phallic. Some of these songs we have recorded and give the substance of them here with a translation ; it being understood that all songs are sung with almost endless variation and repetition.

> 1. Kwezhiwa, musale umambako,
> Koya musolobole !
> Mama ! Musale,
> Koya musolobole !

" Come, select your paramour : go take her out.
Dear oh dear, select her, go take her out."

Photo E. W. Smith.

A GROUP OF MOURNERS.

2. Ni wakudi ku mayoba
    Buka, untebe wo !
    Buka, untebe wo !

" You who were at the rains get up and lie with me, get up and lie with me."

3. Mu lubambo shinaile mo ;
    Mu lubambo shinaile mo ;
    Mu lubambo uiye !

" I have not yet been concerned in *lubambo*
I have not yet been concerned in *lubambo*.
    Have a try at *lubambo* ! "

4. Ma ! Ma ! Ma ! Diakomena itoni diakwe !
    Ndia mulolobozho
    Kudikwete kudilolobola.

" Dear ! dear ! dear ! His great penis is a size ! It is a thing without an end. It must have had a long unwinding ! "

5. Munkundanguzu,
    Chanda ncha masanga.

" Most energetic in copulation (remember that) the old house is only made of grass."

6. Uswe kesu kabanga kadibangamene
    Umwe chenu chishinshi chidishinshibele.

This has a double meaning. Literally : " As for us, our little axe is long ; as for you the stump is short." The secondary meaning is : " As for us the penis is erect ; as for you the clitoris is small."

7. Umwa mukazhima ikongo mbi mbi !
    Ome mwangu mudi tushino tubotu.

" In my fellow wife the clitoris is very black,
    In myself there are small and pretty labiae."

When we have expressed our astonishment at women singing such songs—for it is the women that sing them— the elders have quoted the proverb " *Ushidilwe taitwa ku bushu* " (" A mourner is not to be passed before the face "), *i.e.* he or she has licence to do whatever he or she pleases. Under ordinary circumstances it would be reckoned taboo for women to utter such things in the presence of men ; but at funerals all restraints are removed. People do as they like. Grass may be plucked out of the thatched roofs ; the fields may be robbed of the growing corn ; all passions are let loose ; and no complaint for damage, theft, or adultery can be made.   This last item used to be the case ;   nowadays fines are claimed.

In old times a funeral of an important person at Nanzela was the scene of much violence.   As old men have described it to us, it seems to have been like this.   When a chief died, a great pit was dug and a mat spread at the bottom. Upon this were laid the bodies of several slaves, who had been knocked on the head for the purpose ;   and upon these was placed the chief's corpse ;   on either side bodies of his wives and at the head and feet bodies of his children.   Over all these were placed other corpses and the grave was filled in. If any stranger happened to pass he was promptly killed and added to the pile.   Women would voluntarily jump into the grave and suffer themselves to be buried alive with their husband.   This custom, which seems never to have existed among the Ba-ila proper, has now happily died out.

So far we have dealt with normal or natural deaths ; we may add a few notes on special practices on other occasions.

Among the Bambala it is the custom not to bury a child who dies before cutting its teeth but to throw it out into the bush.

When a woman dies in childbirth, it is customary to bury the child, alive or dead, clasped in its mother's arms. We have been instrumental in preventing this in a few instances ;   but have reason to suppose that it is still done. In one case we remember it was the woman's mother who was most insistent upon the usual custom being carried out.   We gave the child into her charge and showed her how to feed it artificially, but only succeeded in prolonging its life for a short time, for the old woman so neglected it that it soon died.

A pregnant woman must have the child removed before she is buried.   An example of this was reported to us by Rev. W. Chapman from Nambala.   In Feb. 1912 there was a woman at Mpone's village, seven months with child.   She was taken ill and died four days after.   While she was lying ill nobody attended to her.   The husband was away at a beer drinking. When she died, the child was taken away by the husband's mother. At first it was arranged that the husband himself must do it. Then the mother came forward and cutting into the upper part of the abdomen, while her son held the light, brought out the child. When it was taken out, she held it up, saying : " Here it is, now you must not say I have not taken it out." It was then taken and buried in another grave. No one must be near at the time. If this were not done, the woman would rise up and her ghost would kill people. The husband had to remain in the hut during the burial.

If a person after death is suspected of harassing people by killing them or bringing other misfortune upon them, the corpse is taken up and burnt. Or in some instances, where through ill-treatment or sheer malice, a person has expressed an intention on his or her deathbed of returning to haunt the living, then no burial takes place ; the corpse is simply thrown out into the bush or burnt.

Rev. W. Chapman writes us : " A man came to me one day, saying : ' Will you please come and see my wife who is ill and give her medicine ? ' I accompanied him to the village, and on entering his hut a most sickening and repulsive sight met my gaze. An old woman about seventy was lying on the ground by the side of the fire with arms, legs and parts of her body a mass of deep-seated fetid sores. Her surroundings were indescribably filthy. The miserable little hut was full of blinding smoke ; a pot of coarsely ground meal was simmering over a low fire, a putrid stench pervaded the whole place, and there were abundant signs of neglect. It was a hopeless case, indeed the wonder was that she was still alive. The following morning when I enquired of the husband how his wife was, he replied, ' She is no better, other sores are breaking out ; she will most likely die to-day for the rats have begun to eat her already.' That day the poor soul was released from her sufferings. But to my surprise there was not the usual mourning. The reason, as I afterwards learnt, was this : The old woman had said just before she died : ' You people neglect me, you do not bring me water and food as you ought ; when I am dead I will come back and trouble you.' So a noted doctor was sent for from a neighbouring village and after various incantations had been gone through and the people protected by his various medicines from the power of the old woman's ghost, the corpse was taken into a lonely place in the veld. And there a huge pile of firewood was collected and set alight. The doctor then cut up the corpse and threw it on the fire bit by bit, going through numerous incantations the while. When the process of cremation was completed, the ashes were scattered to the winds so that the old woman's purpose might be completely frustrated."

In case of a person drowned, whose body is not recovered, or of any one who loses his life in such a way that the body is not available for burial, the funeral rites are gone through and some of the person's belongings are buried. Sometimes a person gets burnt in a veld fire; if the remains are discovered they are taken to the village, unless it is too far and then they are buried on the spot; but in any case the ceremonies take place at the village. The same is done if a person dies far from home, if his absence was only a temporary one. As for a woman who is married into another district, she is buried there and some of her people will travel to her funeral; others remaining behind *bunga idilwe* ("hold the funeral"), but without any burial of things. In all these cases the ghost returns to the paternal home of the deceased.

Suicides are buried in the usual way, and their ghosts are not feared more than others. All they think is that the ghost of a suicide is a *shingonzunzu*, discontented, rebellious, headstrong, and will be likely to cause whoever it is reincarnated in to commit suicide. In one case we knew, of a man who blew out his brains in the bush some distance from the village, the body was carried back to the village for burial, but all the funeral rites took place on the spot that was bespattered with his blood; and the little spirit-temple was erected there. We were told that the ghost is where the blood is, hence this practice.

The funeral rites of a stranger are carried out in the usual way in the village where he dies. The news is sent back to his home and the relations have to provide a *musambo, i.e.* something to cleanse the village—*kusalazha munzhi*—from the defilement of the corpse. This generally takes the form of an ox, which is killed and eaten by the villagers. This done, the ghost returns to its home.

So much for facts : what can we learn from them ?

We may say here, that we have always tried to ascertain what meaning the people give to their own practices. Generally speaking, they can give no reason other than that they do as their fathers did. Sometimes we have got a reason, and have noticed often that their theories do not coincide with the theories deduced by anthropologists from similar or identical practices elsewhere. This is not to say that the theories of anthropologists are unsound ; they may be truer than the explanations given by the people to inquisitive enquirers. For, leaving out the fact that has always to be borne in mind, that people seek often deliberately to mislead enquirers, the original intention of a practice may be forgotten and a purely fanciful one put in its place.

So with regard to the things buried with the corpse and the cattle slain at the funeral. These world-wide practices seem to point to a belief in a spirit-world where life is lived much as it is lived here on earth ; where men and women need the things they needed here, food and drink and tobacco, hoes and spears and cattle and slaves ; so that food is buried in the grave that its shadowy counterpart may be taken by the ghost of the deceased whither it goes ; and the cattle and slaves and wives and children are killed for the same reason, that the deceased may continue to derive from them the comfort and joy he experienced on earth. This appears to be a rational explanation of the customs. But if a Mwila is asked why they kill the cattle, he will answer that they are to feed and comfort the mourners. We have heard men strongly deny that the things buried with the corpse are taken by the ghost ; they say the reason for burying them is that they belonged to the deceased, and if they were not buried the ghost would be angry and would return to trouble them. When we asked about the custom of killing slaves, etc., we were told that it was, not to provide the ghost with a retinue, but simply to show their grief. And as for the wives throwing themselves into a grave, which we interpreted as due to their desire not to be separated from their husband, had we not, they asked, heard of people in our country killing themselves out of sheer grief? What about a certain European who had recently committed suicide, was not that due to some sorrow? We should say that a child is buried with its mother in order that the mother may keep it in the spirit world, but they will not have it so: the child is buried simply because of the impossibility of rearing it artificially and because women will not, and may not, nurse children other than their own.

As to the noise at funerals, and the deshabille of the mourners, some would say that they were due to fear of the ghost, and a desire to drive it away, others to the desire to show respect to the deceased; but the Ba-ila give the meaning simply as grief. How can any one, they say, be happy and clothe nicely when a friend is dead? At Chongo's funeral, after watching the men charging up and down, all dressed in war toggery, we suggested to some that it looked as if they were engaged in a battle with death. This was taken as a huge joke and was quickly passed round: " The missionary says you look as if you were fighting death."

We notice, therefore, a tendency to give these practices a meaning other than a spiritistic one; but at the same time there is no doubt in our minds that the Ba-ila believe implicitly in the survival of personality after death. They state this without reserve, and, as we shall see, seek to come into communion with the departed.

Most significant of this are the last words sometimes addressed to a corpse: "*Kochiya! Kukashimuna kabotu kudi babo bakatanguna kufwa, ati, Ndabashia balalanga kabotu*" ("A good journey! Tell them well who died before you: I left them living well ").

2. THE DESTINATION OF THE DEPARTED

We have not met with a Mwila who would dogmatise as to the destination of the dead. We may sum up as

follows the answers to our inquiries : the ghost goes underground or somewhere to the east, or hovers in the vicinity
of the grave or lives in the houses of the living ; it becomes
an animal or lives in a tree, or rock or ant-hill ; it becomes
an evil spirit or a divinity that is worshipped : it may for
a time possess a person ; sooner or later, unless prevented
by certain untoward circumstances, it is reincarnated.

We will take up these points one by one ; and here deal
with the first.

Many place the location of Hades (*Kubashikufwa* :
where the dead are) deep down under the ground. They
say that there are collected the spirits of all cattle and wild
animals as well as the ghosts of men. In that shadowland
things go on much as they do here : the hunters still hunt,
fishers fish, and there is marrying and giving in marriage.
This, however, is not a conception prevalent widely among
the Ba-ila proper, but seems to be that of the Bambala.

Among the Ba-ila, we have often heard it said that Hades
is somewhere in the east. Thus one old man said their
fathers told them the *basangushi* ("ghosts") went *Kwiwe*,
" to the east," but he did not know just where, nor whether
their fathers had ever been there to see or how they knew.
When a man dies they often say to him : " *Utakunjila u
manda a bantu, koya kwiwe kwa Chilenga* " (" Do not enter
into people's houses, go to the east, to the Creator "). Of
a corpse it is said sometimes : " *Utamutanzha a mwaka, no
mupuule ambo, utamululamikidi a mwaka, wachita bobo
ulazhimina* " (" Do not turn his head to the south, put it to
the west : do not lay him north and south, for if you do he
will lose himself ").

The corpse is placed, as we have seen, west and east,
with the head to the west ; but the head is bent down so
that if the corpse could see it would look towards the east ;
if at one time the custom was to bury in a sitting position,
it would be looking towards the rising sun, *i.e.* in the direction
whither the ghost is supposed to go.

We believe that this has to do with the direction from
which the Ba-ila immigrated into this country ; for as we
have seen, there is a vague tradition that they came from
the east.

Another idea among the Ba-ila is that the ghosts of the dead continue to hover about the place they used to inhabit ; either near the grave or actually in the houses of the living. Certain practices appear to be founded on this belief.

It is the general custom to plant a circle of sticks, chosen from trees that easily sprout, around the grave, so that in a few years there is a grove of trees to mark the place. These groves are called *mabwabwa*. Over the grave and

Photo E. W. Smith.

THE *MABWABWA* AROUND A GRAVE.

within the circle of sticks, a small hut is erected, consisting simply of a few short uprights and a roof of grass. Sometimes these " temples " are situated other than over the graves. On moving his village to a new site, a chief will often move the temples of his fathers and rebuild them near his huts in the new village. One chief we know has no fewer than six of these outside his principal hut. In this way the ghosts are brought to the new habitation of the living.

It is at these temples that offerings and prayers are made to the ancestral spirits. This shows that the ghosts

Photo E. W. Smith.

GRAVES.

are supposed to be near the place where they lived their mundane life.

If ever there was a people conscious of being surrounded by a great cloud of witnesses it is the Ba-ila. They might say with Milton :

> " Millions of spiritual creatures walk the earth
> Unseen, both when we wake and when we sleep."

In and around the village and in the huts themselves they are continually present.   There are certain people who, in virtue of *musamo* ("medicine"), can see them ; and occasionally a ghost appears to a person when he is awake. But the latter is an ill omen, and, generally speaking, though the ghosts are everywhere they do not appear to men. They are, however, visible to dogs and other animals.   We were in the early days of our residence foolish enough to smile when an old man was telling us about the ghosts. " Ah ! " he said.   " You do not believe.   But will you tell me why your dog barks so much at night when all is quiet ? He sees the ghosts, to be sure."   Many are the tales told of the ghosts.   Here is one native account of their doings.

" This is what a ghost does.   He comes back to his house and taking hold of its door like a living man, opens it as if to enter.   His widow, if awake, calls out : ' Who are you, opening the door ? '   Getting no answer, she rises from the bed, dresses, and goes to the door.   She finds it open—the door removed.   She says nothing but replaces the door ; she knows that it is the master of the house, the ghost, her dead husband, who opened the door.   Perhaps she will ask her new husband : ' You, lying there, didn't you hear some one open the door ? '   And he may answer, ' No, no, I heard nothing.'   Then she may tell him how she found the door open.   When this happens, the widow and the eater of the dead man's name do not make the door fast : they simply lean it up against the doorway, so that the ghost may have free ingress.

" The reason why people are forbidden to stand about a doorway is that ghosts are always near the doorways of houses, wanting to enter, and if a man stands there they will make him fall to the ground.   And if a man comes

with a big heart (*i.e.* with evil intentions) into any house
where there is a ghost, he will stumble and fall just there
at the doorway. Why? Because the ghost seeing that
he has not come with kind intent will throw him down.
Seeing which people say to him : 'Come graciously, not
with a big heart, that is why you fell at the doorway.'
That is how a ghost helps the people in his house ; and
that is why the ghosts' people trust them. The ghosts save
them from their enemies, those who would kill and harm
them in any way whatever.

" Again, when a man coming in from a journey drinks
water he begins by pouring out a few drops ; before he
eats, he throws a little piece of the bread on the ground,
and after that he can eat well. If he doesn't do that, but
simply eats at once, and a piece falls from his hand, he
knows that the ghosts are asking for a taste. That is how
all Ba-ila do. They pay regard to the ghosts. When they
smoke, they first throw a piece of tobacco on the ground
for the ghosts. Should a man eat without recognising the
ghost, he would vomit and grow sick and people know he ate
by himself. He lived with a ghost and forgot to make an
offering."

The Matongo[1] are the sites now unoccupied once
inhabited by people. They are found all over the country,
for within certain areas the Ba-ila move about every few
years—because the soil is exhausted or because a new chief
does not want to disturb the ghosts of the ancestors. Or
it happens that a community dies out or is dispersed by
war or plague. These Matongo are held sacred. People
are as afraid of passing by them at night as villagers in
England are afraid of passing the churchyard. Here live
the ghosts of the people who once resided on the spot.

They are not happy in their deserted position, but live
disconsolately in the trees, cold and hungry. When one of
the writers took up his residence at Ibamba we had an
interesting conversation with an old chief on this topic.
Many years before there had been a large community living
at Ibamba but it had come to an end. Ghosts, he told us,

[1] The Zulus call the spirits of the dead Matongo. The Ila word
muzhimo is rarely heard among them in the form Umzimo.

are always glad when there is a village near, so that they can come and warm themselves at the fires and have friends to bring them food and drink. Since the Ibamba people died out, the ghosts had been living in the trees, now they would rejoice as the place was to be occupied once more. Here, evidently, is the other side of the truth that the living reverence and worship the dead : the dead are dependent upon the living for their happiness.

3. METEMPSYCHOSIS

The Ba-ila are firm believers in the doctrine of metempsychosis : that is, that at death a person passes into another living creature, man, animal, or plant. We deal now with the transmigration into animals.

We will first by means of a story which gained universal credence throughout the country some years ago, illustrate their belief in metamorphosis—the change that a living person may undergo (temporarily) into the form of an animal.

A man in the Bunkoya country was in time of famine searching for roots. He sat down after a while to rest and suddenly descried several lions dragging an eland. He hastily climbed a tree under which the lions finally deposited their spoil. Then they turned themselves into men and after eating lay resting, when one of them looking up observed the man in the tree. They thereupon begged him to descend, which he naturally refused to do. All then began pushing and swaying the tree until the man dropped down. They then having questioned him gave him a leg of eland and warning him to say nothing of what he had seen, sent him home. The frightened man, however, no sooner got a short distance away than he dropped his meat and fled for safety. The men promptly reassumed the form of lions, chased and caught him. They brought him back to the tree, and one of the young lions strongly urged that he should be put to death. The elders, probably in a good humour from a plentiful meal, forbade this and after again warning him sent him off home. This time he obeyed and reaching his village informed the people that he had found a dead eland. To his wife only he related what had actually happened. She naturally told others, with the result that when her husband went out two days afterwards to gather firewood he was killed and eaten by lions.

Many men, it is said, have the power derived from powerful medicine to turn themselves into a lion or hyena or wild dog, and to go out at night-time to hunt animals. It is even said that they will take people out of their huts into the forest and eat them. We remember a strike amongst some of our workmen because, as they said, a stranger whom we had just engaged had this unpleasant power ; he was a were-wolf. They refused to work with him or to have him on the premises. Needless to say, could they be sure of any man thus changing his shape the *mudisanguzhi* (" the self-changer ") would have short shrift. Under the old conditions any one suspected of such doings would have met with a swift fate as a *mulozhi*.

Believing then in metamorphosis, it is easy for them to believe that the dead can become animals. Numerous people are said thus to change. It depends upon their own wishes and whether they can obtain the necessary medicine.

Curiously enough, it is only more or less dangerous beasts that men choose to become : the lion, leopard, hyena, wild dog, elephant, the *shimakoma* snake, and the (fabulous) Itoshi monster. Sometimes a person may choose to become all the first four or five of these. A doctor provides the necessary medicine. He cuts small pieces of the hide of each animal chosen and puts them to soak in a potful of water to which he adds certain roots. The pot is carefully covered and put away. After a time they find worms in the pot and these are removed. If it is a quadruple operation the doctor professes to pick out the worms that represent the four animals and puts in the man's mouth two of the lion, two of the leopard, two of the hyena, two of the wild dog. Sometimes they are added to porridge, but in any case the man must swallow them without chewing, so that they enter his body alive. He is not allowed to eat hot food, nor must he get wet. If one should pour a little water on him he would go mad, showing the strength of a lion and roaring and barking like all those four animals, until they bring live coals, on which some drug is sprinkled, and make him inhale the fumes. And at a funeral, when he sees the blood-stained earth where cattle have been killed, the frenzy may return. He rushes to the grave, and if not speedily prevented will dig down to get at the corpse. When he comes to die, he roars like a lion, cries like a leopard, howls like a hyena, barks like a wild dog, and then expires. When he is buried, a long hollow reed is inserted in the ear and the other end of it left to protrude above the surface, the opening being carefully covered over with a potsherd. Along this channel emerge the worms from the corpse and grow into the animals named. Or, before the man dies he may vomit up the worms, and these, after his death, become the animals.

Two points must be noticed. The person does not enter into an already existing animal, but becomes an animal. The animal is not born, it simply develops out of the worm. The ghost of the man has already taken its course, gone to the east or taken up its abode near the grave. While the hyena or lion is wandering about, the people will still come to the grave to make their offerings. And the fact of having become a lion is no bar against being reincarnated.

It was like this with the old chief Sezongo at Nanzela. Some time after his death we visited his grave and found some men sweeping the hut in which he was buried. There was a tortoise in the hut and we were informed that it was Sezongo. They scraped some earth from the grave, disclosing a potsherd, which they moved, shewing the orifice of a reed. It was along this the tortoise had come, so they said, but they meant that worms had come along the reed and changed into the tortoise. We heard subsequently that two lion cubs had appeared in the hut and it was an accepted fact that Sezongo had become two lions. A year or so later a number of lions, ten or a dozen, came one night and made the earth shake with their roaring. The people were much impressed. They said the lions had come from afar to salute the two who were Sezongo.

Some time afterwards, Sezongo's son had a son born to him, and it was proved to be the old chief who had returned to earth.

The question occurs to a European—it would not occur to a native—where is Sezongo ? At the grave where to-day he is "worshipped," in the tortoise, in the lions, or in the boy running about the village ? There seems to be either a curious confusion of thought or a conception of the "soul" as bipartite or tripartite.

Photo E. W. Smith.

THE GRAVE OF SEZONGO II. AT NANZELA.

Leaving that for discussion later, another question arises : What is the relation between the people and the lion who was once their chief, and in particular what is the relation between the lion who is Sezongo and the boy in the kraal who is also Sezongo ?

Some people would answer that the lion was the boy's external or "bush" soul, and the relation between the two was so close and intimate that the well-being of the one depended upon that of the other. But the Ba-ila have no such belief. As we shall see presently, the boy has a guardian which seems at first almost like a fourth Sezongo, but which certainly is not the lions.

To the community that lion is more or less sacrosanct. They will not kill it if they can avoid doing so, and further, they will seek to prevent a European from killing it. Should, however, it take to man-eating they will give their scruples to the wind ; be he ten times their chief, they are not going to let him devour them !

We were once asking a man about his totem and he said he was of the Banashumbwa or lion clan. Asked if he would eat lion flesh, he said he would though the elders would not ; there was but one lion that he would not eat. It seems that a man named Nachibanga of the lion clan had turned into a lion and none of the clan, not even the young men, would eat it if they got the chance.. Nor would they attack it, nor would it attack them. If they were to meet, so this man told us, the lion would simply look at them and seeing that they were his clansmen would wag its tail and trot off. Sometimes a lion, that is one of these persons in lion-form, will chase one of his old friends, but he is only having a game with him. If instead of running, the man stops and addresses the " lion " by name (*i.e.* the name of the deceased), " he " turns away. If a man meets a wild-dog and recognises in it an old chum, he says : " Go and get me some meat, there's a good fellow ! " It goes off, finds some game, chases one in the direction of the man's village, then kills and leaves it. The vultures soon congregate, and so the man finds the meat his friend has got for him.

Sometimes going through the forest, people may disturb a lion at its meal and perhaps the lion will leave its kill for them. In such a case the party will recognise the lion as one of their friends and will loudly thank it for remembering them and killing them such a fine animal.

The imagination of the Ba-ila has peopled the rivers and hills and pools and forests of their country with a great many monsters, which, without more proof of their existence than we have at present, we can only consider to be fabulous.

Chief among these is the nix, the great water monster, named Itoshi by the Nanzela people and called by the

Ba-ila simply *mupuka,* or *muzoka* (" reptile," " great snake ").
All rivers and lakes in Africa are probably thought to
be inhabited by similar monsters. In the Victoria Nyanza
there is Lukwata.[1] The Batonga speak of the Maloa in the
Zambesi and the Barotsi of the Lengongole. Mr. Worthington tells us that Lewanika informed him he once
saw the latter when he was a young man. It was walking
along the bank of the river ; it had a body like a hippopotamus in size and a tail like an iguana, which swung from
side to side as it walked. From Stow's *Natives of South
Africa* (pp. 131-2) we learn that the Bushmen painted
animals that are not seen in these degenerate days. One
of these described by an old Bushman woman was *'Kow-
kign 'koo-ron* (" Master of the water "), of enormous size,
far larger and more formidable than the hippopotamus.

There was talk some years ago of an expedition to
Central Africa to search for a dinosaurus whose existence
was reported by the natives, described as having the
head of a crocodile, with rhinoceros horns, a python's
neck, the body of a hippo, and a crocodile's tail, all of
great size.

It is to this class of creature that Itoshi belongs. It
has been described to us as big as a very large Ihunga
thorn-tree, with the body of a crocodile, the head of a
man, and the fins of a fish, and upwards of fifty feet in
length. It is generally invisible to all but those who have
the proper medicine ; should it appear to others it means
death. It seizes people and takes them into its burrow
under the river-bed. When this happens, a person duly
protected by medicine goes along the bank and sits there
praying for the captive's release, and maybe succeeds.
Numerous adventures are related by people of their narrow
escapes from these monsters.

What concerns us here is the fact that many people,
especially chiefs, enter the water after death and become
these monsters. Along a short stretch of the Kafue at
Kasenga, no fewer than ten chiefs have been named as

---

[1] H. H. Johnston, *Uganda,* vol. i. pp. 79-80. The author thinks the
lukwata may be a small cetacean or a large form of *manatee* or a gigantic
fish.

living in the river, and our informant added that there were many more whose names he did not know. Nor is it only in the Kafue that they are found ; its tributaries abound in them. At Nanzela, Namongwe, who was the chief some generations ago, and Shantalo, one of his successors, are both now in the river in the form of *matoshi*.

Here is a description, given to us by a doctor, of the way a man is treated in order to become an Itoshi :

" You go and dig up musamo, bring the root, scrape off the bark, and spread it out to dry. When it is dry you grind it into a powder. Then you bring a scale of the Itoshi, the head of a python, the head of a Mulala (dragon), heads of other snakes, and a powdered reed, and mix them all up together. Of these you make a little bread. You break off a bit, put it on the ground, pick it up with your mouth and swallow it. When your health begins to fail, you will be very quick in dying unless they go to the river, bring some wet mud, and smear it on your heart. Then they must bring you a little bit of python skin and after soaking it in water put it in your hands. They also put palm-string in your hands, because being long it is like a snake. When you die, from your decaying body there will come out an Itoshi and a python ; indeed many snakes. When grown the Itoshi goes into the river and the snakes go into the veld."

At the funeral of Chongo, mentioned by us already, we learnt from Mungaila that, being of the Bakubi clan and having " eaten " the necessary medicine, Chongo was to become an Itoshi. In two days' time they expected him to emerge through the reed in the grave and take up his quarters in the hut where he used to live. There the people would feed him on lizards and fish until he was full grown, when his clansmen would accompany him to the river. He added that the place in the Kafue destined to be his home was at Munga-wa-nkanga. We saw Mungaila again a few days later and were told that Chongo was then in the hut. We wanted very much to go in and watch him enjoying his lizards and fish, but were told it was impossible just then. The next time we were at the village Mungaila said they had already been in procession to Munga-wa-nkanga and put Chongo into the river. So we had missed the chance of seeing him.

Besides these in the rivers, there are said to be various *bapuka* inhabiting ant-hills, rocks, and trees, who once were men. These places are regarded with great awe by the people; they are *tonda* ("taboo"): no firewood may be gathered there nor earth taken for building purposes.

There is a grove of trees in the Mala chishi, for example, said to be inhabited by a monster called Shichonka. A very long time ago it was a man. It is regarded as the guardian of the Nyungwe clan. If enemies come, it makes them weak at the knees.

At Chitumbi there are several of these sacred places. The ancient chief of the place, Shikadio, lives in the form of a *mupuka* beneath a great ant-heap; others say he turned into the ant-heap itself. When the Mission was founded there, an old chief came from a distance to warn us that this ant-heap must not be touched. Close by is another great heap called Kafumpa, inhabited by another ancient. We were warned that if we dug at these spots we should die.

Besides creatures such as these, there are various sprites living in pools and trees and forests which are difficult to classify. According to some people they once were men, but others deny it. They may be nature spirits, or they may be transformed men: it is impossible to say. These are the names of some of them: Luwe, Kaluwetoba, Chibinda, Mwabi. Of these Luwe is a one-legged goblin that rides about the forest mounted on an eland. He prevents people from killing game but is himself a great hunter. They say the antelopes are his cattle. Some people say it is possible to get medicine from Luwe for hunting.

On the top of Nambala mountain there is said to be a very deep pool of water in which one of these beings lives.

There is Chobochobo. A man told us once that he had not seen it but had heard of it from his father. It lives in a certain pool in the forest. He told us of a man who long ago dived into this pool and was given very powerful medicine for hunting elephant and buffalo. It gives others good luck. It is a benevolent fairy.

4. VARIOUS KINDS OF GHOSTS

We have spoken of various kinds of ghosts ; it will be well at this stage to attempt some kind of classification of them.

The general name for them is *basangushi* ('' the changed people''). The word is derived from *kusanguka* ("to be metamorphosed "). They are regarded generally as beneficent or neutral, but may be induced by neglect to make people sick. They enter certain people and speak through them to men ; or they appear in dreams.

The *mizhimo* (sing. *muzhimo*) are *basangushi* in their capacity as divinities, " worshipped " by the people.

Some people at or before death are, as we have seen, " pressed " and their ghosts taken as slaves by the witches. These ghosts are variously named : *mazwa, tuzwa, bashi-kazwa* (sing. *chizwa, kazwa, shikazwa*)—all forms of the same word.

There is some idea that these are not always in the charge of witches ; perhaps they escape or survive them ; anyhow they act as free agents. They cause disease, sometimes, by entering into a person. They waylay people and strike them dead. They act, sometimes, in sheer devilry, it seems, knocking burdens off people's heads, breaking hoes, unhandling axes, upsetting pots of beer, and so on.

Another kind of ghost, closely allied to the *mazwa*, is the *tuyobela* (sing. *kayobela*). They are also the ghosts of men and women who have been " pressed " by witches and are now in their service. They have two characteristics peculiar to themselves : first, they chirp and twitter like birds—hence the name (*kuyobela*, " to twitter "), and second, they are dwarfish. We might call them elves. Some people have seen them. Mungalo told us that he had : and he was amazed to find what funny things they were. " What are all these children ? " was his first thought. On looking again he saw that, although they were very short, only about eighteen inches high, they had the bodies of full-grown men, only they were turned round the other way, so that the bellies and faces were at the back ; their hair was all standing upright. They live in and around their master's hut, and his wife must cook plenty of food for them, or they would beat her. They are sent out to steal, to make people sick and to kill. We knew of one boy who was said to have been bitten by them; he fainted and the people had to doctor him. They sometimes enter into people and *kosaula mala* (" cut up the intestines ").

Another species of evil ghosts is the *tunchinya* (sing. *kanchinya*) The *mutalu* is the vengeful, destructive demon of an aggrieved person. The *malendela* are said to be the ghosts of particularly brave men. Another species of ghost, not regarded as malevolent, is the *bashituta*, the characteristic of which is their silence (cf. the Zulu, *isituta*).

Here is a typical ghost story. There was once a witch who, beginning with those of her relations, had " pressed " many ghosts. She was quite used to doing that. This is what befell her. One day she found a ghost up in a *namuzungula* tree, eating the flowers (they are called *chishonsho-momba*). She called the ghost, saying, " Come, let me carry you on my back." The ghost left off eating the flowers, came down from the tree, and got on to the woman's back. She went off home, and on arrival there said to the ghost, " Get down off my back." But the ghost refused, saying, " No, I won't. You yourself called me there where I was eating *chishonsho-momba* and bade me get on your back."

Hearing this, the witch fetched some porridge and invited the ghost to get off her back and eat. But the ghost refused. She found some honey and *miseza* and other delicacies and offered them to the ghost, but it refused to get off her back. She then said, " Come off and I will give you whatever you like." But the ghost refused, saying, " No, I won't. You asked me—there where I was eating *chishonsho-momba*—to get on your back and here I stay." So the woman was in a bad way. She could not eat, nor lie down, nor sit: she could only stand there with the ghost on her back. Six days she neither sat, nor ate, nor lay down. Then she began to totter at the knees and get dizziness in the eyes. Then she lost the power of speech. And on the ninth day the witch died and the ghost left her and went its way.

5. DREAMS

According to the Ba-ila, the ghosts often make their appearance to the living in sleep. To them the dream world is as real as the waking world. When a man sees in his sleep the phantom of a person he knows or used to know, he has no doubt that the person, or the person's ghost, has actually visited him. These appearances may be beneficent or maleficent in intention. Missionaries find that very often a dream is the turning-point of a man's life; many a convert, now doing useful service in the Mission, traces back his conversion to a dream. One such bright young man gave this as his experience. In sleep he stood on a high mountain and saw the villages and people below. Coming down he found a crowd collected at a river. There was a missionary there, who lifted up his hand, with something in it, and immediately water flowed from it. The people fell to the ground amazed, thinking the end of the world had come. He (the dreamer) stood with folded hands praying. Suddenly the scene changed. Now he was in the river fishing and heard a voice saying, " Follow me and I will make you fishers of men." Then he woke up. We have been asked sometimes to interpret dreams, and can bear witness to the extraordinary impression often made by them on the minds of the people. But not all dreams are caused by the ghosts. Some arise they know not how and need interpretation. Like some civilised people the Ba-ila interpret them often by contraries.

The following translation of notes dictated to us will illustrate this :

It may be that when a person is lying asleep a ghost comes to him and says: " Go and pluck such and such leaves and use them as medicine for such and such a disease." He gets up and in the morning he goes just where the ghost told him, he goes and plucks that medicine and uses it just as he was ordered. To others the ghost comes in sleep and on arrival says: " To-morrow go to such and such a place and you will find such and such a thing." So in the morning he goes and finds it. To another, who has a case in court, a ghost comes in sleep and says: " As for

this affair, you must speak in such and such a manner."
He does just so, he speaks and all believe what they are
told, and say: "He does not speak of himself, it comes
from dreaming." That is how they are convinced at the
court.

Or a hunter when he is lying asleep, a ghost comes and
tells him: "In the morning take your gun and go to hunt
at such and such a place." So next morning he goes and
finds game; just where the ghost told him. The thing he
went for, he goes and kills just in the way he was told.

It may be that a man in sleep dreams, perhaps that
his father or mother or kinsman is dead; that means, it
is not that one but another who is dead. It may be he
dreams his father is being carried or that he is nicely clothed,
or that he is fat—that means he is dead. He knows that
he is dead. If it be that he dreams his father is bathing
at the river, or that he is very white and thin, it means
that he is alive. If he dreams when asleep that a dog bites
him, it means that he must not go about that day, or he
will be bitten by a lion. Or if he dreams that his father is
bitten by a dog, it means it is another not his father who is
bitten by a lion.

If he dreams of marrying his relation, or embracing her,
it means meat; he must go and hunt. If in sleeping he
dreams of pieces of tobacco, it means meat—the livers of
animals. He who dreams of weeping says: "There is a
person dead, there is mourning."

If there be a sick person and there come two ghosts
to fetch him, and if they fight, it means they will kill him;
he knows that he will die. If they simply come and tell
him about medicine, and say, "Do so and so," why, he
goes and does so and recovers. On the other hand, if the
sick man tells his friends, "I dreamed of ghosts who were
fighting about me," at once they go to a diviner and the
diviner divines, and having consulted the oracle he tells
them: "There were two ghosts fighting about him, one
is a deliverer, the other is the one who wants to kill. Now
go and make an offering to the deliverer, that he may go
on delivering. And the one who did not deliver, to him
also make an offering at the cross roads, at the foot of a

tree, that he may pass away." At once they go and make offerings just in that way. They say: "You must never return, pass away for ever." And they motion him off with medicine.

The following, from another source, gives some more of these dream omens :

"Again if you dream of fish it is *malweza*. That dream tells that next day a person will die. Truly he will die. If next morning you tell people, "I dreamt of fish, let us go to-day and kill fish in the water," the elders will interpret, saying, "A person is going to die." Afterwards a person who was sick will be wept for. If he dreams of flying through the air, going flying over the trees, and next morning tells them, "I dreamt of flying," they will tell him, "You will live very well. It is life. That is a great dream." If a person dreams of red beads it means meat, he will kill an animal. Next morning he goes hunting in the forest and kills an animal.

"Again if a person dreams of falling into a game pit, next morning he tells people, "I dreamt of a game pit and fell into it," and they answer, "You will die." Truly he gets sick and dies."

6. SPIRIT POSSESSION

A ghost may, according to the belief of the Ba-ila, enter into a living person, temporarily, intermittently, or permanently. The reincarnation of spirits falls in a different category, for, as we shall see, it is not a case of a spirit merely possessing any one but of its becoming actually re-embodied in a new physical organism.

1. Temporary, transient, possession is conceived to take place in the case of a person who commits murder. The uncomfortable feelings that seize such a person, which we should call remorse and attribute to conscience, they attribute to the ghost of the murdered man. It is then said: "*Chia chamukwata*" ("The *chia* seizes, possesses, him "). The ghost is supposed to take up its lodging in the region of the epigastrium and can be expelled by the taking of an emetic or by cupping. The physical basis for such a belief

is, of course, that the solar plexus becomes disturbed by excitement of the higher centres.

There is another idea that seems more like obsession than possession. A murderer or other evil-doer is said to have Chanzu or Lwanzu, that is, the ghost of the murdered man, or some other spirit, haunts him, or is in him—the idea is very vague. A man we knew of went to stay at a village and fell sick. The diviner declared that he was a murderer and had Lwanzu. He was therefore driven away. If he had been allowed to remain many others would have died. At Munkwasa's village, at Nambala, there were two men who had Lwanzu. One was a boastful person (*wadikankaika*) so they beat him, and he repented and got well. The other, who was an adulterer, was sold into slavery.

These conceptions remind us of the Erinnyes.

2. Temporary possession is also the cause assigned to many cases of illness. As we saw before, delirium is put down to the *basangushi*. We were called once to see a man who was said to be possessed. We found him lying in his hut wrapped in a blanket. He was conscious and could answer feebly our questions. He was in a state of prostration ; his pulse weak, his temperature below normal. He had pains in the frontal region of the head and in the nape of the neck. Two days before he had come from across the Kafue at midday : and it was an extremely hot day. That evening he complained of being sick and fell into convulsions. They thought it was a ghost, and as is the custom, asked him who he was. The answer was, " I am Shacheza "—a brother who had died recently. He recovered in a few days. We diagnosed this case as heat-stroke.

3. There are people who are intermittently possessed. They might be called demoniacs. A description of such a case has been furnished us by Mr. L. C. Heath, the A.N.C. at Chinenga, who had a good opportunity of watching it and recording his impressions at once. He writes :

" Last night I was called to see a woman who was dancing *busala*. I found the wife of Chungwe face down on the ground and covered with dust. The limbs were rigid, the eyelids quivering, and only the whites of the eyes visible. The feet moved spasmodically and the head wagged

from side to side.   This morning on inquiry I heard that
she was still in a fit and leave was asked to play drums
for her, a certain cure, it was said ; after dancing to the
drums she would sleep and recover.   The woman was still
on the bed apparently unconscious when they commenced
to bang these drums immediately outside the hut.   With
me in the hut there was a second woman who was said to
be similarly affected at times.   As soon as the noise began
the woman on the bed began to twitch and jump about,
and would have fallen from the bed had I not directed the
other women to help her to the floor.   She then grovelled
on the floor with her head in the dust, but presently began
to crawl on all fours to the door, still keeping her forehead
on the ground.   The other woman gave a native rattle into
her hands which she grasped and shook violently and did
not at any time release her hold of it.   I was surprised to
see her take it, as she appeared to be otherwise unconscious
and her eyes were still only showing their whites.   The
drumming continued and the woman kept on throwing
herself about and kicking and rising to her knees, but no
further.   She made noises at times with her mouth and the
drums were suppressed in order to accompany her ' song.'

" I became aware that the dinning sound of the drums
produces a perceptible feeling of vibration in the chest
which may be the cause of the excitement they produce.

" While the above was in progress the other woman
mentioned suddenly developed the complaint in a most
alarming manner.   Her body moved like a whiplash with a
big knot at the end, her head, which seemed in danger of
being flicked off.   She also had a rattle, and dropping it
during her contortions made several ineffectual efforts to
pick it up again, but was prevented apparently by the
action of her body.   She had also a battle-axe, and I was
glad to see a man remove the sharp edge therefrom by
grinding it on the ground.   Woman number one, then, was
more or less on the ground and kicking, and number two
in a state horrible to witness, when a third woman came
and made obeisance to the possessed.   This was because
she felt the spirits calling her to dance but she was unwilling
to do so.

" The cure seemed to be out of order somehow and the complaint too catching to be safe. So I had the drums stopped and the women taken wriggling to their beds, and after bathing their heads with cold water they are now quiet and apparently asleep.

" (Next day.) There is more to chronicle on those cases, though I had thought the incident closed.

" Woman No. 2 recovered yesterday afternoon and is well again. She still has pain but in her neck only, where the spirits congregated. (I wonder it is not dislocated.)

" Woman No. 1 had another attack last night and was once more grovelling in the dust. Bathing her head with cold water had no effect, and I was besought to have the drums beaten for her again and refused.

" This morning she was much better again and able to talk. She had pains in her neck of course. She was not quite well, however, and I found they had given her a rattle soon after I had been to see her and done everything in their power to encourage her malady. They have now taken her to their village.

" The following points may be noted :

" (a) The drum is played on these occasions in a peculiar way described as *kunzuma, kunzuma, kunzuma, kunzuma,* and the vibration is felt by all the natives in the manner I mentioned as having been apparent to myself. Playing the drum, on other occasions, as at dances, does not have this effect, and I have not myself noticed it before.

" (b) On hearing a drum so beaten any *busala* dancer within earshot, it may be miles away, they say, must needs hurry with great speed to the spot and commence the contortions described. In corroboration of this it may be noted that the sick woman left her bed at once to go to the drums, that the woman No. 2 came and danced to the drums, and that woman No. 3 was affected and would probably have started had I not stopped them.

" (c) Had the drums been beaten for long enough the sick woman would have risen to her feet, spoken the name of the spirit troubling her and then recovered, or she might have gone on in this manner for several days and the drumming should be carried on at intervals until she recovered.

" (d) The afflicted will not eat, and can only drink water with a little meal stirred into it. Children, even small babies, are affected in this manner, and are to be seen wagging their heads while on their mothers' backs."

4. The kind of possession we have just described may pass into another, not different in nature but in degree. The persons may go on to deliver messages from the unseen world and so be named *bashinshimi* or *baami*. *Kushinshima* is to prophesy, the word being applied primarily to the low muttering tone in which the person speaks.[1] The name *basala* applied to them indicates the people of the Busala country, and is said to be given to them because the first prophets came from that country. Most of them would be called " mediums." The entering or using of such a person by a ghost is described by the Ba-ila as *kukwata* (" holding " or " seizing ").

A few notes (translated) written by one of our informants will serve as an introduction to them.

" These are the affairs of a prophet. When a ghost enters his chest he will prophesy. It will be that that ghost causes him to prophesy. He enters his chest and then he prophesies : ' Hi ! Hi ! ' The people answer him : ' Tell who you are ! ' He answers, ' I am So-and-so.' They say, ' We are humble. Tell the news that you have got so that we may hear.'

" Then that prophet tells all the news, saying, ' I am So-and-so, I have come to tell you the news. There is here at the village a warlock who bewitches. Look out for him and seize him, or here in the community you will all die of disease or something.'

" Or he tells them if there is going to be a famine here, or much grain this year, or whether there will be drought and the rivers will not be full of water ; or whether the rivers will be full, or whether this year it is to be abundance and much grain.

" Or the prophet will prophesy after a man's death. If he has been bewitched he will enter into a person and cause him to prophesy, saying, ' I have come, why did I die ?

---

[1] The word seems to be equivalent to the Arabic نَبَأَ, to utter a low voice, whence نَبِيّ a prophet ; cf. Hebrew נבא

Why was I simply killed when I had no fault ? ' All the
people hear the news and say, ' So-and-so is possessed by
a ghost and he prophesies of So-and-so, he is asking about
his death. Says he, Why was I killed seeing I have no
fault ? '   Then his relations discuss those affairs of the
prophet. Again they will ask the prophet, ' Who is the
warlock ? '   He will tell them, saying, ' It is So-and-so.
He is the warlock who killed So-and-so.'   Then the men
will kill the accused or they will drive him out of the
community—out he goes.

" The ghosts tell many things when they enter the chests
of people. One spirit when he seizes a person and prophesies,
will speak and say ' There will be a ravening here by
a lion.' Another will prophesy : ' So-and-so is pregnant,
I shall come to be born by her.' Another ghost seizes a
person and speaks to the people of the community : ' At
such and such a community they are plotting to kill you.'
Another ghost seizes and causes a person to prophesy, saying,
' So-and-so I shall kill if he does not brew beer and make
me an offering.' Or he says, ' He who ate my name does
not look after my children well : I shall kill him, or I shall
kill all the children and he will be left alone to his sorrow.'
He will say, ' Let him go out of the community, let him
build elsewhere if he does not make me an offering. Let
him brew beer.' That is how the ghosts speak in the chests
of people. That is how they cause them to prophesy and
tell all the news."

These prophets play a very important part in the life
of the Ba-ila. As the mouthpieces of the divinities they
are the legislators of the community and, generally speaking,
they receive a great deal of credit. Sometimes the message
they deliver is harmless enough, sometimes it is distinctly
good, but sometimes it is noxious. The word of the prophet
is sufficient to condemn to death for witchcraft a perfectly
innocent man or woman. And such is the extraordinary
credulity of the people that often they will destroy their
grain or their cattle at the bidding of a prophet.

We must distinguish two methods in which the message
is supposed to be conveyed to them. The Ila account
quoted above speaks only of the first, and most common

method : the message comes from the ghost " in the chest " of the prophet. This is possession proper : a disembodied spirit enters into the sensitive medium and uses his brain and organs of speech. The communicator takes more or less permanent possession of him : he may continue for a long time to speak his messages, and the medium may even call himself by the name of the spirit and be so named by the people. Or the ghost may only occasionally use the medium ; or again a medium may only once or twice be so used. There are some mediums who are regularly possessed by their own particular controls ; so that whenever a *muzhimo* communicates with his people it is through this one individual.

The other method is different : it is that of ecstasy. The spirit of the prophet makes an excursion into other realms and comes back to tell what he has seen and heard.

There are some prophets who enjoy a very wide reputation, and their names have been handed down for generations. The Bambala speak of no less than five famous prophets of the past, of whom Mukubwe was the greatest. Another most famous one was Longo, the mother of the chief Shakumbila of the Basala. She was once captured by the Makololo chief, Sekeletu, and taken by him as far as Ianda on the way to Barotsiland. It is said that when on the Kafue, Sekeletu ordered her to call Chinga—the chief at Kaingu, thirty miles away. She went down to the river and shouted his name : " Chinga ! Chinga ! " and then came back to Sekeletu to say that Chinga had answered and would be in the camp next morning. Sure enough he was. On another occasion the Makololo set her to stamp grain in a mortar, and she had no sooner started the work than a stream of water gushed out of the mortar. She performed such marvels as these, until the chief grew afraid of her and sent her back to her home.

We will give some account of the prophets we have knowledge of.

In December 1911 the chief Sachele, who had died about six months before, began to speak through a woman : he told the people that he had not been allowed to go to his mother—the Longo spoken of above—in the spirit world because she was angry with him for having been buried with dogs in his grave instead of slaves. He told them that he was living in the neighbourhood of the village and going about hunting as he used to do in life. This prophet, like most others, had a message demanding something from the people ; in this case she gave out that all who went to pay respects would be given rain and those who refused would experience famine.

At the same time there was a man prophesying at Kakoma's village, near the Nambala mission station. His message was that there was going to be a lot of rain and an abundance of fish of all kinds ; they would be found on the banks of the river, and some would be already cooked. He called the chiefs of the district to him but they refused to go. He named one lad as his slave to do his bidding, and the people insisted upon the lad doing it. As a proof that it was going to rain he ordered a clay pot to be put out, but unfortunately it was never filled and somebody threw it away. The old women of the village used to tell the children of the greatness of the prophet : last year, said they, he told us that we should find an eland in a game-pit and we found one, so you must honour him and listen to what he says. The missionary was not very pleased with him, as he told the people that praying to God was all nonsense and that they would get no rain at the Mission !

The prophets claim sometimes to be possessed by beings superior even to the *mizhimo*. It was so with a man who called himself Chilenga, " the Creator," and who appeared in 1909. He announced that he could destroy a grub that was spoiling the crops. In obedience to his commands the people brought him specimens of the grub and he burnt some amidst incantations. But the grubs did not cease their ravages. One would have thought they would have lost faith in him, but undaunted he ventured on loftier flights. He said that in a short time he would turn the sun black for six days, destroy the bridge over the Kafue, tear up the railway, and cause all the Europeans to leave the country. To enable all this to happen the people were to destroy their cattle. The unfortunate Batwa, to whom he told this tale first, had by long exertions managed to scrape together a few head of cattle; believing his story they killed them; but before the sun turned black the false prophet was arrested for sedition and put into prison by a Government not inclined to be sympathetic with such things.

Another professed to be Mwana Leza ("the Child of God"), *i.e.* to be possessed by Him. He came to the people at Nanzela at a time when there was a very heavy rain (1909), and the crops were in danger of being spoilt. He made his appearance in one village and ordered the chief to build him a hut which was to have two doorways in it, one facing east, the other west. "When you have finished the hut," he said, "bring me some grain and I will pray to Leza so that these floods may cease." They all believed him and built the house and brought the grain. "But," said he, "this is no good; there's too little of it, bring more." He went to another village and ordered the headman to produce grain, to another and to still another, until all the villages, believing his story, were doing their utmost to provide him with grain. It was at a season when grain is very scarce. They came flocking with what grain they could gather, but he looked at it disdainfully and said, "I cannot pray for you, because you give me such a little. If you want me to pray for you, you must give me cloth and shirts." Some believed and produced cloth and shirts, even cattle and goats. Then at last he offered his prayers, but the rain did not cease. He then declared that it was against Leza's will and that He had ordained there was to be a great flood of water that year. The people then began to get restless and to demand the return of the things they had given him. "Don't be in a hurry," he told them; "presently I will beseech Leza very earnestly to hear my prayer." He put them off in this way, until they became convinced that he was a false prophet. We have never heard that they got back the things they gave him.

And who, may we ask, is Mwana Leza?

Our first acquaintance with the name came in this way. We quote from the diary of one of us:

"July 1, 1906. Visiting Mala. After service this

morning three women came and talked with me. They
are *baami* (' prophetesses'right). Had not been at service, but
had heard I had been telling people about the Son of God.
Told me spontaneously about Mwana Leza. Came down
long ago in the country of Lusaka ; was kind and gentle,
went about telling people to stop fighting. After a time
people killed him ; *bamuyayil'a musune* (' they killed him
on account of an ox'). Was killed at Chongo. His spirit
enters into many *baami*, who foretell events and tell people
to stop fighting, to live in peace and cease shedding blood.
Mungaila brought one of them here because of the fighting
between him and Mungalo and through her they have
peace to-day. They are light-skinned women, with a curious
far-away look in their eyes ; hair is twisted into small knots
with ochre and fat in the way called *shimbulumbumba*."

Later in the year (1906) the people of the country were
weeping because Mwana Leza was dead. It appeared that
a certain man living in some district in the north was out
hunting one day and following a wart-hog he had wounded.
As he was going through the veld, a bright, dazzling object
appeared before him, reaching from the earth to the sky.
The man fell to the earth as one dead. Then he heard a
voice saying, " Have you not heard that it is taboo to
eat the flesh of wart-hog ? Stop following the spoor and
tell people that if they persist in eating that flesh there
will be trouble. And—stay! Why is it you people on
earth have never lamented the death of Mwana Leza who
died so many years ago ? Bid them weep!" The man
presently returned to his senses, and made his way home.
He told the people what he had seen and heard ; they
only laughed at him. A few days afterwards two people
died very mysteriously in the village. That was sufficient
to set them mourning. The deaths were accepted as a
sign : " Leza is angry with us," said they, " come, let us
weep." They commenced the mourning ceremonies as if
it were for a friend. Moreover, they sent messages to the
neighbouring villages, who sent farther on, and in a very
short time all over the country the people were mourning
on account of the death of the Child of God. In some places,
perhaps most, the matter was regarded in a most serious

way. The people would gather outside the village and be solemnly warned by the elders that there must be no joking or playing. For upwards of a week the mourning would be carried out and the ashes from all the fires collected and placed in a heap outside the village. Then a pole would be erected by the heap, to give proof that they had carried out the command, so that Leza would pass them by and not destroy the village.

This was one of the most remarkable occurrences we have experienced among the Ba-ila. It will be said at once that the story of Mwana Leza is nothing but a corruption of the teaching of the missionaries. In the district where we first heard of it there were then no missionaries, nor in the districts of Lusaka and Chongo named by the *baami*, nor in the northern district where the hunter saw his vision. Moreover, there is every sign that the story is much older than the advent of the missionaries among the Ba-ila. Mwana Leza is a figure introduced into the folk tales. We are inclined to think that the story is an offshoot of Christian teaching grafted upon an old idea of their own ; and that while it may have come to the Ba-ila through other tribes from the teaching of Dr. Livingstone, yet it is more probably an infiltration from the old Jesuit mission in Portuguese East or West Africa.

That it is not recent is shown by the fact that the first missionaries among the Ba-ila heard about Mwana Leza. The Rev. A. Baldwin has given us the following quotation from his diary of August 26, 1895, a time of severe famine and rinderpest :

" Chungwe's son was here this afternoon with a wonderful story which he had got first hand at Mosanga's to-day. A woman belonging there was out in the forest getting roots for food, and in the midst of her digging she looked up to find herself confronted by a big man. She had heard no sound of his approach and could tell neither how nor whence he came. Naturally she was afrighted, whereupon he told her not to be afraid, for he was Mwana Nyambe (Leza) who had come to make a revelation to her. She was to pick up her basket and hoe and follow him. On and on he led her far away until they came to a kloof overspread with beautiful

white sand.   He bid her look down into it and she saw all
the cattle that had died of this disease—thousands of them,
all alive and healthy.   (We did not know at the time that
the disease was rinderpest.)   He asked, ' What are these ?
She replied, ' Our cattle which have died.'   ' Yes,' he
went on to say, ' You are right.   I have taken all your
cattle away from you.   I am not going to allow you Mashukulumbwe to have any more.'   Again he called her to
follow as he left the kloof and on and on they went.   At
last they sighted a town, but nearing it she discovered that
what she thought were huts were granaries, and he told her
this was where he kept his stores.   He then showed her
grain of all kinds—mealies, kaffir corn, small corn, nuts, etc.,
in such abundance as she had never seen before.   She had
carried her few roots in her basket all this time, and now
he told her to throw them away and filled her basket
with corn.   Then he commanded her to return home and
tell the people all she had heard and seen, and that he
promised they should all have an abundance of food this
next harvest.

" He was intensely excited as he told his story and all my
questionings failed to change his belief in it.

" The story puzzled me for some time, until it occurred to
me that it must have been a dream.   The woman was
tired and hungry and had fallen asleep in the forest and had
dreamed the experience she related when she got home."

Whether Mr. Baldwin's explanation is the true one or
no, this story admirably illustrates the way in which some
prophets receive their messages.

In June 1913 another prophet arose in the neighbourhood of Nanzela.   His name was Mupumani, and he was a
leper.   According to his own account, he was not given to
dreams, and had only the one vision.   This is what he told
us of his experience.   He had gone to sleep as usual in his
hut, when he heard a movement above, and looking up saw
a man's leg dangling down from the roof, then a body, and
at last the person reached the floor and stood by his side,
but he could not see his face.   The man (Mupumani said he
must have been a *musangushi*, " a ghost ") lifted him upon
his shoulders and carried him off, where to, he knows

not, but he found himself in the presence of Namulenga ("The Creator"), or Mulengashika ("Creator of Pestilences"). The first thing Namulenga did was to take Mupumani's leprous body and throw it away and then

Photo E. W. Smith.

MUPUMANI THE PROPHET.

begin to mould a new body with complete fingers and toes. But another figure intervened and said, "No, do not do that. If Mupumani goes back to earth with a new body the people will die of amazement to see him." So Namulenga desisted and gave him messages to take to the people. One was to the effect that he would give him a *kankudi ka buloa* (" a small calabash of blood "), which he was to pour out and all the people would die. But once again the second figure, wishing to save the people, intervened and restrained Namulenga from doing this. Then Namulenga gave him a message that people when mourning were to cease killing cattle, throwing themselves violently on the ground (*kudikankata*), and rushing about with spears (*kuzemba*). He had often, He said, sat by invisible and watched people mourning and had split His sides with laughing (*kuzumininina kuseka*) to see their antics. He took men from earth, and caused men to be reborn, as it pleased Him : it was not for people to mourn. He also gave a message denouncing witchcraft. " Go down again," he concluded, " and give my words. Perhaps the people will revile you, perhaps they will listen and treat you well. I shall see." Mupumani found himself back in his house ; how he got there he does not know. He began to tell of his vision and soon the fame of it spread abroad, and people began to flock to him from all quarters. We ourselves were at the time travelling in the northern districts and met many parties, some from as far off as the Lukanga swamp, on their way to him. In those villages whence the people had already been to him, a long white pole was erected as a sign. Ultimately, people came from districts as remote as Ndola and Mwinilunga. To all of them he gave the message. At first he accepted nothing from them, except the small ring of beads for the little finger which seems to be given to every prophet. But what preacher is accepted without signs and wonders ? And the people demanded " medicine " of him to make their corn grow and give them good luck in hunting, and Mupumani had to yield to their insistence. He gave them drugs, and they gave him money in return. Later, before the magistrate, Mupumani said the Ba-ila did not accept his messages : " They still kill cattle at the funerals. You know the Ba-ila never listen well to people who tell them to do things. At first I told the people about the calabash of blood and then I did not Perhaps I made a mistake in not always speaking about it ; they would have been afraid of that and listened to Leza's voice."

A man from Mala, named Mungaba, while on a visit to Lubwe, heard of Mupumani, but scoffed and refused to go on to him. Shortly after his return to Mala, one of his people died suddenly, and while he was wondering what had caused the death, one of the mediums of the communal demigod, Shimunenga, fell into a trance. The people sat round, as usual, waiting for the message, and presently it came: " I am Shimunenga. Mungaba's child has been slain by Leza because he scoffed at Leza's messenger. It is your habit, it seems, to scoff at those who come from Leza. The missionary, too, you do not listen to him. Look out for yourselves." This message made a very deep impression upon the people, and it was further deepened by several strange portents that happened at the same time. Some of the women at Mala had been going for some time to collect firewood from a great tree that had been blown down in a gale. One morning when they went they found it standing upright! Imagine the excitement. We were taken to see the tree and there was no question about its having been lying flat—there were the marks left by the termites on the bark and on the ground, and the sides that had not been in contact with the ground were charred by the fire that had swept over the country just before. There was no question about its being upright; we saw it and saw too that it had not been raised by human hands. The explanation soon occurred to us, but did not commend itself to the people: they were sure occult powers had been at work.

Mupumani was taken to the magistrate's camp for examination, it being suspected that mischief was afoot with all these people flocking to him. He gave his story in a straightforward manner which showed him sincere and innocent. The most extraordinary rumours were meanwhile floating about the country.

It was said that while being taken to the Magistracy he told the people in one district that if he were put in prison he would stop the rain; curiously, there ensued a drought in that district and the people drew their own conclusions. The day after his arrival, a trader's store near by was burnt down, and this was regarded by the people as another

IN A BALUBA VILLAGE.

(Notice the long pole.)

display of his supernatural power. Some said that Mupumani had sent an oribi with a letter to the magistrate, and there was a still more extraordinary story of two monkeys, each with two tails, that had come down with a letter for him from the sky. The excitement died down after a time, and it seems that the only result of his visions is the inauguration of a new kind of salutation on solemn occasions. Mupumani greeted people with the formula used in prayers to the divinities—"*Ndakabomba*" (" I am humble "), and taught them to raise their hands high over their heads and reply "*Twakabomba*" (" We are humble ").

7. REINCARNATION

Sooner or later, almost every person now living will return to earth. Such is the belief of the Ba-ila. The exceptions seem to be two : the ghosts who have been pressed into the service of the sorcerers ; and the great *mizhimo* of the various communities, such as Shimunenga.

The Ba-ila seem to think that a certain number of spirits were created at the beginning and given bodies : when the bodies wear out or are destroyed, the ghosts live for a short time free and then have other bodies prepared for them. They seem to regard this as the best of all possible worlds, for the disembodied spirits clamour to be reborn.

The process of discovering the identity of the reincarnate person may be described here in the (translated) words of one of our informants :

" Before the mother emerges from the hut, if the child cries they go to divine, and a female spirit comes in the divining rod and says : ' Go on sacrificing, it is So-and-so come to be born, give him the name (*lit.* call upon his name).' They return from divining, and on their arrival they offer water at the door, saying, ' You, So-and-so, we see you. Now as you have come back to earth, do not come with two hearts, suck well and grow ! ' Some of the water remaining in the mouth they spurt over the child's body, and call him by that same name ; then the child starts up and cries. The child cries because fearing the water. But if he goes on crying all the time

when he is called by that name they will go and divine a
second time, and bring another spirit, for it seems the first
spirit should be conquered.   Then as they call that one's
name the child leaves off crying.   Calling they call aloud,
and the first spirit is conquered.   This is the birth name,
the great one, the one of the spirit, he is called by it by all
the people who have the right.

"It is taboo to address an elder by his birth name.   It is
to *shokolola* him, and he will be angry.   Because it is the
great name, which is to be honoured.   If his contemporary
shokolola him by the birth name it is to despise him, but
he does not get angry, he simply laughs, saying, 'It is my
musama.'   The mothers and fathers are they who *shokolola*
him by his birth name, and his elder relations, his younger
relations, no.

"Often a spirit of a woman comes to be born in a
male.

"When they say, 'Do not come with two hearts,' they
mean, 'Do not be in a hurry to die.'   The spirit may choke
himself through being angry.   If he hurries to go away
again they say he has choked himself."

This is one method of identifying the child.   Another,
similar, consists in placing the child to the breast and
pronouncing the names of its grandfather and other fore-
bears.   If at the mention of a name it begins to suck, they
are satisfied as to the identity.

There is some difference of opinion as to the precise
time when the ancestral spirit becomes the child.   Some
hold that it is at the mentioning of the name in this ceremony
that the child becomes So-and-so, or, rather, that So-and-so
becomes the child.   That is the reason of the cryptic remark
quoted above : "They bring another spirit—for it seems
the first spirit should be conquered "—*i.e.* driven away, as
not being the legitimate one.   But we have again and again
heard men say: "I am my grandfather, I entered my
mother's womb to be born."   In that case, either at conception or some time later, the spirit enters the embryo.   If
there were unanimity upon this point, it would help us to
determine their ideas of the soul.   If the spirit only comes
at the naming ceremony, then, before it, has the child no

soul, or has it a secondary, a nutritive, sensitive soul, and the spirit comes as the rational soul ?   What is the relationship between the ancestral spirit and the body ?   Does it simply live in it as a guest, or does it animate the body, making it perform its functions ?   These are questions to which they can supply no answer.

It seems certain, however, that there is no relation between the incarnate ancestral spirit and one of the most important functions of the body, viz. the sexual function ; for a woman may return as a man, or a man as a woman. This seems to show that the spirit animates the higher and not the lower centres ; a person, *i.e.* the true self, the self continuous through all the reincarnations, may take the form of male or female ; it itself has no sex.

In accordance with this belief, we find many men with feminine names, and females with masculine names.   The name prefix *na-* is a shortened form of *Nina* (" his mother") ; Nachibanga means " mother of an axe."   The prefix *shi* or *sha* or *she* represents the word *ushe* (" his father ") ;   so that Shimunza means " father of the day."   The following are the names of some males we know : Nakadindi ("mother of a pit ") ; Namamba (" mother of hoes ") ; Nabanyama (" mother of animals ") ; Namabuzo (" mother of baobab trees ").   And the following are names of females : Shimbala (" father of palm string ") ; Shamakowa (" father of wild cucumbers ") ; Shachifua (" father of a bone ").

Furthermore, there is a double incarnation in some cases, for a discarnate spirit may return to earth in two bodies. Suppose there are two brothers who separate to live in different districts, and each has a child born to him about the same time.   They go to the diviners in their respective districts, and each is told that it is the grandfather who has returned in the flesh ; the child confirming this in the way we have described.   They are satisfied, then, that this is so. Up to this time no communication has taken place between the brothers as to the children, but now that the names are given each sends to the other to say, " Our father has returned to our home."   No conviction arises in their mind that a mistake has been made ; they simply accept the situation.   If a spirit so wishes, why should it not occupy two bodies ? It does not occur to them to question the possibility of one person being in two places at once.

The Ba-ila, then, are at one with Wordsworth :

> The Soul that rises with us, our life's Star,
>   Hath had elsewhere its setting,
>   And cometh from afar :

But with the next lines they would not agree :

> Not in entire forgetfulness,
>   And not in utter nakedness . . .

For no man can remember, they say, what he was when he lived on earth before, or what he was and did in the spirit world. The memory—shall we put it so ?—and all intellectual activities are outside the scope of the spirit ; which determines who the man is, not what he is. With us personality is somehow bound up with memory ; we are conscious of our identity through all the changes the years bring. But to the Ba-ila, it would seem the soul—the man himself—is more like a tenant, a lodger, in a house where all the daily avocations are carried on apart ; he has no share in them, but is like a star and dwells apart.

Consequently, there is no morality in their ideas of incarnation. They are far removed from those of the Brahmans and Buddhists,[1] where the conception of metempsychosis is dominated by the idea of moral retribution ; where the successive migrations through ten thousand millions of lives, as ordained in the code of Manu, are steps through punishment to redemption. A man is blind now owing to his lust of the eye in a previous birth. The Karma (doing or action) in the one life determines the position of the individual in the next. Nothing of this kind is found in the Ba-ila ideas of reincarnation.

---

[1] Buddha denied the soul. With Plato he said that the desires, cravings of a man determined his future ; there was no passing over of a soul. The cravings made a new body ; how is not said. There is something like this in Bwila. A man wishes to be a lion and he gets medicine and becomes so. But in regard to reincarnation, no medicine is required ; whether he craves it or not he returns.

8. The Genius, or Guardian Spirit

Here is a short account given to us of the Guardian Spirit. It is called *musediakwe muntu*, " a person's namesake."

" When a person sneezes, he makes an offering by spitting, and says, ' *Tsu !* My namesake, stand by me always ! '

" If he is minded to go hunting he gets up early ; and at the Lwanga makes a heap of meal—fine meal—and offers, saying, ' *Tsu !* My namesake, let us go out together and hunt ; bring the animals near to me, let the sharp stick sleep, let all biting things sleep, let the fierce snake be far away. I want only meat. Give it me, O hunter.'

" When he has finished the offering, he goes out. When he finds animals and kills one, he cuts up the liver, and off the rump he cuts morsels, as well as from the heart and foreleg and leg, and begins to make an offering, saying, ' Thou in the East, here is meat ! ' He throws a morsel from the leg, one from the rump, one from the foreleg, one from the liver, and one from the heart. Having done so he makes another offering, saying, ' Thou in the North, here is meat ' ; (and another) ' Thou in the West, here is meat ! ' (and another) ' Thou in the South, here is meat ! ' When he has done this, he lies on his back, does obeisance, and claps his hands, saying, ' To-morrow and to-morrow give me meat ! '

" Having finished, he makes an offering to his namesake of liver, roasted or boiled, heart and liver, and says, ' Here is meat, O my namesake. *Pambala, pambala*, a spirit does not refuse his own anything. To-morrow and to-morrow may I kill even more than this animal ! Be thou around me, O hunter ! '

" He claps his hands. And at the village when he returns, he does the same, he makes an offering at the Lwanga to his namesake. Then also he claps his hands. He will in this way put his trust in his namesake all his life through."

Several points call for elucidation. And, first, as to the name. *Musediakwe* means " his namesake." One never hears the word *musedi* without the enclitic possessive, but we may here use it alone. As already explained, there is

something about a man's name that must be respected.
For any one to call a man by his birth name is a fault ; it
is also a fault for a man to pronounce his own name, that
is, his birth name.   If another person has the same name
as you, you may not speak to him or of him by that name,
but must use the word *musediangu* (" my namesake ").

Now, in this connection, *musediangu* is not used indis-
criminately by a man, as if just any one bearing his name
stood by him always in spirit.   He is not thinking of any
of his friends or relations on earth.   The namesake upon
whom he calls for help, and to whom he makes his offerings,
is the one whose name was given him after birth—his grandfather, probably.   Thus a boy is named Mungalo after con-
sultation with the diviners, and by his solemn act of accept-
ing the breast at the mention of the name he shows his
acquiescence.   Mungalo was his grandfather.   And when
he speaks in his prayer of his namesake he means Mungalo,
his grandfather.

But he was named Mungalo because he actually was and
is Mungalo, that is, he is his grandfather reborn !   Quite
so !   He is Mungalo, and Mungalo is his grandfather and
Mungalo is also his guardian spirit.   That is to say, a man's
guardian spirit, his tutelary genius, is the reincarnate spirit
within him : shall we say, is himself.   The genius is not
only within him, but, in a sense, external to himself, protecting and guiding him.

Now, at first sight, this appears to be an incongruous
conception, resulting from the fusion of two disparate ideas
derived from different sources.   One might imagine that
one set of ancestors believed in reincarnation ; that another
set believed in a guardian spirit, a father or grandfather
who, while not actually reincarnated, constituted himself
the genius of his descendant.   These two sets of people, we
say, might have coalesced and one belief become superimposed upon the other in the minds of the children, and
hence to-day they say in one breath that Mungalo No. 1 is
Mungalo No. 2, and that Mungalo No. 1 is the guardian
spirit of Mungalo No. 2.

That is a possible explanation ; but may there not be
something deeper in it ?   Some doctrine of the soul, implicit

if not explicit in their beliefs, which though not explicable
by modern Ba-ila was clearly grasped by their ancestors ?

That the soul, or part of it, may also be a man's guardian
spirit seems to be a belief shared by Plato.[1]   " As concerning
the sovereign part of the soul within us," he says, " that
which we say and say truly, dwells at the top of the body
and raises us from earth towards our heavenly kindred,
forasmuch as we are a heavenly and not an earthly plant—
φυτὸν οὐκ ἔγγειον ἀλλ' οὐράνιον—we ought to believe that
God has given it to each of us as a daemon "[2]—a kind of
genius or guardian angel for the direction of our lives.

The Ba-ila would agree that we are a heavenly and not
an earthly plant and that our kindred are in the regions
above.   They would certainly subscribe to the doctrine of
daemon.   And they would also agree that the sovereign
part of us is the daemon guiding our lives.   It seems that
Plato and the Ba-ila philosophers are not far removed from
each other in this matter.

As for the doings of the guardian spirit, it is not necessary that we go into details.   Briefly, whatever good fortune
a man may have, whether it be by way of gaining wealth
or fame, or escaping from danger, it is ascribed to the good
offices of his namesake.   The apparent contradiction that
he also has medicines for the securing of safety and prosperity is no greater than the contradiction between praying
for rain and yet working medicines to induce it to fall.   The
two things work together.   The *musedi* is the man's own
personal god, devoted to his interests.   Accidents, of course,
happen ; a man may have his life endangered in a thousand
ways.   When such happens he wonders what his *musedi* was
doing to allow him to get into danger like that.   He makes
an offering and reproaches his *musedi*, saying, " Why did
you leave me ?   I nearly died.   Where were you ?   See, I
make you an offering : do not leave me again."   Should
the accident be fatal, his friends can only suppose that for
some reason the guardian spirit was vexed and had abandoned him to his fate.

As for the way the guardian spirit conveys his admoni-

[1] *Timaeus*, 90 A.
[2] Jowett translates, " divinity."

tions, he comes in dreams, or he speaks in a low voice heard only by the man himself within his breast.

It only remains to be said that all people have these attendant spirits, from the time the birth name is conferred until death.

We may compare this Ba-ila belief with the Zoroastrian doctrine, founded on primitive Sumerian beliefs, of the fravashis, and also with the idea of the genius (or of a woman, the Juno) or divine double of the Roman, accompanying him during all his lifetime, who was also an object of worship. In America also a very widespread belief assigns to each individual an attendant guardian spirit, independent of, but attached to the physical self, which warns the self through the intuitions of impending dangers and the like.

This widespread belief cannot but remind us of the conception of the subliminal consciousness formulated by modern psychologists. Here in the secondary self, that part of us that lies beneath the threshold of consciousness, we have, it seems to us, the psychological basis for the Ba-ila belief. That secondary self is more sensitive than the primary self with which we normally identify ourselves : it receives impressions from the world without, which our ordinary senses cannot perceive, just as a photographic plate will record things which the eye cannot see. And it sends up into the supraliminal consciousness messages in the form of monitory inhibitions and impulses. Such seems to be the explanation of the daemon of Socrates, the Voice, the sign that guided him in all the affairs of life. Numerous instances have been recorded since the days of Socrates, where a sudden presentiment of danger has saved a person from violent death, or where in answer to a strong overmastering feeling a person has hurried off to a fateful meeting to which he had received no call in the ordinary way. There is no reason to suppose that such experiences are confined to civilised beings ; indeed we can well understand that they should be more common among the uncultured races. Granted such phenomena we can see how naturally they would suggest to the savage mind the presence of a spiritual guardian, directing his movements and shielding him from danger.   For the voice or sensation arising from the subliminal region seems actually to be external to himself. He does not see the hidden danger, or opportunity of fortune ; it must therefore be some being wiser than himself, who is interested in his welfare and who directs him accordingly. We do not suggest that every time a man thinks that his guardian has prompted him there has actually been a message from his second self, for many an escape or meeting may be only an accident or coincidence, though interpreted by the savage in accordance with his dominant idea.   All that we ask for is that such messages have been sent up at some time, and have really been the means of helping ; such instances would be sufficient to start the idea.   Once started it would be handed down from generation to generation and become firmly established as a universal belief.

Whatever may be thought of this, the close correspondence between the Ba-ila idea of the guardian spirit and the psychologist's theory of the subliminal consciousness cannot but strike our readers.   Here is the secondary self, so mysterious and elusive, guiding the primary self by virtue of its hyperesthesia ; within and yet seemingly without, so that often its extraordinary performances suggest rather the action of some extraneous being ; oneself and yet not oneself.   In this strange conception, which yet explains so much, the Central African savage and the European (and American) psychologist once again clasp hands.

9. THE PSYCHOLOGY OF THE BA-ILA

We are now in a position to estimate the contents of the Ba-ila psychology. We have certain facts before us, how can we explain them ?

Let us note first the important distinction to be drawn between what the natives say about these and what we say.   One is apt to read into things more than the people do.   It is not easy for us to realise that the African does not systematise as we do.   To explicate what lies implicit in his ideas is legitimate enough, provided always that we state clearly which is our deduction and which are his ideas ; and that we clearly understand what his ideas really are.

Some writers present to us a very elaborate analysis of the soul of the people they are describing ; and we wonder whether the people would recognise the description or whether the writers have not made out to be separate entities what are really only different aspects of one entity in the minds of the people.

It is well known, for example, that the ancient Egyptians had a very complicated idea of the human ego ; we are told of about ten entities comprising it. Many of these bear a striking similarity to what we find among the Ba-ila ; indeed it would be easy to compile a Ba-ila psychology as complicated as the Egyptian.

There is the Egyptian *Ab*, translated " heart " or " inside," the will or intentions. This corresponds with the Ila *mozo*, of which, as we have seen, the Ba-ila speak much. The ḥaibit corresponds to the *chingvhule* (" the shadow "). The Egyptian *ba* was " a sort of agile principle whose habitat is chiefly in the skull " : one writer compares it to those little genii or " spirits " that savage peoples locate in the nape of the neck ; that is to say, they (for people had more than one *Ba*) may correspond with the Ba-ila *shiu* and *Bashimpulukutwi*, of whom we learnt in Chap. X. In many respects the Egyptian *Ka* corresponds to the Ba-ila *musedi*. It has been variously described by different writers, but we may be content to say that it was the man's double, second self. Perhaps, too, we may take the Egyptian *Ran* as like the Ba-ila *izhina*, the name ; for the Egyptians had similar ideas as to names. If the *Ran* was part of the personality, so is the *izhina*. The Egyptians thought that these elements of the personality were not enough to make up the living being, they constituted merely a being capable of life. Then came into the man's nostrils the vital breaths of Nature, wafted by the breeze ; this we may compare to the Ba-ila *moza* or *muwo* ; and as a result of its entrance life came ; what the Egyptians called Aonkhu and the Ba-ila, *bumi*.

On these lines, then, we might speak of the Ba-ila *Ego* as composed of *mozo, chingvhule, shiu*, etc., *musedi, izhina*, and *moza*. But this would be an over-elaboration and would, we believe, misrepresent Ba-ila ideas.

The *chingvhule, e.g.,* cannot be taken as a separate entity. It is true that it is sometimes spoken of as if it were. If you want to take a portrait of a child, its father will object on the grounds that you will take away its *chingvhule* and it will die. We have seen how witches can take away a man's " shadow." But on the other hand, when the question as to the identity of the self and the shadow is pressed home, they will always deny it. We remember talking this matter over with one of our closest friends among the elderly Ba-ila chiefs ; he emphatically declared that the shadow was only a thing seen when a person stands in the sunshine, and had nothing to do with the man himself. You say, we went on, that when a man is dead he is not done with. " Yes, true," said he. " He enters the womb and is born again." " Well, what is it that enters : the man's body or his *chingvhule,* or what ? " " I don't know, perhaps it is *muwo.*" *Muwo* is the wind. Sometimes they talk of the *moza,* " breath." But we feel sure that all three terms are used metaphorically. They know the difference between a corpse and a living being ; they have watched the last breath and know that when it has come out a change takes place. And that breath is evidently akin to the wind. Breath—wind—shadow—these are not to be regarded as three distinct entities ; rather are they words with which the Ba-ila seek to express the mysterious self-evident thing that possesses them. We should be nearer still to their attitude if we said that they think of a living being as a *muntu*—a person, without asking questions as to what constitutes his personality. There is something strange about him, as mysterious, intangible as the shadow, or wind, or breath ; but what that is they cannot say. Suffice it to call him a person.

The soul as we speak of the soul, it is doubtful whether the Ba-ila believe in it. Certainly we have never found a word that would be a satisfactory translation. *Muzhimo, musangushi* : these are discarnate spirits. There is no word, and apparently no idea, of a " soul " as such.

Can we formulate an explanation that will cover all they think and say ? Shall we say that a man is full of soul-stuff just as the world of Nature is pervaded by those mysterious forces manifest in medicines, etc. ; that this soul-stuff pervades his whole body but is specially active in some organs—in the blood, heart, and genitals ? It is also specially prominent in the senses of taste and hearing, so much so that there the soul-stuff appears to become a self-acting distinct individuality. This soul-stuff is ethereal, impersonal, animating the whole body, giving it life. The essence of it may, with the aid of drugs, be separated from the body and be hidden for safety as an "external soul" in other things. Into the body comes the spirit from the spirit-world, which gives the person his identity, his name, his position, all that we mean by personality.

At death the man *wasanguka*, becomes metamorphosed. The spirit is freed from the body and enters the unknown spirit-world where it awaits the time of its reincarnation. The "soul" of the man now changes, it is no longer mere "stuff" but a person—a *musangushi*—which hovers around the grave, lives in trees and houses. This is the normal process ; but it may be disturbed by the action of the mysterious force in *musamo* (medicine), by taking which a man may extract an essence from his body which transforms into an animal. So that the one person now becomes three distinct entities. On the other hand, a magician may, by means of his art and medicine, destroy the spirit entirely, so that it cannot be reincarnated, and the soul-stuff instead of becoming a *musangushi* is transformed into a malevolent *chizwa*. Between the body mouldering in the grave and the spirit no connection exists after death, but until the process of decay is complete the *musangushi*, as well as the *chizwa*, remains in some way attached to the body, so that to destroy the body is to destroy the *chizwa*.

CHAPTER XXII

*

THE DIVINITIES

THE *basangushi* (" ghosts "), regarded as objects of adoration, are named *mizhimo*. Strictly speaking, not all *basangushi* are *mizhimo*, but only those more or less helpful to men, not those who, for some reason, are inimical; though in a loose way the word is applied to all ghosts. The root of *mizhimo* is no longer a living one in Ila, and it is impossible to give a derivation of the word. That it is an ancient one is shown by the fact that in various forms (*umzimu, muzimu, mudzimu, mdzimu, musimo, mushimu, modimo, morimo, elimu*) it is the common name throughout the Bantu field for the divinities; indeed we may take this as an indication that before the Bantu tribes emigrated from their original home they already had this name and this cult of the dead. One other significant fact may be mentioned: *muzhimo* is not a personal name, but neuter or collective; the plural, as almost always in Bantu languages, is *mizhimo*, not *bazhimo*. It would seem as if the dead were regarded as having lost their individualities and become mere potentialities. But whatever may once have been, it is impossible now to deny all personality to the Ba-ila divinities. Other names of the ghosts, *basangushi, bashikazwa,* etc., are personal in form; and there can be no question that such *mizhimo* as Shimunenga stand out clear and distinct in their individuality.

For the purpose of description we may divide the *mizhimo* into three classes: personal, family, and communal divinities.

1. Personal and Family Divinities

We have already had occasion to describe the Genius, or Guardian Spirit; it is what we mean here by a personal divinity. It is, in a sense, the man himself; his spirit moving on a higher plane, watching over him and his interests. " Every person," said one of our informants, " trusts his own *muzhimo* : whether he is travelling or whether he stays at home, he does not forget his divinity." It would, of course, be a poor man who had only one divinity —the Ba-ila call such a person *shikazhimo-komwi* (" a single-divinity man "); every one not isolated in the world has his family divinities all around him. Hence when a hunter is successful he throws morsels of meat as offerings north, south, east, and west, that none of his divinities may go neglected. If you had only one, and that one should absent himself, you would be in a bad way; but having many, if one should neglect you, others are sure to be there, and not knowing who is present it is better to cast your offerings in all directions and give thanks by expressing confidence in their continued beneficence : " To-morrow and to-morrow, give me meat." But, says our informant quoted above, " however many may be a person's divinities there is always one that is thought of first, whose name and help are first invoked, and that is the man's own personal *muzhimo*."

The family divinities are the ghosts of one's grandfathers, grandmothers, father and mother, uncles and aunts, brothers and sisters. In the unseen world they continue to take an interest in things mundane and, in particular, in the welfare of their relatives on earth. They are never far away. Theoretically their number is indefinite; all the deceased members of a man's family are his *mizhimo*, but in practice it is mostly only those who have recently passed over that are thought of.

There is one law of spiritual etiquette that rules in this region; that is, a man has to do only with the divinities of his own family; looked at from the other side the law is expressed in the formula : *Pambala-pambala, muzhimo tokaki mwini* (" Pray pray, a divinity does not refuse his own "), with the implication that he has nothing to do with others.

A man and his wife, being of different families, have different divinities ; and it would be an offence, coming under the category of *buditazhi*, for a man to appeal to his wife's divinities or she to his.   More curious is the application of the word *buditazhi* to the divinities themselves—to any who should presume to go beyond their province and affect, for good or ill, members of another family.

This is what one of our informants says on the matter :

" Married people have their respective divinities : the husband his, the wife hers—that is to say, the divinities of their families.   When they are married their divinities remain distinct, only when a child is born is there a partial assimilation.   If the child gets sick and they go to divine, the diviner finds usually that the one who causes the sickness is the divinity belonging to the husband—his father's ghost, or his mother's, or his own genius, or his grandparents' ghosts, or his sister's.   Those are they who have the right to sicken the child.   Should the diviner declare that it is the wife's divinities that cause the child's sickness, the husband's family would wax exceeding wroth and say, ' How comes it that the woman's divinity sickens the child in the house ?   That *muditazhi* of a divinity has no right to act thus.'   The divinity of the wife may sicken her ; the husband's divinity may not : nor may hers sicken him. That is how the divinities are separate : yet they live together in the house together with the man and his wife. When the husband makes an offering to his divinity he does it at the doorway of the house—on the right-hand side : the woman makes the offering to her divinity on the left side. That shows that the divinities of the husband are superior to the wife's.   The same divinities of the husband's are the divinities of the children in the house ; the wife's are her own, and only to a certain degree of the children, in that they help the father's a little in shepherding and guarding the children.   The father's divinities are superior in the house and over the children ; and quite distinct from the woman's in regard to the husband and wife : the husband's do not help the wife : only her family divinities help her ; and the wife's divinities do not help the man."

From what we have said, it will be seen that the Ba-ila

are well provided with divinities : for a man has his own attendant genius, his family gods, and, moreover, superior to all, the great communal divinities watching over the interests of the commune as a whole.   If we add to these all the various charms whose use we have already described, it is apparent that the Mwila strenuously guards himself against the ills of life.   Nor is there any incongruity in his mind in the simultaneous resort to both divinities and charms.   There are, he recognises, many forces, personal and impersonal, seeking his destruction, and the wise man will enlist the aid of all the help the universe provides.

Their attitude towards the departed is a twofold one, founded on a sense of mutual need.   In the close community between the living and the dead neither can do without the other.   The living need the help of the ghosts in battling with the evils of their present existence, and on the other hand the departed depend for much of their well-being upon the living.   Out of this there grow apparently contradictory ways of regarding the ghosts.

From one point of view, we may define their attitude by the word *shoma* (" trust ").   The meaning of the word is quite clear.   On the first occasion we heard it we were standing on the top rung of a rickety ladder, papering a room in our house, and were just reaching up to place the paper in position when we heard a boy below saying, " If I were the master, I would not *shoma* this ladder, he will fall and break his neck."   The word means to put reliance upon, have confidence in, to trust.   The ghost has some power that the living man has not, power largely in that it lives invisible (seen at any rate only on rare occasions), independent of the laws of space and time.   Things hidden to the mortal eye are no secret to the ghost.   And normally it is devoted, or one may suppose it devoted, to the interests of its family.   The attitude of trust would seem then the proper one to adopt towards this unseen but powerful being.

But, on the other hand, in putting off the flesh the ghosts have by no means divested themselves of human nature.   The best of living men are subject to moods : ordinary people are jealous, touchy, fickle ; you have to be on your guard not to offend them, for if put out they are apt to be vindictive. And so it is with the ghosts ; you can never be quite sure of them ; any omission on your part to do them reverence will be visited on your head or on the head of some one dear to you. Then they must be placated by offerings. It is a good thing they are placable, for if they kept up resentment where would you be ?

There is, then, both trust and fear in their attitude towards the divinities ; in a word, awe, what the Ba-ila call *mampuba*—the proper disposition, including reverence, fear, trust—in which to approach both chiefs of dignity and the divinities.

But there are ghosts that are deserving of no trust whatever, only unmitigated dread. They are the larvae who have gone into the other world embittered by their treatment in this, and now work off their spleen upon the living. This is what we are told about them : " One divinity of a man is not good, no, he is bad. It is a person who was not pleased in his death because he was bewitched by a relation, desirous of ' eating ' his name ; so he goes off indignant when he dies saying, ' We will see to that one who killed me.' But it does not mean that he straightway kills that warlock ; he begins to cut down (*kutemenena*) outsiders—any one he sees—and their relations, seeing the deaths, go to the diviner. The diviner declares the deaths to be due to this divinity, saying, ' It is So-and-so who killed this person ; he is fighting about his own death at the hands of his relative : he wants to kill him.' Thereupon that warlock gets into trouble with those people and has to pay over one of his slaves as a fine. So the divinity goes on troubling him who caused his death. The man will have to be purged (*pupululwa*) with medicines, to drive away that divinity, or else he will be the death of many and himself will die *inzanganzanga*—a violent death."

A man is *pupululwa*'d by being held forcibly with his face over a potsherd upon which are placed live coals and medicine. He inhales the pungent fumes. Presently he struggles and breaks away from his captors : they follow him with the potsherd until he falls down. Just then they throw away the sherd, and after a time he gets up and returns home free of the tormenting ghost. The " medicine " has somehow driven it off; others say it goes at the moment the sherd is thrown away. This purging is resorted to in any case where a person is possessed or obsessed by a harmful ghost.

Not only are the divinities offered various things, but they are kept in good humour by having their names given to one's spear, ox, canoe, slave, dog, or drum—anything that one has. Every time you have need of the thing you remember the divinity's name and pronounce it, and that is highly pleasing to him.

There are places consecrated to the divinities, but the Ba-ila proper neither make images of them, nor portray them in any way whatever. It is only on the north-eastern border of Bwila and under the influence of Baluba, that one finds graven images. Chibaluma, chief of the Lusaka commune, who is of mixed Baluba and Ba-ila blood, took us into his sanctum—an ordinary hut surrounded by trees, entry to which is forbidden to ordinary people—in the centre of the village. There he keeps the most valuable of his movable property—drums, guns, etc.; they are safe in the guardianship of the divinity, safer than if behind locked and bolted doors. Here also are deposited his hunting trophies. There is also a bed upon which occasionally he sleeps. And in the hut there are two figures about ten inches high, roughly carved in wood. They are named *mituni, bangosa,* or *tunkishinkishi.*[1] In the heads of these images there are holes into which " medicine " is poured. The hut is sacred to Chinenga, an ancestor of Chibaluma, removed three generations back, who was chief of the district and had his village farther west. He is reincarnate in Chibaluma and is his genius. It is believed by some of his people, and some of his sons, that Chibaluma's life is hid in these images; he himself told us that they preserve him from witchcraft. In some way his genius is bound up with the images, and the " medicine " is poured in at times to renew their power. On occasions, such as departure for a trading or hunting expedition, or before going to war,

---

[1] This name is evidently related to *nkici,* the name given to the " fetish " among some Congo and Western tribes.

A Feast in Honour of the Dead outside Chibaluma's Sacred Hut.

and when he is sick, he makes an offering before these images and implores the help of his divinity.

This hut we have described was not built over a grave. Among the Ba-ila proper, as well as among the Balumbu and Bambala, a tiny temple, consisting of a small conical grass roof supported on sticks, is built over the grave. This also is a sacred spot. Within the temple one usually finds an earthenware pot, sunk into the ground above the grave, as a receptacle for beer offerings. Around this, living poles

Photo E. W. Smith

A *LWANGA* AND GRAVE-TEMPLE.

are planted which soon sprout and in course of time grow up into a circular grove. On these trees one notices at times maize cobs, heads of Kaffir corn and other offerings, also heads of game. Some chiefs are buried in their huts, which are kept in repair for some time and then replaced by others, smaller and flimsier. In them are kept various articles that belonged to the deceased. After the death of Sezongo II. at Nanzela we saw in the hut various drums, stools, and spears—among them some very handsome elephant spears. One would think they would be preserved inviolate, and so we were told at the time ; but some years later we found them all gone. They had been removed by relations of the deceased. When we expressed surprise at the impiety, we were told : " It is all right. When a relation wanted anything, he made an offering to Sezongo, told him what he desired, and took it."

Another sacred spot, which we might dignify by the name of the village altar, is the *lwanga*. It takes different forms. Usually it is a long many-pronged pole planted near the centre of the village ; sometimes it is composed of four or five poles planted in a row and joined by a cross-

Photo E. W. Smith.

THE GREAT GATEWAY WITH SMALL SACRED ENCLOSURE AT EACH SIDE.

beam ; sometimes a quick-growing tree, such as an Isole, is planted for the purpose. In any case it has a close relationship with the divinities, localising, as it were, their presence in the village. Upon it various charms are hung to put them in the guardianship of the divinities ; men hang on the prongs, or place at the foot, their hunting trophies as offerings ; here, too, the spears are often deposited ; when meat is brought to the village it is first placed at the foot of the *lwanga* and an offering made. When a man has bought a new slave, he stands him at the *lwanga* and makes an offering to the divinities by filling his mouth with water and spitting it out upon the slave

and upon the *lwanga* ; he then gives the slave a new name :
this rite is to bind the slave to his master.

The *lwanga* is the public altar. In addition each family
has private altars in the house. We say " altars," but in
reality they are sacred spots without anything to mark

Photo E. W. Smith.

A NEAR VIEW OF THE SACRED ENCLOSURE AT THE GATEWAY.

them off. One is at the foot of the musemu, the central
pole of the hut ; the others are on either side of the main
doorway—on the right the husband's, on the left the wife's.

Another sacred spot in the village is at the great gateway, through which the cattle are driven. There is often
nothing to mark the spot, but at some villages there is a
small enclosure formed by the fence poles on each side of
the gateway. It is here that offerings are made to the

divinities to secure the well-being of the village, and of the cattle in particular.

To make an offering to the divinities is *kupaila*, a form of the word *kupa* (" to give "), and signifying to give repeatedly or frequently. The offering itself is *chipaizho* (" that which is given," or more accurately, " that by means of which one gives "). Two other words, *impaizho* and *mapai*, meaning the same, are formed from the root. Another word often used is *kutula* (" to offer "), and *chituzho* is the thing offered. A place at which things are offered is *chipaidilo*, or *chitudilo*.

These words are not restricted entirely to the service of the divinities, but are occasionally (and *kutula* more frequently than *kupaila*) used of presents given by one person to another, and especially of gifts to a superior. The word *kukomba* corresponds very well to our " worship " in the broad sense.

Many things are offered to the divinities, anything indeed that has value, or may be thought to be valuable to the divinities. Beer, grain, tobacco, hemp, hoes, bells, impande shells : all these among others are offered. The commonest of all is water ; a person fills his mouth with it and spits it out upon the ground. Simpler still is it to offer the saliva ; but here a necessary distinction must be made. A violent expectoration, such as may be represented by *Thu !* is a curse ; a gentle expectoration, *Tsu !* is an accompaniment of an offering, or an offering in itself, to the divinities.

The occasions for offerings are numerous ; they are made whenever there is need to approach a divinity, either to propitiate his anger or to entreat some blessing from him, or whenever his devotee wishes to do him honour. We may specify some of these occasions.

As we saw in a previous chapter, various things are placed in the grave and vocally offered to the deceased. The beer and beef consumed by the mourners are also to be taken as a form of offering, though perhaps not always regarded as such by the people themselves. Two or three days after the funeral ceremonies are completed and the crowds have dispersed, the relatives meet to drink beer named *funku owetwe* (" beer of the ash "). The occasion of this is the sweeping up of the ashes left from the fires made by the mourners : they are carefully gathered and thrown away into the veld. After some time they meet again for the *funku owa nsako* (" beer of the shafts ")—meaning the shafts of the deceased's spears, which are then broken and thrown away. Then comes *funku owa kuzhola munganda mufu* (" beer to bring back the deceased into the house "). It is a kind of welcome home to the ghost. A month or two after the funeral is *funku owa mapai* (" beer of the offer-

Photo E. W. Smith.

THE GRAVE OF OUR FRIEND MUNGALO.

ings ")—a simple feast in honour of the deceased, at which an ox is killed and eaten and beer is drunk. The next and last of the series is called *funku owa madidila* (" beer of the final weeping "), probably a year after the funeral. Thereafter there are no set occasions upon which an ordinary divinity, as distinguished from a communal divinity, is to be celebrated : only when they need his help or he makes his needs known by bringing some trouble upon them.

Such an occasion is the illness of a member of the family. The diviner on being consulted may say that the sickness is caused by a divinity who thinks himself neglected. So the head of the family makes an offering in his house : and prays: "*Tsu! Na ndiwe wasasha mwanesu, ngu wezo mukuku ng'ulanga, o tombwe aze. Uwe Leza na ndiwe ukunjaya n'apone kabotu* (" Tsu! If it be thou who art causing our child's sickness, see, here is the beer which thou wantest, and also some tobacco. And if it be Thou, O Leza! who art destroying me, I pray Thee let him recover "). Here is another prayer offered by a man on behalf of his child: "*Akaka, tata, na ndiwe muleke mwanako adiendele. Tsu! Akaka, tata, no kambonzhi? Anu tamuboni nu mizhimo nimudi kunze. Tsu! Akaka, muchembele, muleke. No uladila kudya, ulakukumbila mukuku ng'udila, ulakupaila. Akudi ndiwe, muleke, aende bubona bushiku. Tsu! Akaka, tata, twakukomba* ("Oh, my father, if it be thou (who art troubling him) leave the child alone that he may go about alone. Tsu! Oh, my father, what is the matter ? You divinities who are without, he doesn't see you (*i.e.* doesn't recognise you). Tsu! Oh, old man, leave him alone. If thou art crying for something to eat, he shall brew thee the beer thou criest for and make thee an offering. If it be thou, leave him alone that he may walk this very day. Tsu! Oh, my father, we worship thee ! ") If it is the head of the house himself who is sick, he makes an offering on his own behalf: "*Tsu! Na ndiwe akaka ndeka, ndeendele, no chinzhi uch'ukapula? Kai, tombwe ngu wezo, menzhi ngazo, ibwantu ndi ledi. Ndeka ndikusobanina budio*" (" Tsu! If it be thou, O leave me alone, that I may be well. What is it thou requirest ? See, here is tobacco, here is water, here is beer. Leave me alone that I may enjoy myself ").

Before a hunter sets off on the chase, he takes water in a dipper, together with tobacco, or hemp if he is a smoker of that narcotic, and places them at the foot of the musemu. He may add a little meal to the water. He spits out a mouthful of the water and prays : "*Tsu! Nini, ngu wezu tombwe o lubange, ndakupa ; ndaya mwisokwe atuende tonse ; kutabi uchebuka munshi, atuendele tonse. Chisamo chikadi na ch'one, inzoka inkadi nesakane, shiluma shonse kashisakana, pele kuyana chimana malweza, muzovu ngu wakuwula kulota, pele kusamba*" (" Tsu! So-and-so, see here is tobacco and hemp that I give thee ; when I go to the veld, let us all go together; let there be none who looks back, let us go on all together. Let the sharp stick sleep! May the fierce snake be far away! Let all biting things be far away! Let there only be found the end of that horror—the elephant that was picked up dead in a dream! Let there be good fortune!") He makes his offering after killing game, by throwing morsels in all directions, and on returning home deposits the meat first at the *lwanga*, where he makes another offering, to his own genius first and then to the family divinities.

Photo E. W. Smith.

A *LWANGA* AND GRAVE-TEMPLE.

An unsuccessful hunter will consult a diviner, saying, "Who is it that prevents my killing game? Is it Leza, or is it a divinity? Tell me." He consults the oracle, finds it is a divinity and tells the man to make an offering to his father or uncle. "And when you have done so, go to bed, and early in the morning go into the veld and you will kill an animal." He does so and is successful. When he has skinned the animal and cut it up, he makes an offering of pieces of meat in the manner already described, and again afterwards at the *lwanga*.

When a man's son returns home from a long journey, or after a lengthy residence elsewhere, he takes him into the

hut and *paila*'s him by sprinkling water on him and giving
him beads or other things ; they are named *impaizho*, and
are intended as an offering to the divinities, who have
guarded the man's son and brought him safely home. It
would be *buditazhi* for a person to *paila* in this way any
one not related to him (see Vol. I. p. 287).

Sometimes people gather around the grave of a departed
relation or chief. The chief takes a calabash-cup of beer or
water, pours a little upon the grave, and passes it to the
person next to him, who does the same. So the cup circu-
lates and each person pours out in turn a little of the contents. This is *kulazha muzhimo* (" to greet the divinity ").

When a village is moved to a new site the goodwill of
the divinities must first be obtained so that they will consent to remove with the people. Further, care must be
taken that no malign influences destroy the felicity of the
removal. The chief goes to a doctor to enlist his aid ;
together they visit the proposed new site, and the doctor,
if he approves of it, doctors (*wainda*) it with his "medicines."
They return to the old village and after a time set out again,
accompanied by the people, and preceded by a woman
(sometimes a child) carrying a pot of " medicine." Some
poles are first planted in a small circle where the gateway
of the new village is to be, and the woman places her pot
of medicine within them. Then an ox is killed and some
of its blood added to the contents of the pot. Then the
chief offers a prayer : " Hear us, O divinities, that our
village may be firm and strong." As an additional safe-
guard, the doctor drives in pegs of *musamo* around the site
to keep off witchcraft and other evils from the new village.

In a case like the foregoing, it is primarily the divinities
of his own house that the chief addresses, and each man as
he speaks the prayer directs his thoughts to his own family
divinities. It will be seen that there is no organised priesthood in this cult. The head of each family acts as the
priest, as far as his divinities are concerned, and his wife
approaches hers ; the chief of the village appeals to his on
behalf of the village, for they are on a different footing
from the ordinary family divinities who do not act outside
the family limits ; like him they have a representative

capacity, acting in the other world, as he acts in this, as the guardians of the village.

Photo E. W. Smith.

THE CHIEF, KAKUA, AND HIS *LWANGA*.

When the early maize is ready, the people go through the ceremonies of *kusomya* : that is, before they eat any of the grain (*kusoma*) they make an offering to their divinities.

The man goes to the field and plucks a few ripe ears of maize and takes them to the village. He strips off the husks and takes the cobs to the grave of a certain ancestor. He sweeps around the grave and then kneeling before the grave, says, " So-and-so, here is some of the maize which is ripe first and which I offer thee." Having done this he returns to his home, and at the threshold of his hut makes another offering in the same way : afterwards hanging some of the cobs over the door, or in the rafters.

2. THE GREAT MIZHIMO : COMMUNAL DIVINITIES

The genius is the man's own personal divinity ; each family has its own ; and the chief's or headman's divinities are in a way the guardians of the village. Over and above all these, are the great *mizhimo*, whose function it is to care for the common interests of the communes to which they belong. They are distinguished from all others by their greater permanence ; within the family the ghosts of one's remote ancestors cease to be regarded, but the respect paid to communal divinities lasts as long as the community survives. And they are unlike in this respect also : the communal divinities are never reincarnated, but remain in the spirit world. While the Ba-ila give them all the same name, *mizhimo*, we may, to mark the grades in the hierarchy, call the three classes : Genii, divinities, and demigods.

First let us transcribe what one of our informants had to say about the demigods.

" The divinities of the community are common property, there is no man who can claim them as his own. As at Kasenga, for example, where Shimunenga belongs to the whole community and all, whether chief or slaves, put their trust in him for what they need. They do not rely upon him in case of ordinary sickness—that is a matter for the family divinities—but for wealth, for victory in war, for protection against lions and in pestilence ; against all things that fight against them they trust him, saying, ' Shimunenga, our *muzhimo*, will save us.' In all the communities it is just the same ; they have one, or two, or three demigods. If a lion is killed the chief takes it to Shimunenga's grave

and the *muzhimo* is grateful for it shows the trust his people
have in him—a trust shown in the offering. If one kills a
leopard he does the same, taking the head to show that it
is the great *muzhimo* of the community who gave the good
fortune to kill that fierce beast. If there should be a
pestilence, all the people have faith that this *muzhimo* will
remove it so that they die not. Every community that
God created is the same, there is none that has not its
muzhimo to whom offerings are made. The divinities of
men are not assimilated ; a man who is not your relation
does not join you in making offerings to your divinities ;
he would be doing wrong. But it is otherwise with the
communal demigod : none refrains from calling upon him ;
he belongs to all. In a household there are various divinities ; a husband prays to his, a wife prays to hers ; but as
members of a community they all pray to one and the same
demigod.''

As we look back into the past, there emerge from the
hazy gloom the figures of these demigods who are regarded
with such impressive reverence. This is a list of some of
them and the communities to which they belong :

At Kasenga :	Shimunenga.
,, Kabulamwanda :	Zambwe.
,, Bambwe :	Sheebelelwa.
,, Bunga :	Kazua.
,, Kasamo :	Shibulwe.
,, Ianda :	Mushanana.
,, Lubanda :	Namashaka.
,, Lubwe :	Mwanachiwala.
,, Ngoma :	Shanyimba.
,, Basanga :	Ngala and Namadila

,, Nalubanda, Chiyadila, Munga,
Naluvwi. Maulizhi, Byangwe,   } Malumbe.
Kabanga, Nzovu, Nyambo, Lusaka.

In other districts N.W. : Munyama.

These demigods vary in importance according to the
extent of the territory over which they are the guardians,
the number of their present adherents, and the length of
time that has elapsed since they left the earth. Some of
these named above are, in these respects, of inferior note :
three stand out pre-eminent, viz. Malumbe, Munyama, and
Shimunenga.

Of Malumbe—who to-day is worshipped over a larger area than any other demigod of the Ba-ila—it is said that his father was named Mungalo, who came from the far east. Mungalo had two children, Malumbe and Chintu, the latter being the ancestress of the present Basala chief, Shakumbila. Others say that Malumbe was the son, not the brother, of Chintu. In accordance with his origin in Busala is his praise-name : Mwana-Musala. Others say that his father was Shitemambalo, and his mother Nachisanto. The latter died, it is said, of hunger, and people all over the land pray to her in time of drought.

When Malumbe grew into a man, he became famous as a wonder-worker. Then he came from Busala among the Ba-ila and gained the submission of the people in the districts where to-day he is reverenced as a *muzhimo*. He did not gain sway by means of the spear, but by reason of the fear he inspired. He is said to have struck with blindness all who opposed him. He was contemporary with Munyama and they were rivals. To settle their claims, the two chiefs agreed to appeal not to the spear but to a trial of skill in the *chisolo* game, which, according to one tradition, had been introduced by Malumbe. They met near the hot springs—Isho dia Mwino, in the neighbourhood of Mafwele. The first game fell to Munyama ; the second to Malumbe ; a third to Malumbe and the fourth to Munyama. Munyama wished to play one more game to settle the question, but Malumbe refused. By so doing he forfeited his claims to the country he was contesting, and it fell to Munyama. This tradition comes to us from a descendant of Munyama and is contradicted by another from the other side, according to which Malumbe was victorious, and gained in consequence much territory which hitherto had been Munyama's.

Another tradition assigns the creation of Isho dia Mwino to the agency of Malumbe. He had seen farther north a similar spring from which the possessors drew a considerable income by making salt ; and Malumbe thereupon made Isho dia Mwino to spring up for the benefit of his own people, and caused the other to dry up.

Malumbe's end on earth is said to have been very

mysterious. He simply disappeared. His spears, clothes, and ornaments were discovered by the side of a deep pool, but he himself was never seen again. Before leaving earth, he parcelled out his territory among several chiefs.

Of Munyama it is said that his mother and father came down in a rainstorm from heaven, and afterwards gave birth to him. One tradition is that he, or his parents, were immigrants from the Lunda country in the far north-west. He became a very powerful chief, had a great many people under him : so many, his descendant Mulendema told us, that no trees were left in the land, and as for his village, you could travel a whole day and yet not get through it ! After his death, different chiefs set up for themselves, and one by one hived off. So that to-day Mulendema sits alone with his family in a village of about ten miserable huts and complains much as he thinks of the departed glories of his family.

Shimunenga is the communal god of the ba-Mala, the people of the Kasenga district. How long ago he lived it is impossible to say. He is spoken of as *Mukandonokwabo Malumbe o Munyama* ("the ancient one who was contemporary with Malumbe and Munyama"), but little is known of him, and we cannot even guess when he lived. It is significant that like the other two great *mizhimo* he was an immigrant. His praise-name is Munambala ("the one of the Mbala country"), *i.e.* he came from the north somewhere. His father is said to have lived at Kaundu.

Besides Shimunenga there is at Kasenga a female divinity named Nachilomwe. She is said to have been a contemporary of Shimunenga ; some say she was his mother, others his sister.

In the other communities there are the demigods we have named, but often it seems that the most ancient ones are not those most regarded to-day. They lived so long ago that the people prefer others who were more recently in the flesh among them. Thus at Lubwe, Mwanachiwala is to some extent displaced by Shepande.

In each commune there is a grove of trees consecrated to the demigod. It is called Isaka ("the thicket"), or Isoko ("the place of origin"). Malumbe's grove is at

Malende in the Mauluzhi commune, Munyama's is near
Chikuni's village, and Shimunenga's at Mala, within the

Photo E. W. Smith.

OFFERINGS UPON A GRAVE.

Kasenga district. Besides the principal grove each has
subsidiary groves or single large trees where the demigod
at times takes up residence ; thus Shimunenga has a large
fig-tree at Chitumbi and another at Busangu.

The origin of the groves may be the poles planted around the graves. In course of time they would grow into large trees, decay, and be replaced by younger ones growing up around them. As it is taboo to meddle with the trees and the brushwood springing up under and around them, a dense impenetrable thicket is formed. Shimunenga's grove at Mala covers at least an acre of ground ; on its outskirts there stand several large wild fig-trees, upon one of which, in particular, various skulls of cattle and animals hang bleaching—remains of past offerings. We have tried

Photo E. W. Smith.

SHIMUNENGA'S GROVE AT MALA.

many times, but always unsuccessfully, to induce the Kasenga chief to take us into this grove. Sometimes we imagined that we had persuaded him, but always at the last moment, and once after he had got as far as the grove itself, he found a polite excuse for declining. It would not be easy to enter. There is no path into the interior. Only the " priest " ever enters and he but once a year, when he has to cut his way in.

Sometimes in travelling one comes upon a beautiful grove in a region destitute of inhabitants. It stands as a witness to the denser population of former days, for it was at one time the revered centre of a community that has now died out or been dispersed. Such a grove is that of

Maundu between Kalundo and Ngabo. It stands at the summit of a slope and is about half an acre in extent. There is but one entry. Creeping in there, between and under the thickly massed trees, you enter what is a fit temple for a sylvan god. There is a vacant space in the centre, the heads of the tall evergreen trees arching overhead and almost shutting out the sky. Long twisted vines hang down from them. The ground is strewn thick with leaves. Here is a bone, bleached with age, the remains of some offering. But there are no signs of any recent sacrifice. The grove no longer resounds with the rejoicing of the yearly festival. For the *chishi* has vanished and no devotees now forgather here. In such a case the ghosts continue for a time to haunt the trees, but they are cold and hungry and lonely, and should no fresh inhabitants take the place of the old the memory of them dies out—which is as much as to say that they themselves perish. And the communal demi-god shares their fate : maybe his very name is forgotten.

Besides these groves there are in some communes other sacred spots, associated in some way with the demigod. At Mala there is such a spot named Nakatunda. It is a bare place about an acre in extent, with a solitary palm-tree growing upon it. It is strictly taboo : nobody may cultivate there, nor build. Nobody has been able to give us an explanation of the name. It is one of the places that are reckoned as *chikomo* : an obscure word which is applied to places, rites, and customs traditionally associated with the demigods. It is here that the communal gatherings take place before and after war : where the warriors are doctored, where war is decided upon, where the cattle are killed in ratification of peace ; and it is here that the chiefs and people meet to discuss what shall be done when a murder has been committed.

In past days it was no uncommon thing for an embassy to arrive at Mala from a neighbouring community to solicit aid in war. The request was made in this form : " *Kamwiza bakwesu, mukatutemene kasanzhi oka meya kapatizhile* " (" Come, brothers, and cut down for us a twig covered with thorns "). A ready response was generally forthcoming, for the ba-Mala were always spoiling for a fight, and dressed and armed for war they collected quickly at Nakatunda, where oxen were killed—called *ing‘ombɛ sha makulo*—to seal the compact. At the close of the war, the opposing parties would meet at Nakatunda, and again oxen would be killed—*kuyaya kakosa*—and partaken of by all, as a declaration of peace. When a murder has taken place within the community, the people assemble at Nakatunda, singing an old song that runs something like this :

Nguni wabisha kono ?	Who is it that has been doing wrong here ?
Wa-wo-o, katuyabuenda.	Wa-wo-o, let us all go.
Ye-ye ! Wo ! We !	Ye-ye ! Wo ! We !
Kwabula bapanda bwanga,	There are none who can purge it with medicine.
Wa-wo-o, katuyabuenda.	Wa-wo-o, let us all go.

Shimunenga's medium delivers a message to the effect that the demigod is offended by the murder, and that steps must be taken to discover the impious criminal. He is made to pay *lwembe* ("weregild") of from ten to twenty cattle, which he collects from among his friends and clansmen. Two of the oxen are killed at Nakatunda : they are the *luloa*, offering to Shimunenga ; the flesh is eaten by the people and the heads deposited at the grove. One, or two, are reserved for the representative of the demigod, *i.e.* the "priest." The rest are distributed among the chiefs : so that each subdivision of the commune has one at least.

In all these observances the community as a whole is regarded as assembling in the presence of the demigod. The affairs are those in which he takes an immediate personal interest.

There is no organised priesthood associated with the demigods. But they have their representatives on earth, one class of whom seems to be a rudimentary priesthood. Presiding over the central grove in each commune is a custodian whose duty it is to receive and make the offerings on behalf of the people, to summon the people to the periodical feasts, and it is he who takes as his perquisite two of the cattle paid as *luloa*. In the former capacity he is *mupaizhi* ("offerer") or *mupaidizhi* ("offerer on behalf of others") ; in the latter he is *mukonki* ("a summoner").

This office is generally hereditary. At Mala it is held by a man named Kabombwe, whose son is now associated with him in the duties. The other men who figure in the rites are the mediums through whom the demigods make their will known. At Kasenga there are two of these ; one is a middle-aged man named Nakahunga. At times one of them falls into a trance (*mu chiyu*). It happened thus in June 1911. Nakahunga was sitting quietly with his friends in the evening when he was " seized." The people carried him into the veld where he remained unconscious till next morning. They told us he was convulsed with contortions and twitchings (*wazuzuba*). On being questioned the communicator announced himself as Shimunenga and proceeded to give a message to the community. Nakahunga told us afterwards that he was quite unaware of what had happened. In reply to a question he said that he first became " possessed " when a child. We always wanted to see him in that state, but never had an opportunity.

We have mentioned that when a lion is killed the trophies are offered to the demigod. One night shortly after our arrival at Kasenga we were awakened by a sudden outburst of drumming from the cattle outpost close by and the simultaneous shouting of our workmen aroused from sleep. On inquiry next morning we learnt that the drums had been beaten to convey to the community the news of the death of a lion. About midnight it had sprung over the high fence and seized a cow. The three or four herdsmen had issued from their huts and attacked it with their spears —a plucky thing to do in the dark. We were in time to see the little procession of men, carrying the skin and head, set out on its way to Shimunenga's grove. In such a case, the skin would be taken by the chief, and the " priest " would deposit the head in a tree of the grove as a solemn recognition of and thanksgiving for the demigod's assistance.

Another occasion for approaching Shimunenga is at the sowing season. The " priest " goes to the Isoko and plants a few seeds as an offering ; before this is done nobody may sow his fields, but once the demigod has been recognised they may set to work. Early in the season when the corn begins to show above the surface (*kuvhwa busonga*) the priest makes another offering.

Apart from these occasions, every demigod has at least one annual festival in his honour. It is called an *ikubi*. At Kasenga, the *makubi* of Nachilomwe and Shimunenga are held some time in September, *i.e.* at the close of the old and beginning of the new year, according to their reckoning, in connection with the opening of the cultivation season and the departure of the cattle for the outposts (*kuwila*, see Vol. I. p. 131).

We will translate an account of this *ikubi* given to us by one of our informants :

" The festival of Shimunenga is called (*diakonkwa*) at the new year (*kumwaka*) according to his sacred custom (*chikomo*). It is said, ' The year has come round again.' Kabombwe goes to Mala and enters Shimunenga's grove and holds conversation with him. This finished he goes round to all the villages and says, ' Gather firewood and begin the brewing of the beer.' After several days, thinking that by this time they have gathered the wood and the malt has sprouted, he returns to Mala and gives a second summons : ' Now put the beer to brew.' So on the morrow they begin and for four or five days are busy with the beer. On the fifth day all the cattle are collected to sleep at Mala and the drums begin to sound throughout the commune. On the sixth day, all the men plaster themselves with white clay, and they and the women adorn themselves in their finery. And they call upon his name : ' Shimunenga, Lobwe, Udimbabachembe ! ' (' Shimunenga, Gatherer of men, Giver of virility to males ! ') Then they all drink beer. The men make compacts with the women, that is to say, give them cattle, and the women rejoice and give their lovers leopard skins and cloth and other things as they wish. All join in these things. On the morrow the same things happen. And they drive out the cattle, and *wila*, *i.e.* go down to the outposts on the river bank. In leaving Mala they are preceded by Shibeenzu's herd ; his is the one to lead the way and goes by itself ; the others follow after. They go down to the Lubunda ford and there they cross. When all are on the other bank, they recross them to this, separate the herds and each goes off by itself. Before leaving Mala, and while the men are all charging up and down (*kukwenzha*), all the women lululoo and cry : ' *Ulu !* Let the cattle beget and bear coloured calves ! O Shimunenga, Gatherer of men, Giver of virility to males ! Let them bring forth coloured calves ! ' This is how the festival is celebrated. They drink plenty of beer and are all very happy. When it is over they leave the villages and go off to the fields to cultivate, and things go on until the year comes round again."

We will now supplement this account by some notes written by us after being present at a festival :

" Went to Mala to-day to witness some Shimunenga celebrations. Came to Chidyaboloto's and finding they had not yet started, sat there. The women were busy getting their finery ready, many wearing the *mukaku* girdle, others with strings of white beads around their waist. Presently women began to pass by the village singing. Then a party of men came in, singing and beating sticks together to make a noise. They came and knelt before Chidyaboloto, evidently singing his praises, but I couldn't catch the words. My boys said the men go all round the villages doing this and in return the headmen give them beer. I went off, leaving the men there. Long lines of women were converging from all the villages towards Shimunenga's grove. They wended their way there and joined company outside the grove, singing with all their might and clapping their hands. Presently a man came with a drum and started beating it to help the women in their singing. This being the women's day the men simply stood and watched. Presently the men we had seen at Chidyaboloto's came round singing. What they sang I could not distinguish, nor the songs of the women. One of my boys said, ' They're singing about us,' and another replied, ' Why, they sing about anybody.' Shambweka came up and said it was their custom thus to pray for rain. In the midst of these proceedings, which lasted about an hour, a ceremony took place which struck me as very incongruous." (This has been described in another chapter : it was the Lubambo ceremony.)

This we found was the song of the men as they knelt before Chidyaboloto :—

Boloto wakakala shishishini
Muwale kashishi, akuuluke !

> " Boloto sat as an owl,
>   Throw a firestick at him and make him fly away ! "

The men on the path sang :—

Umudi Shimunenga
Mwenzu ndi abia taumwa :

> " Where Shimunenga is, a visitor, however ugly he may
>   be, is not to be beaten."   (This about us !)

The songs of the women are the same as those sung at funerals, *i.e.* mostly phallic in character.

On this first day of the feast, the women's day, Nachilomwe, the female demigod, is associated with Shimunenga in the celebrations. The display of the cattle on the second day, the men's day, seems to ·be for the purpose of showing them to Shimunenga. We cannot say whether the demigod is thought of as partaking in the feast of beer. We should rather say that just as a living chief is pleased and complimented by an exhibition of his people's happiness and wealth, so Shimunenga is thought to be gratified by this display—so gratified that at this critical season of the year he will in return do his utmost to increase their prosperity in field and herd.

There is a monotonous sameness about all the *makubi.* There is always plenty of beer ; much dancing and singing ; charging up and down by men with their spears ; lewd songs and a general license. In many points the annual feast is comparable with the Saturnalia.

At the end of 1914 something happened at Kasenga that had never been known before : the months slipped by and no festival was held for Shimunenga. When January came in and still Kabombwe gave no signs of summoning the people, a meeting of the chiefs was held to discuss the matter. The reason was found to be that Kabombwe was angry. He made this declaration : " This year I have not inaugurated the festival because when, two years ago, one of

Shimalondo's people committed murder you never gave me part of the *luloa*, but nevertheless I held the festival. This last year there have been two murders and I have received no cattle. Now, I, Kabombwe, how can I hold the festival in the face of these things ? Is it not always so, that when a murder takes place you give me a cow and you also collect two great oxen to be killed for Shimunenga ? " The assembly could only answer him in the affirmative : and it was decided that the cattle should be collected. Why they had never been paid we do not know. All three of the murders had been committed by clansmen of one chief, and the old man addressed the assembly in a great state of mind. Said he, " You are killing me altogether ! How can I find thirty head of cattle to pay these fines ? " They insisted, until Nalubwe called for silence and spoke : " I say, my brothers, that Shimalonda cannot find these thirty head of cattle. Let him bring one, a fine big ox, to die at the grove. And let Machacha, at the *chisungu* feast of whose daughter the other murder took place—let him bring a cow in calf and give to Kabombwe. And let the clansmen of the third murderer all contribute ten cattle for the damages and one big ox to die at Shimunenga's grove. This is what I say, I Nalubwe ! " And it seemed good to all the chiefs and they ordered this to be done. But as a matter of fact, when we left Kasenga in March 1915 the feast had not been held.

3. BULONGO

Of all the figures in the Ila pantheon, the most elusive is the arch-demigod Bulongo. We put him in a class by himself because, according to the imperfect information we have collected, he seems not to be a local demigod such as Shimunenga, but to be regarded over a wider area than even Malumbwe : as one of our informants says, " He is the *muzhimo* of the whole country : there is no community that does not pray to him." He has no grove such as the others have, but has temporary huts built for him. At Mala, his representative is an old blind chief named Nalubwe, who is said to be a lineal descendant from Shimunenga. The latter, we are told, was the first to ordain that an annual *ikubi* should be held in honour of Bulongo, and the dignity of Bulongo's priesthood has descended not to the chief who has inherited Shimunenga's chieftainship, but in Shimunenga's family. Nalubwe has the clan-name borne by Shimunenga, *i.e.* Nyungwe ; and this is an interesting example of how exceptionally the clan may descend through the father, and not through the mother. His ancestors since Shimunenga's time have all, he tells us, lived where he lives now.

We will transcribe three accounts of Bulongo that we have received from different men :

" That Bulongo," said our friend the Mala blacksmith, " is the greatest on earth. Every person puts his trust in Bulongo at all times, for when they pray to him at a time when they have no water falling from Leza, it will come— Leza will let fall much water. But they do not know who he is ; all they know is they found him (*i.e.* his name) here on earth. It is said of him : Bulongo, greatest on earth among those earliest ancients, is earth only. They praise him thus : ' Bulongo, Mwanamungo, we are humble before thee.' When they call thus upon him, rain falls. Again, after the grain is ripe they make a festival for him in the winter. The first in the year is Bulongo's ; afterwards comes Shimunenga's. It is said again he is the friend of God (*mwenzhina*, comrade, equal, fellow). When they pray to Bulongo, Leza throws down (*walosha*) water, so they suppose that the two are together (*badibwenene*, ' in each other's sight'). Some suppose Bulongo is the greater, and Leza to be as his friend only, or as his ' child.' Only really nobody knows these things. Our fathers never saw Bulongo, but perhaps their grandfathers knew better about him ; perhaps they saw him himself. This is all that can be said of Bulongo. He is earth only, not a person."

Another man said, " Bulongo is simply a *musangushi*, he is not a person. Nobody knows him. The ancients simply found him here when they descended long long ago, and they sacrificed to him in blindness because of what they had heard by the ears. The Ba-ila found their fathers of long long ago doing this, so those who came after them did as they did, simply carrying on the tradition. Bulongo

speaks to us only through Shimunenga. When he wants
to have beer brewed for him he seizes Shimunenga in the
usual fashion of a control (*mu chisoko cha kushinshima*) and
Shimunenga in turn seizes his medium and tells his name.
The people ask, 'What is it you say, sir?' and he
replies, 'I say, brew beer for Bulongo.' The Ba-ila at
once consent and say, 'We are humble, O Chief! we
will brew beer.' When he has given that message, Shimunenga leaves the medium, and he who had been entered
recovers and becomes a man again. The Ba-ila get to work:
the whole country puts malt to soak and brews beer. On
the day for drinking it, all the ba-Mala go to the little huts
yonder in Nalubwe's village, every person with a calabash
of beer to offer to Bulongo. They pour it on the ground
and cry, 'We are humble, O Bulongo! See here is beer
which we give you.' He who calls that feast is Nalubwe,
and in doing so is carrying on the sacred custom (*chikomo*)
left by his fathers, and they who begat his fathers found
it being done by those who begat them. But not one of
that line of descent knew him; they heard only by the
ears that Bulongo is—whether a man, or a ghost, or whoever
he may be, they do not know. Another time Bulongo
'seizes' by means of Shimunenga and tells people to do
so-and-so according to his wishes. And Nalubwe himself,
as it is his *chikomo*, if he wishes to call a festival, tells
the people, 'Let Bulongo be built a house.' Then all
the people bring every one a bundle of sticks and the
women small bunches of grass, and build those small houses
for Bulongo. And if he wants beer brewed for Bulongo
he gives his orders, whether it be the winter or any other
time. But as for knowing him, nobody knows. They
simply imagine things. And in plastering those huts, all
the people join, bringing small lumps of clay. As the
people of Mala are so numerous, some of them can't get
near with their contribution, but they try, and they who
struggle forward do well. Again it is said: Bulongo
belongs to all the communes, there is no commune where
Bulongo is not. No, in all the world his existence is
recognised—everywhere. But as for seeing him, among
all the people there is none who has seen him, no, no, they

imagine things only. Some say : He is earth ; others : He is a ghost ; others : He is just wind (*muwo*) ; others say : He is a man who came from the Sala country. He never was seen ; that is all we can be sure of."

The third account says :

" Bulongo also was a man and had his origin in the Sala country at Nashamwenda's. He also was a fellow of Shimunenga, for those two were living at the same time. It is from the Sala country that the impande shell came, because when Bulongo's people descended they brought the shells with them—shells and all kinds of wealth, such as *bukolwe* and *mambulukutu*, *i.e.* large beads. People of to-day have never seen these, but in those old days you took a string of beads, long enough to go round your neck and down to the navel, and bought an awfully nice girl with it. All these are things heard by the ears, even Kabombwe and Nalubwe, the masters of these ceremonies, never saw them. Bulongo has a festival made for him at Nalubwe's. They meet to drink beer, dressed in their finery, and they praise him, saying, ' Bulongo Mwana-mungo, Mwanakumpande, Upaokutuba' (' Giver even to the whites,' *i.e.* to unfortunates, wasters). He is worshipped in the summer, whenever rain does not fall and there is great heat. They build a little hut at Nalubwe's, on the western side of the village near the big gate. There are three altogether : Nachilomwe, elder sister of Shimunenga ; Shimunenga himself and Bulongo ; they are the three great ones of the Mala community. If it should be that these three did not speak as usual at the change of the year, the ba-Mala would be perplexed and say : ' Where have our demigods (*mizhimo*) gone to-day ? The year has gone without our hearing their words.' That is how the people speak. They haven't a lot to say for nobody has ever seen them, but this is the way in which these three are worshipped."

We have had many talks with Nalubwe himself about Bulongo. He is a very intelligent old man—the most intelligent of the Ba-ila chiefs, we should say ; and he is not one who puts you off with fancy legends, but discusses a matter reasonably. But we have not been able to add much to the accounts given above. Nalubwe will not dogmatise as to who or what Bulongo is. It seems to him that he could not have been a man ; he still lives, that is certain, but whether as *muwo* or *musangushi* he does not know. We discussed the question of the identity of Bulongo with Leza, for some people confuse the two. When you ask for Bulongo's praise-titles they answer : Mwanamungo, Chiotamaila, Nakumpande, etc. " And what are Leza's ? " Lubumba, Chilenga, etc. " You do not praise Bulongo as Lubumba ? " Oh, no. " Nor Leza as Nakumpande ? " Certainly not. Well, that shows they are not the same. Nalubwe agrees to that. Ba-ila and Bambala make an annual festival in Bulongo's honour and build houses for him ; the other demigods have their groves. But nowhere in Bwila has Leza a local habitation, natural or artificial, and nowhere is a festival held for him. The little houses built for Bulongo remind one of similar structures put up for every prophet that arises in Bwila. And we imagine that Bulongo is the name of a very ancient prophet, either contemporary with Shimunenga or more probably prior to him, who gained an unrivalled influence all through the Ila countries, so much so that since his death he has remained the one *muzhimo* that is venerated in all the districts. There is probably some truth in the tradition that he came from the Sala country : he may have come with other emigrants from some country farther north and introduced the impande shells and other things mentioned above.

We ought to mention before leaving the subject, that one of our informants had the idea of Bulongo being the earth (the name means clay) and Leza the sky, and the union of the two producing grain and all other things.

We have been mounting through the stages of the Ila hierarchy—genii, divinities, demigods, arch-demigod—all spoken of as *mizhimo*, but having an ever-widening scope of action ; it remains now to deal with Leza, the Supreme Being, whose sphere is cosmical.

CHAPTER XXIII

*

THE SUPREME BEING : LEZA

THE Ba-ila tell a legend of a very old woman, who in ancient times, being perplexed by the riddle of this painful earth, set out to seek for Leza and to demand from him an explanation. The legend runs thus :

She was an old woman of a family with a long genealogy. Leza being Shikakunamo—" the besetting One "—stretched out his hand against her family. He slew her mother and father while she was yet a child : and in the course of the years all connected with her perished. She said to herself : " Surely I shall keep those who sit on my thighs "—but no, even they, the children of her children, were taken from her. She became withered with age, and it seemed to her that she herself was at last to be taken. But no, a change came over her : she grew younger. Then came into her heart a desperate resolution to find God and to ask the meaning of it all. Somewhere up there in the sky must be His dwelling : if only she could reach it ! She began to cut down trees, immense trees and tall, joining them together and so planting a structure that would reach to heaven. It grew and grew, but as it was getting to be as she wanted it, the lowest timbers rotted and it fell. She fell with it, but without being killed or breaking a bone. She set to work again and reared the structure, but once again the foundations rotted and it fell. She gave it up in despair, but not her intention of finding God. Somewhere on earth there must be another way to heaven ! So she began to travel, going through country after country—nation after nation—always with the thought in her mind : " I shall come to where the earth ends, and there where earth and sky touch, I shall find a road to God, and I shall ask Him : ' What have I done to Thee that Thou afflictest me in this manner ? ' " She never found where the earth ends, but though disappointed she did not give up her search, and as she passed through the different countries they asked her, " What have you come for, old woman ? " And her answer would be, " I am seeking Leza." " Seeking Leza ! For what ? " " My brothers, you ask me ! Here in the nations is there one who suffers as I have suffered ? " And they would ask again, " How have you suffered ? " " In this way. I am alone. As you see me, a solitary old woman : that is how I am ! " And they answered again, " Yes, we see. That is how you are ! Bereaved of friends and kindred ? In what do you differ from others ? Shikakunamo sits on the back of every one of us, and we cannot shake Him off ! " She never obtained her desire : she died of a broken heart (*yamuyaya inzezela*). And from her time to this, nobody has ever solved her problem !

That is legend. Let us hear what living men say themselves of the Power they dimly discern working in the world. We have talked with many old men who had not come under the influence of Christian teaching, and will transcribe here the actual words of two of them—both intelligent old chiefs.

This is Shikanzwa's version :

Sunu Leza waalaula, waleka mianza yakwe ya kalekale, sunu ngunji, udi bunji chinichini, ukuti tadi mbu akubele miaka mile, kabatana kwiza bami batuba. Nakudi Namese chinichini shonse shintu kashichizudile sh'anshi, shakasokasoka ku masokelo. Ledio Leza kachidi mupya. Anukuti sunu kwina muyoba, kwina shoye, shivhulamabwe shinjishinji. Indaba Shikanzwa,

To-day Leza has turned over, and abandoned his old ways. To-day he is not the same, he is altogether different, for he is not as he was in distant years before the white chiefs (*i.e.* the Europeans) came. At that time he was truly the Water-giver and all things were still sufficient on earth as they had been established from the beginning. Then Leza was still fresh (or young or new). Whereas to-day there is no heavy rain, no continued rain and no great hail-storms. As I am Shikanzwa ! to-day we say :

sunu tulaamb'ati : Leza wache-mbala, waba muntumbano, ubele kale. Mbu tuzunga bobo ukuti menzhi aza ng'alosha izungwa bu misozhi ivhwa u menso a bantu ni badila, bu bafumbi aba mupami adile nakasozhi kalosha a chamba chakwe, mbu tumuzunga. Sunu Leza ati udimwi tamwizhi sunu, tulaamba, tulazeka, kudi ukazumya mutwi, ukakusakulwa, ulabona okubonesha shikaba kwa Leza nshi akachita bwasunu. Miaka yedia katuyene shimuno sha mikumo mikumo sha mbono, anu sunu, kwina pe, pe. Ngu Shatwakwe, shintu shonse nshina-kwakwe. Talandwa, taambwa, aze tabuzhiwa, takolombwa, tachitilwa shonse nshi tuchitila bantunokwesu anshi ano, pe. Ulapa o kubozha. Muzhololosha ngwakwe mwini. Kwina mwenje sunu, kwina shi-mwenje mukando. Mbu azungwa-zungwa bobo, usunu Leza ulasha-shitizhiwa. Kalekalc kadi su-ngwasungwa kuchitila kabotu, pele waleka.

And Kambunga said :

Kalekale Ba-ila tibakumwizhi Leza makani akwe, pe, pele kaba-mwizhi budio ati, ngu akatulenga, o kutachimwa kwakwe. Leza ubudi-sunu mainza mbu akatazha sunu, mbu atawi, intela kai balatamauka, ati, Leza watukatazha kutawa. Odimwi awisha, ati, Leza wawisha.

Leza has grown old, he has become the ancient one, of long ago. That is what we suppose, because the water which he rains down is supposed to be like tears from the eyes of men when they weep. So it is when one becomes aged, when he weeps tears he lets them dribble down his chest — and that is how we judge Leza to be. To-day we say again, we do not know Leza now, we speak, we imagine there is one who will harden his head by being shaven, and he will see and see clearly what will be from Leza and the things which he will do nowadays. In yonder years we found wealth of various kinds of property, but to-day there is none —no, no. He is Owner-of-his-things : all things are his. He cannot be charged with an offence, cannot be accused, cannot be questioned, cannot be claimed from : none of the things can be done to him which we do to our fellow-men on earth. He gives and rots. Vengeance is his own. There is no flood to-day — no great giver of floods. This is how he is judged of ; to-day Leza is not as he is wanted to be. Long ago he was the One who could be urged to do well, but to-day he has left off being so.

Long ago the Ba-ila did not know Leza as regards his affairs— no, all that they knew about him, was that he created us, and also his unweariedness in doing things. As at present when the rainy season is annoying and he does not fall, why then they ask of Leza different things : they say now, " Leza annoys us by not falling " : then later when he

Achita impeyo, ati, Leza wachita impeyo. Abala lumwi ati : Leza wabadisha, na kuvhumba-vhumba. Nikubabobo Leza mbwadi Shintemwe, kwaamba, mbwadi Shiluse, talemani, taleka kuwa, taleka kubachitila shintu shonse, pe, obatukana, obamuchopa, obamuvwiya, bonse wabachitila kabotu shikwense. Mbu bobo mbu · bamushoma shikwense. Kwakudi kubona makani akwe shikwense, pe, tabezhi Ba-ila, baamba budio, ati, Leza ngu shichenchemenwa, ngu natamaukilwa. Tu Ba-ila twina ntu twizhi.

falls heavily they say, " Leza falls too much." If there is cold they say, " Leza makes it cold," and if it is hot they say, " Leza is much too hot, let it be over-clouded." All the same, Leza as he is the Compassionate, that is to say, as he is Merciful, he does not get angry, he doesn't give up falling, he doesn't give up doing them all good—no, whether they curse, whether they mock him, whether they grumble at him, he does good to all at all times. That is how they trust him always. But as for seeing always his affairs, no, the Ba-ila do not know, all they say is : Leza is the good-natured one ; he is one from whom you beg different things. We Ba-ila have no more that we know.

In these native-told accounts, certain epithets are applied to Leza which need, and will repay, reconsideration. He is called *Shikakunamo*. *Kukunama* is to beset any one—to cling to, adhere, persecute by unremitting attentions. The phrase gives the idea of Leza plaguing the old woman, castigating her by killing off her relations. Again he is called *Sungwasungwa*. *Kusunga* is to stimulate, stir up a person to do things, good or bad, by repeated solicitation. Long ago, says Shikanzwa, you could get Leza to do what you wanted by constant entreaty, but not so to-day. He is called *Shichenchemenwa*. *Kuchenchemena* (the active form of the verb) is to trade on a person's good nature, by asking for various things without a sense of shame, which you know you have no title to ask for. That is how Leza is regarded. He is called also : *Natamaukilwa*. *Kutamauka* is to be changeable in speech. To *tamaukila* a person is to ask him for something, and when you get it, say, " No, that's not what I want, give me something else." So is Leza treated by men. When no rain falls they say, " Leza you annoy us, give us some rain " ; and when he sends plenty of rain they say : " You give too much " ; when he sends cold they want heat ; and when he sends heat, they want cold.

These are epithets that might be applied to any person whose character warranted it ; they are different from the praise-names, which are peculiarly his. As we have seen in another connection, a praise-name is descriptive of qualities, capacities, possessed or supposed to be possessed by a person. What a man's character is, in the opinion of his fellows, may be gathered with accuracy from these names. So is it in regard to Leza. In no way can be better determined the Ba-ila theology than by a study of these praise-names.

Chilenga [1] (also Namulenga) "The Creator." The word is derived from *kulenga*, to make, to originate, to be the first to do anything—not necessarily to create out of nothing, but certainly to produce something that did not exist before. The word is sometimes used of men ; for instance, when one of us commenced to make bricks the people said of him : "*Ngu akalenga shitina um Bwila*" (" It is he who was the first to make bricks in the Ila country.") It is also used in the sense of establishing, instituting a custom. By calling Leza Chilenga, they mean that He made things and established the tribal customs. We were talking in our room one day with an old man ; he picked up a beautiful wild-cat skin lying on the floor, and with some enthusiasm said, " Who but Chilenga could colour a skin like that ? Yes, only He who is above. And all these things "—with a wide sweep of the arm to indicate the world in general—" He only ! "

Lubumba (" the Moulder ") is a title made from the common Bantu word *kubumba*, to mould, shape, as a woman moulds her pots (cf. Kongo, Zulu, *bumba* ; Suto, *bopa*).

Shakapanga (" the Constructor ") is from another common root : *kupanga*, to put together, set in order, construct. The verb is not used commonly in Ila to-day, but occurs in many other Bantu languages (Lenje, Lala-Lamba, Wisa, Bemba, Swahili, Nyanja ; Kongo, *Vanga*).

These three titles indicate that Leza is the maker of

[1] Among the Awemba Mulenga is said to be the chief *mulungu* or nature spirit distinct from Leza : a benevolent spirit who can grant abundant rain. Mlengi is a title given by the Manganja to Chiuta.

things. If we ask, what things? the answer is " all."
Necessarily the " all " of a Central African native is restricted, but it comprises all that he knows, and the word
to us could mean no more.

Mutalabala is a name derived from *kutalabala*, to be
age-lasting, to be everywhere and all times, equivalent to
the phrase, *Uina ng'aela* (" He has nowhere, or nowhen,
that he comes to an end ").

Namakungwe is a title said to mean " He from whom
all things come." The etymology is obscure. *Kukungwa*
means to be well-dressed, and if derived from that root the
name would mean " He (or rather, she) who is well adorned "
—and might be taken to refer to the beauty of the world as
the garment of God, but that is doubtful.

Other names bring Leza into relation with men : Muninde
(*kudinda*, to watch, guard), " The Guardian"; Chaba (*kuaba*,
to give, to allot to), " The Giver "; Ipaokubozha (*kupa*, to
give ; *kubozhu*, to rot), " He who gives and causes to rot."
He gives things, but His gifts are not permanent : fruits
fall from the trees and decay ; the rainy season passes into
winter : the corn in the bins is spoilt by weevil, etc.

Ushatwakwe means " Master, Owner, of his things."
Leza is not only the master but the owner of all, and the
ordainer of the fate of all. Life, as an old man said to us
once, is like a labour ticket that the white men give to
their workmen ; before your time is up you cannot leave,
but as soon as it expires you have to go. So Shatwakwe
disposes of men. When we killed a deadly snake one day,
a man greeted it by saying, " To-day you are dead ! Killed
by the white man ! So was it ordered by Shatwakwe that
you should come and be killed." The name gives expression
to the deep underlying fatalism of the Ba-ila.

Other names have reference to the elements.

Shakatabwa, " The Faller " (*kutabwa* is to fall ; used
only of the rain : *Leza watabwa* : rain falls).

Lubolekamasuko means " He who causes the *masuko*
fruit to rot." Mangwe is said to mean " the Flooder ";
Shakemba, or Kemba, is said to mean the Rain-Giver ; but
the etymology is obscure. Namesi is " The Water-Giver."
(*Mesi* is an older form of *menzhi* : water, cf. Yao, *mesi*.)

Munamazubạ means " He of the suns " (or " days ").
Luvhunabaumba : " Deliverer of those in trouble."

Other less familiar titles are : Mukubwe (*Kukubula*, to
cut down and destroy) ; Chembwe, said to mean " He who
takes away till there is only one left " ; Munakasungwe,
" Leader " (*kusungula*, to lead) ; Munakachulwe, or Nama-
chulwe ; Namazwingwe (or Namazungwe) ; Kayuyu ; Mu-
ndandamina-Kalunga ;[1] of the last four we have been unable
to find any meaning.

These are some of the descriptive *tembaula* titles applied
to Leza : *Lubombolangulu-maumbuswa-nchi-atalana* (" Dis-
solver of ant-heaps, but the *maumbuswa* ant-hills are too
much for him "). *Wakazuzha-kalambwelambwe, katende-ka-
nakasha-kamukachila* (" He can fill up all the great pits of
various kinds, but the little footprint of the Oribi he cannot
fill "). *Chaba-wakaaba-ochitadiwa* (" The giver who gives
also what cannot be eaten ").

These are names commonly applied to Leza. They are
in no sense esoteric, but may be heard on the lips of anybody. It is just possible that some of the obscurer names
may at one time or another have been of human beings, or
mizhimo, though now applied only to Leza. We have heard,
e.g., among the Bambala the name Lukele given to Leza ;
and He was described as having been the piler-up of the
Nambala mountains. But it seems that Lukele was at
some ancient date a human hero. At Lubwe we have heard
Leza called : Bulongo-Namesi. Bulongo, as we have seen,
is the arch-demigod of the Ba-ila, probably once a man. If
we did but know, the same might be true of other names ;
but at the same time we are certain that in the consciousness of the Ba-ila at present these names do not imply that
Leza is the totality of ancient heroes ; nor do they imply
a recognition of many gods. To conclude that the Ba-ila
were polytheists on the strength of these titles would be as
accurate as saying it of the Parsis who are said to have
a thousand and one names for the Supreme Being. The
Parsi names, *e.g.* Purvedegar, the Provider ; Purvurdar, the

---

[1] We have heard these other names for Leza among the Bambala :
Nzumakule ; Mulundumuna ; Mundobwe. The Baluba and Balamba
have the names Shakapanga ; Mande.

Protector, etc., are similar to those of the Ba-ila: not names of multitudinous deities but praise-names of the one.

So much for the titles. What in everyday talk do the Ba-ila say of Leza? Now, when we say "it rains, it blows," grammarians call the word " it " a prop-word; it remains in our language probably as evidence of an ancient belief that the sky fell in the form of rain: just as the Greeks talked of Zeus raining and afterwards dropped the noun and simply said: "it rains." And that is how the Ba-ila speak to-day. Where we say " it " they say " Leza." *Leza wabala* ("it is very hot"); *Leza ulaunga* ("it blows"); *Leza wawa* ("it rains"), literally " Leza falls." When it lightens they say: *Leza wakalala* (" Leza is fierce "); when it thunders, *Leza wandindima* (" Leza makes the reverberating sound *ndi-ndi-ndi* "). *Chandwa-Leza* is the name given to anything struck by lightning: " that which is split by Leza." *Leza watikumuna masalo akwe* (" Leza is beating his rugs ") is another way of describing thunder. *Leza wazhika mai* (" Leza buries eggs ") is another description of thunder. Just as a crocodile buries its eggs in the sand and returns to the spot unerringly, so does the thunder return in its season. *Leza wabwanga bushiku* (" Leza ties up the day ") is said of a disappointingly short rainy season. *Leza wabonzha bushiku* (" Leza softens the day ") is said of the beginning, and *Leza wabusangula bushiku* (" Leza changes the day ") is said of the end of the rainy season. The rainbow is called *Buta bwa Leza* (" Leza's bow "). In regard to a death they may say: *Leza wakombola mungo wakwe* (" Leza snaps off his pumpkin"). The name is further used in solemn affirmation: *Leza! ngu Leza!* are common oaths. It is used also in cursing: *Leza wakuanda* (" May Leza split you! ").

It is not altogether easy to say to what extent these names and phrases imply belief in a personal Being. The curse just quoted might be the invoking of the wrath of a person, or merely calling down lightning. Many of the names might very appropriately be applied simply to the elements.

The rain and the phenomena associated with it are the most important, the most striking, the most useful. In

the Ila country it is supremely so.   From the end of March
till the end of October not a drop of rain falls.   The small
rivers either disappear entirely or remain as shrunken, broken
pools.   The water-holes dry up.   As winter passes and
August comes in, the sun grows in power until in the weeks
preceding the rains the heat is almost unbearable.   And
then in the most impressive manner imaginable the welcome
clouds gather, the wind suddenly veers round to the west,
and a great storm passes over the country, heralding the
incoming of the new season.   And what a transformation !
A day or two after the storm, nature is wearing a new face.
Millions of little seedlings are pushing their way through the
earth.   The people have been hoeing their fields, and now
the work is pressed on.   To them, of course, the rain comes
just at the time when they are wanting it : not that they
cultivate in preparation for, and at the coming of the rains ;
but it comes when they cultivate.   For months there has
probably been a scarcity of food ; and the coming of the
rain is looked forward to eagerly and anxiously.   Should
its coming be delayed, or be scanty, great is the trouble.

Any one understanding these things, could appreciate at
once the calling of the rain and thunderstorms by such
names as Chaba : the giver of all good things ; and Muninde,
the Guardian of Men ; seeing that it is from them that we
derive directly all the material blessings we enjoy.   And
those other names are so aptly descriptive of the rain-
storms that sweep the country: " The rotter of the
masuko fruit "—the " Flooder."   And when a man tells you
that Leza is Shichenchemenwa (" the good-natured one ") ;
Shintemwe (" the Compassionate "), you can see he has the
rain in mind.   The rain falls on the evil and the good, the
just and the unjust : and falls, in greater or less amount,
with regularity year by year.   When it falls they say, "Leza
falls " ; although they have the common Bantu word for
rain—*imvula* (cf. Luba, *imvura* ; Suto, *pula*, etc.), yet they
always speak of the rain as Leza.   And the wind is Leza :
thunder is Leza, the lightning is Leza.   That is to say, those
elements themselves, not any personal being working in and
through them.   To generalise : Leza is the sky and what
comes from it.

Such is one's first impression of the Ila theology: but two facts must be remembered which correct that impression. The names are proper names. In form, Chaba, Lubumba, Chilenga, etc., appear to be neuter, but are personal really: the use of the pronouns *wa* and *mu*—" he " (or she) and " him " (or her) is conclusive of this. Some of the names—those beginning with *na*—are really feminine : *Namesi* would mean, literally, " The mother of Water." And, further, the people themselves recognise that the water falling to earth is not really Leza, but is water sent down by him. *Walosha menzhi*, they say sometimes, " Leza drops water." There is much confusion in the minds of many of them, and the way in which they speak sometimes might lead one to think the contrary, but we have never yet met with any one who on being pressed would confound the one with the other. It is very likely that the metonymical use of " Leza " for rain is a survival from a time when the two were actually identified. We can think of them revering the elements themselves, then rising to the thought of a power behind the elements, and finally coming to think of that power as a person.

There is certainly in these names a personification of the powers of nature. But it is clear that the Ba-ila have gone a step beyond that and attained to the idea of a personal god. There is, of course, a vital distinction between the two stages of development. To personify simply means that you recognise the thunder, for example, as He instead of It. You get then a special god, one whose activities are confined strictly to one sphere, that of thundering. If you pray to him, or make offerings to him, it is only to avert disaster from the thunderbolt : you would not ask his help in case of ordinary sickness, for that would be outside his sphere of operations. But a personal god exercises a wider influence ; if he begins as thunder, he comes to control the clouds, to feed his people, to watch over their interests, and so become the Father of men. That seems to be how the Ba-ila now regard Leza ; not simply as a sky god, but as their god ; though sufficient of the old views remains to make him in the minds of many little beyond a dispenser of the rains.

It is no mere sky god of whom the woman in the legend already related went in search, though his home was in the space above. And in the aetiological myths we have indications of a similar kind. In a later section we give the tale of how Leza in the beginning gave men grain (see p. 348). Here Leza is evidently more than the sun and rain which cause fruits and grain to ripen ; in his solicitude for the well-being of the people he has placed on earth, he shows personal feelings : he provides for them, is grieved at their foolishness, and takes steps to repair the damage they have done to themselves.

In the story of Chikambwe — the blue jay who married the daughter of Leza (see p. 347)—Leza is more than a sky god. The lightning is the opening of his mouth, his voice is the thunder, his sweeping descent is that of the tempest or thunderbolt. But he has some relationship to men ; he speaks in the imperative, he imposes a taboo, he punishes Chikambwe, holding him responsible for her death. He is very human in his affection for his daughter : human, too, in his desire to avenge her.

It must be added that the Ba-ila are far from being convinced of the benevolence of Leza. He is over all— *watuvhunikila*, they say, " covers us " as the sky above, but this is not altogether a comfort. He is mostly regarded as an all-powerful Fate, to whom they trace much of the evil and sorrow of life. A person who is bereft of his children is called *mulabile-Leza* (" one upon whom Leza has looked ").

We have been trying to reconstruct for ourselves the theology of the Ba-ila. We conclude that they have risen to the conception of a being closely related with the phenomena of the sky, who is also the maker of all things, and the guardian of men. Such cognition does not, of course, constitute religion, which is primarily a matter of emotion —an impulse to enter into mystical communion with the Being whose existence is felt in the world around them. What is the nature of that communion ?

We notice, first, the disparateness of Leza from the *mizhimo*. Everybody will admit that the *mizhimo* were once men ; but we have never once heard a suggestion that Leza was ever a man, nor is he ever named a *muzhimo*. He stands in a class by himself. It is true that legends assign to him a wife and family, but that does not imply his humanity. The *mizhimo* are near to men : they are of the same nature, know human life from the inside, realise the wants of men ; Leza, on the other hand, is remote and takes little or no cognisance of the affairs of individuals.

Hence there arises a difference in the cult. Many tribes, indeed, that acknowledge Leza do not pray to him ; he is otiose—too far removed from men to heed them. But the Ba-ila do seek to come into touch with him. They regard the *mizhimo* as intermediaries between themselves and Leza ; but on occasion they address him directly. They say (with no irreverence) "*matwi akwe malamfu*" ("his ears are long"), *i.e.* he can hear even words whispered in secret. But Leza has no *ikubi* as the great *mizhimo* have ; there is no individual who periodically summons the people to sacrifice to him. Generally speaking, it is only on occasions of special need, when the help of lesser beings is of no avail, that they seek him.

As might be expected, it is in time of drought that the help of Leza is much sought after. In the proceedings now to be described, it will be seen how dynamistic and religious conceptions may be combined. The prayers are a definitely religious act, but the rain-making process is as definitely dynamistic in character. They not only pray, but employ the mysterious powers in *misamo* to compel the rain to fall.

When there is a drought, the people repair first of all to the *musonzhi*—the diviner. After consulting his oracles, he informs them perhaps that a certain *muzhimo* is preventing the rain from falling and bids them go and make him an offering. Or he may announce that there is no obstacle on the part of any *mizhimo* : in that case they are at a loss. Then appears another functionary—the *mushinshimi*, the prophet or prophetess. With all the people kneeling in a circle around him, clapping their hands, he works himself up into an ecstasy. Presently he delivers his message, which may be of drought, famine, or only of delayed rains.

He orders them to build one or two prayer-huts, to pray and go through the rain-making ceremonies (*kupuka*). In probably every *chishi* there is a person or more who has the ability to *puka*. His services are now called into requisition. Taking a pot he puts into it some roots of the Mutimbavhula tree and some water. Then holding a small forked stick between the palms of his two hands he twirls it round in the liquid, producing froth (*iovhu*). Some of this froth he throws in all directions, the idea being that it will collect the clouds. Then another kind of medicine is burnt, and throws up a dense smoke which is supposed to have some connection with clouds. The ashes are put into a pot of water, so that the water becomes very black—another reference to black clouds. Then he once again twirls his stick (*lupusho*) in this mixture—to gather the clouds. As the wind brings up clouds, so will the movement of his *lupusho*. All the time this is going on the people are singing and invoking the praise-names of Leza. One refrain is :

Tuendele o muyoba, Leza, kowa !
" Come to us with a continued rain, O Leza, fall ! "

When the operation is completed, the medicine is poured on the ground, the pot is covered and left there by the little huts.

When rain first falls, they do not work for two or three days : nobody makes any attempt to hoe. This is an act of reverence towards Leza. They say : " *Mutayasi iyamba, mutayasi menzhi akwe, mushu akwe* " (" Do not wound (him) with a hoe, do not wound his water, his urine ").

Here is an account given to us by a native at Nanzela of prayer offered to Leza by a party of hunters :

" Again they pray also to Leza, Muninde (" The Guardian "). When they go into the forest hunting and stay there many days without success, they build a shed, and in the evening find out whether any of the company is able to divine. They inquire of him what divinity it is that keeps them from killing, and maybe he finds it is Leza himself. ' What are we to do now ? ' they ask, and he replies, ' Let us go out of the shed and sweep a clear space outside.'

They do this, and then with all their things assemble at that clear space. The eldest of them takes his place in the centre, with all the others sitting round, and begins to pray : ' O Mutalabala, Eternal One, if it be Thou that keepest us from killing animals, why is it ? We pray Thee, let us kill to-day before the sunset.' When the elder has finished his prayer, all fall to the ground and cry : ' O Chief, to-day let us kill.' Then they break up and go to the shed to rest awhile. In the afternoon late they separate and hunt. One kills an animal and at once calls his fellows, and they clap their hands. One cuts off bits of meat and makes an offering, throwing a piece in the air and saying : ' I thank Thee for the meat which Thou givest me. To-day Thou hast stood by me.' They clap their hands. Then they take the meat to the space cleared for Leza. The oldest man arises, cuts off bits of meat and makes an offering, saying : ' Chief, here is some of the meat Thou hast given us. We are very grateful.' Then he throws the morsels of meat into the air, and offers again between the horns of the beast. Then they *shuwelela*—utter the shrill greeting and divide the meat. They say : ' Who gave us the meat ? It was Leza who gave it to us, not a divinity.' "

There are cases of sickness when, after praying in vain to the divinities, direct access is sought to Leza. The head of the household fills a *lukoma* with meal and water, and pours some of it on the ground on the right side of the threshold and prays like this : " *Leza ndakukomba na ndiwe wasasha wezu mukwesu, muleke adiendele muzhik' ako. No nu wakamulenga anshi ano waamba akeende, akanshome, muleke mwanako, akakushoma. Mutalabala twakukomba, ndiwe mwami mukando.*" (" Leza, I pray Thee. If it be Thou who hast made our brother sick, leave him alone, that Thy slave may go about by himself. Was it not Thou who createdst him on the earth and said he should walk and trust Thee ? Leave Thy child, that he may trust Thee, Eternal One ! We pray to Thee—Thou art the great Chief ! ").

He then fills his mouth with water and squirts some out as an offering.

We have mentioned, too, that access is sought to Leza when offspring is desired.

In the early morning, when a man smokes his pipe for the first time that day, he may blow some smoke into the air as an offering and say : "*Mwami, wambusha kabotu. Muntu owakunditaya, muzovu owa kuwula, chibosha nda-bweza chinyama*" ("Chief, Thou hast caused me to rise in health. A man who shall *ditaya* me, an elephant who shall be found dead—it is good that I should take such a great thing" *i.e.* "give me happy fortune to-day ! ").

When, in travelling, a Mwila arrives at a river, he some-times takes the opportunity of offering a sacrifice. Filling his mouth with water, he squirts some of it on the ground and says this, or something like it : "*Ndiwe unyenzha. Inzho koko nkwinja nkazhoke o cholwe chako uwe Leza. Koya bu nyembela kabotu, Shimatwangangu*" ("It is Thou who leadest me. Now may I return with Thy prosperity from the place where I am going, O Leza ! Go on shepherd-ing me well, my Master ! ").

We have seen that Leza is regarded as having founded many of the customs, and that certain laws or regulations are said to be *shifundo shaka Leza* ("God's prohibitions"). But too much must not be made of that. The relation between Leza and men is not to be described as ethical. He has no title of Judge. It is true that at times when they see a circle around the moon the Ba-ila will say : "To-day there is a *lubeta* above" (*Kudi lubeta kwizeulu*), using the word describing the meeting of the chiefs and people to try a case. But this is no more than a picturesque description to-day, whatever it may once have meant. That Leza should take cognisance of all the doings of men, and regard them with approval or disapproval, is an idea quite foreign to their minds. In all their invocations of Leza there is no confession of sin. Indeed we have never met with the idea of sin against Leza except in one instance. That is in connection with the *luloa* or blood-offering made on account of a murder. As we have seen already (p. 187), among the cattle paid as a fine, one or two are offered to the communal demigod. We once amused an old man

by asking whether in such a case Shimunenga would eat
the ox offered to him. " No," said he, " we eat the
ox.   Shimunenga takes the *chingvhule* (the shadow-soul)."
The offering is made to him as the head of the community,
for in killing one of his men a crime has been committed
against him.   But that is not all.   They have the idea that
Shimunenga is in some degree responsible to Leza for the
lives of the community, and should any one be slain he
(Shimunenga) is in fault to Leza.   Hence they say Shimunenga
takes the *chingvhule* of the ox and conveys it to Leza as a
propitiation.   The old man went through the action of
Shimunenga approaching Leza with the offering in his hand.

PART V

CHAPTER XXIV

*

MISCELLANEOUS NOTIONS

1. RECKONING TIME

THE Ila word *chindi* means " space, period," and *chidingo*,
a definite point of time. As the people have no clocks
and no calendars, one is prepared to find much vagueness
in their expressions.

The day-period of twenty-four hours is called *bushiku*,

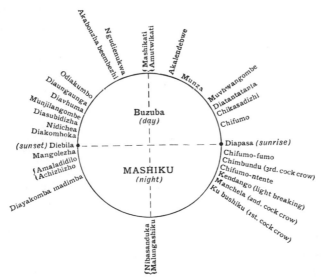

DIAGRAM OF TIME RECKONING.

a term which is also applied specifically to the time of
dawn. The *bushiku* is reckoned from one sunset to another.

One plural form of the word, *inshiku,* means " days," the other, *mashiku,* is " night." *Mashiku aza* (" this night ") is the night coming ; *mashiku adia* (" yonder night ") is the one passed. The period of daytime is called *buzuba* (from *izuba,* sun), or *munza,* a term applied specifically to the forenoon. The mode of dividing the *bushiku* may be seen from the diagram on the preceding page. Many of the names indicate what is done about that time. Thus, *muvhwang‘ombe* is when the cattle go out to graze ; *munjilang‘ombe,* when the cattle return in the afternoon ; *akabonzhabeembezhi* is the time in the early afternoon when the herdsmen begin to get weary ; *ama-ladidilo* is when the last meal is eaten (*kuladila*), and *achizhizho* the time for which food is prepared (*kuzhia,* to grind meal). Other names trace the course of the sun : *diapasa* (" sunrise ") ; *akalendebwe* (" when the sun rests on the fontanelle "), *amutwikati* (" when it is on the middle of the head "), *diakumbo* (" when the sun declines," *kukomboka*), *diaungaunga* (" when it gets a bit cool "), *diasubidizha* (" when the sky reddens "), *diavhuma* (" when the sun is diminishing "). When speaking of time, a Mwila points to the position of the sun in the sky ; thus he will say, " We will arrive when the sun is so high," and point.

There was no division of the month into weeks, but they are learning it from Europeans. Sunday is named by a corruption of the English word, *nsunda,* which is also applied to " week." For Saturday and Monday they have taken Tebele words learnt at the mines : *imbelekelo* (" the end of work "), and *mushimbuluko* (" the opening day ").

The year, *mwaka,* is a very indefinite period. In common speech *ku mwaka* means the spring, or the point when the old year merges into the new ; others speak of the *mwaka* as the six months from October to March, *i.e.* covering the sowing, weeding, and early harvest seasons. Yet they recognise the cycle of the year, and say *mwaka wazhinguka* (" the year has revolved, has come round "). The number of months in a year is not a thing they think about, and we have never met a man who could say off-hand how many there are. Even when you ask them to give you the succession of the months, some will give ten, some twelve,

and some thirteen names ; and no two of the lists we have
written down agree.

By months we mean, of course, moons (*miezhi*). The
Ba-ila reckon from the first appearance of the moon to its
disappearance, and the dark interval is *inshiku sha ntatano*
("the in-between days"). The new moon is *mwezhi
mucheche* ("the infant moon") ; and at the full it is
called *mwezhi uzhuka* ('the moon which comes out of the
ground"). *Chonancheche* ("when the children sleep") and
chonankando ("when the elders sleep") are terms applied
respectively to the full and waning moon.

Reckoning the year from about the time of the appearance of the Pleiades, there are three seasons : *Chidimo*,
("the cultivation-period"), *i.e.* spring ; *mainza* ("the rainy
season"), and *mweto* ("winter"). *Kunkosoko* is a name given
to the change of season, as from *chidimo* to *mainza*, *mainza* to
mweto, and *mweto* to *chidimo*. The following is a list of the
moons in as accurate a succession as we can determine :

CHIDIMO
- *Kavhumbi kashonto*—the time of new grass and leaves.
- *Ivhumbi ikando*—the time of full grass and leaves.
- *Shimwenje*—when the rains are fully developed.

MAINZA
- *Kukazhi*—the women's month, *i.e.* when they are busy weeding.
- *Kuyoba*—the time of continued rain.
- *Kulumi*—the men's month, when they hunt.
- *Itaano*—"pass here" literally ; *i.e.* come and get food : there is plenty.
- *Chisangule*—the time of change, *i.e.* the rains are lessening.
- *Chibuantimba*—the time of little rain.
- *Inkombolabulezhi*—the breaking of the Pleiades.

MWETO
- *Ikonaula masanga*—breaking of the long grass.
- *Kazhalakonze*—when the hartebeeste calves.
- *Kaabanino*—change in the season, beginning to get warm.
- *Kapukupuku*—the time of much wind.
- *Katente kashonto*—the time of the first veld fires.
- *Kasangabimbe*—when the *bimbe* bird appears.
- *Katu*—the shooting of the first leaves.

Several of the "moons" have more than one name.
But none of these names is constant. With us January
is always January, and June, June : but, as the Ba-ila name

the moons according as to what is done at the time, if the season is retarded, or hastened, the name varies accordingly.

2. IDEAS ABOUT THE WORLD

The creation of all things is, as we have seen, ascribed to Leza. The blue arch of heaven they call *Izeulu* ; some speak of it as a solid thing, others confess they do not know what it is. The earth they think of as flat, and somewhere on the far horizon is where earth and sky meet. Somewhere in the east, on that bordering line, they say, is the home of the Bashikampinukila—a race of dwarfs of whom their forefathers told them : men about two feet high, living in holes in the earth. When you visit them and inquire about your sleeping-place they point to crevices in the rocks, or say, " *vhungulula ibolo diako, uone mo* " (" loosen out your scrotum and sleep in its shade "). But nobody has seen them : their existence is only a tradition.

The sun is called *izuba*. It is to some extent personalised by the name *Chisowa* (" Mr. Disperser "), whose rising is the signal for men and women to go about their daily work. The sun, said Sir W. Scott, " is every wretched labourer's day lantern—it comes glaring yonder out of the east, to summon up a whole world to labour and to misery."

When the sun appears above the horizon a man expectorates on the ground as an offering, " *Tsu ! Wavhwa chisowa* " (" Mr. Disperser has emerged "). This is to avert ill-luck and give him good fortune during the day. They have the idea that the sun, after declining in the west, comes back to the east at dawn, leaping across from stump to stump on the earth. Nobody sees it ; indeed to see it would be *malweza*—and death. Eclipses of the sun are regarded with fear ; they speak of the sun as rotting away (*kubola*) ; as dying and rising again (*kubukuluka*).

The moon is *mwezhi*, and every month they think a new and different moon appears. When it is first descried, a person takes a piece of charcoal (*kashimbi*) in his hand, waves it round his head, and throws it towards the west. This is *kudikusha malweza*, to remove ill-luck from himself. In its early days the moon is *tonda*: the ill-luck attached to it has not yet been thrown away. When six days have passed, and it has reached its first quarter, the ill-luck has gone, and the people dance in joy. A tale tells how Sulwe, the hare, got up into the moon; he is still to be seen there.

Remarkably little attention is paid to the stars (*intongwezhi*). When one thinks of the magnificently brilliant nights and their habits of sitting around the evening camp-fires, one wonders that they should not have figured out constellations and formed myths of the stars. We have many times drawn their attention to the stars and tried to get their names, but without success. It is not reckoned taboo to attempt to count the stars, but any one who should try it would be laughed at as a fool. The only planet they name is Venus; but, not knowing that she appears as the evening and as the morning star, they give her two names. Because Venus is often seen very near the moon in the evening she is named *Mukamwezhi* (" the moon's wife "); or she is named *Inangabadya* (" seen of the eaters "). As the morning star Venus is *Intanda*, and plays a considerable part in their life, for her rising is *bwacha* (" the dawn "), and is the signal for travellers and hunters to rise and go about their business.

The Milky Way is named *Mulalabungu*, from some fancied resemblance to the hair on a person's chest.

The only constellation named is *Bulezhi* (the Pleiades, " the shewer "), so called because it indicates the beginning of the new year and the time to begin cultivating.

We have heard the stars spoken of as the eyes of Leza.

A falling star is named *itanda*; and they say of it, not that it falls, but *diakosoka* (" it is cut off "). When seen it is greeted with curses; a man spits violently on the ground in the direction it is falling: " *Thu!* " he says, " may the people in that direction come to an end ! " But this means little or nothing.

In May 1910 we saw Halley's Comet. The people made little comment upon it, and did not seem to take much notice. Four years afterwards we had some difficulty in recalling it to their memory. Perhaps there is some notion we have not discovered which forbade their noticing it, or remembering it; otherwise, it is certainly remarkable that the most glorious celestial phenomenon we have ever witnessed should have made so little impression. When we afterwards heard of King Edward's death and spoke of it to Mungaila, he at once connected it with the Comet.

The rainbow is named *buta bwa Leza* (" Leza's bow "). They have the curious idea that just below where the bow touches earth there is a very fierce goat-ram, which burns like fire. When the bow is very brilliant they take a pestle (*munsha*) and point it to the bow, without speaking, to drive it away; for they think it prevents rain from falling.

Their ideas of lightning and thunder have already been illustrated when speaking of Leza. Lightning (*lulabo*) is said to be the wide-opening (*kulaba*) of Leza's mouth; it is also spoken of as the quick, fierce glance of his eyes. Things struck by lightning are not specially regarded, except that a portion of a tree that has been struck is burnt and the ashes mingled with the ash from a tree named Mwande Leza (" struck by Leza "), mixed with fat, and forced down the throat of an ox or cow; this is to ensure the beast wasting away and dying if ever it is acquired by the owner's opponent in a lawsuit.

Thunder (*makadi*) seems to frighten them more than lightning. When it thunders you will hear a man shouting to the sky : " *Kowa budio, tulalanga menzhi ; twina kambo o muntu ; ukwete kambo o mwenzhina makani akwe mwini* " (" Please simply fall, we want water. We have not offended any one ; if any one has offended his friend it is his own affair, not ours "). This is to *disansulwila*, to defend himself against any possible evil results of the thunderstorm ; as he is innocent, he does not deserve to die. A person will also pray in the presence of thunder and say : " *Tubantu tulaamba, okuvhuya, uamba buti ; utababiki ku mozo, bape budio menzhi* " (" We people talk and complain and speak all sorts of things ; do not put them in your heart (*i.e.* do not cherish resentment against them), but simply give them water ").

The rain (*leza, imvula*) is thought to be sent by Leza ; some say, through small holes in the vault of heaven. The rain may be prevented from falling by those who have the proper medicine and released by others with more powerful stuff.

The hail is called *chivhulamabwe* ("abundance of stone") ; if it falls during the season, they take it as a sign of *cheyo* ("an abundant harvest") ; if the stones are very big, it is the maize that will be plentiful ; if small, the sorghum.

Water is *menzhi*, a plural term. It is reckoned taboo to drink water in the early morning unless one has first expectorated as an offering ; for you may have had the company of a ghost during the night, and it is right to offer him something, or he may be vengeful. When crossing a stream it is the custom to bathe and cook on the farther side, not on this side ; the idea being that somebody may be drowned, and it is better to get the crossing over first before refreshing yourselves. Streams are, as we have seen, often regarded as being occupied by ghosts in the form of monsters.

The wind is called *muwo* ; they do not know its nature, it is a mysterious thing, to be identified with the breath of a person, and the ghosts. They have names for winds. The cool wind of the rainy season is *katengezhi* ; the burning wind of October is *ikasazhu*. The whirlwind is named *kambizhi*, and also *shikwidikwikwi*. Some fancy it to be a cock with a long tail. When they see it coming towards them, one stretches out his left arm, and points with his little finger, moving it slowly round in the direction in which they wish it to go. Or they point with a pestle (*munsha*). If, notwithstanding this, it whirls the grass off a roof, the owner consults the diviner, for he concludes it to be no mere whirlwind but *katumwa* ("one sent" by an evil-wisher). If it assaults a person himself, he spits as a curse : "*Thu! Bulozhi bwako twakubona ; ndiwe nini*" ("We see your witchcraft. You are so-and-so"). This averts the evil.

Earthquakes are a very rare occurence in the Bwila. On May 28, 1910, there was a slight shock, lasting about

thirty seconds.   It was in the morning as we had finished
dressing ; we heard, or felt, it coming from the west and
wondered what it could be ;   then we felt the tremors
beneath our feet, and felt it passing east.   Two miles in
that direction are the Mala villages, and as the shock
reached them we could hear the shrieks from the people.
They called it *mududumo* (" the rumbling ").   Some ascribed
the shaking of the earth to Leza, others to the white men ;
all agreed it was a tremendous portent.   Old men told us
they had heard from their fathers of a very violent earthquake, when the ground opened and swallowed villages.
They gave us a fragment of an old song which celebrated
the event.   A dearth of ground-nuts the next year was
attributed to the earthquake.

The metals known to the Ba-ila were only two—iron
and copper.   Brass came later in the form of thick wire
introduced by traders.   Even now, when they have had
money for some years, they have no idea of the value
of gold and silver, and have formed no names for them.
They know that the mines produce gold for making
money, but do not appreciate its value when not coined ;
a gold ring being no more in their eyes than a brass one.

The Ba-ila have well-known names for the points of
the compass : *Kwiwe* is the east (" at the rising ") ; *kumbo*,
the west (" at the setting ") ; north is *kumbala* ; south is
kububizhi (" to the Butonga country ") or *kumpusu*.

But the Ba-ila are not a travelling people, and therefore
have very little knowledge of countries around them.   In
fact, many of them know little about their own country
outside their immediate neighbourhood, for until recent
years they mostly remained at home.   One does, however,
meet great travellers even here, such men as were taken
captive by the Makololo in their youth, and afterwards
accompanied their captors on their expeditions.   Old
Mukubu, for example, can tell of travelling with Livingstone, the discovery of the Victoria Falls, and the journey
to the west coast, of the raid to the upper Kafue by the
Makololo, etc.   Another old man told us of a year's journey,
during which he visited Kanyemba, the Chikundi chief in
Portugese territory south of the Zambesi.   Such men have

some idea of surrounding people, but even their knowledge is not extensive. In later years many adventurous spirits have gone to labour at the mines in Southern Rhodesia, and a few farther, to Katanga in the Congo Belge, and even to Kimberley. But they return with hazy notions of those countries. In Kimberley, *e.g.*, which they call Deemani, they think, some of them, that the white people dig for big white things like impande. We have told them of our country, but they cannot, of course, realise it. We have shown them pictures of houses taller than their highest trees—taller than three or four trees on end ; but all such wonders are received incredulously ; they only pity the narrator as a clumsy liar.

Kumbulawayo ("at Bulawayo") is the Ultima Thule of most Ba-ila, and they think all white people come from there. When European traders and hunters began to visit the Bwila, we were solemnly asked whether Bulawayo was being deserted.

They have ideas of the sea derived ultimately, it seems, from the early Mambari traders from the west coast. They suppose that all European merchandise is thrown up out of the "big water" by monsters—some think they are men who have been transformed by the magic of white men to work for them under the sea—and traders pick it off the shore and sell it. So easily procured and yet so hardly obtained by them in exchange for their precious cattle and grain ! They think we white people are very selfish.

3. Ideas about the Animals and Plants

When we turn to the Ba-ila knowledge of the animal kingdom, whose representatives are so numerous around them, we are struck equally by their shrewd observations and by their ignorance. They have accurately observed many habits of the animals, but there comes quickly a point at which they go wrong. Their notions are interesting, not because of their scientific importance, but largely because of their fantastic nature. Many of them have been already mentioned, others will be described in connection with the tales : a few of a miscellaneous character regarding insects and reptiles may be introduced here. This is their classification :

Banyama : quadrupeds.
Bapuka : creeping things, reptiles.
Tupuka : insects.
Bazune : birds.
Inswi : fish.

The *banyama* are divided roughly into hoofed animals : *obadi nfumba* ; and *bachele*, soft-footed animals with *shituta* (" noiseless feet "). But lions, leopards, and cheetahs are not included in the latter subclass.

Among the Annelida they name the leech (*musundu*). They speak of the leech getting into an elephant's trunk and thence into the brain, and so torturing the huge beast that it commits suicide in vain attempts to free itself of its tormentor. Because of its " sticking " quality the leech is made into " medicine " to prevent women rebelling and running away, and also to prevent riches from vanishing.

Among the Myriapoda, the *shongolwe* (" millipede ") is a very familiar object in the rainy season, winding about on the ground, much as one imagines a train would appear to a man from a balloon. The Ba-ila have a dread of the innocent creature, because, they say, long ago it entered the vulva of a woman and she died. They take it up on a stick and throw it and the stick away so that it may not return ; and if any one should bring a *shongolwe* to a house, the owner would give him things and salute him humbly by clapping hands and then throw it away. Hence the proverbial expression, used by a person repenting of a wrong action : *Sh'enda dinji kodia, ndapanga ko, ndasowa ko chongolwe* (" I won't go in that direction again ; I have deserted it ; I have thrown *shongolwe* there ").

Of the Arachnida, the scorpion is named *kapididi* or *kabanzi* ; the centipede, *ilumabanduwe*, also *shimukosola-mukongo* (" the cutter of the clitoris "). They dread the sting of these.

Spiders are of many kinds, but we only know two named by the Ba-ila. One is the *shilubidila*, which makes its circular white silky nest (*namundelele*) on the hut wall—

used to give resonance to the Budimba—and the other is the *shilutangatanga*, which weaves its web from tree to tree, from grass to grass. These are lucky things to the hunters, for if they find them on their gun they know they will be successful in killing.

They name two varieties of tick : the ordinary one which is found on dogs and cattle is called *malumabatolo* (" the biter of the lazy "), because only lazy people would refrain from picking it off themselves ; and the *insengele*, which, they say, if it keeps its grip on one's head, will cause baldness.

Itch (*bwele*) is a common disease, but they do not know it is caused by a minute insect.

The *inkofu* is a kind of bug which infests many houses and whose bite may make you feel very sick. They say that if you are bitten by *inkofu imishi*, a pregnant bug, you will swell up.

Of the Orthoptera, locusts have in past years done considerable damage to crops among the Ba-ila : we have not seen them in swarms during the last twelve years. The swarming kind is named *chikwikwi* or *chisozhi* ; the voetganger, *shinchuta*. Locusts are eaten, roasted, with salt, in an earthenware pot on the fire.

The Mantis is named *namutekamenzhi* (" drawer of water ") or *lulukwati*. Women drawing water are careful not to kill one, or their pots would break.

There are numerous stick-insects, whose appearance can with difficulty be distinguished from twigs and grass ; but the Ba-ila do not seem to pay attention to them.

Lice are named *injina*. They infest the houses.

Of the Neuroptera, the house-fly is called *inzhi* ; the hippo-fly *mazhimbwa*. There is a fly which inserts an egg under a person's skin, where it becomes a worm ; we have taken a dozen out of a European, and some out of ourselves ; but the Ba-ila do not seem to be aware that it is a fly that deposits the egg. They think the worms simply appear ; they say they are not troubled by them, and if any one gets them he is very unlucky and will die.

Mosquitoes are *mamwe*. There are several kinds : both culex and anopheles. Surely no country in the world can produce more mosquitoes than the Kafue valley during the greater part of the year. They are a great nuisance to the natives, who, though ignorant of the connection between the anopheles and malaria, try to protect themselves from them. They have an aromatic plant called Muvhumbane, which they say drives mosquitoes from their houses, but, judging by their complaints of sleepless nights, it is not very efficacious.

Fleas are called *imbwenjina*. They wrongly imagine it is an ordinary flea which burrows into the skin and produces the chigoes (*maundu*). Only recently introduced, the chigoe for a year or two was quite a scourge at Kasenga, but it seems to have disappeared again. If fireflies (*kamweshimweshi*) are caught in the evening and placed under one of the clay cones of the fireplace, next day there will be heavy rain.

Dragon-flies have the name *shimukundanchela*; they say that if one sits on an *inchela* (the earthen spout of the blacksmith's bellows), it dies.

Termites of two kinds infest the Bwila: one, a small kind, is *lumoma*; the other, a large variety, is *mulanzhi*. Some people eat, and find nice, the earth of which the termites make their tunnels. In the flying stage they are called *inswa*, and are eaten.

There are many kinds of ants. The *busulubi* is the vicious little beast that drives you out of your home and eats up every living thing in it, that kills fowls, and even, it is said, calves. *Shimwenzhalubilo* is a black biting-ant. *Manjenji* is a large kind that bites grass. *Bumbuswa* is a small ant that makes mounds; its larvae are eaten by guinea-fowls.

Of the Lepidoptera, butterflies are named *inkongolokwa*; moths, *mampempe*. They do not know that a butterfly develops from a caterpillar. There are many caterpillars: one is *shichisuntaboza*, a hairy kind found on trees, which causes intense irritation if you come in contact with it. *Inzala* is another kind.

Beetles are in great variety. There is the borer (*shika-busumpwe*) which drills holes in all one's woodwork. The *ing'ombemuka* is a kind that we have seen tied alive into a man's hair; some say it is with the object of killing lice, others that it makes *buyebuye*, scratching movements, which are very refreshing!

Kankontyontyo is the cicada, whose " voice " is heard in the early spring heralding the rains.

Chitolamatuzi (or *shafumbula*) is the scarab beetle, whose indefatigable energy in pushing balls of dung is the admiration of travellers.

Namudilakushobwa is a beetle found in the hard bark of trees: it has a rough back (*tuyabizhi*). A piece of the bark containing the beetle is stored in a calabash and the beetle is used, alive, to rub the gums of a teething child to facilitate the cutting of the teeth.

Of the Hymenoptera, the Ba-ila name two wasps— *mangvhu* and *malumansha*—which build their nests on palm bushes and trees, and whose sting is very painful: the latter is said to be capable of stinging a reedbuck to death. The mason-wasp, *namuzhingididi*, figures in folklore as the fire bringer (see p. 345).

There are two kinds of bees. *Inzuki* makes its nest in the hollows of trees, whence it is smoked out and robbed by the Ba-ila, guided by the honeybird. They divide the bees into *bachende* (" males ") which make a dark-coloured honey which they call *kansama*, and which is taboo to children; and the *inzhazhi* (" females ") which make the ordinary honey (*buchi*). That which the bees extract from flowers they call *buluba*, but do not know exactly what it is. The larvae, *mana*, are eaten; and are taboo only to those who have an aversion from them. The wax is used in mending calabashes, and is put on arrows and the cupping horn. It is also used in a kind of divination; if some one is suspected as a thief, a lump of wax is held over a flame, and as it melts and drops, he is named, and if the wax burns he is guilty, if not, not. The honeycomb, *mankanza*, is chewed.

The other bee—named *bwanshi*, or *shikangulwe*, makes its nest in a chamber under the ground. The honey (called by the same name as the bee) is said to be very nice indeed. It is not often one finds these nests: only those with good luck, or the necessary medicine, do so.

Of the Mollusca—the mussel (?) found in the rivers is called *lwidi* : sometimes, they say, a pearl is found in it. Snails are *inkolakola* ; their shells are used to pour medicine into the ear. Neither is eaten.

There are three frogs : the ordinary one, *kabombwe*, found in the pools ; *mazhibongo*, a huge kind, and *kangvhungvhwe*, turned up out of the ground in cultivation. This latter characteristic is celebrated in its praise-titles : *Shamanungo, Kanyama ok'ona mwivhu.* From the frog is made medicine administered to cattle, which will ensure their swelling up and bursting if taken from their owner ; and also medicine to render warriors invisible.

Tadpoles, *balube*, are said to metamorphose into barbel fish (*babondo*).

Crabs (*inkala*) are eaten.

Among Reptilia the Ba-ila name four kinds of lizards : *Intombela, bulube, shachikanka* and *sosolwe*, the last of which they say is *mukadi* (" fierce ") when in its *bwina* (" burrow "), and bites.

The chameleon, *nanundwe*, is dreaded : they fear its bite ; and they hate it as the cause of death being in the world (see p. 100).

Four kinds of tortoises are named : *Fulwe* and *inkaka* —water tortoises ; *kalalamina* and *shichanga*, land tortoises. *Fulwe* is a prominent figure in folk-tales.

Snakes (the generic name is *inzoka*) are much dreaded by the Ba-ila, who almost invariably describe every one as dangerous. They name many kinds. Of the puff-adder, *chipile*, the fat lazy snake that lies in one's way and whose bite is death, they say that if you tread on it it does not bite, but only if you step over it. In the latter case, the snake feels insulted : they imagine it to say : " I am regarded as an insignificant thing and despised," and to bite in revenge. Whereas if you tread on it, it feels flattered by your attention, and so merely hisses its gratification.

Of *chisambwe*, another poisonous kind, they say that a person bitten by it will surely defaecate and then die : whence the name.

The *ingongoki* is a rare snake : we have seen only the one shot at night by Captain Lynch. To see it is a good omen ;

others say it is a bad omen. It is a prettily marked snake, with its scales pricked out with white in the centre and turning to a greyish blue towards the edges. The ridge on the back is very peculiar—very hard and bony and marked by a series of white horny scales. The head of this specimen was shot away. It is said to be purely nocturnal in its habits, going to earth during the day.

The *shimakoma* is a cobra with the unpleasant habit of spitting at one's eyes.

The *shibudikila* is a short dark-coloured snake thought by the Ba-ila to have two heads. Its name is used as an idiom "to come suddenly." It is regarded as bad luck to see it.

Chidingadinga is a small snake with a blunt tail. Said to be *tonda*, to see it means ill-luck, not to oneself but to one's friends and relations. It is called the *mwenzhina* (" the fellow ") of *shibudikila*.

There are other snakes whose real existence is believed in by the Ba-ila, but which we prefer to call fabulous, because of their extravagant descriptions which we have never been able to verify.

Such is *ikonkola*—a huge snake two hundred yards long, which leaps over trees : in colour red and black mixed. Shapela, one of the chiefs, says he has seen it. A person would go carrying on his head a huge pot full of medicine ; the snake always aims at one's head from a tree, so it would strike the medicine and die.

Another such beast is *mulala*—which we call a dragon (see our note on p. 380). Riding across the veld one misty morning we asked our groom if he had ever seen one : promptly he replied : " Yes, I saw one yesterday when the horse was grazing just over there ! "

The Ba-ila name a great many trees, plants, and grasses. Trees have the generic name *masamo* ; bushes are *shivhuna* ; grass is *mani* ; leaves eaten as vegetables are *shishu*. Under each of these heads we could give a long list of names, but they would serve no useful purpose : we have already mentioned many of those that are eaten and used as medicines. Of trees we have seventy and of grasses twenty-four names ; and there are others we do not know.

4. THE BAKAMIPILWI

One curious thing that has been described to us by several elderly men is the Flying People, *bakamipilwi*. We were showing old Mungalo a picture of an aeroplane and trying to make him understand that we white people were so clever that we could now fly ! He was not so impressed as we expected him to be. " Oh ! " said he. " We saw them long ago." He went on to tell us how that, say, twenty-five years ago they came from the north-west and passed over Mala : he didn't know what they were, but they seemed to be men flying over the tops of the trees : whether they were men, or enormous birds or ghosts he couldn't say. We heard of them again from Chibaluma, who said he saw them flying between his place and the Nambala mountain, going south-east. He added that there were several companies of them and they were several days in passing over. Some Bambala say the trees were turned into people and passed away east.

5. IDEAS OF COLOUR

The colour-sense of the Ba-ila is undeveloped. There are but three special names : *kusubila*, is " to be red " ; *kutuba*, is " to be white," or rather, light-coloured ; and *kushia*, " to be black," or rather, to be dark-coloured. But it would be wrong to suppose from this that they can only distinguish those three. We have many times tested them with coloured wools and other things and found they had some ideas of the differences even when they could not name them. They give some colours the names of objects so coloured : *e.g.* a yellow thing is named from the butter-fly (*inkongoloko*) or cattle-urine (*ishudiang'ombe*) ; *ifumba-lushi* and *ishishi* are browns ; *shimufula-mwemvu*, a snake of that colour, gives its name to a green ; and *injanjabizhi*, a water plant, to another green. The names given to cattle, from their colours, are very interesting. Every variety has its special designation.

6. IDEAS OF NUMBER

The Ila system of counting is decimal. They have distinct names for the numbers up to ten : one is *mwi* ; two is *bidi* ; three is *tatwe* ; four is *ne* ; five is *sanwe* (these are adjectival roots and take the qualifying substantival prefixes) ; six is *chisambomwi* ; seven is *chiloba* ; eight is *lusele* ; nine is *ifuka* ; and ten is *ikumi*. Eleven is ten and one ; twelve is ten and two, etc., twenty is two-tens, etc., twenty-one is two tens and one, etc., a hundred is *mwanda* ; a thousand is *chulu* : the word is also applied to any great number. We have had workmen, ordinary unschooled young men, whom we could trust to count the number of poles in a waggon-load, say—361. Men can very quickly tell whether a beast is missing from a herd : tell it more quickly than we could ; but that is probably because, not of their facility in counting, but of their ability to recognise each beast by its colour and other characteristics.

CHAPTER XXV

*

NOBODY who has watched Ba-ila at play would ever again regard them as without energy. They may be addicted to lolling about in a very listless fashion, but the sound of a drum awakens their energy : and when engaged in the dance they may keep it up most of the night, or in case of a sham fight, a large part of the day with magnificent élan. Many of the dances are associated with serious occasions, but we are here concerned only with amusements. In these, all the people join : from early childhood to an advanced age they have their various recreations. The asking of riddles, and telling of tales, both favourite amusements, are dealt with in later chapters.

1. ADULT GAMES OF SKILL AND DEXTERITY

(*a*) *Chisolo*.—Foremost among these games is one that in different forms is found over a large part of Africa. It is what the Bathonga call *tshuba* ; the Banyanja *mchombwa*, or *msuo* ; and the Ba-ila *chisolo*. This is not a children's game, though we have seen lads engaged in it with adults as their opponents, evidently a case of teaching the young idea how to shoot.

This popular game is played by two men sitting on opposite sides of a " board," consisting of a series of shallow holes in the ground. The number of these varies ; we have watched games with as many as twenty holes on each side, but a more common number is fourteen. In any case they are arranged in four parallel lines, two to each player. Small stones, called *lubwe,* are used as " men " : and of them each player has an equal number.   The motive of the game is, by moving these stones in certain directions fixed by rule, to get them into positions relative to your opponent's and so sweep him off the board.   The skill lies in selecting

Photo E. W. Smith.

PLAYING *CHISOLO.*

your move so as to bring your men into the required position.

There are several varieties of the game : the following is a typical example of the kind named *natatu* (" the one of three "), so called because most holes contain three stones to start with.

Each player has 33 stones, which he proceeds to place in the holes nearest to him—this is called " planting " (*kushanga*)—three in each hole, except the last four on his right hand in the second row which have 2, 1, 0, 0. They are now ready to start. They may move only in one direction : in the line nearest the player from right to left, in the farther row from left to right. Thus in the plan here given A moves in the direction *n—h—g—a* ; and B, 7—1—14—8.[1] The opening move is called *kubingula*, subsequent moves *kuteka* ("to draw water"). The player selects the hole to move from ; takes out the stones and drops them one by one in the following holes. The secret is to plan a move so as to leave the last of these stones in an otherwise empty hole, immediately opposite the opponent's occupied hole. If he succeeds in this, he takes all directly opposite that hole : this is "to eat" (*kudya*) ; and he has also the right to remove all the stones in any other hole of his opponent : this is *kusuwa* ("to snatch"). In the plan the "eaten" holes are marked ● ; the "snatched" holes ⊕.

Another form of move is called *kusuntula* ("to lift up"). You drop the men in the holes as before, but having come to the end of those you hold you take out all the stones from the last hole you come to and drop them one by one in succeeding holes : you can continue this till your last stone drops into an empty hole. At times one sees a player going round the board, twice or even three times, dropping men in successive holes and taking them out. They do it so rapidly that it is difficult to see what they are doing. The following will illustrate this *suntula* move :

DIAGRAM OF *SUNTULA* MOVE.

The top row shows the holes before the move takes place ; and the lower, after he has moved. He takes 4 out of 1, drops one in each of 2, 3, 4, and 5 : he takes the three out of 5 and drops 1 in 6, 7, and 8. As 8 was empty he has to come to a stop ; but if there had been one or more in

---

[1] This applies to the first move : in the second move the player may, if he chooses, reverse the direction, but if he does he must keep to it through the rest of the game. A did so in the game here recorded.

that hole he could have gone on moving. The point where the move culminates is marked X on the diagram.

The following plan shows the actual moves in a game recorded by us on the spot.

    I. The holes arranged for playing.

    II. *B* moves first. He takes 3 out of 12 ; puts 1 in 11 ; 1 in 10 ; and 1 in 9. This brings him immediately opposite the holes *f* and *i*, each of which has three stones : he therefore " eats " these ; and " snatches " 3 out of *h*.

    III. *A* now follows and makes a corresponding move. He takes 3 out of *e* ; puts 1 in *d*, 1 in *c* ; and 1 in *b* : he eats 3 out of 13 and 3 out of 2 ; and snatches 3 out of 1.

    IV. *B* takes 3 out of 11 ; puts 1 in 10, 1 in 9, and 1 in 8 : he eats 3 out of *g* ; and snatches 3 out of *d*.

    V. *A* takes 2 out of *c* ; puts 1 in *d* and 1 in *e* : he eats 3 out of 10 and 3 out of 5 ; and snatches 2 out of 9.

    VI. *B* takes 3 out of 14 ; puts 1 in 13, 1 in 12,[1] and 1 in 11 : he eats 1 in *d* and 3 in *k* ; and snatches one out of *b*.

    VII. *A* takes 3 out of *m* ; puts 1 in *n* ; 1 in *a* ; and 1 in *b* : he eats 1 out of 13 ; and snatches 3 out of 3.

    VIII. *B* takes 3 out of 6 ; puts 1 in 5, 1 in 4, and 1 in 3 : he cannot eat because of his own 2 in 12 (and there are none in *c*), *i.e.* he is not immediately opposite *l*.

    IX. *A* takes 4 out of *n* ; puts 1 in *a* ; 1 in *b* ; 1 in *c* ; and 1 in *d* : he eats 1 out of 11, and 4 out of 4 ; and snatches 1 out of 12.

    X. *B* takes 3 out of 7 ; puts 1 in 6, 1 in 5, and 1 in 4 : he can't eat the 1 in *d*, because he is not immediately opposite.

    XI. *A* takes 2 out of *b* ; puts 1 in *c* and 1 in *d* ; he now *suntula's*, *i.e.* takes both out of *d* ; and puts 1 in *e*, and 1 in *f*.

    XII. *B* takes 2 out of 5 ; puts 1 in 4 and 1 in 3 ; he *suntula's*, *i.e.* takes out the 2 from 3, and puts 1 in 2 and 1 in 1.

    XIII. *A* takes 2 out of *e* ; puts 1 in *f* and 1 in *g* ; he eats 1 out of 8, and snatches 1 out of 6.

    XIV. *B* takes 2 out of 4 ; puts 1 in 3, 1 in 2 ; he *suntula's*, *i.e.* takes the 2 out of 2, and puts 1 in 1 and 1 in 14 : he eats 2 in *a*, and snatches 3 out of *l*.

    XV. *A* takes 2 out of *f* ; puts 1 in *g* and 1 in *h*.

    XVI. *B* takes 2 out of 1 ; puts 1 in 14 and 1 in 13.

    XVII. *A* takes 2 out of *c* ; puts 1 in *d* and 1 in *e*.

    XVIII. *B* takes 2 out of 14 ; puts 1 in 13 and 1 in 12.

    XIX. *A* takes 2 out of *g* ; puts 1 in *h* and 1 in *i*.

    XX. *B* takes 2 out of 13 ; puts 1 in 12 and 1 in 11 : he eats 1 out of *d*, and snatches 3 out of *j*.

    XXI. *A* takes 2 out of *h* : puts 1 in *i* and 1 in *j*.

---

[1] There is an error in the plan : hole No. 12 at this point should have an only stone (not two) ; the error is continued in VII. and VIII.

XXII. *B* takes 2 out of 12 : puts 1 in 11 and 1 in 10 : he eats 1
out of *e* and 1 out of *j* : and snatches 2 out of *i*.

XXIII. *A* has now no stones left : *B* has 1 in 3 ; 1 in 10 ; 2 in 11.
B therefore wins : *Wamwanga* ("he ties him up").

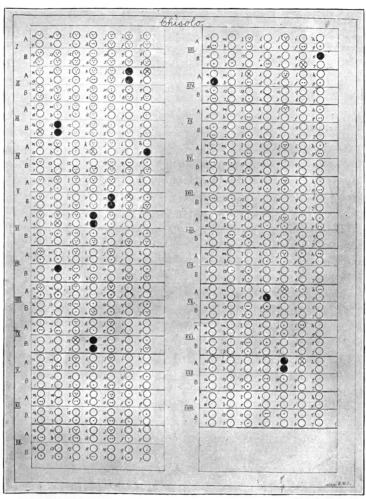

A PLAN OF A *CHISOLO* GAME.

This game was complete in twenty-one moves ; but
some, especially when the number of the holes is increased,
are much more complicated and lengthy. One we recorded

was not complete until the 117th move. The game is frequently lengthened by one or both players " passing in foreigners," as they say, *kuisha Balumbu.* When one is getting beaten he has this privilege of adding six or seven fresh stones to his depleted holes and continuing the game. His opponent may elect to do the same. But unless he does, the other may not enjoy the privilege in two successive games.

There are varieties of this game. One variety is played with only one stone in each hole. As there is no empty hole to act as the goal, the starter without moving one of his own stones makes a vacancy by eating two of his opponent's men opposite his own and snatches another. That empties three holes ; and his opponent does the same. As there are now vacant holes, the game can proceed as before. The players manœuvre about to get their men into " eating " positions and also to avoid being eaten themselves.

Another variety is named *namudilakunze* ("eating on the outside ") ; and is also played with one stone in each hole, but with the hole on the player's extreme left, on the outer row, empty. As the name implies, instead of eating stones on the inner row only those on the outer row can be eaten. This is the " eating " position :—

$$\left. \begin{array}{c} \odot \\ \bigcirc \end{array} \right\} \text{A}$$
$$\left. \begin{array}{c} \odot \\ \bigcirc \end{array} \right\} \text{B} \qquad \text{B eats A.}$$

Nambidi is played, as its name indicates, with two stones in each hole. The opening move is the same as when one stone is in each hole.

(b) A Hunting Game.—A favourite sport indulged in by adult men is an imitation lion hunt. This is not mere sport but serves a utilitarian purpose of practising the tactics actually pursued in the real thing.

One man (or two) takes the place of the lion, and dresses in character, with ruffs on his arms and legs and round his neck, and a most realistic tail attached to a belt and projecting behind. Some unfortunate herdsman has been attacked and now lies in the grip of the lion. The hunters,

befeathered and beruffed, with long wands as spears go out
to attack it.   They advance to the combat.   One more bold
than his fellows advances and throws his spear.   It hits
and with a growl the lion turns and bites savagely at it.
The others advance and menace the lion—distracting his
attention, so that they may seize an opportunity of rescuing
their comrade.   The beast charges and they retreat, but at

Photo C. Earee.

THE HUNTERS AND THE "LIONS."

last achieve their object.   The fun waxes fast and furious.
The growls and roars of the lion, the shouts of the hunters,
the beating of a number of drums and the singing and
cheering of the spectators, the women cheering on the
men—all make up an exciting scene.   It is intensified
when with a loud roar a second lion bounds into the
midst and the hunters execute a strategic retreat.   But it
ends, as all hunts should, in the defeat and slaughter of
the lions.

Photo G. H. Nicholls.

A SHAM LION HUNT: THE LION AND HIS VICTIM.
Scouts (in the distance) report the misadventure.

Photo G. H. Nicholls.

A SHAM LION HUNT: THE HUNTERS ARRIVE ON THE SCENE.

A Sham Lion Hunt: Attacking the Lion.

A Sham Lion Hunt: Rescuing the Lion's Victim.

A SHAM LION HUNT : SAVED !

A SHAM LION HUNT : THE HUNTERS ATTACKED BY TWO LIONS.

(c) *Spear Throwing.*—Practising with spears is one form of sport. They compete in throwing—to see who can throw farthest. In this many men are very expert. Shooting at a moving target is also practised. A large seed-pod of the Namuzungula tree is fastened to a long string and a man drags it at racing speed along a line of young men, making it bounce and jump. As it goes past they take aim. It is

A SPEAR-THROWING COMPETITION.

(The target, drawn by the running man, is hidden in the dust.)

no mean test, for to spear the darting object requires considerable skill.

2. CHILDREN'S GAMES

Here as elsewhere, the labour of adults is the play of children, that is to say, many games are simply an imitation of the serious pursuits of the elders. Boys very cleverly mould clay oxen and clay herdsmen—long *isusu, impande* and all. They build small kraals of sticks and spend happy hours putting the cattle in and out. Nowadays, figures of white men, mounted on horses and wearing monstrous hats, are introduced into the scene. Boys have fierce mimic battles, using long shafts of grass as spears. They charge and retreat and charge again and shout with glee when they succeed in transfixing the enemy. Generally speaking, such games are carried out with good temper, but sometimes a sham fight develops into a real one, when sticks are grasped instead of grass and broken heads result. We

Photo E. W. Smith.

BOYS PLAYING WITH CLAY OXEN.

remember one instance when a little boy of ten gravely brought a charge against another of the same age for hurting him in one of these sham fights, and claimed an ox as compensation.

Here are two tiny naked boys sitting with legs stretched out. They have a wild cucumber which they cover with sand. Each has a spear—a grass stem with a thorn tied on the end—and they take turns in stabbing the heap to see who can impale the cucumber. "*Ndawala! Ndawala!*" they say in their pretty baby Ila.

Boys are fond of dressing to imitate their elders ; if they have no bangles of ivory or brass they make them of grass, or mould clay on the arms to represent them.   A

Photo E. W. Smith.

VERY MUCH A MAN.

very favourite sport is to plait a grass *isusu* and fix it on the head by a string passing over the forehead.   With this on his head and a play bow and arrows in his hand, or a small spear of wood, the boy is proud and thinks himself very much a man.

Girls play with dolls—carved out of wood and decked with beads, or simply made out of a mealie cob. They build tiny villages, with all the feminine appurtenances—the grinding stones, mortars, and all.

Another favourite sport among the boys is the imitation, and caricaturing, of the movements of animals and birds.

One of the best things of the kind we have seen was performed by a lad of about eleven, who mimicked the antics, real and supposed, of the Honey-Guide (*solwe* : called for the purposes of the game *mwana miyange*). He had on a scanty loin-cloth, into the tail-piece of which he put a few handfuls of sand and tied it in a knot. Giving this a twist and working his loins, he kept the cloth whirling round in a circle, in imitation of *solwe's* tail. He drew in his stomach and pushed out his chest, drew in his cheeks and pushed out his lips to imitate a beak, and then began his antics by dancing about on his toes. There is a post near, and towards this *solwe* advances mincingly—hoping to find honey, but fearing the stings of the bees. He pecks at the tree, to hop away with a cry and painful grimaces : presently he returns with bits of grass with which he proceeds to make a mock fire to smoke out the bees. Then he brings a dish and scrapes at the tree, while a friendly bystander drops a clod into the dish, and off he skips delightedly. All the time a man sits strumming a *kankobele* and the spectators sitting around laugh and cheer. It is a most amusing sight, and not the least amusing part is the severe gravity with which the youngster goes through his performance. He keeps it up to the point almost of exhaustion. Presently, with giving his tail a too vigorous shake round, the cloth drops off, leaving him exposed and shamefaced, to the merriment of the onlookers.

We have seen other antics of a similar kind. One was in imitation of the *Katongotongo* bird (the Jacana ; called also *inandananda*). A chorus is formed of a line of boys, who clap their hands and sing ; while the performer dances in front imitating the movements of the bird. One sings a solo : *Katongo Katongo ntumina mudilo* (" K., send me fire ! "), and the others chant in chorus—*Tewe ! Tewe !*

In their set games the motive is largely the same—an imitation of birds, animals, and objects.

The game *kabombwe* ("Frog") is played by boys who squat on the ground, with their arms passed under their knees. They hop about after the manner of frogs and sing : "*Chibombwe chakundelela mwana*" ("The great frog was nursing a child for me"), or this : "*Bombwe ati ku Fulwe, tuye tudye boa*" ("Frog said to Tortoise, let us go and eat mushrooms").

Photo E. W. Smith.

THE GAME *KU LUMAMBA LWA MAINZA.*

The game *chikwekwe* is supposed to be a representation of the *lwando*—the long mat of reeds stretched across a small river as a drag-net for fish. Boys and girls make a long line, holding hands, and then the leader starts off in a circular movement, all the rest following, and each dragging the other. The game is to see how long they can keep it up without any one loosing hold. As they go they sing : "*Chikwekwe chilambuzha mudimo*" ("Chikwekwe is asking me about the work").

Another game is supposed to be an imitation of a battle fought in marshy ground, where the warriors in charging sink deeply into the mire at every step. The boys form up in two lines, kneeling on one knee, and advance, changing from one knee to the other, and clapping their hands. They sing :

Ku lumamba lwa mainza !—" To the war of the rainy season."

In the game *chitendebele* the motive is to represent a *lukwi*—the flat basket with sloping sides used in winnowing. The boys stand in a ring holding each other by the wrists. They dance round, and, as they go, throw themselves back as far as they can. They run round, sloping their bodies until it seems they must fall backwards. They keep it up till one, to save himself from falling, jumps back to regain the perpendicular. One boy sings and the rest join in chorus :

    Solo : *Chitendebele*—" The backward sloping thing ! "
    Chorus : *Kamuchileka*—" Leave it alone ! "
    Solo : *Chitendebele*.
    Chorus: *Chitumbwa, kamuchileka*—" Leave the old basket alone."

Another game, *lutambo lwa ng'ombe*, is, as its name suggests, a representation of a calf, tied by the leg and trying to break free. Boys stand in a ring holding each other by the wrists. One boy is inside, and as they stand still he rushes, throws himself on their joined hands and endeavours to break through. Should he succeed, the boy who looses his hold takes his place in the ring. The boy within sings : " *Lutambo lwa ng'ombe* " (" The reim of the ox ! "), and the others answer : " *Talukosoka* " (" It won't break ").

Intululu represents an animal going into its burrow (*bwina*). The boys stand in file with their legs stretched apart. The hindmost boy creeps through between their legs and takes his place in the front, while the next follows. The boy sings :

Intululu yenjila—" The intululu is entering."

And the rest answer :

Yenjila ku mudiango—" It enters by the door."

This game, under the name of *chombombo*, is played by

others to represent foreigners stealthily creeping into a
village.   The boys, standing, sing :

> *Chombombo, akaka, balumbu benjila.*
> " *Chombombo !*   Dear, oh dear, the foreigners are entering."

Kulea miumba is a game in which the players are supposed to be fish dodging the fish-spears aimed at them.
They stand about with their arms stretched up over their

Photo E. W. Smith.

PLAYING *INTULULU* OR *CHOMBOMBO*.

heads.   One dances round his fellow, and he round another,
until they all are dancing round each other.   Of course
they sing.

> Solo : *Kulea miumba*—" To escape the spears ! "
> Chorus : *Midimo nji yatuleta*—" That's the work that brings us ! "
> Solo : *Kulea miumba*—" To escape the spears ! "
> Chorus : *Kwesu ku Butwa*—" There at our home in the Batwa
> country."
> *Midimo yatuleta*—" That's the work which brings us ! "

In another game the boys represent a reedbuck wounded
by the hunter.   They stand in line with their legs apart,

and come jumping in halting fashion as if their legs were
broken. They sing :

Solo : *Banakasha mba lubilo*—" The reedbuck are swift."
Chorus : *Ati mfuse chini chakonoka*—" When I said I would
shoot, the leg broke ! "

Another game is in some imaginary fashion a caricature
of birds, the secretary bird and the *ingoane*. Two boys
kneel on the ground, facing each other, with a pole over

Photo E. W. Smith.

BOYS PLAYING THE *BANANSAKWE* AND *INGOANE* GAME.

their shoulders. They clap on the ground with their hands,
and, as they do so, have each to dodge his head underneath
one side of the pole to the other. They keep it up until
one of them, in moving his head, knocks the pole off his
shoulders.

They sing :

Banansakwe tabapumbani
Ingoane nshi shipumbana.
" The secretary bird doesn't move his head from side to side,
the *ingoane* are they who move their heads."

In another game boys form up in two lines to represent
flocks of two carrion-eating birds — *bashikube* and *mwa-
ngvhwa*. The idea is that these two birds always avoid each

other when they come to feed on a carcase. The boys kneel
in lines facing each other, with a boy in between them to
represent a carcase. They advance on their knees and retreat in alternation : as one approaches the carcase the
others retire. They sing :

> Bashikube tabadiatana o mwangvhwa.
> " The vultures do not stand together with the *mwangvhwa*."
> Badiatana balweza !
> " It would be horrible for them to stand together."

Another game is representative of animals at play. Two
bands of boys are drawn up facing each other, with their arms
around their neighbour's neck. One company advances,
singing :

> Solo : *Mwanamukopwe yaya.*
>   " Our brother Mwanamukopwe."
> Chorus : *Woona, shamukola imbwila.*
>   " He is asleep—the ground beans have intoxicated him."

The other line now advances, singing :

> Solo : *Nu banyama kubingwa.*
>   " You animals to be driven."
> Chorus : *Nu banyati nkwaya ku mulonga.*
>   " You buffaloes, that is where he goes to the river."

The two lines pass by each other, wheel round and return.
Then they dance up to each other and charge with wild
yells : " U ! U ! U ! Ah ! Ah ! " Once again they form
in two lines, with arms round each others' necks, and advance
and retreat, singing :

> Ku manyama, kubinga ku manyati.
> " To the many animals, to drive to the buffaloes."

Ing'ombe ingofu (" the blind cow ") is like our blind-
man's buff. The " cow " is not blindfolded, but simply
closes his eyes. He has a reed in his hand with which to
touch any of the boys springing about round him. He
sings : " *Ing'ombe ingofu* " (" A blind cow ! ") The others
answer : " *Teboni* " (" It can't see ! ") The first one touched
has to take the " cow's " place.

The game *kabia* is supposed to be a representation of a
small earthenware pot. Boys stand in a close ring, holding

each the other by the little finger of one hand and grasping
the thumb of that hand with his other thumb, all knuckles
up.   Their hands, lifted above their heads, make a circle ;
they raise and depress it, to show the form of a pot.

The leader sings :

> *Kabia*—" A little pot ! "
> Chorus : *Kabwengo*—" A relish ! "

In the *shikamimbia a Mala* game (" The swallow at
Mala ") the representation is of a swallow.   The boys stand
in a circle, with their arms crossed so that each grasps his
neighbour's knee.   They dance round : leave hold of the
knees to clap their hands and regrasp them : singing all
the time :

> *Ibia diakamutola Shimunenga a Mala.*
> *Okoko disanduluke, isamo diabola,*
> *Okoko disanduluke.*
> " The big pot took him, Shimunenga, at Mala !
> And there change over again, the tree is rotten.
> And there change over again !"

As they pronounce the word for " change," they alter their
grasp.

Mambwanyanga is supposed to represent the long stems
of the pumpkin and melon plants.   The boys stand in a
long line, grasping each other by the wrist.   The leader
sings :

> *Mambwanyanga !*

Others in chorus :

> *Shibalabala shiboni matanga.*
> " I do not see the melons."

As the leader sings he goes through under the arms of the
next pair, then through the next, dragging the others after
him.   It is like a long chain, threading one end through
the links.   When all have passed through they reverse and
go back, singing :

> *Lushi ! Lushi ! twenda nu bana, tumuswanganye tumwikate.*
> " Round and round it goes, oh children, let us meet him and
> seize him."

Another game is supposed to be a representation of a
tortoise with its hard shell.   It is called *namakaka a fulwe.*

One boy kneels, all fours, on the ground.   Two boys lie at
right angles to him, one on each side, and put their legs
over his back : each then grasps the other's feet and raises
himself slightly off the ground.   The boy in the middle
moves off with his burden ; as they go they sing :

> *Namakaka fulwe mbweenda.*
> " That is how hard-backed tortoise walks."

There is a game called *inyundo* (" the hammer ") which
is a representation of the blacksmith's work.   There are
two bands of boys, sitting on the ground.   One leaves his
company—walking on hands and heels, face upwards—and
goes across to the other and begs a hammer.   They answer :
"*Mukafula o bani?*" ("With whom will you do the smithery?")
The other company answer :   " We will do it with *machende.*"
He returns as with the hammer and starts knocking.   Another boy from the opposite company now comes with the
same request.   They ask what he wants to make, and his
company answer : " *Tulafula intongwezhi* " (" We shall forge
a star ! ")   They give it to him, saying :   " Here it is ! "
Then they begin to fight over the hammer.   A boy, going
along in the same position, charges the company opposite,
shooting out his foot and giving one of them a kick—if he
can—and quickly retreating.   They charge and recharge—
darting about with remarkable quickness in this strange
attitude.

In the game *banakabwenga*, stronger boys take the
juniors on their shoulders—their feet hanging over the front
and their heads hanging down behind.   They go about
singing.   There is some imaginary reference to hyenas carrying their young in this fashion.

In the game *shikoswe* (" rats "), boys squat on the
ground, with their hands through under their knees to give
the appearance of four legs.   They dance about.   The leader
sings :

> *Shikoswe ! Shikoswe !*—" Rats ! Rats ! "
> Chorus : *Nkwatile mbeba*—" Catch me a field-rat."
> Leader : *Mbeba waunka*—" The field-rat has cleared."

Then they dance back.   Another takes up the song as
before and they go dancing about.

There is a game played which is a kind of dramatic representation of thefts from a melon patch. One boy stands with his hands lifted above his head—he is a *lubange* bush growing in the garden ; kneeling on the ground around him are five or six other boys, with their faces hidden low down : one of them has his head between the " *lubange's* " knees. These are the melons, one of them being caught fast in the *lubange* bush. The owner comes round to examine his melons, and thumps each one as he says : " *Matanga*

BOYS PLAYING THE GAME " IN THE MELON-PATCH."

angu mudizudile ? " (" Are you all here, my melons ? "). They answer : " Yes, we are all here." He goes away : then comes the thief, who, stealthily and with much looking about, carries off one of the melons. By and by the owner comes again to count his melons and, tapping them, asks again : " Are you all here, my melons ? " They answer : " *Kamwandamwanda ng'uteo* " (" K. is absent ") This is repeated again and again, until the thief, having removed all the loose melons, tries to dislodge the one fixed in the *lubange* bush. While he is at it the owner comes upon him, and asks who has taken his melons. The thief answers that he doesn't know : he also has lost a lot. He persuades the owner ; they pluck off each a branch of *lubange* (by pulling down the boy's arms) and go off. Later, the owner discovers the thief in the very act of bearing off the last melon. The game is up and the thief is chased by all—owner, *lubange*, melons and all.

Other games can be classified only as play. There are numerous such games, and it would be impossible to give an adequate idea of them. The boys enter into them with immense zest. It would be as easy to describe them as it would be to describe young colts at play. Some of them might be regarded as trials of skill and dexterity : in others the only motive is to make as much noise and kick up as much dust as they can.

In the game *lutu* a boy sits on the ground holding a long string, to the other end of which is attached a bunch of grass. He whirls this round his head, at a distance of about two feet from the ground. As it whirls round, the boys rush in and jump over it, perhaps as many as three at once. One boy lies crouching near the whirler, and the jumper in the intervals between his jumps has to bend down and pinch him, and then jump over the string as it comes round to him. The boy who is pinched is called *kamwale* (" the maiden ").

In *katundulwa* the boys stand closely together in a ring, with their arms round each other's waist. One boy is in the centre and may have rather a rough time, for the idea is for the circle gradually to press in upon him, closer and closer, while he makes frantic efforts to escape between the legs. The boy inside sings : " *Katundulwa !* " The others answer : " *Uvhwile kwi ?* " (" Where will you escape ? ").

In *kanyanja* the boys form a ring, holding each other by the wrist and dance round. One boy crouches inside and hops about trying to escape. They sing :

> Solo : *Kanyanga kadila*—" Kanyanga cries."
> Chorus : *Kadila mwitanga*—" He cries in the enclosure."

Impila is a ball game, played with a ball made of resin or rubber. No sides are chosen, but each boy throws to a friend, while the others try to intercept it. As one throws

he claps his hands, and the boy preparing to catch it must
first clap his hands.

Another favourite sport is *kuuma bungo* (" to beat the
ball "). It is a kind of hockey, played by two parties with
sticks and a palm-nut as a ball.

In the *muneke* game they stand in a ring holding hands
and dance round, singing :

> *Tuleebela mbu aika muneke,*
> *Mulumi adye muneke.*
> " We will watch how she cooks *muneke,*
> That her husband may eat *muneke.*"

Still holding hands, two of the players bend to the
ground and the one between them has to step over the
hands, turn round and regain his position, all without
releasing his hold. Should he bungle this and, not being
sufficiently lithe, be forced to leave hold, then they deride
him by saying he is the cooker of *muneke* (" ill-cooked
food ").

Another ring game is called *nzenze*. One player squats
on the ground in the ring, and the others join hands and
sing :

> *O Nzenzele ukamukume Kanza.*
> " Oh, you Nzenzele, you may mention Kanza."

One of the players, still holding hands, springs forward
and must leap round the inside boy without touching
him, while the others do their best to pull him so that
he falls over the boy. The boy in the centre doesn't
have a very good time. He is relieved by the first who
touches him.

One game is unique among these youngsters' gambols.
In all except this they strive to outdo each other in noise :
in this, silence reigns. It is called *muvhumuko* (" the
silencer ! "). The boys stand in a ring with one inside.
Mum's the word : the first who speaks has to take his
place within. This is not by any means a popular game.
We have only seen it once.

Buwawa (" tickling ") is a game played by boys in the
evening. A number of them sit in line with their legs
stretched out, and one goes along the line, drawing his

hands along each boy's legs in turn. As he does so he
sings :

Tandabale—" Stretch out."

They reply in chorus :

Buwawa !

He goes round a second time, lifts up one leg of each
boy and plants it with knee flexed. As he does so he tickles
the boy's knee-cap. He goes round a third time and puts
up the other legs, and the boys all sit with their arms on
their knees. Then he sings :

Adikuluke ikumbi—" Let the cloud descend ! "
Adibwele ikumbi—" Let the cloud return ! "

As he sings the first line they shoot out their legs, and
return to the former position as he orders the " cloud "
to return. He goes round again, separating the knees and
knocking them on the ground. They sing in chorus :

Tupampe insanya o baina shabaluma.
" Let us shake out the bugs, they bite my mother."

He separates their feet and draws them together, saying as he
does so : " *Twabona mo !* " (" We see (the bugs) in here ! ").
He does this to each in turn : at the end he takes each boy
under the arms and lifts him up rigid, without the legs
bending. As he does so, he says : " *Bwasuntuka butala bwa
kanini* " (" the grain bin of So-and-so is raised "), naming
each boy's village in turn.

In *katantaile*, a number of boys stand in file, each
with his hands on the shoulders of the boy in front of him.
The hindmost boy runs back a short distance, charges
and jumps with all his force upon the back of the next
boy. As he does so he sings :

Katanta katantaile—" Let the jumper go on jumping up ! "

They answer :

Katanta kadinyelele—" I can bear the jumper."

The boy upon whom he springs carries him off to the
front, deposits him there and returns to take his turn at
jumping. The game goes on until all have jumped in turn.

BOYS PLAYING THE *KATANTAILE* GAME.

Kanzhinge is a game very similar to the Oranges and Lemons familiar to our own younger days. Two boys stand making an archway with their arms, while the others form in file and march round. As they go the boys standing sing :

> *Banangu bamanina mukasaka kazhinge.*
> " My children make a circling movement in the forest ! "

And the players answer :

> *Sansadi bombwe.*

They pass through the arch and the boy in the rear is cut off, and takes his place behind one of the two pillars. It goes on till one boy only is left. He makes strenuous efforts to break through without being trapped. He sings :

> *Kanga kazhinge kaladikumbakumba mu twembezhi.*
> " The little, little quail scratches about among the herd-boys."

The others answer :

> *Kaladikumba* —" It scratches about."

He circles round and round, with many a feint, and manages perhaps to break through. It goes on until he is caught.

Lembelembe is a kind of " Follow my leader," each boy having to do as the leader does. The boys sit down in a ring. The leader kneels on one knee, and sings : " *Ilembelembe musamo mukololo.*" They repeat it in chorus. Then he chants to one boy : " *Uwe, choka* " (" You, be broken ! "). The boy answers : " *Nchoke* " (" Let me be broken ") and kneels on one knee. When they have all done this, he begins again : " *Uwe, vheketa.*" The boy answers : " *Nvhekete,*" and sits on one hip-joint with the legs at the side. He goes the round and sings again : " *Ilembelembe musamo mukololo.*" He says to one, " *Uwe, ona* " (" You, sleep ! "). The boy says " *Ngone* " (" Let me sleep ") and lies down. He goes the round with this. Then he begins again. He makes a ring on the ground before the first boy and sings : " *Umwesu umwesu mudi ng'ombe !* " (" At our home there is a cow ! "). The boy imitates him. He goes to the next. " In my place there is an ox." The

boy follows him. He goes the round, varying his song—
" There is a grain bin," " There is a stamping block," etc.
At the end he jumps up suddenly and says: " *Ushadila
wamuluma luka* " (" A tsetse-fly will bite the last one ").
They jump up and rush off with gleeful shouts, not forgetting
to jeer the last one to rise.

There is a girls' game in which they squat on the ground,
one line facing another. One girl takes a bit of grass and
makes her way, without rising, in a series of short jumps,
to the other side, singing :

> *Kanyama ntole kwa tata.*
> " Let me take a little animal to my father."

The other side sings :

> *Leta ! Leta !*—" Bring, bring."

In another game, a boy sits on the ground with his
legs stretched out, while another lies on his stomach with
the other's body between his legs. The sitting boy then
gaily sings, while smacking the other on the buttocks :

> *Bombambomba, tusalumuke, kuya kutanguna kuzuma
> Tu sandumuke !*
> " Submit to me till we turn over. Go and be the first
>   to be tired.
> Let us turn over."

And the spectators keep on chanting : " *Bombambomba !* "
When he reaches the last word of the song there is a
sudden twist, and lo ! they have exchanged positions, so
that the boy who was at first sitting up is now lying on
his stomach and has in turn to be smacked. As the second
boy smacks he sings the same song.

Another game consists in a number of boys squatting
on their heels in a close circle and beating the ground with
the palms of their hands. The object seems to be to make
as much noise and dust as they can. All the time they
sing : " *Wansomba wansomba.*"

In the game *bwato* (" a canoe ") a pole about 3 feet
6 inches long and with a pointed end is planted in the
ground. A longer pole has a hole made in it, into which
is loosely fitted the upright. A boy sits on each end of

this longer pole, and by the help of long sticks they set
it revolving.   Faster and faster they go, in a way to make
the spectators dizzy.

Nyumbe is a swing   The one swinging sings :

Nyumbe !—" Let me swing."

Photo E. W. Smith.

THE GAME *BWATO*.

While the others answer :

Nzemwa kalando, ndamukula dino.
" He who gets in the way, I will knock out his tooth."

Shikonkobele is a hopping race.

There is a whistling race too.   One boy trots alongside
the competitor, who walks as fast as he can, whistling ;
the moment he stops whistling his companion halts and

marks the ground to show how far he has got; and the next tries to go one better.

3. LEGERDEMAIN AND PUZZLES

We have often heard of wonderful conjurers among these people, but have never succeeded in witnessing any

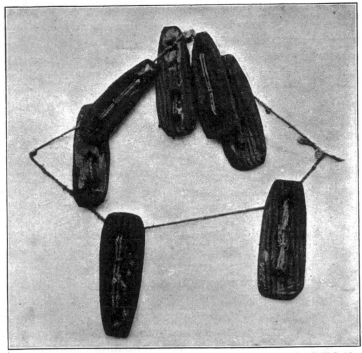

Photo E. W. Smith.

JEU DE PATIENCE.

of the tricks—they are called *mabibo*. For some reason they have been hidden from us. We are not sure even that we are correct in classing them here as amusements: they may have some mystical significance. We have heard of such things as these: handling and swallowing fire; gashing the tongue, and then putting medicine on it and showing it healed instantaneously; chopping the leg with an axe and healing it in an instant, so that no scar shows, by application of medicine ; sitting on a fire. We should like to have seen these, but can only mention their reported existence. Some say the tricks are only done by " drunken " men. It is said of such conjurers that they cannot be bewitched—they are impervious.

We have seen only one puzzle among these people. This was made of two small pieces of flat wood, each having three holes pierced in it. A piece of string is taken and the ends spliced : the string is doubled and passed through the holes, so that when complete the puzzle consists of the pieces of wood and a double cord joining them, some twelve inches apart. The puzzle is to unthread the sticks without breaking or unsplicing the string. A man will say to another who doesn't know the trick : " Untie this, and I'll give you a spear." The other accepts the challenge and promises a spear if he cannot do it. It is quite a clever puzzle, and it took us a long time to master it. It is complicated when four or five pieces of wood or more are used. Our illustration shows seven of them.

4. MUSICAL INSTRUMENTS

The Ba-ila have no great range of musical instruments, and none that has not been already described in books dealing with other African tribes.

The stringed instruments are very simple. The *katumbu* is a musical bow, with a calabash as a resonator. A second and rather more elaborate form is made up of a piece of wood shaped into a shallow bow, and having at one end a number of notches used for tightening the cord (see illustration).

The *mantimbwa*, used only by girls in the seclusion of the initiation huts, consists of two rough bows cut by the girls from a Munto or Muntembwe bush, and stringed with a twisted cord of palm-leaf. The girl sits with a pot between her knees (nowadays often a tin pan, as giving more resonance) ; the bows rest on this, one supported on each shoulder, and are kept in place by a stick passing over the bow under her knees. She twangs with both hands, holding the cord of one bow between her lips to vary the tone. She sits and plays this by the hour together (see p. 22).

Percussion instruments are of some variety.

The xylophone (*budimba*) is made of about ten wooden slats fastened lightly with cords, passing through holes in them, upon a framework. On the reverse side of the frame are fixed a number of elongate calabashes, of various sizes, each under one of the slats : these are the resonators. If a calabash of suitable size is not to be had, the maker neatly joins two smaller ones together. In the

Photo E. W. Smith.

TWO KINDS OF *KATUMBU*, MUSICAL BOW.

lower two-thirds each calabash has a small hole pierced in it, over which is fixed the thin tough web of the *shilubidila* spider. A large bow is fixed on to the instrument, to keep it at a distance from the player's body when playing it. The player stands upright, or squats on the ground, a cord round his neck supporting the instrument. He plays on the keys with two sticks—the heads of which are covered with string and a rubber substance. The tone is sweet, and a good player can produce very pleasant sounds from the instrument.

The *imbila* is a very simple form of the *budimba*, consisting of a single wooden slat, fixed on a frame above an

open calabash with narrow mouth.   It is struck with a
stick.   It is used by hunters in the veld and is also played

Photo E. W. Smith.

A MAN PLAYING THE *BUDIMBA.*

when, on their return, they make the thank-offering at the
lwanga.   It is said to have been introduced from the
Bambwela.

The *kankobele*, or native piano, consists of a keyboard with about twelve metal keys, superimposed on a small open calabash. The player holds it in his hands and strums with his fingers.

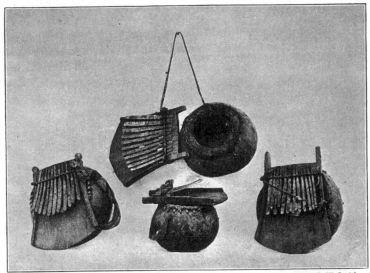

Photo E. W. Smith.

FOUR BA-ILA PIANOS.

There are several varieties of the drum proper—all called *ingoma*.

The *namalwa* is a friction drum—a hollow cylinder

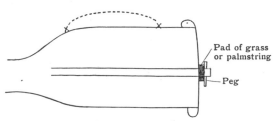

Pad of grass or palmstring

Peg

DIAGRAM OF THE PUSH-DRUM.

carved from a solid log. It is open at the base. The head is covered with a skin, like the *kayanda*, but has a hole in the centre through which passes the end of a reed, secured outside with a peg.

To play the *namalwa* a man takes some sodden grass in his hand and grasps with it the reed inside the drum, and then draws his hand backwards and forwards along the reed. He sits with the drum between his legs, the head outwards : and as he plays with his right hand, with his left he grasps the string to steady it. This drum produces a deep, booming note. It is used in giving announcement of war, or accident or disaster of any kind. Also, when

Photo E. W. Smith.

MAN PLAYING THE *NAMALWA*—"PUSH-DRUM."

cattle are to be crossed over a river, they send this drum ahead in a canoe and the cattle follow.

The *mwandu* is formed by placing an *inkidi* ("grain mortar") on the ground and covering the top with dressed leather. A woman dips one hand in water and draws it up and down a reed stood upright on the leather. This produces a deep, raucous note. It is used in connection with the girls' initiation ceremonies.

The *kayanda* is the ordinary drum or tom-tom. They vary considerably in size and the quality of their workmanship. A well-made, well-preserved drum is a handsome object. One is made from a solid block of a light, tough wood—usually Muntuntumba or Mulombe ; and is hollowed out, of course, by hand with spears and other rough tools. The shape is seen in the photo. The head of the drum is formed of skin, which is put on wet, with the hair side upwards, left to dry, and the hair then shaved off. The skin is fastened on by means of pegs. The drum is played

Photo E. W. Smith.

THE *KAYANDA* DRUM.

by one man with his hands. He stands it up between his feet, holding it between his knees. He hits with the lower part of the palm and first phalanges, sometimes with the tips of his fingers.

This drum plays a large part in the life of the Ba-ila. It has serious, as well as recreative, functions. It figures at all the dances : there is no more common sound in Bwila than its *dum-dum-dum-tum-tum-tum-tur-r-r-r*.

From the Barotsi has come a certain way of beating the drum called *kutambausha*, and Lewanika granted the right to Kaingu and Sezongo of having their drums so played—no other chief may do it ; the attempt by a sub-ordinate chief to usurp the right caused much trouble.

And on this drum signals are conveyed. Constantly when travelling we have heard the drum beating on our leaving a village, and on arrival at the next have found ourselves expected. It is awkward when the government official is thus heralded, and on arrival

Photo E. W. Smith.

THE *INGOMANTAMBWE* AND *INDANDALA*.

finds tax-defaulters absent. The drummer of the chief Sezongo once initiated us into the code of signals, but we found it impossible to record them. There were signals to call the people to the chief's village to discuss business ; to announce the arrival of visitors ; a special signal for the government official's approach ; and others to proclaim tidings—as of war, and disaster and triumph.

The *indandala* is a small drum or tambourine, 6½ inches in diameter and 4½ inches in height. The wooden rim is carved out of a solid block, the one end covered with skin. It is beaten with a short stick. It is used in hunting and war to carry signals.

The *ingomantambwe* or *iyavukuvuku* is a small push-drum. It consists of a hollow cylinder of wood, carved out of a single block, about $5\frac{1}{2}$ inches in diameter and 9 inches high. It is made on the same principle, and played in the same way, as the *namalwa*, except that, being small, it can be carried in the hand.

Wind instruments include the *impeta*—a horn of the reedbuck, pierced with a hole at or near the tip, used much by herdsmen when bringing home the cattle; and the *mwembo*, a larger kind of the same.

Rattling instruments include the *injua* or *insakalala* : a simple thing like a child's rattle. Nowadays it is made of a condensed milk tin containing a few mealies or pebbles, and a handle passing through it. This is much used by travellers on the march to make a diversion.

The rattles on the legs of dancers may be mentioned, and the bits of iron strung on the sporran. The *ingonji* are iron bells, made in pairs, and used by the Balumbu.

5. SINGING AND DANCING

Through ignorance of technique, we find ourselves at a loss when we come to describe the music and dancing of the Ba-ila. We can give, and have already given, the words of many of the songs, but to illustrate the music and to detail the steps of the dances are beyond us.

The Ba-ila are great lovers of song. Hardly any game mentioned in this chapter is complete without singing. They sing, when travelling, to keep up their spirits ; they sing at funerals and at all public celebrations. They are particularly fond of a chorus, and most of the songs consist of a line sung as a solo by one man, followed by several lines in which all the party joins. And a man feeling lonely will start up a song, very often in the middle of the night, all by himself : this is *kuyabila*. To sing ordinarily is *kuimba*, and a song is *lwimbo*. To dance is *kuzhana*.

There are a great number of names describing the various dances.

The dance plays an important part in the life of the people. On the whole, theirs is a monotonous existence, a rarely broken round of work and idleness. For many of them the day passes without any physical exertion. The heat is enervating during much of the year, and it is far more comfortable to loll about in the shade of the verandahs than to perspire in the hot sun. Ceremonial occasions, such as the initiation dances, the Makubi, and funerals, supply the necessary stimulus to energy ; and the fine moonlight nights give a welcome occasion for throwing off the lassitude attendant upon the hot days.

The dances are a revelation of the latent energy of the people. Often when irritated by the idle ways of one's workmen, one thinks of Triptolemus Yellowley and his complaints about the Zetlanders : " Give them a spade and they work as if it burnt their fingers ; but set them to dancing, and see when they will tire of funking and flinging." Many of the dances are merely a matter of *gaieté de cœur*. Those associated with the rites may have some mystic significance, though we cannot say what that is. The dances associated with the *Basala* certainly are not a mere recreation.

Many of the dances are patently mimetic. Occasionally one finds a man who dances a description of some event. A chief on the confines of the Bwila produced for our inspection a huge knife which he said was a precious heirloom, and derived originally from the Congo country, and in the evening he danced a most vividly realistic representation of a fight between two men, including the hacking off of the head of the defeated.

Many of the set dances are also mimetic. For example, that named *malasha* is nothing more than an imitation of the actions of a man suffering from venereal disease. Each dancer in turn goes through his painful way of limping about.

In some dances the women act alone, the only men taking part being the drummers. The women form up in line, standing close together and clapping their hands,

Photo M. A. Daffarn.

BA-ILA WOMEN DANCING.

shuffling their feet, and moving their bodies backwards and forwards. Then one springs forward and executes a *pas de seul* and returns to the line, her place being taken by another. Other dances are danced by both men and women. They stand in two lines—one of men and the other of women—and sing and clap hands. Then a person from each line advances and they meet and dance round each other without touching. Their place is then taken by others.

They are very quick in learning new songs and dances. You arrive at a village accompanied by a host of carriers and in the evening a dance takes place. The carriers join in, and then perhaps in an interval take charge of the proceedings by seizing the drums and starting a dance of their own. Tune and song and dance, maybe, are all totally strange to the villagers; you see them intently listening and watching, then they begin tentatively clapping their hands; they get into the swing of it, quickly catch the tune and words of the song, and in a very short time are singing and dancing with all their might, as if they had known it intimately all their life.

We have watched many of the dances without detecting any improprieties. The words of many of the songs are innocuous; often they are quite irrelevant or the merest nonsense. On the occasions, especially in the Mwandu and Chisungu, connected with the initiation of the girls, both dances and songs are grossly obscene. There may be some hidden significance in them—that there is such attached to the songs we have already seen—but the apparent motive is to excite the passions to the highest pitch.

The occasions when lewd songs are not only permitted but are regarded as essential to the ritual, are at sowing-time; at the *Lwando* fishing; when a new canoe is taken to the river to be launched; when smelting iron; at the Initiation; and at funerals and the Makubi. They are also employed in the Kashimbo dance. In these dances a man may not have as partner his sister, niece, aunts, nor any of his *bazhile*.

We will give here the words, with a translation, of some

more of the songs. It is not easy, even for one well acquainted with the language, to translate these songs They abound in words and phrases of not a bit more meaning than " Hi-tiddeley-hi-ti " or " Ta-ra-ra-boom-de-ay." And to a philologist it is especially interesting to find in the songs grammatical forms which are not in the ordinary speech, but which he can recognise in other Bantu languages. For instance, one finds in Ila songs the impera-

Photo Rev. J. W. Price.

THE BAND AT A DANCE.

tive suffix *-ni*, which is never otherwise used by them, but which is the ordinary form in Zulu and Xosa. And, again, one finds the possessive *-mi* suffixed to the noun *mwana*,—*mwanami* (" my child," " my dear child ") ; we have never heard it outside of the songs, and only know of its existence elsewhere in the Suto language.

1. Women's song at funerals and when sowing :

> *Tu bana Leza, Yeye. Tu bana Mwami, Yeye.*
> *Tu bana Leza, Kemba watubona ;*
> *Tu bana Leza, Muninde watubona ;*
> *Tu bana Mwami, Yeye, tu bana Leza, Yeye.*

" We are children of Leza, *Yeye.* We are the Lord's children, *Yeye* !
We are children of Leza, Kemba sees us,

We are children of Leza, the Watcher sees us.
We are the Lord's children, *Yeye* ; we are the children of Leza,
Yeye."

2. Men's song ; funeral song :

Mb'uunga musanza, Yeye !
Waunga musanza, utelele,
Mb'uunga musanza, Yeye !
Waunga musanza, utelele.

" This is how the forest shakes in the wind, *Yeye*,
The forest shakes in the wind, listen."
Etc. etc.

As they sing they raise their spears aloft and crash them
together.

3. Song for the Baami (prophets) when rain is scarce :

Chongo-chongo, nu baami, nu bana bakunzuma
Nkambileni milonga yaka Mwanza idi musa.

" Chongo-chongo, you prophets, you children of the thundering
east,[1]
Clap for me, for the rivers of Mwanza are only half-full."

4. Song sung by the Baami :

Bulongo akaka !   Bulongo mbwezha kwiwe,
Ya-ye-ya, ingala, mwadi,
Ya-ye-ya, ingala, mwadi,
Shimushimbula kolanga mwinangu,
Ya-ye-ya, ingala, mwadi.

" Bulongo oh !   Bulongo, take me back to the east.
Ya-ye-ya, an ornament to the head she is here.
Ya-ye-ya, an ornament to the head she is here.
Pucker-up of the brows, look at my wife,
Ya-ye-ya, an ornament to the head she is here."

5. A warrior's song, sung at the Mwandu and any time :

Ndawala, ndawala, kwiwe-e, kwiwe-eyè,
Ku buyasanino kwiwe,
Ndawala, ndawala, kwiwe-e, kwiwe-eyè.

" I threw a spear, threw a spear, in the east, in the east, away yonder,
On the battlefield of the east,
I threw a spear, threw a spear, in the east, in the east, away
yonder."

---

[1] The reference is to the thunderstorms gathering from the east.

BA-ILA WOMEN DANCING: A *PAS DE SEUL*.

6. A song sung of a man escaped from a lion :

> *Kubulwabulwa kavhuluma namaundu*
> *Wo ! Wo ! Yeye ! Wo ! Tadi munyama, mawe !*
> *Munyama udi mubumbe.*

" At the place of many islands, roared the dweller in the veld !
Wo ! Wo ! Yeye ! Wo ! He is not a wild beast, oh dear !
No, but one moulded in wild-beast form."

(*I.e.* Is one made by the art of a warlock.)

7. A song made by dancers on hearing a woman mourning for her child :

> *Kachila, maloama, mwezhezhe.*
> *Ambwene ndawezhezha twambo twaleta lundu,*
> *Twala oto ntu asama kakasowaila mulwenge,*
> *Kabakasakila bachiwena, mawe ! mwanangu.*

" Kachila, blood of my blood, let me think of you,
Perhaps, thinking of you, the whole world will know of my grief.
These little hair-ornaments let them be thrown into the river
That the crocodiles may wear them. Oh dear ! my child."

CHAPTER XXVI

*

THE ILA LANGUAGE

THE languages of Northern Rhodesia belong to the Bantu family. The following grouping is founded upon suggestions made by Father Torrend, S.J., in a letter to the writer, and upon Sir H. H. Johnston's article on Bantu languages in the *Encyclopædia Britannica*.

1. Ila, Lenje, Sala, Tonga, Totela, Subia.

2. Sodi, Bwini-Futwe.

3. Lamba, Rwano, Bulima, Lala, Maswaka, Tabwa, Twa, Bisa, Bemba. This is the most widely spread group.

4. Masasa or Mbwela.

5. Kaundi, closely allied to the Kanyoka of the Congo.

6. Lui, to which may be related Mbwe, Bukushu, Kwamashi.

7. Nyanja, Senga.

1. Phonetics

The writer is mainly responsible for the present orthography of Ila,[1] and he confesses that if he had to do the work again he would adopt the alphabet of the International Phonetic Association, of which he was ignorant at the time but which now seems to him to be the best system in all respects. The chief fault of the present system is the use of the compound symbols *sh*, etc., for what are really simple sounds. The following are the Ila consonants in the I.P.A. script, the ordinary letters, where they differ, being given in brackets.

[1] E. W. Smith, *Handbook of the Ila Language* (Oxford University Press, 1907), and other books.

TABLE OF ILA CONSONANTS

	Bilabial.		Alveolar.		Palatal.		Velar.	
	Breath.	Voice.	Breath.	Voice.	Breath.	Voice.	Breath.	Voice.
Plosive .	p	b	t	d	c (ch)	ɟ (j)	k	g
Nasal .		m		n	ɲ (ny)			ŋ (ng')
Lateral .				l			'	
Fricative	f	ʋ [1] (vh) v w	s ʃ (sh)	z ʒ (zh)	j (y)			

Glottal, breath, fricative : h.

[1] This sign ʋ is not used by the I.P.A.

We use these signs in this section, but in the other sections of this chapter, as in the rest of the book, we are content to spell Ila as it is now written.

The free breath (*spiritus lenis*), which we show by ', is not distinguished in Ila books but it must find a place here. If Ila were correctly written, a vowel would no more stand unsupported than it does in Hebrew and Arabic ; such words as *amba, ita* would be preceded by a sign like Aleph or Alif-hamza to mark the emission of the breath, the weak guttural effort made when one passes from silence to the pronunciation of a vowel. Although for practical purposes the ' is not necessary, a recognition of it is essential to an understanding of the phonetics and morphology of Ila.

The plosive sounds :

The breath in its passage from the throat to the lips may be completely blocked at various points. By the pressure of the back of the tongue upon the soft palate and sudden withdrawal two Ila sounds are formed, viz. *k* and *g*, as in *kama, guna*.

The tongue pressed against the palate farther forward and suddenly released produces the sound phonetically written *c* which is represented as *ch* in Ila books. It is

heard in such words as *chaba, chita, chinichini*. The sound
varies. Sometimes *ci* is heard more like *ki*, that is, the
point of articulation is drawn back nearer to the position of *k*. Sometimes the sound resembles more the *ch*
in English *church, i.e.* the composite sound *t∫* ; and
sometimes, when followed by *u*, it approximates to the
sound in *tune, i.e.* the breathed fricative sound written
phonetically *tç* (*tç:un*).

The voiced sound corresponding to *c* is ʓ written *j* in
Ila books and heard in such words as *njeko*.

The plosives written *t* and *d* are usually described as
dental, but as the Ba-ila have no top front teeth it is evident
that they can have no dental sounds. *T* and *d* are formed
by pressing the tongue upon the edge of the gum behind
where the front teeth should be.

The teeth can also have no part in forming *p* and *b˙* ;
they are both bilabial sounds.

The nasals :

By dropping the veil of the palate the intonated current
of *b, d,* and *g* is allowed entrance to the nose and exit there,
and so the three nasals are formed, *m, n,* ŋ. Further,
m as the labial nasal nasalises the labials and we get the
compounds *mp, mb, mf, mv, mw* ; *n* nasalises the alveolars
and palatals, hence *nt, nd, ns, n∫, nz, nʒ, nc* ; ŋ nasalises
the velars, hence ŋ*k,* ŋ*g.* ŋ*k* is the sound of *nk* in *ink* ;
ŋ*g* is the sound of *ng* in *finger* and is written simply *ng*
in Ila books (*tenga =* tɛŋ*ga*) ; while ŋ is the sound in *singer*
and is written *ngʻ* in the books. The ŋ plays an important
part in the morphology of Ila ; it is the resultant of *n +* ʼ
before *a, o,* and *u*, followed by a nasalised consonant. For
example :

> *ʼamba*, speak ; ŋ*ambe*, let me speak, for *nʼambe*.

While before *a, o,* and *u* with no nasalised consonant
following *n +* ʼ becomes ŋ*g*. For example :

> *ʼona*, sleep ; ŋ*gone*, let me sleep, for *nʼone*.

There is a fourth nasal in Ila, ɲ, the sound in Italian
campagna, a sound distinct from *nj* (*ny*) = *ni* in *onion*.
though closely resembling it. It is formed when *n* is

placed before roots beginning with '*i* and '*e* followed by a nasalised consonant. For example :

'*imba*, sing ; ɲ*imbe*, let me sing, for *n'imbe*.

There are really two *m*'s in Ila : a light nasal as in *map*, e.g. *mata*, and a heavy nasal as in *ember*, e.g. *imbuta*. The latter should properly be distinguished as *m̥*. Similarly there are two *n*'s, as in *ine* and *n̥dapa*.

The lateral *l* is sounded as in English. Nasalised it becomes *nd*, e.g. *lwila*, fight for ; *ndwila*, fight for me. When followed by *i* it is often heard as *d*.

The fricatives :

F and *v* are formed by the passage of the breath through the lips. Another bilabial fricative is the sound written *vh* in Ila books and here represented as *v̥*. The difference between *v* and *v̥* is often very difficult to detect and is not significant. The *v̥* is pronounced with lips more rounded and with a more distinct emission of the breath.

W and *j* are semi-vowels. The former is the sound in *watch* ; *j* that in *yet*. *W* is often inserted in Ila words to separate *a* from a preceding *u* or *o* ; thus *bo:a* may also be written *bo:wa*. *J* is often inserted to separate *i* or *e* from another vowel ; thus *i:i*, an egg, appears as *i:ji* (*iyi*) ; ɛ*:a* as ɛ*:ja* (*eya*), yes.

S and *z*, ʃ and ʒ, are formed by the passage of the breath between the tongue-tip and alveolus ; *s* and *z* are pronounced as in English *seal* and *zeal* ; ʃ is the sound of *sh* in *show*, and ʒ that of *z* in *azure*.

No two consonants can come together without an intervening vowel. This does not, of course, apply to the semi-vowels, *w* and *j*, and such nasal compounds as *mb* are treated as one consonant. All syllables are open and each word must end in a vowel. No consonant is doubled.

The Ila vowels are :

	Back.		Front.
Close . . .	u		i
	ʊ		
Half-close . .	o		e
Half-open . .		ɔ	ɛ
Open . . .		ɑ a	

U is the sound in Italian *uno* ; *o* that in Italian *come*. The ʊ is intermediate between *u* and *o*. ɔ is pronounced with the back of the tongue lowered from the *o* position and with the lip-opening further enlarged. It is the sound in Italian *notte*. The ɑ is similar to the *a* in *father*, perhaps more like the *a* in French *tasse*. The *a* is not the sound in *man*, which is written phonetically œ, but *a* in French *patte*. The ɛ is the open sound of *e* as distinguished from the closed sound ; it is heard in the Italian *cielo* (t͡ʃɛ:lo). The *e* is the sound in Italian *bene*, French *été* ; perhaps it has a tongue position a shade lower than cardinal *e*. The *i* is the sound of *i* in *machine*.

As an illustration, we give the Lord's Prayer in Ila, first in the usual orthography and then in the I.P.A. script.

1. Ushesu udi kwizeulu, nadiile izhina diako, nabuzize Buoneki bwako, naluchitwe luzando lwako anshi ano ubudi kwizeulu. Shidyo nshi tubula utupe bwasunu. Utulekelele milandu, bubona mbu tubalekelele kale obadi milandu kudi uswe. Utatuenzha mu kutepaulwa, utuvhune ku bubiabe.

2. U'ʃɛ:su udi kwiʒɛ:'ulu, 'na:dijile i'ʒi:na djakɔ, 'na:buzi:ze buo'nɛ:ki bwakɔ, 'na:luci:twe luʒandɔ lwakɔ, 'anʃi anʊ ubudi kwiʒɛ:'ulu. ʃi:djɔ nʃi tubulɑ utupɛ bwa'sunʊ. utu'leke'lɛle milɑndʊ, bubɔna mbu tuba'leke'lɛle 'kɑle ʊbadi milɑndʊ kudi 'u:swɛ. u'ta:tuĕnʒɑ mu kutɛpa:'ulwɑ, utuʋune ku bubi'ɑbe.

(: lengthens the preceding vowel ; ' indicates stress falling on the next syllable.)

The tone in Ila is often very important as distinguishing words of different meaning ; thus the difference between *chiwa*, drought, and *chiwa*, the outer appearance, depends entirely upon the pitch of voice. Ila sentences often begin on a high pitch and end on a low one. The stress, if any, usually falls on the penultimate, but in long words there is also a secondary stress on the stem-vowel ; compare the word *utu'leke'lɛ:le* given above, where the stem is *lek-*. Monosyllables are largely treated as enclitics and draw the stress forward to the final syllable ; for example : *amb'i:la*, speak to ; *uambila:'nʒi ?* Why do you speak ? The stress often marks difference of meaning ; for example, *'ɑze*, with him ; *ɑ'ze*, he also.

HISTORY OF THE SOUNDS

The phonetic laws of the Bantu languages are very obscure, more obscure perhaps than those of the Indo-European languages. Much light has been thrown upon them by the researches of Meinhof, Jacottet, and Homburger,[1] and we propose here to apply some of their conclusions to Ila.

According to Meinhof the original Bantu language possessed nine primitive consonants—three gutturals, three dentals, and three labials. They may be shown as follows :

	Voice—fricative (Sonants—continuous).	Breath—explosive (Surds—explosives).	Nasals.
Gutturals	γ	K	ŋ
Dentals	L	T	N
Labials	V	P	M

From these primitive consonants all the others have been derived, either (1) by nasalisation, or (2) by the influence of the vowels *i* and *u* upon the preceding consonant.

What Ila phonemes correspond to these of the ur-Bantu ? We shall find out by comparing words taken from various Bantu languages, selecting as typical the Nyanja, Bemba, Kongo, Xosa, and Suto, of all of which there are excellent dictionaries published. The last-named is said by Meinhof to be "the phonetically best-known Bantu language."

The primitive sound γ, a voiced guttural written *g'* by Mlle. Homburger, is alveolarised in Ila into *z* ; that is, the enunciation is formed not at the back of the mouth but at the front. The primitive *γaka*, to build, becomes *zaka*; *γada*, to spread, becomes *zala* ; *γanika*, to put out into the sun to dry, becomes *zanika*. In other languages the γ becomes *j* or ' ; thus in Nyanja we have *yaka* or *'aka* ; in Xosa *'aka*, in Suto *'aha*. In Ila we have also a number of roots beginning with ' which, when a nasal is placed before it,

[1] Meinhof, *Grundriss einer Lautlehre der Bantusprachen*, 1899; *Grundzüge einer vergleichenden Grammatik der Bantusprachen*, 1906. E. Jacottet, *Bantu Phonetics* (Supplement to Christian Express; Lovedale, S. Africa, 1907). L. Homburger, *Étude sur la phonétique historique du Bantou* (Paris, 1914). In this section the writer closely follows Jacottet, who was his first teacher in Bantu studies.

reverts to the original γ and is shown as *g*; for example, *'ala* becomes *iŋgala*; *'ulube* becomes *iŋgulube*; *'oma* becomes *iŋgoma*.

The original dental represented by Meinhof as *l* and by Mlle. Homburger as *d*, appears as *l* in Ila, as also in Nyanja, Bemba, Xosa, Suto, and Kongo; thus *lala*, lie down, has the same form in these and most Bantu languages.

The original fricative bilabial *v* is the plosive bilabial *b* in Ila, so *vala*, to count, becomes in Ila *bala*, which is the common Bantu form, except in languages such as Nyanja and Bemba, where it becomes the peculiar *w*, a sound between our *v* and *w*, formed by the teeth and lower lip.

K remains firm in the languages we are comparing, except in Suto, where it is *h*; so we have *kama*, to squeeze, to milk, in all the five = Suto, *hama*; *kala*, to sit, in Ila, Nyanja, and Kongo; *kanda*, to knead, in Ila, Nyanja, and Bemba. In Ila as in Xosa the *k* is followed by a slight aspirate (*k'*) when in the first syllable of the stem.

The ur-Bantu breathed dental has also persisted in these languages except Suto, where it is *r*; thus the word for "three" is *-tatwe* in Ila, and *-tatu* in Nyanja, Bemba, Xosa, and Kongo, and *-raro* in Suto; and "my father" is *tata* in Ila, *tate* in Nyanja, *tatu* in Bemba and Kongo.

The ur-Bantu breathed plosive labial is *p* in Ila, Nyanja, Bemba, and Xosa, and *f* in Suto; as *pa*, to give (Suto *fa*); *pala*, to scrape. In Kongo it becomes *v*: *vana*, give; *vala*, scrape; that is, the breathed phoneme becomes a voiced. In Ila the initial *p* of words often disappears; thus the common locative *pa* becomes *'a*. A curious feature of Ila is the presence of double forms, such as *'aŋgika* and *paŋgika*, which both represent the more archaic *paŋgeka*, to hang up.

These comparisons show that in all but one of these languages the original breathed phonemes have remained plosives; the voiced phonemes have mostly remained fricatives, with a tendency to become plosives, *e.g. v* becomes *b*. The other language, Suto, does not show the same steadiness, for the breathed phonemes become fricative, *i.e. p* becomes *f*. The voiced phonemes have remained voiced, and the breathed have remained breathed, except in the instance given from Kongo.

These, then, according to Meinhof, are the primitive Bantu consonants from which all the consonants in the modern dialects have been derived. The distinction between voiced and breathed phonemes in the table given above is of great importance, for the sounds derived from the one are quite distinct from those derived from the other. As Jacottet says, the distinction is " one of the most important phonetic features of Bantu speech."

The derived sounds are produced (1) by nasalisation, *i.e.* by the influence of a nasal upon the following consonant, and (2) by vocal influence, *i.e.* by the influence of the vowels *i* and *u* upon the preceding consonant.

The nasalisation of the primitive ur-Bantu phonemes probably gave the following results :

Voiced.	Breathed.
$ŋ + γ = ŋg$	$ŋ + k = ŋk$
$n + l = nd$	$n + t = nt$
$m + v = mb$	$m + p = mp$

The nasal is guttural before a guttural ; dental *n* before a dental ; labial *m* before a labial. The voiced fricatives *γ, l, v* become plosives ; the breathed plosives *k, t, p* remain plosives.

Except in Suto the results of nasalisation in these languages are the same as in ur-Bantu ; but the original *γ* having become *z* or ' in Ila, the *ŋg* appears as *nz*, as well as, sometimes, *ŋg*. These results are very different from what we get in Suto where $ŋ + γ = k$; $n + l = t$; $m + v = p$; $ŋ + k = kh$; $n + t = th$; $n + p = ph$; that is, the voiced fricatives have become breathed plosives, and the breathed plosives have become aspirated plosives, and the nasal usually disappears when the stem is not monosyllabic. Hence the Ila *iŋkani* is the same as the Suto *khaŋ*. In Ila and Xosa, instead of *ŋg* we often have *ɲ* ; *e.g. mu-ɲati*, or *iɲati*, a buffalo. In Xosa we may have *ɲ* corresponding to Ila *nz.* *iɲoka = inzoka*. The words in Suto are *nare*, buffalo ; *noha*, snake. The law governing this change is very obscure.

There are two principles which appear universal in the

Bantu languages : (1) that nasalisation never causes a consonant to change from one articulation class into another, that is, labials remain labials when nasalised, gutturals remain gutturals, dentals remain dentals ; (2) that the phonemes which were voiced fricatives become plosives after nasalisation. There is a third principle which applies in Ila and some other languages, namely, that the nasalised phonemes produced from the voiced fricatives are sharply distinguished from those produced from the breathed plosives. In some languages ŋ + γ and ŋ + k both produce ŋg ; n + l and n + t both produce nd ; and m + v and m + p both produce mb. .

In Ila nasalisation accompanies morphological change, that is, when the morphons in-, im-, n-, and m- are prefixed to roots. Im , in are used to form nouns and adjectives of classes 8, singular and plural, and 9, plural ; m and n represent the personal pronoun " me," or in the subjunctive mood of the verb, " I." Here are some examples :

From the root	'anda	iŋanda, a house	= in-'anda
	bona	imboni, pupil of eye	= im-boni
	pela	impezho, brush	= im-pezho
	limi	indimi, tongues	= in-limi

lemeka, honour ; wa-ndemeka, he honours me.

zaka, build ; nzake, let me build, that I may build.

When these morphons are placed before stems beginning with b and l which already contain a nasalised consonant, the b and l are changed into m and n respectively. It is as if the so-called " heavy " nasals m and n would not tolerate in the same word another heavy nasal. For example :

bamba, to arrange ; ba-mmambila, they arrange for me = bambambila
lumba, to praise ; ba-nnumba, they praise me   = banlumba.
From the root -banza : immanza, courtyards   = imbanza.

It is a matter of instinctive economy of effort.

Another use of nasalisation in Ila is worth mentioning here. It expresses often the grammatical copula ; for example, buzani is " meat," bobu buzani, this meat, bobu mbuzani, this is meat. In the case of nouns of the in- class the copula is formed with n-, e.g. iŋombe, a head of cattle, niŋombe, it is a beast.

The changes of *mu* into *um*, and of *n(i)* into *in* are of frequent occurrence in Ila; one hears *umbwa*, dog, for *mubwa* ; *ndombona* (= *ndaumbona*) for *nda-mu-bona* ; and *ulenta* (*u-la-inta*) you call me, for *u-la-nita*. *U* resembles *m* in its place of articulation, just as *i* resembles *n* ; and when, as happens, *m* and *n* are pronounced so like vowels as to cause the disappearance of the vowel following them, the prolongation of the sound becomes *um*, *in*. In some languages the change uniformly takes place in the noun prefix *mu*, which then appears as *um-* or *m-*. This prefix coming to stand immediately before the initial consonant of the stem produces what is termed " improper nasalisation," the effects of which are sometimes very different from those of " true " nasalisation, with which we have been dealing. In Ila the prefix before consonants other than *b* always preserves its form *mu-*, and so this " improper nasalisation " does not enter.

We have so far accounted for ten Ila phonemes, viz. *z*, *d*, *b*, *k*, *t*, *p*, ŋ, ɲ, *n*, and *m*. We have now to deal with the others, which are mostly fricatives. These can be shown to derive from the primitive sounds through the influence of vowels and semi-vowels.

Of the three primitive Bantu vowels, *a*, *i*, *u*, *a* does not, it seems, have any part to play in producing other sounds. *I* and *u* cause many changes, and still more when they become *y* and *w*. Meinhof recognised the presence of two " heavy " vowels which cause changes often very different from those caused by the ordinary *i* and *u*.

Meinhof also came to the conclusion that in the proto-Bantu there were sounds, not primitive in the same degree with those we have been considering, which were due to the palatisation, under the influence of the semi-vowel *j* (*y*), of the primitive guttural sounds *k* and γ, and probably also of the dentals *t* and *l*. We may write these mixed sounds γ', *l*', *k*', and *t*', two being voiced fricatives and two breathed plosives ; nasalised they become ŋg', *nd*', *nk*', *nt*'.

What Ila sounds correspond to these mixed phonemes ?

The γ' has become *iz*, that is, *z* modified by the vowel

sound *i.* For example, we have in Ila *izula*, to be full, *iza*, to come ; which correspond to *dzala* and *dza* in Nyanja, *isula* and *isa* in Bemba, *tlala* and *tla* in Suto, and *zala* and *za* in Xosa. Nasalised, the sound is *inz* in Ila, *e.g. ni-inzuzhe*, let me fill, *n-inze*, let me come.

The *k'* has become *ik* in Ila, corresponding to *ik* in Nyanja and Bemba and *hl* (*ḷ*) in Suto and Xosa, as shown in these words : *leka*, for *la-ika*, (Ila, Nyanja, Bemba) = *lahla* (Suto, Xosa), to reject ; *ikala* (Ila, etc.) = *hlala* (Suto, Xosa), to stay.

The *t'* becomes *s* in Ila ; thus *sanwe* (Ila), *sanu* (Nyanja, Bemba), five = *hlano*, *hlanu* (Suto, Xosa). In ur-Bantu, *t'anu.*

The *l'* in ur-Bantu is represented in Ila by *dy* ; *dya*, cat – *lya* (Bemba), *dia* (Nyanja), *ja* (Suto), *dla* (Xosa).

What we have just said, however, does not exhaust the matter, for sometimes the *l'* becomes *ts* in Suto, *sh* in Bemba, *j* in Nyanja, and *zh* (ʒ) in Ila, as is shown by the words for "road" : *tsela, in-shira, n-jira, in-zhila* = Xosa, *indhlela ;* and the *k'* appears, not as *hl* but as *ths* in Suto (*thseha*, to laugh), and not as *ik* but as *s* in Ila, Bemba, and Nyanja (*seka*, to laugh = Xosa, *hleka*). This is apparently due to the influence of the vowel *i* or *e*. And that there is still something to learn is shown by these other correspondences : Ila, *chaba* = Suto, *tshaba* = Xosa, *hlaba*, to rise (of the sun) ; ur-Bantu, *k'aba.*

The same Ila phoneme *ch* (*c*) has been produced by the influence on the primitive *k* of the vowel *i* ; *e.g. mu-chila*, a tail (Nyanja, *mchila*, Bemba, *umu-chira*) = Suto, *mo-sela* ; Xosa, *um-sila.* In Swahili the original *k* has been preserved, *m-kia.*

The semi-vocal *i* and *u*, *i.e. y* and *w*, cause certain changes which chiefly affect the gutturals and labials.

Thus the ur-Bantu *kya*, to dawn, is in Ila *cha* (so in Nyanja and Bemba) = Suto and Xosa, *sa*. The primitive *pya*, to burn, retains its form in Ila, Bemba, and Nyanja = *tsha* in Xosa and Suto.

The " heavy " vowels *î* and *û* are now only recognisable in a few languages like Suto ; in most of the others they have become exactly homophonous to the primitive *i* and *u*. They are probably the result of a blending of *i* (or *y*) and *u* (*w*) with *i*. It was the presence of these vowels in Suto that led Meinhof to the conclusion that many obscure phonetic changes in the modern Bantu languages were due to the presence in the ur-Bantu of such heavy vowels.

The primitive *γî* becomes *zhi* (ʒi) in Ila (*munzhi*, a village), *zi* in Xosa (*umzi*), *tse* in Suto (*motse*), *dzi* in Nyanja (*mudzi*), and *shi* in Bemba. So, again, Ila *menzhi*, water = Xosa *amanzi*, Suto *metsi*, Nyanja *madzi*, Bemba *amenshi*.

Lî is also represented in Ila by *zhi* (ʒi) (*imbuzhi*, a goat), *zi* in Xosa (*imbuzi*) *li* (= *di*) in Suto, (*poli*), *zi* or *dzi* in Nyanja (*mbuzi*), and *shi* in Bemba (*imbushi*). So again, Ila *izhiba*, a pool = Xosa *isiziba*, Suto *seliba* (= *sediba*), Nyanja *dziwe*, Bemba *icishiba*.

Vî is also represented by *zhi* (ʒi) in Ila (*zhimba*, hide, cover up), by *vi* in Xosa (*vimba*, shut up), by *bi* in Suto (*bipa*, hide), by *vi* in Nyanja (*vimba*, to thatch), and by *fi* in Bemba (*fimba*, thatch).

Kî has become *shi* (ʃi) in Ila (*bushi*, smoke, cf. *buka*, to rise), *si* in Xosa and Suto (*umsi*, *mosi*), *tsi* in Nyanja (*utsi*), and *shi* in Bemba (*ichushi*).

Tî again is *shi* in Ila and Xosa (*shiya*, to leave), *si* in Suto (*siea*), *shy* in Bemba (*shya*), and *si* in Nyanja (*sia*).

Pî also is *shi* in Ila (*ishishi*, dimness), *fi* in Suto (*lefifi*, darkness), *fi* in Xosa (*ubufifi*, dimness), *fi* in Nyanja (*chimfimfi*, secret) and *fi* in Bemba (*imfifi*, darkness).

Thus we see the remarkable fact that in Ila the primitive voiced fricatives with the heavy vowel *î* are all represented by ʒi (*zhi*), and the breathed plosives by ʃi (*shi*). The primitive sounds have been assibilated. Probably the removal of the front teeth has had much to do with this; certainly the first impression one has on hearing Ila spoken is that it is made up of *shi*'s and *zhi*'s.

When *î* becomes semi-vocal (*ŷ*) other changes are produced. They may be seen when the causative suffix *ya* (ur-Bantu, *ya*) is added to the verbs.

In Ila when *ya* is suffixed to verbs whose stems end in *l* the resultant is *zha* (ʒa), e.g. *katala*, to be tired, becomes *katazha*, to make tired. In Xosa it becomes *za* (*katala*, *kataza*), in Suto *tsa* (*khathala*, *khathatsa*); in Nyanja it is *tsa*, preceded, however, by a vocal element that is written *e* when the stem-vowel is *o*, and *i* when it is *a*, *e.g. ola*, to be rotten, *oletsa*, to make rotten ; *ala*, spread, *alitsa*, help, or cause to spread. In Ila the corresponding words are *bola*, *bozha* ; *zala*, *zazha*. In Bemba the *ŷa* becomes *shya*, *e.g. bola*, *boshya*.

The primitive *vŷ* is also *zh* (ʒ) in Ila ; *e.g.* from *samba*, to wash oneself, is formed *sanzha*, to wash (clothes). In Xosa it is *z* (*hlamba, hlanza*) ; in Suto *tsw* (*hlapa, hlatswa*) ; (*i*)*ts* in Nyanja (*samba, sambitsa*) ; and in Bemba *by* (*samba, sambya*).

The primitive *kŷ* becomes *sh* (ʃ) in Ila ; thus by adding *ya* to *buka*, to rise, we get *busha*, cause to rise. In Xosa it is *s* (*vuka, vusa*). In Suto it is also *s* (*tsoha, tsosa*) ; in Nyanja *ts* (*dzuka, dzutsa*), and in Bemba it is *shy* (*shibuka, shibushya*).

Tŷ is also *sh* in Ila ; thus we get *chisha*, cause to do, from *chita*, to do. In Nyanja this word appears as *chitsa* from *chita* ; and in Bemba *chishya* from *chita*. The stem does not seem to be found in Suto and Xosa, so we may take another example ; in Xosa we have *ambesa* formed from *ambata*, which words appear in Suto as *apesa*, from *apara*.

Pŷ in Ila does not as a rule change into *sh* but remains as in the ur-Bantu ; thus the causative of *papa*, to be shrunken, is *papya*. In Nyanja *pŷ* appears as (*i*)*tsa* (*papa, papitsa*) ; in Bemba also it is *pya* (*papa, papya*). There are, however, instances in Ila of *pŷ* becoming *sh*, *e.g. lansha*, to make sharp, from *lampa*, to be sharp.

We get much the same results in Ila from the influence of *ŷ* as we got from *ı̂* ; under their influence the primitive voiced fricatives all become the voiced fricative ʒ and the primitive breathed plosives become the breathed fricative ʃ.

$$\left. \begin{matrix} \gamma\hat{\imath},\ l\hat{\imath},\ v\hat{\imath} \\ l\hat{y},\ v\hat{y} \end{matrix} \right\} = \mathrm{ʒ} \qquad\qquad \left. \begin{matrix} k\hat{\imath},\ t\hat{\imath},\ p\hat{\imath} \\ k\hat{y},\ t\hat{y},\ p\hat{y} \end{matrix} \right\} = \mathrm{ʃ}.$$

It will be noticed that the changes produced under the influence of *ı̂* are different from those produced by *i* ; thus *ki = chi* ; *kı̂ = ʃi*.

We now come to changes wrought by *û* and *ŵ*.

The original Bantu *γû* has become *vu* in Ila (*e.g. muzovu*, an elephant), and the same in Nyanja (*njovu*) and Xosa (*indlovu*). It is *fu* in Bemba (*insofu*) and *u* in Suto (*tlou*).

The *lû* of ur-Bantu is *vu* in Ila, *vu* in Xosa, *lu* in Suto, *e.g.* Ila *vumina*, to agree = Xosa, *vumela*, consent = Suto, *lumela*.

Vû becomes *vu* in Ila (*imvula*, rain) and Xosa (*imvula*), *pu* in Suto (*pula*), *bvu* or *vu* in Nyanja (*mbvula* or *mvula*), and *fu* in Bemba (*infula*). Compare also Ila *vukuta*, work the bellows = Nyanja *bvukuta*, Bemba *fukuta*.

The ur-Bantu *kû* has become *fu* in all these five languages, *e.g.* Ila, Xosa, Nyanja, Bemba, *fumbata* = Suto *fupara*, to close the fist.

Tû is also *fu* in Ila and Xosa, *e.g. fua = fuya*, to possess ; in Suto it is *ru* (*rua*, possess). In Nyanja it is *pfu* and in Bemba *fu* ; Xosa *funda*, to learn = Suto *ruta*, to teach = Bemba *funda* = Nyanja *pfunitsa*.

Pû becomes *fu* in Ila, Suto and Xosa, *pu* in Nyanja and Bemba ; compare the root in the words " to blow " " to breathe " : Ila, *fula* ; Suto, *phefumuloha* ; Xosa, *pefumla* ; Nyanja, *puma* ; Bemba, *umupu*, breath.

We see then that the primitive voiced phonemes + *û* (*i.e. γû, lû, vû*) are all represented in Ila by the same, viz. *vu* or *vu*, and the primitive breath plosives + *û* (*kû, tû, pû*) by *fu*. The voiced phonemes are represented by a voiced phoneme, the breathed by a breathed.

When *û* becomes semi-vocal (*ŵ*) much the same changes are produced in Ila as those we have just described.

Thus the ur-Bantu *lŵ* becomes *v* in Ila (*vwa*, to go out) ; in Xosa it is *v* (*vela*), in Suto *tsw* (*tswa*), in Nyanja *low* (*lowa*).

Kŵ becomes *fw* in Ila (*fwa*, to die) and Bemba (*fwa*), *f* in Xosa (*fa*), *shw* in Suto (*shwa*).

With two exceptions we have now traced the origin of all the Ila consonants given in the table on p. 278. The exceptions are **J** and *h*. Neither of them is a common sound in Ila ; **J** is formed by the nasalisation of *y*, thus = *ya*, to go, *nJe*, that I go ; and also when *n* is affixed to verbal stems beginning with *i* which do not contain another nasal : *ita*, to pass, *nJite*, that I pass. The aspirate *h* is heard in some parts of the country, *e.g.* among the Balundwe, in place of ʃ; they say, for example, *hakahina* for *ʃakaʃina*. It is heard, too, instead of *ʋ*; *huluma* for *ʋuluma* (Bemba, *buluma*), to growl. Other words in which it occurs are foreign, *e.g. hola*, to earn.

2. WORD FORMATION

The rudimentary germs of the Ila language are monosonants, *i.e.* sounds capable of separate pronunciation, whether represented by a vowel, semi-vowel, or consonant. If now we take the consonants given in the table on p. 278, and fit each one with the five chief vowels, in the manner following

| pa | pe | pi | po | pu |

we shall have a list of 115 monosyllables. These can be modified by nasalising the initial consonant or by the insertion of the semi-vowels *w* and *y*—what is called "mouthing." Thus :

mpa	mpe	mpi	mpo	mpu
pwa	pwe	pwi	pwo	pwu
pya	pye	pyi	pyo	pyu
mpwa	mpwe	mpwi	mpwo	mpwu
mpya	mpye	mpyi	mpyo	mpyu

This gives a further list of potential monosyllables, making with the former 485 in all. Ila does not make use of all of these, but probably 400, and it is not too much to say that they are the materials out of which the vocabulary is made.

A large number of these syllables are used alone with more or less definite meanings ; there are, for example, such particles as *pe*, no. The first column contains many monosyllabic verbs, used as imperatives without any modification ; *e.g. pa*, give; *dya*, eat. These nasalised gain the added signification of the first person personal pronoun ; *mpa*, give me. The corresponding forms in the second column, ending in *e*, are jussive and subjunctive ; *mpe*, let me give, (that) I give. The same forms ending in *i* are negative and require an auxiliary particle, *t'a pi*, he

does not give. Others of these monosyllables are pronominal
suffixes : *nda, ndi, ndu,* I, *twa, tu,* we, etc. Others again are
tense formatives, *chi, ka, la,* etc. Others are nominal roots,
needing only a prefix to define them ; *e.g. -bwa, -twi,* from
which are formed *mu-hwa,* a dog, *ku-twi,* an ear. The
great majority of the monosyllables can come together in
pairs to make verbal base-words, *ma-na, mi-na, me-na,*
mu-na, etc., to which other monosyllables, as formatives,
may be added. So from these four hundred or so syllables,
by a process of agglutination, a vocabulary of at least
fifteen thousand words is formed.

In addition to the uses of the monosyllables just
mentioned there is another, which, as it is one of the most
remarkable features of Ila, it will be worth while to illustrate
further.

Many of these monosyllables are holophrastic. They
stand entirely alone, conveying a definite meaning, or, with
modification of stress and tone, a variety of meanings.
Or they may stand closely connected with verbs, whose
signification they serve to extend, define, or emphasise,
without the connection being at all necessary to their own
being. They are somewhat of a puzzle to grammarians, for
they stand outside the conventional parts of speech. They
have been termed "interjections," "onomatopoeic vocables,"
" onomatopoeic substantives," " descriptive adverbs," but,
properly speaking, they are a new part of speech. Whatever
they may be called they are certainly the most interesting
feature of a Bantu language, and have been all too rarely
and insufficiently studied. It may well be, as Mr. Madan[1]
thinks, that in them we have the ultimate elements of
speech—the survivals of the earliest form which human
language assumed. They stand midway between the
gesture and the articulated sentence. We might indeed
call them spoken gestures, conveying in sound the impression
given by a motion of the arm or a movement of the lips.
They are commonly accompanied by their proper gestures.
They are very numerous in Ila. There is hardly a sound,

---

[1] A. C. Madan, *Living Speech in Central and South Africa,* 1911. The
writer had studied these particles closely long before Mr. Madan wrote
this stimulating book, but he owes to it many suggestions.

action, movement, sensation but has its expressive descriptive particle. They are usually monosyllabic, but often the monosyllable is repeated or is combined with another.

Let us take some examples.

Mba! expresses falling headlong to the ground. *Muntu wawa*, a person falls, is a tame generalised phrase. *How* does he fall? That is what the Mwila, with his vivid appreciation of fact, desires to know. Does he fall lightly, heavily, or how? *Wawa mba!* There is no mistaking that, even if no swift vertical motion of the arm accompanies it. He falls headlong. But there is no need to make a grammatical sentence of it. *Mba!* expresses all you want to say.

Mbo! is another kind of falling. You can see the person in the act as the native says, *Mbo! mbo! mbo! mbo!* with a lowered intonation on the last syllable. He falls gradually, easily, floatingly.

Mbwa! is the action of falling heavily, wearily, flopping down on a bed or chair. It is expressed still more vividly as *Mbwa! mbwala! mbwa!*

The word *wa*, the ordinary verbal word for "fall," is descriptive of continual pattering as of the rain—*Wa! wa! wa! wa!*

There is in one of the tales in a later chapter a very expressive representation of the falling of Tortoise from a very great height: *Pididi, pididi, pididi!* How could you express that in English? Here it comes, rolling over and over, unhasting, down inevitably, inexorably—down! It is all there in the Ila phrase.

Ti! expresses striking the ground. You may say *Ndamuchina anshi* ("I throw him down"), but it is much easier and more trenchant to say simply *Ti!*, and it means the same. "The spear thrown comes to a rest in the ground short of its target"—you can say it all by *Ti!* Nor is there any confusion in actual usage; in the one case and the other the context is sufficient to show what you are talking about.

Te! is "tearing," the sharp rending of a thin dry skin or piece of calico. Hence, as rending means that the thing is divided, perhaps ended, you can say of a case in

court, a lengthy discussion or argument, *Amana te!*
(" The affair is finished ! ") or simply, *Te !*

To-o! with the vowel drawn out expresses quiet,
peacefulness. *Tontolo t-o-o !* (" All is calm ! "). *Wi !* and
Ne-e! express different shades of the same thing. The
line of the hymn " Peace, perfect peace " is translated in
Ila *Ne-e, pele ne-e.*

Tu ! is spurting or pouring or ejection, according to
the pronunciation. With a short vowel, *Tuh!* it represents a gun going off ; *Tu tu!* is spurting ; *Ntu-u!* is
pouring water from a pot.

Pi ! is the sensation of heat ; *Lu !* the sensation of
bitterness ; *Bu-u!* that of sourness—the restringency
caused by a lemon, for example. *Lwe!* is the sensation
of sweetness ; " *Lwe! lwe! lwe! lwe!* " a Mwila will say
on tasting a lump of sugar.

Mbi! expresses darkness, blackness. When a Mwila
says *Mbi! mbi! mbi! mbi!* what he means is, " It is
altogether and entirely dark, pitch-black, with not a ray
of light anywhere."

Mi ! is " drinking " and *Mu !* " sucking." *Mi !* uttered
as a command means " Down with it ! Swallow it all ! "
Mu! means " Go on sucking, don't chew it ! " *Mo!*
expresses the action of shedding off, peeling. You may say
of a leper, *Chinsenda chamumonkaola* (" The leprosy causes
his flesh to peel off "), but you can say all you want to say
by using *Mo ! mo !*

Ka! gives the idea of firmness, tightness. *Ka!* you
say after driving home a roof-pole : " It is firmly in, it won't
move ! " *Nka!* describes the action of striking ; *Nka!*
nka! nka! nka! (" Thump ! thump ! thump ! thump ! ").

Di ! is the sound of footsteps. *Didi didi* means " Listen !
here they come ! " *Ndo !* is a rumbling sound, and *Ndu !* a
dull thudding sound ; *Ndi !* is a reverberating sound. *Ndi !*
ndi ! ndi ! ndi ! is thunder reverberating in the distance.

Pyu ! expresses redness (" How red ! Altogether red ! ").
Bu ! expresses whiteness.

It is needless further to multiply instances. The reader
will now appreciate, perhaps, the extraordinary vividness
given to conversation by such particles.

We have in languages nearer home expressions that may remind us of these. One recalls the French comedy the heroine of which was Mademoiselle Frou-frou, so named from the rustle of her silk skirts. We have borrowed the word from the French and have many similar expressions of our own. When the Italian says *Andava torno-torno* he is using a phrase exactly like the Ila *Weenda zhingo-zhingo* (" He went meandering about.") But that phrase represents a further development of the germs we have been discussing ; it is well on the way to being a regular adverb. In Hebrew we meet such expressions as *taurouph touraph* ("rending he has been rent") where we have first the infinitive verb followed by the same verb conjugated. The Ba-ila have precisely the same construction, but once again the phrases we have described are in quite a different category. There is nothing of articulated speech about them ; they are interjectory as Whew ! is interjectory, but they are some-thing more. We may say they are echoisms, but they echo not only natural sounds—as *Nka !* echoes the sound of a hammer—but also, and more often, the sensation caused in the mind by outside things. *Pyu !* is evidently not an ordinary echoism ; it does not repeat anything heard as the onomatopes, of which there are plenty in Ila, do ; it represents the immediate percept of redness. There is a word for " red," *subila* : we can trace its history, know exactly what it means, put it into its place in a sentence ; it is just an ordinary conventional sign. *Pyu !* is also con-ventional in the sense that it has been handed down, but there is something natural and immediate about it that *subila* has not.

It is tempting to see in these particles the germs out of which the extensive Ila vocabulary has developed. Is there any indication of their being ultimate roots ?

Many of these particles, like *zhingo-zhingo*, are intimately connected with fully formed verbs. They consist in repeat-ing all or some of the syllables of the verb with perhaps an altered and stressed final vowel to give emphasis. Thus :

> *Chalemana lemanè !* How heavy it is—so very heavy !
> *Chabota botè !* How delicious it is—so delicious !
> *Chachisa chisè !* How painful it is—so painful indeed !

Very evidently these are not on the same footing with the others ; they are probably modern derivations from the verb.

In another category we can place the onomatopoeic words. The Ba-ila aptly describe the flying of the goose as *sekwè sekwè!* imitating the sound of its wings ; and the bird is named *nachisekwe.* They imitate the cry of the crested crane by *o-anè* and name the bird *namuoane.* These are evidently true onomatopes.

Besides these there are many verbs which we should say have been formed from the particles rather than that the particles have come from the verbs. From *lwe* we have the verb *lwela,* to be sweet ; from *mi* we have *mina,* to swallow ; from *nka* we have *kankamina,* to hammer ; *ndi! ndi! ndi!* which stands for a reverberating sound, is reproduced in the noun *indindima,* distant thunder. And so on. An illuminating word in this connection is *Chimbu-ndungu.* The first syllable is simply a formative, *chi,* which, as often, gives the general idea of " time." *Mbu!* describes the break of day ; *bushiku mbu,* or simply *mbu!* means " the day has dawned." *Ndu* is not only, as we have seen, a thudding sound, but with a varied intonation, mistiness, haziness, twilight ; *ngu* is expressive of emerging from within ; *Wavhwa ngu!* (" He comes out "). These syllables put together, *chi-mbu-ndu-ngu,* mean " the time at break of day, while it is still twilight, when you come out of your house," and that is precisely the sense in which the word is used to-day.

Now Mr. Madan's theory, if we understand him aright, is that the vocabularies of the Bantu languages have been formed in this way ; that these expressive monosyllables were the germs of speech, that the process of language consists in adding one syllable to another, thus increasing and varying the meaning, and that the first syllable, or the initial consonant, of a word retains the root-meaning, all others being formative.

If this attractive theory were true we should expect that the various Bantu languages would show some measure of agreement in the words whose first syllables are identical. And if the root-meanings survive in the descriptive particles still in use, we might expect some agreement in regard to them also.   That is to say, if the original speakers said *Za !* as the Ba-ila say it to-day, to express breaking, splitting, rending, we should expect *za* to show with some such meaning throughout the Bantu field.   There should be, in other words, some permanence of root-meaning.   As a matter of fact, the Bantu did not say *Za !* for *z* is, as we saw, not a primitive sound.   What they must have said is *ɣa !* which becomes *ya* in Nyanja, Bemba, and Kongo. Let us refer to the excellent dictionaries of those languages.

In Nyanja we find these words :

> *yala*, arrange, spread out.
> *yamba*, begin.
> *yambakata*, spread out upon the ground.
> *yandama*, float.
> *yanika*, spread.
> *yangalala*, be spread out.
> *yanja*, spread over.

The idea common to these words is that of " spreading."

In Bemba we get these words :

> *ya*, expand, grow.
> *yaka*, catch fire.
> *yanika*, spread out in the sun.
> *yankula*, catch up a chorus.
> *yaula*, yawn.

Again, the idea of spreading.

In Kongo we get :

> *yaluka*, migrate.
> *yalula*, roll up (something that has been spread).
> *yalumuka*, spread out.
> *yalumuna*, expand.
> *yambana*, be placed upon (used of something spreading).
> *yanda*, spread and peg out.
> *yangama*, float.
> *yanga*, spread out in the sun.

Once again, spreading.

Now take the Ila words :

> *zaka*, catch fire.
> *zala*, spread out.
> *zamba*, bind.

zambukila, be contagious.
zamuka, migrate.
zandala, grow, spread out.
zangadika, be a vagabond.
zanzala, stir up grain spread out to dry.
zazambe, an endless thing.

Running all through these words there is the idea of " spreading," and as the one syllable common to all is *za* or *ya*, which represents an original *γa*, we may, if it is legitimate to judge from these four representative languages, conclude that *γa* is an original root with that meaning, and that the extended significations have been given by the added syllables. But when we inquire what the Ba-ila mean to-day by *za*, we find that it is not spreading but bursting, tearing asunder. When, for example, the cattle burst through the cattle enclosure, they say *Za!* Of course we may say that there is some connection between the two ideas ; when cattle break through they spread out. The verb corresponding is *zapuka*, burst, split, be torn, and we might say, perhaps, that the second syllable gives that special meaning, for *po!* conveys the sense of " appearing through " (cf. Bemba, *lepuka*, burst), so that the word might signify " be in a state (*ka*) of spreading (*za*) through (*pu*)."

We might, if space allowed, go through other syllables and determine their meaning by comparison in the four languages. We should find that *pa* has the root idea of putting together, causing to adhere, giving, increasing, filling ; *pe* that of light motion, winnowing, grinding, skimming, spinning ; *pi* that of rolling, twisting, wringing, folding ; *pu* that of separation, stripping, cutting, threshing, aborting, uprooting. We should find that *ka* expresses the idea of hardness, tightness, firmness ; *ke* that of cutting, depriving, decreasing. *Ta* gives the idea of extension, from one to another, one place to another, growing, also of rending, splitting ; *te* that of looseness, shaking, slipping, swinging, quivering, creaking ; *ti* that of tenseness, flexibility ; *to* that of piercing, ramming.

We might conclude from these facts that there is much to be said for the view that the root meaning of Bantu words is contained in their first syllable. Or perhaps, more correctly, we should say in the consonant of the first syllable.[1] As to the so-called interjections in everyday use by the Bantu representing these primitive germs of speech, we can only say that as far as we have studied the matter we do not find that identity between them that the theory would seem to demand. *Ka,* it is true, as a root means "firm," and on the lips of the people it has that meaning as an exclamation ; but *pi,* which as a root means "rolling" or "twisting," as an exclamation means "hot." Of course we have to make allowances for changes, for conventionalising, during the two thousand or so years since the Bantu migrated from their original home. The subject would repay more extended study.

Formation of the Verb

Let us now leave these interesting speculations and get back to the firmer ground of plain fact.

Ila has properly three parts of speech : Verb, Noun, and Particle.

It is an agglutinative language. Its words are formed by adding one syllable to another, each of which brings an added signification to the whole. These syllables may be divided into (1) basic, (2) formative. Thus to take an example : *Chintamwizhi* ("I did not know him"). The base upon which it is formed is *izhi,* the shortened form of the verb, *izhiba,* to know. *Chi* is a tense particle ; *n* represents *nda* = I ; *ta* is a negative particle, "not" ; *mw* = *mu* the accusative pronoun "him."

Take another example :

> *Wa-ka-ba-sasidilá-nzhi ?*
> Thou-didst-them-sew-for-for-what ?

Here the root element is *sas* ; all else is formative.

Learning Ila resolves itself into gaining an intimate acquaintance with these formative elements, their right

---

[1] This brings us back, of course, to Plato, who observed that *p* is expressive of motion, the letters δ and τ of binding and rest, the letter λ of smoothness, ν of inwardness, etc. (Jowett's translation of *The Dialogues of Plato,* vol. i. p. 311).

use, the minute shades of meaning they convey, their correct order in making the word.

Most Ila verbs in their simplest form are disyllabic. Hundreds are formed by the simple coupling of the monosyllables given on p. 291. Thus : *kamba, kemba, kimba, komba, kumba.* Indeed the writer, when learning the language, speculated by forming scores of words on this model and then seeking their meaning. He did not often draw a blank. One felt there should be such words, and there were.

The final *a* is properly a formative, so that, *e.g., kamb* is the base-word. The formatives may be prefixes or postfixes, but whatever is added this base-word remains invariable, except that occasionally assimilation causes a change in the vowel ; you cannot take it to pieces and add letters to it as you can to the triliteral roots of Arabic. You may, as we have just been doing, go behind it in the endeavour to discover the ultimate meaning of the syllables *ka-mb(a)*, but for all practical purposes *kamb* is a root. There are some monosyllabic roots, but they are exceptional ; the normal Ila root is on the form : consonant + vowel + consonant. Any further syllables, whether their meaning can be determined or not, are formatives.

We may represent the verb in this way :

PREFIXES.		POSTFIXES.
Tense (negative)		Voice
Subject	Root	Tense (exceptional)
Object		Mood
Voice (exceptional)		

The Ila noun always stands in apposition and is represented by a pronominal suffix to the verb, as if we said " John he-eats." The object may be represented also by a prefix inserted between the subject and the verbal root, just as in Italian *Io vi do* ("I give you") = *ndamapa* ; only in Ila it is written as one word.

The tenses of the Ila verb are very numerous ; more have been made out since the Ila Handbook was published. All of them but one are formed by means of suffixes ; the exception is the perfect, a tense that is different from the others in that it has something of an adjectival significance. These are some of the chief tenses of the verb, *kubona,* to see :

INDICATIVE MOOD : AFFIRMATIVE TENSES

(ʃ = Simple stem, *bona.*   ß = Modified stem, *bwene.*)

Tenses.	Tense Sign.	Example.
1. Aorists.		
(1) Adjectival	-ʃ	1. *tu-bona*—we (who) see.
	-ß	2. *tu-bwene*—we (who) have seen.
(2) General	-a-ʃ	3. *tw-a-bona*—we see (saw, have seen, etc.).
	-a-chi-ʃ	4. *tw-a-chi-bona*—we continue seeing.
	-a-ya-bu-ʃ	5. *tw-a-ya-bu-bona*—we are engaged in seeing.
2. Presents.		
(1) Imperfect	-di-mu-ku-ʃ	6. *tu-di-mu-ku-bona*—we are seeing.
	-chi-ʃ	7. *tu-chi-bona*—we continue seeing.
	-la-ʃ	8. *tu-la-bona* — we are constantly (usually, certainly) seeing.
	-la-ya-bu-ʃ	9. *tu-la-ya-bu-bona*—we are being engaged in seeing.
	-la-ya-ku-ʃ	10. *tu-la-ya-ku-bona*—we are habitually in the act of seeing.
(2) Perfect	-di-ß	11. *tu-di-bwene*—we have seen.
	-chi-ß	12. *tu-chi-bwene*—we have been seeing.
3. Pasts.		
(1) General	-a-ka-ʃ	13. *tw-a-ka-bona*—we saw.
	-a-ka-chi-ʃ	14. *tw-a-ka-chi-bona* — we continued seeing.
	-a-ka-ya-bu-ʃ	15. *tw-a-ka-ya-bu-bona*—we were engaged in seeing.
	ka-ʃ	16. *ka-tu-bona*—we saw.
	ka-ß	17. *ka-tu-bwene*—we did see.
(2) Imperfect	-a-ku-ʃ	18. *tw-a-ku-bona*—we were seeing.
	-a-ku-chi-ʃ	19. *tw-a-ku-chi-bona*—we were continuing to see.
	-a-ku-ya-bu-ʃ	20. *tw-a-ku-ya-bu-bona*—we were engaged in seeing
(3) Pluperfect	-a-ku-ß	21. *tw-a-ku-bwene*—we had seen.
4. Futures.		
	-ka-la-ʃ	22. *tu-ka-la-bona*—we shall soon see.
	-ka-la-chi-ʃ	23. *tu-ka-la-chi-bona*—we shall continue seeing.
	-ka-la-ya-bu-ʃ	24. *tu-ka-la-ya-bu-bona*—we shall be engaged in seeing.

These are affirmative tenses; they may be modified by the use of various negative particles : *ta-tu-boni*, we do not see ; *ta-tu-na-ku-bona*, we have not yet seen ; *ta-tu-chi-na-ku-bona*, we have still not yet seen, etc. And besides the Indicative mood, there are the Subjunctive, Conditional, Jussive, and Imperative moods. These are formed by means of prefixes, the final vowel of the verb changing to *e* in the Subjunctive and allied forms.

By the addition of various suffixes the meaning of the verb is extended in a manner that reminds us of the forms of the Arabic and Hebrew verb. These forms are variously called Voices or Species. It will be worth while to give a list of them. No one verb that we know of takes all these forms and great care has to be exercised in their use, as often they have idiomatic meanings which are not apparent.

1. Simple verb : *bon-a*, see.
2. Relative : suffix *-ila*, which by assimilation may be *-ela*, *-ina*, or *-ena* ; *bon-ena*, see to, or for, in connection with.
3. Extended relative : suffix *-idila* (*-elela*, *-inina*, *-enena*). *Bon-enena*, see to for somebody. Often gives an absolute meaning ; *e.g. ya*, go ; *ila*, go to ; *ididila*, go right away.
4. Causative : suffix *-ya*, which undergoes many phonetic changes, see p. 288. *Chita*, do ; *chisha*, cause, or help, to do.
5. Causative : suffix, *-ika* or *-eka*. Meaning : cause to be in a certain state. *Mena*, grow ; *meneka*, cause to be growing.
6. Capable : suffix, *-ika* or *-eka*. Meaning : corresponds to the English suffix *-able*. *Chit-ika*, be doable.
7. Passive : Like Arabic, the Ila makes use of the vowel *u* to express the passive ; but instead of changing a root vowel (Arabic, *qatala*, he kills; *qutala*, he is killed) it is suffixed in the form of *w* ; *e.g. chita*, to do ; *chitwa*, to be done.
8. Middle : suffix *-uka*. Meaning : to be in a certain state. It differs from the Passive in that the action is not referred to any agent. *And-uka*, be split. The Passive, *andul-wa*, means that it is split by somebody ; *anduka* refers simply to its condition.
9. Stative : suffix *-ama*. Meaning : to be in a certain position. *Lul-ama*, be straight; *kot-ama*, be bowed. Unlike the other voices this is dead, or at least moribund ; it cannot be used with the same facility.

10. Extensive : suffix -*ula*. This corresponds to No. 8 as transitive to intransitive. Meaning : to put into a certain state. The suffix translates " up " " through " in such words as, break up, bore through. *Sand-ula*, turn over. *And-ula*, split up.
11. Extensive : suffix -*aula*. Gives meaning of " keep on doing, do in degrees, gradually, with repeated action." *And-aula*, chop up firewood.
12. Repetitive : suffix -*ulula*. Answers to our prefix *re-*. *Ula*, trade ; *ululula*, trade a thing over and over again.
13. Reversive : suffix -*ulula*. Answers to our prefix *un-*. *Amb-ulula*, unsay, retract.
14. Reflexive : prefix *di-*. Throws the action back on the subject. *Anga*, tie ; *dianga*, tie oneself ; *pa*, give ; *dipa*, give each other.
15. Reciprocal : suffix -*ana*. Expresses mutual action. *Bona*, see ; *bon-ana*, see each other.
16. Intensive : suffix -*isha*. Meaning : to do forcibly, heartily, lengthily. *Ang-isha*, tie tightly.
17. Reduplicative : repeating the verbal stem. *Ambuka*, turn aside ; *ambukambuka*, keep on turning aside.

Besides these seventeen forms, others are formed by adding one form to another ; *e.g. langidizha* (No. 1 + 3 + 4), cause to look on behalf of.

Each form of the verb can take the various prefixes to mark tense, etc. In this way most formidable-looking polysyllables may be, and commonly are, formed ; for example :

Tamuchinakubaangulwilanzhi ?
Why have you still not yet untied them ?

The root, which seems lost amid the multiplicity of syllables, is *ang*, tie.

Formation of the Noun

The Ila noun includes not only the substantive, but also the pronoun and adjective ; everything that is formed of a root and the noun prefixes. Like the verb, the noun has a basic portion and a formative portion, but its formatives are as a rule prefixed. The final vowel may undergo significant changes, and there are a few suffixes, such as we find in *muntu-ma*, " my fellow-man."

The Ba-ila, like all Bantu, conceive of all things as

distributed in a certain number of categories. The *funda-mentum divisionis* is not very clear to the European mind, but would seem transparent to theirs, for they never have any hesitancy in allotting new things and new conceptions to their proper places. The division is not on a sex basis, like our familiar masculine, feminine, and neuter. It is marked by the use of certain prefixes, thirteen in number, which again are roughly divided into two, marking the singular and plural numbers. We may arrange them as follows :

Class.	SINGULAR. Prefix.	Significant Letter.	Class.	PLURAL. Prefix.	Significant Letter.
I.	*mu-*	*u-* (*w-*)	I.	*ba-*	*b-*
2.	*mu-*	*u* (*w*)	2.	*mi-*	*i* (*y-*)
3.	*i-* (*di-*)	*l-* (*d-*)	3.	*ma-*	*a*
4.	*bu-*	*b-*	4.	*ma-*	*a-*
5.	*ku-*	*k-*	5.	*ma-*	*a-*
6.	*ka-*	*k-*	6.	*tu-*	*t*
7.	*chi-*	*ch-*	7	*shi-*	*sh-*
8.	*in-*	*i-* (*y-*)	8.	*in-*	*y- sh-*
9.	*lu-*	*l-*	9.	*in-*	*y- sh-*
10.	*lu-*	*l-*	10.	*ma-*	*a-*

The third columns contain the significant letters of the prefix which are used in forming pronouns, etc.

All nouns whatever carry one of these prefixes which places it in its proper category ; the base of the word serving to define its proper nature.

We will not enter into the never-ending discussion as to the precise nature of these classifiers. Suffice it here to say that as far as Ila is concerned, Class 1 contains persons ; it contains also the names of most animals, many of them being proper names and as such not having the prefix *mu-*, but belonging unmistakably to this class. Class 2 contains things with a less degree of personality ; Class 3 contains many augmentatives. The nouns of Class 4 are abstract or collective. Class 6 is the diminutive class. Class 7 contains many names of worn-out, defective things. Class 8 contains names of things. Classes 9 and 10 contain many abstract or semi-abstract things. We noticed that when new words were being formed for the purposes of

Christian teaching, such words as " love," " will," were at once given the prefix *lu-*.

We will give one example. The root *-ntu* has some such meaning as " entity," and with differing prefixes it becomes as follows : *mu-ntu*, personal entity, a person ; *ba-ntu*, people ; *i-ntu*, an important entity (compare the word *muka-intu*, a woman, *i.e.* the one belonging to a human par excellence) ; *bu-ntu*, status, quality of a person, also *virtus* ; *ku-ntu*, where an entity may be, a place ; *chi-ntu*, a thing ; *shi-ntu*, things ; *ka-ntu*, a little thing ; *tu-ntu*, little things ; *ma-ntu*, a great many things all together.

The noun roots are either verbal roots, or else are a class by themselves, that is, are quite different from the verbal roots.   In making nouns from the former, great care is exercised in the choice of the final vowel ; *a* and *i* give the noun an active meaning, *e* and *u* a passive meaning ; *o* is either one or the other or something between ; *i* and *e* are the vowels mostly in use.   For example :

> *mu-yas-i*—one who spears.
> *mu-yas-e*—one who is speared.

Nouns are formed, not only from the simple verbal root but also from any of the voice-forms. *Mu-kumb-izhi*, a beggar, is formed from No. 2, the relative form, *kumb-ila*, with the suffix given a definitely active form.

The Ila adjective proper is formed in the same way as the substantive, with a prefix and stem, the difference being that the stems are more mobile and can take whatever prefix the qualified substantive takes ; *e.g.* *muntu mu-kando*, a great man ; *chi-ntu chi-kando*, a big thing. Besides this normal way adjectives are formed in other ways.

It would take us too far afield to enter into a description of all the various kinds of pronouns—relative, demonstrative, personal, indefinite, etc.   Suffice it to say that they are all closely related to the noun prefixes, being formed by reduplication or by being attached to certain special roots. Each noun class has its own proper set. In all, these forms number some hundreds.

A word should be said of what are called the locative prefixes.

mu = rest within, motion into or out from.
ku = position at, motion to or from.
a = rest upon, motion on to or from off.

These are prefixed not to the noun roots but to the complete substantive. They afford an example of the remarkable precision of the Ila speech. If we say in English " the house is dark," our meaning is, if we think of it, very vague. Do we mean " it is dark " within or without ? No doubt is caused by the way the Ba-ila say it :

> *mu-ng'anda mulashia*—the interior of the house is dark.
> *ku-ng'anda kulashia*—around the house is dark.
> *a-ng'anda alashia*—darkness is upon the house.

If they said *ing'anda ilashia*, they would mean that the structure is dark or black.

From these locative prefixes another series of pronouns, etc., is formed, all bringing with them the defined meanings of the original *mu, ku, a*.

We need not enter into a description of the particle. The preposition, apart from the prefixes we have just mentioned which are used as such, is not greatly developed, its place being largely taken by the suffixes of the verb. The adverb and conjunction would repay further study could we give it here. We may just illustrate the way in which the meaning conveyed in some of the noun prefixes is carried beyond the noun itself. Thus the prefix *bu* gives an abstract meaning to the noun, and, used as a particle, has the meaning " as, how, in the way that." *Twandana bu bakaandana shempela o chivubwe*, " let us separate as the rhino. and hippo. did." It is as if in the mind of the native the whole phrase *bubakaandana* formed an abstract noun. So in the tense already quoted, No. 5, *tw-a-ya-bu-bona*, " we are engaged in seeing," *bubona* seems to convey the sense of an abstract noun.

A Page from the Ila Dictionary

To show how Ila words develop from roots, we now give an entry from a dictionary as it might be written. As a matter of fact, abundant material for such a lexicon exists, but whether it will ever see the light is doubtful. There is nothing artificial about this. No words have been coined for the purpose of exhibition : all are in actual use.

'Amb-

(**Ur-Bantu,** *γamba* ; usual modern forms, **amba,** as in Ila, Swahili, etc., **gamba,** in Ganda, etc.).

1. **Amb-a**—speak, say, talk, utter.
    Inf. **kuamba** (*kwamba*) ; perf. **ambile.** *Uambai ? Uambanzhi ?* What do you say ? *Wangamba*—he says to me. *Makani ngwingamba*—things which I say. Usually followed by *ati* ; *ulaamb'ati*—he speaks and says. Idiom : " about to " ; *mubwa aambe avhwe wapatila mu chibia*—when the dog was about to withdraw it stuck in the pot ; *mwaba aambe achebuke munshi*—when the jackal was about to look behind.

2. **AMB-ila**—speak to ; **ambil'a,** say about, on account of. *Wangambila*—he says to me ; *ndamuambil'ati*—I tell him that . . . ; *muambilanzhi ?*—why do you speak ?

3. **AMB-idila**—speak on behalf of.

4. **AMB-ya**—cause, help, to say. (+14) **Diambya,** speak to oneself, or to one another ; *wadiambya mu chamba*—he talks silently to himself ; *badiambya beni o beni*—they discuss a matter between themselves.

6. **AMB-ika**—be tellable, speakable ; *makani taambika*—the affairs cannot, may not, be spoken of ; *makani ataambika*—unspeakable things.

7. **AMB-wa**—said, spoken ; *kwambwai ? Kwambwanzhi ?*—what's the news ?

11. **AMB-aula**—keep on saying. (+2) **ambawila ;** perf. *ambaudile.*

13. **AMB-ulula**—unsay, retract ; *sh'ambulula*—I do not unsay what I said ; (+8) **ambuluka,** unsaid, retracted, reversed ; perf. *ambulukile* ; *makani adi ambulukile*—the affairs have changed. Hence the following, apparently of different meaning, but all from same root :
    (8) **AMB-uka**—turn aside, leave path when travelling ; leave path of rectitude, go astray, fall away ; also, of children going to the bush. (17) **AMB-uk-AMB-uka,** constantly to leave the road ; *twakeenda obach'-ambukambuka* (riddle) we travelled with those who were always leaving the path. (10) **AMB-ula,** put, take, out of road ; (+2) **AMB-wila,** turn—for ; (+4) **AMB-usha,** cause to turn aside, lead astray.

14. **diAMBya**, see 4. (+1) **diAMBa,** speak of oneself, confess. (+2, 3) **diAMB-ila, diAMB-idila,** speak for oneself, plead one's own cause.

15. **AMB-ana,** converse, dispute, argue, quarrel ; perf. *ambene.*

16. **AMB-isha,** talk much, loudly. (+2) **AMBishizha ;** *muambishizhanzhi ?*—why do you speak so loudly ?

Derived Nouns :

Cl. Mu-ba- **MwAMBi,** speaker. **MwAMBilwa,** person spoken to ; proverb : *kaluba mwambi, mwambilwa taluba*—the speaker (insulter) may forget, but the one spoken to (insulted) does not forget. **MwAMBididi, MwAMBidizhi,** advocate, intercessor. **MwAMBidilwa,** one interceded for. **MwAMBushi,** one who turns out of the road. **MwAMBuzhi,** one who turns another aside. **ShikuAMBisha,** one who speaks loudly. **MwAMBuluzhi,** one who retracts. **MwAMBani, ShimwAMBana,** disputer ; proverb : *Shimwambana o mwami walekela o mano* ; the disputer with a chief has thrown away wisdom.

Cl. Mu-mi- **MwAMBo,** word, speech, language. **MiAMBoMiAMBo,** various kinds of languages.

Cl. I-ma- **IAMBo,** a great saying. **MAMBo,** a great many sayings. **MAMBAMBa,** chatterings, one's own affairs, particularly in contrast with a message with which he is entrusted. *Mambamba budio !*—He is speaking for himself, not what he was sent to say ; also a confused talking, of many people speaking at once.

Cl. Bu-ma- **BwAMBE,** speaking, manner of speaking. *Wabosha bwambe*—you speak well. **BwAMBI,** loud talking.

Cl. Ku. **KwAMBa,** speaking, talking.

Cl. Ka-tu- **KAMBo,** thing spoken of, affair, fault, crime, court-case, reason. *Kambonzhi ?*—Why ? *Kambokakuti*—because. **TwAMBO,** sayings, utterances, reasons. **ShikAMBoma,** my opponent in a case ; **shikambonoko,** thy—— ; **Shikambonina, shikambonokwesu, shikambonokwabo,** his——, our——, their——. **KAMBile,** something spoken of already, decided upon, plot, plan.

Cl. Chi-shi- **ChAMBa,** the chest, thoracic cavity (as seat of thought). **ChAMBa - chilemu,** forbearance. **ShichAMBachilemu,** a forbearing person. **ShichAMBa,** a sincere, truthful person. **ChAMBo,** speech, language, dialect. **ChAMBukilo,** place for turning aside. **ChAMBilo,** time for speaking, opportunity ; **+a,** locative particle : *achambilo*—at the time ; *ano ng'achambilo chakwe*—this is the time for him to speak.

Cl. In-In- **IngAMBAMBi,** persistent talking ; **ShingAMBAMBi,** a persistent talker.

Derived Adjectives :

1. **-AMBi,** speaking ; **-AMBe,** spoken.
6. **-AMBishi,** speakable ; proper, right, to be spoken.
8. **-AMBushi,** errant, fallen astray.
13. **-AMBulule, -AMBuluke,** unspoken, retracted.

Here we have, in all, nearly sixty words formed from the one root AMB ; not all that could possibly, by the rules of the language, be formed from it, but those we have recorded as in use. The Ila dictionary would be made up of similar pages.

Sentence Formation

The noun is the chief word in the sentence ; it is the master, so to speak, and every pronoun, adjective, verb, that is dependent upon it takes its prefix (or the significant part of the prefix) as a livery or mark of subservience. This is the principle of the alliterative or euphonic concord. For example :

> *Mu*-ntu *u*-umwi *mwi*-botu *mwi*-ni-*mwi*-ni *wa*-ke-za
> One really good person came.
> *Ba*-ntu *ba*mwi *ba*-botu *be*-ni-*be*-ni *ba*-ke-za.
> Other really good people came.

In a subsequent chapter we give many of the Ila folk-tales ; it will help to an appreciation of these and of the language if we now transcribe one in the original with a word-for-word translation :

> *Sulwe*　　　*mbwakatizha*　　　*Muzovu.*
> Hare　　it-is-how-he-made-fear　Elephant.

Usulwe　*wa-ambila Muzovu*　*ati :*　" *A-tu-ende*　　　*tu-ka-zube*
The-Hare　he-spoke-to Elephant he-said : " Let-us-go　(that) we-may-hide

tu-ka-bone　　*u-kwete*　　*mano*　　*a*　*ku-zuba.*"　*Inzho*　*Muzovu*
we-may-see　who-holds　cunning　of　hiding."　　Then　Elephant

wa-ambila Sulwe,　*ati :*　" *Ome ndi-kwete*　*mano*　*ku-bazha uwe,*
he-spoke-to　Hare,　he-said :　" I　I-hold　cunning　to-surpass thee,

uwe kashonto　*to-mbadi*　*mano.*"　*Inzho ba-ya.*　　*Ba-shike*
thou little-one　not-me-surpass cunning."　Then they-went. (That) they arrive

budio Sulwe wa-ambila Muzovu,　ati :　　" *Tanguna, uwe uka-zube.*"
simply Hare he-speaks-to Elephant, he-says : " Be-first thou, thou-may-hide."

Muzovu　wa-ya.　　*A-shike ku chivuna wa-zuba ; anukuti u-di-shite*
Elephant he-went.　He-arrive to　bush　he-hid ;　whereas he-is-sitting

a-sweya budio.　　*Walo*　*ati :*　　" *Nda-zuba.*"　　*Walo*　*Sulwe*
on-clear simply.　That-one he-said : " I-am-hidden."　That-one Hare

a-shike wa-mu-zubulula.　*Inzho*　*azè*　*Sulwe*　*ati :* " *Ko-shite,*
he-arrive　he-him-un-hid.　Then　he-also　Hare　he-said : " Stay,

nzube."　*Pele*　*Sulwe*　*wo-ona*　*ku shihuna,*　　*wa-salama*
I-hide."　Then　Hare　he-lay-down　at　bush,　he-lay-on-his-back

wa-tutulula　*menso*　*akwe.*　*Inzho*　*we-ta*　*Muzovu,*　*ati :*
he-protruded　eyes　his.　Then　he-called　Elephant,　he-said :

Kweza u-nzubulule."   Wa-ya   Muzovu,   a-shike   wa-kapaula
Come   thou-me-find."   He-went   Elephant   he-arrive   he-kept-on-seeking

*   wa-amb'ati :   " ngu-di kwi no ? "   A-lang'anshi wa-bona menso*
he-spoke-he-said : " it-is-thou-where ? "   He-look-down   he-saw   eyes

atulukile   wa-zowa,   wa-amb'ati :   " Ya-ndweza inshi, ya-mena
protruded he-was-amazed, he-spoke-he-said : "It-me-horrifies earth, it-grows

menso." Inzho we-ta beenzhina, ati : " Ka-mwi-za mu-bone ya-mena
eyes." Then he-called his-friends, he said : " Come-ye,   ye-see   it grows

menso inshi."   Be-za,   pele Sulwe wa-buka, wa-ambila Muzovu,
eyes   earth."   They-came   only Hare   he-arose,   he-spoke-to Elephant,

ati : " Uwe,   u-di   mudimbushi. Ome nda-ku-bazha mano, ndime
he-said : " Thou, thou-art   fool.   I,   I-thee-surpass cunning, it-is-I

mukando."   Pele Muzovu   wa-usa   budio.
great."   Only Elephant   he-ashamed simply.

How Hare Scared Elephant

Hare once said to Elephant : " Let us play hide-and-seek and we will see who is the more cunning at the game." Elephant replied : " I have more cunning than you in hiding ; a little thing like you cannot be more cunning than I." So they went off. When they arrived at the place, Hare said to Elephant : " You be the first to hide." Elephant went off, and coming to a bush he hid ; at least he thought he hid, really he was lying in the open. He called out : " I am hidden." Hare on his arrival at once found him. Then Hare on his part said : " Stay here, while I hide." He lay down at the bush, turned on his back and protruded his eyes ; then he called Elephant : " Come and find me." Elephant came, and hunted about. Said he : " Wherever can you be ? " Then, looking down, he saw the protruded eyes, and was amazed. " The earth horrifies me," he said, " it grows eyes." Then he called his friends, saying : " Come and see here, the earth grows eyes." They came and Hare arose and said to Elephant : " You are a fool. I have more cunning than you. I am the great one." Elephant was simply crestfallen.

Conclusion

This chapter on the language is not to teach it to our readers (if any have had the patience to follow us so far), but it is meant to leave on their minds an impression of the extraordinary richness and flexibility of the language. It is a fine instrument. One is surprised that the Ba-ila should have such a fine instrument ; it has potentialities far beyond their need of self-expression hitherto. For some years now it has been put into written form for them, books have been written in it, the New Testament has been translated into it.

CHAPTER XXVII

*

PROVERBS, RIDDLES, AND CONUNDRUMS

1. PROVERBS

IN his dealings with the Ba-ila few things help a European more than a knowledge of their proverbs. To be familiar with them gives one a good deal of insight into their character and ways of looking at things, for they express the likes and dislikes of the people in certain directions in quite an unmistakable fashion. And, moreover, these proverbs are taken largely as a rule of life. They are truly " the wisdom of many "—maxims of discreet conduct that have stood the test of ages ; they are equally " the wit of one," showing a remarkably shrewd insight into motives, and expressed in a short, concise manner that reflects great credit upon their authors, whoever they may be. Some of them bear their meaning on the surface and we see at once what their equivalents are in our own language. Of others the meaning is not so apparent, but when once explained their appropriateness to the occasion is immediately patent. A knowledge of the proverbs is, then, invaluable to any who wish to appreciate the character of the Ba-ila and especially to those who have direct dealings with them. Many an angry dispute has been silenced, many an inhospitable chief has been rebuked into generosity, many a forward beggar has been reduced to shame, and many a long, diffuse argument has been clinched by the apt quotation of one of these proverbs.

A study of the proverbs is very valuable to the student of the language. It is not an easy study, but the correct and appropriate use of them will mark the competent speaker. They contain many words that are not heard in ordinary conversation, and also many archaic expressions and grammatical forms. This which, of course, is only a proof of their antiquity, makes translation difficult—natives themselves cannot always explain the significance of these expressions while knowing the meaning of the whole pro-verb—and one cannot always be sure therefore that he has caught the precise meaning. And, of course, the peculiar flavour of these proverbs largely evaporates in the translating. But, with all allowance for these facts, the man is to be pitied who cannot appreciate the wit and wisdom of these sayings.

In the following pages we transcribe a few examples from a large collection of these proverbs, grouped roughly under headings and accompanied by such elucidation as may be necessary.

The first class contains maxims and precepts, truths verified in the experience of the tribe and inculcated as rules of conduct. Many of them are serious enough, but the laughter is never far away. And laughter, Bergson tells us, " is above all a corrective. .- . . Its function is to intimidate by humiliating." The wit pursues a utilitarian aim of general improvement. " By laughter society avenges itself for the liberties taken with it." A Mwila greatly objects to being made fun of, and his susceptibility to ridicule is a powerful instrument in the hands of those who try to improve him. He can often be laughed out of a thing when argument and even force are unavailing.

As a legal maxim we have already quoted : *Kwina mwami owakadizhala* (" No chief ever gave birth to a chief "). The hereditary principle, by which a son follows his father, is unknown to the Ba-ila.

Among the social virtues most appreciated is hospitality, and we are not surprised to find it inculcated in various proverbs. *Mwenzu talangwa ankumu, mulange mwifu* (" A visitor is to be regarded not as to his face but as to his stomach "). *Matako a mwenzu makadikwa* (" The rump of a visitor is made to sit upon "). *Shikwaze tabudi budilo bwa nswi* (" A fish-eagle does not lack fish for food on a journey ") ; he is sure to find some, and so will you ; only trust people. These sayings illustrate also the ironical wit of the people ; they state what ought to be done, pretending that this is just what is actually being done. That is Bergson's definition of irony. We should add that the quickest way of securing hospitality is simply to quote one of these sayings : what ought to be done is done.

Many of the proverbs aim in this way against certain classes of people, who, like the poor, are always with us, whether our lot is placed in civilisation or in heathenesse.

There are Pharisees even among the Ba-ila. *Kabombwe balamusanana, menzhi balanwa* (" They spurn the frog but drink the water "), *i.e.* they don't like to find a frog in their drinking-water, but they will drink it after the frog is removed—an apt description of the unctuous rectitude that strains at the gnat and swallows the camel ! A man who claims to be without fault is rebuked by the saying : *Ushiletekambo wakatea inzoka munzhila* (" Mr. No-fault ensnared a snake in the road "), and left it to bite passers-by. Nobody is without blame for something or other !

" The one failing that is essentially laughable is vanity." So Bergson says again ; and many an Ila proverb laughs quietly at men who puff themselves up and despise others. *Kwina mwami owakadila mumpande* (" There is no chief who eats out of an impande shell "). The shell may show his wealth, but when it is a matter of eating the chief must do as ordinary people do—eat out of a dish. Nature confounds social distinctions. That is a way of reminding an arrogant man that he is only human after all. A person who in his conceit is always running others down will be reminded that *Chizhilo chibe chishinka musena* (" Any old pole will stop up a hole in the fence ") : everybody is useful to the community in some way or other. Or he will be told : *Wabakembetema wasandukila masamo nina* (" An axe-shaft is made out of an ordinary piece of wood "). That cuts two ways : an ordinary person can be made of great use ; but, on the other hand, he is not essential ; like an axe-shaft, he is of use only in connection with others (meaning the axe-head) and can easily be replaced. Or again, the conceited person will be told to remember that *Musongo wakalukanka, takachidyile ; mudimbushi owakweza munshi wakachidya* (" A wise man ran on without eating it, a fool coming behind ate it ")—meaning that the wise in their own conceits often miss the good things in life. An overbearing stranger may be told, *Muchende tafumpuka matanga obili* (" A bull doesn't enjoy fame in two herds ").

A know-all will have quoted to him the Ila equivalent of our saying about teaching one's grandmother : *Uwe muntu takukubudi banoko, kulakubula banji* (" Oh, man, don't try to teach your mother, try others "). Or this : *Mano avhwa mu kaumbuswa* (" Wisdom comes out of an ant-heap "), which means that even a fool knows something. Or this : *Mano takala mutwi omwi* (" Wisdom does not dwell in one head "). Or again, *Mukando mushie lubilo, mano tomushii* (" You may outrun an old man, but you can't outdo him in wisdom "). Or he will be curtly bidden, *Kula ubone twanshi* (" Get grown up and then you will know the things on earth "). These are especially applicable, it will be noticed, to young people anxious to instruct their elders.

Another class needing correction is the grumblers. One who should complain of his food would be exhorted that, *Muchanka wa nyama udi omwi* (" The niceness of meat is one "). That is not true of a epicure, but it is so to a hungry man.

We have many proverbs aimed at evil speakers. *Kamunazaka o mulozhi, shikalaka ulayaya chishi* (" Build rather with a witch than with a false-tongued person, he destroys a community "). *Kaluba mwambi, mwambilwa taluba* (" The speaker may forget, but he who is spoken to does not forget "), *i.e.* you may forget the insult but the person you insult will not, it will rankle. A scandal-monger will be derided thus : *Wakotokela kuvuya* (" He leaves off work to backbite people ") : he's too lazy to attend to his business. The following are two cryptic sayings descriptive of the same kind of person : *Ufulwe mumi tapakwa bwanga* (" A living tortoise is not worn as a charm ") ; which, whether you see it or not, means that you mustn't speak evil of a living man. *Kazune shimuntwanganya imbula watola u muchenji* (" A treacherous little bird took

an imbula fruit to a muchenji tree "—a fruit-bearing tree) :
the idea is that the bird in a fatuous way sought to curry
favour with the tree. It is a proverb describing a person
who runs his own chief down to another chief, and that
chief to his own : a subtle kind of flattery which yet is so
very obvious !

Greedy people do not come off scathless from the makers
of Ila proverbs. *Mulakumune ku kudya kwalo udikwete
insana* (" The great - open - mouth, only in eating is his
strength ! "). He is like a sack, that will take in all that
it will hold ; he is good for nothing else. And if he
clamours for food that is being kept for an absent member,
he is gently reminded : *Udi afwafwi ng'udya twinu, udi
kulale tabudi bwinu* (" He that is near should get a little
of the fat, the one that is far should not lack plenty ").

The Ba-ila are far from being cowards, but they know
quite well that discretion is the better part of valour. Or,
as they say : *Kabwenga moa ng'uongola* (" It is the prudent
hyena that lives long "). A hot-headed man that rushes
into danger, and meets disaster, against all warning is thus
spoken of : *Ubosha obamuweza* (" It pays them out who
hunt for it ! ").

A laggard will be told : *Ing'ombe insolozhi njinwa menzhi*
(" It is the first ox that drinks the water ")—when the
laggards come up they find it all gone. And he will slyly
be spoken of thus : *Inaumpi odia bula* (" The mother wild-
dog of the intestine "). That is a good example of the allu-
sive by-speech of the Ba-ila. Nobody would understand
it who did not know the tale of the wild-dogs : the mother
who used to hunt game for her children until she grew too
old ; then the poor old thing (in the eyes of the Ba-ila she
would be a laughing-stock) had to lag behind, and could
only come up with the pack—her children—in time to get a
bit of the entrails. So to call a man *Inaumpi* is to poke
fun at him, perhaps in a kindly teasing manner.

It is very often said that Africans are deficient in gratitude ; it would be truer to say that they feel thankful but
do not express it in the same way as we do. *Ozona ozona*
is a thanksgiving formula, or, as the Basuto say, *ka moso le
ka moso*, both meaning " To-morrow and to-morrow," *i.e.*

give me it again and again.   The proverbs show that an
ingrate is spoken against.   *Kunavhuna shilumamba, ushi-
nzala udikwete kambukwa* (" Better help a fighting-man
than a hungry person, he (the latter) has no gratitude ").

Squanderers come in for a share of ridicule.   Thus :
Ing'ombe intaka itakanya muchila wayo (" The prodigal
cow threw away her own tail ").   An obstinate person,
who suffers through not taking advice, will have this
thrown at him : *Ngulube wakafwa mu shitamba* (" The pig
died in the trap ")—against which it was warned.

Levellers, despisers of authority, and kickers against
the pricks lay themselves open to many a witty rebuke.
Tatuzanda kasutasuta kei dia namakukwe (" We do not like
the pride of a hen's egg ").   It is difficult to see at first
where the pride of an egg comes in, but if you look at them
lying in the nest you will see that they are all alike ; they
are republicans, every Jack as good as his neighbour—and
that is the pride of an egg !   And a person who sets himself on a level with the authorities will quickly be told that
in this community the pride of eggs is not to be tolerated !
Two proverbs may be quoted which show a discontented
person that, while chastening is grievous, it is for his good.
Nevhuluma tedyi mwana (" Though the lion growls it
won't eat its child ").   *Namakukwe tafwi kabambala ka
nina* (" A chicken does not die of its mother's kicks ").
An incorrigible rebel will be reminded by his father or
chief : *Chikaya ndachileka* (" I throw away an old useless
armlet ")—so take heed !

We may pass now to a series of proverbs which contain
advice for discreet conduct in various relations of life.   A
general proverb, pronounced by the Ba-ila to be a very
great one indeed, is : *Utotakatila mudilo* (" Do not throw
it into the fire ").   We have often heard this quoted to a
person who is about to commit a foolish action ; it means :
Be careful !   You throw away your chance, it won't come
again !   Perhaps we may also put under the same heading
a proverb which is the very reverse of the golden rule :
*Wanchita mwenzha-kabotu, ame ndakuchita mwenzha-kabotu :
wanchita mwenzha-bubi ame ndakuchita mwenzha-bubi* (" If
you do me a good turn, I will do you a good turn ; if you

do me an evil turn, I also will do you an evil turn "). Of a similar effect is the other : *Nvhuna olwaku muma, ame olwa ku menzhi ndakuvhuna* ("Help me in my need on the bank, and I will help you in yours in the water "). This is explained by one of the tales, in which a hare and a crocodile make a compact of friendship ; the hare to help the crocodile on land, and the crocodile the hare in the water.

Advice is given to masters in dealing with their slaves. It will be discreet for them to show no favour but to treat all alike. *Bana ba manga balauminwa dimwi* ("Twin children are both beaten at the same time ")—*i.e.* if one does wrong they are both beaten ; if your servants all do well you must not single out one for praise, nor, on the other hand, if they all displease should you be angry with any particular one—treat them all alike. And remember, too, *Muzhike wako ulumbwa n'aloboka* ("Your slave is praised after he has run away from you ") ; you undervalue him now and treat him with less than justice ; one day, when he runs away, you will begin to appreciate him.

On the other hand, people in a state of dependence are advised against foolish behaviour. *Malelo mazhokaukwa* ("A state of dependence is to be returned to ") : so do not anger your master and get dismissed, for one day you may want to go back to him and he won't have you. And again : *Bomba udye malelo* ("Be humble so that you may continue to enjoy the state of dependence you are in ").

This is a saying conveying advice to a bridegroom : *Kapadingwa kupa banoko, mukazhi nindavu* ("Give to your mother, a wife is a lion ")—which means, treat your mother better than your wife ; you may have many wives, you can have only one mother.

It is a wise saying that a man should be on good terms with his doctor : *Chenjezha nganga, malwazhi eza bu seka* ("Annoy your doctor and sicknesses will come laughing ").

Advice is given to people to keep their friendships in constant repair : *Inzhi ikufwine nj'ikukala* ("The fly that loves you is the one that sits on you ")—visit your friends and so show your affection.

People are warned against not keeping their business

to themselves : *Mankulubwiza atole ku mucheche, mukando-noko ulazukula* (" If you tell jokes about him to a child, your fellow adult will find it out "), so exercise discretion in your gossip. *Mubwa ukuwa twabona* (" When the dog barks we see them ")—you may not notice strangers approaching until the dogs draw your attention to them ; if you want a thing kept quiet don't chatter about it.

So they recognise that walls have ears and little birds carry news. *Kadya maluwo oku mukoa kadikubwene* (" While you are away from home visiting, your own people know all about you "). *Mweemena mu mumbwe umwini mumbwe katelele* (" If you weep in a deep pit the pit even will hear you "). *Udye ka mashiku mashiku adikubwene, u-dye ka munza munza udikubwene* (" If you eat at night the night sees you ; if you eat in the daytime the day sees you ")—whatever you do, it is sure to become known. There is a recognition of the fact that experience teaches ; and young people who want to run before they can crawl may have this saying quoted to them : *Ma mpinika!* (" Mother, give me a turned-up lip "). Here two words, like our " sour grapes," represent a story with a moral. It is the opening of a conversation between Master Wart-hog and his mother ; the little pig wanted a lip turned up by the protrusion of the tusks, like his mother's ; the old dame reminded him in answer that he would have to grow first : " I can't turn up your lip," she said, " it is only Leza who can do that."

Another series of proverbs urges the necessity of a man looking out for himself and getting all he can. *Mudimo wa mwami tokasha kudisala injina* (" The work of a chief doesn't prevent one from hunting out one's own fleas ")—if you are working for a chief that need not hinder you from minding your own affairs. Again : *Kudya mwami omwi wabula matende* (" If you eat with one chief only, it is because you have no feet "). Get all you can out of them all, even if it mean a little exertion on your part. And do not be backward in asking, remember *Muzhimo udiamba ng'udya nyama* (" The god that speaks up is the one that gets the meat "). If a god is easy-going and doesn't trouble those who neglect to sacrifice to him, he won't get anything ;

and if you don't ask you won't get. And, further, if you get a chance do not scruple to extort all you can from anybody : *Kombekache kalazhala bana badi ikumi* (" A young cow will in time bear ten calves "). If you have lent any one anything do not mind playing the usurer ; get out of him all he has. That is just what the Ba-ila do ; they are terribly hard on each other. And if people find fault with you for attempted extortion remind them that *Ushikoswe wakasukusha butale* (" The rat tried his teeth on the iron "). It may have been foolish, but, then, you never know what you can get until you try.

A more pleasant set of sayings are those used to inspire men with patience and courage. *Luvhwavhwa ndu lumana munda* (" Much coming in and out finishes the field ")—so keep at it ! *Bushiku bomwi tabubozha muzovu* (" One day is not sufficient to rot an elephant ")—Rome was not built in a day. *Ukwatakwata tabudididi* (" He who keeps hold does not lack ")—so stick to your work. To a man in great distress one would say : *Ngu menzhi kumbele* (" There is water ahead ")—do not despair. And to a man foolishly afraid : *Ulatia mushinze uina kabwenga* (" You fear the darkness that covers no hyena "). And to brace up a man to a great effort one would say : *Mulombwana muzovu uladikwela* (" A man is an elephant, he is able to draw himself ")—*i.e.* has strength sufficient for his work.

We come now to the second class of proverbs, those expressing what we may venture to call the Ba-ila criticism of life.

Many show a recognition, somewhat cynical, of certain unpleasant facts. For example, that death wipes out our memory from the minds of all but perhaps a few. *Chabola chiya ku beni* (" That which is rotten goes to its owners ")—only a few remember the dead. And the injustice of life finds many an expression. *Mukamwami uleba ubeesha bazhike bakwe* (" When a chief's wife steals she puts blame upon her slaves ")—a poor man is powerless against the rich and influential. *Mubwa n'akuwa impuwo nja mwini munzhi* (" When a dog barks the fame belongs to the master of the village "). A master takes credit for his servant's acts. On the other hand, the master discovers sometimes that his position does not give him everything : *Kwachiswa ng'ombe mabala akaya ku mubwa* (" When the ox was sick its colours went—to the dog ")—*i.e.* the subject married a fine woman, or gained some other advantage that the chief could not get.

The difference between the apparent and the real often finds expression in these proverbs : *Twabona indudi* (" We saw the houses as to the roofs ")—we did not see the interior. There is the suggestion that very often things are not what they seem. *Kusambwa itomba buzhike tabumana* (" You may cleanse yourself, but it is not to say you cease to be a slave ")—let the slave dress as well as he may, he cannot get rid of his real condition. And a man may seem happy and prosperous while really suffering shame and trouble. *Ndaseka budio, meno nchifua*, such a man might say (" I laugh emptily, my teeth are a bone "). Or : *Oka chisa kezhi mwini* (" A man knows his own woe ").

The painful fact that people cannot live long together without some quarrelling is thus expressed : *Matako aswa-ngene tabudi mutukuta* (" Buttocks rubbing together do not lack sweat ").

There is ample recognition of the fact that men follow the inclination of their minds, and that it is useless to try to force them into channels from which they are averse. *Ufuile mubidi, mozo tofuile* (" You have the body but not the heart ")—you may capture me as a slave, or compel me into marriage with you, but you cannot force me to love you. *Kapuka takashinikizhiwa umbwina mbu kata-zanda* (" An insect cannot be forced into a burrow which it does not like "). *Udi kwabo tachengwa inshima inkando* (" The man at home in thought is not to be deceived by much porridge ")—you can't retain a home-sick man by offering him plenty to eat. In brief : *Mozo ngu sungwe* (" The heart leads ").

And it is not for another to criticise me if I choose a thing he doesn't like : " de gustibus," etc. *Chikonda utwele* (" The old thing pleases him who married her ")—whatever others may say about it. *Chibi ku bantu ukudi baina nchibotu* (" What is ugly to other people is fair in the

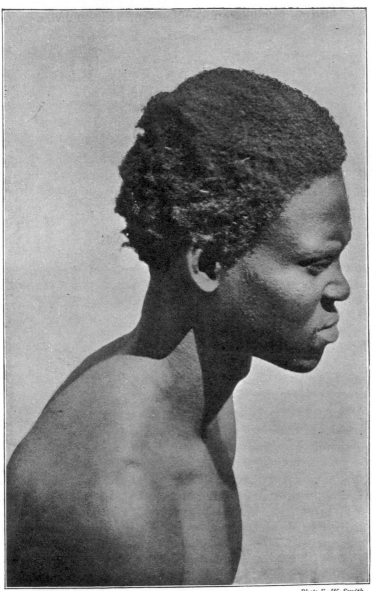

LUKENDO, A BAMBALA CHIEF.

To show style of hairdressing.

sight of its (a child's) mother ")—and it is enough if what a man has satisfies himself.

Of course a man may choose for himself, and choose foolishly, in the face of all remonstrance ; well, he must lie on the bed he made. He can't change later, it's too late. *Mulonga owatakazholwa wakwata makobo* (" A river that would not be straightened has bends in it ")—you cannot do anything for it now.

And so we come to those proverbs which give expression, more or less clearly, to the fatalism that is so characteristic of the Ba-ila. The inexorability of life, the certainty that trouble is the fate of all men, and that it is hopeless to try to avoid it ; those are their feelings. *Ulabuka bwifu* (" It will arise as surely as the stomach "). You don't know how or when ; you only know that some time or other a woman will be pregnant ; and trouble is just as certain. A cryptic saying is that : *Lufu lwina impwizhi* (" Death has no heifer "), *i.e.* it comes to all alike, though we have never seen the connection of thought. *Ushikwaze ulelala* (" Even the fish-eagle has on occasion to go to bed hungry "). *Tangala kabotu, mwana shimatwangangu, mapule adi zile* (" Rejoice circumspectly, son of my master, the enemy has come ")—be moderate in your exultation, Nemesis is bound to overtake you. *Notangala Leza udikubwene* (" When you exult, God sees you ")—and God stands for them as fate, the unconquerable powers of the universe. And if you are very happy, that may be the occasion for a swift disaster to befall you.

We may insert here a number of shrewd sayings of a miscellaneous character : *Mwami tafwi o manza ku matashi* (" A chief will not die with bracelets on his arms "), *i.e.* in a time of famine. You need not worry about a wealthy man, he can always look after himself in time of need. To the same effect is this : *Mukamwini musozha talangwa imfunda inkando* (" You do not look for a big handful for the owner of the provender "), *i.e.* the food is in his power, and he will take what he needs. *Ufwile mpeyo tatondezhiwa ku mudilo* (" He who is cold does not need to have the fire pointed out to him ")—he will go to it without being told.

So we come to the third class into which we divide Ila proverbs : smart sayings and clever metaphors rather than maxims or precepts, though included with the others in the general term *tushimpi* ("proverbs").

Thus a man deceived by another upon whose promises he was relying may say to him : *Wankuluzha olutalampi* ("You shave me with a blunt razor"). When a person is urged to something he is determined not to do, he may close the argument by ejaculating : *Mani nkuvhunika o lukwi!* ("Until I cover you up with a winnowing basket!") —an impossible feat ; he means, never! If a man has done some foolish thing, he will lament by saying : *Ndawala ibwe mu lulu* ("I threw a stone into an ant-heap")—it has gone past recovery.

One of the smartest things of this sort is the saying applied to a person who is overkind, suspiciously anxious to do you a favour : *Ukwete luse lwa mulozhi* ("He has the kindness of a witch").

Thieves are always clever in finding a way out for themselves. It is said of one that he entered a house and stole a mess of boiling porridge ; just then the owner appeared in the doorway, and, slipping his prize under his clothes, the thief gave a yell of pain—not altogether feigned —and shouted : *Nkafwile ansengwe afwila balombwanama* ("Let me get outside to die where my fellow-men died"). The owner, thinking he was dying, let him pass, and of course saw him no more. So when a man makes an outrageous excuse, you say : "Yes, let me die outside."

As we have seen, some of these sayings are allusions to what is narrated elsewhere in the folk-tales. Here is another example. It is said that a blind man was going with a friend along a road carrying firewood ; somehow he got past the other, and when his friend overtook him he was astonished to find some meat lying beside the blind man. "Oh, you've found meat!" he said. "Yes," was the ready answer, "I am waiting for you to put it on my shoulder." The friend was amazed ; how could a blind man find meat ? As a matter of fact, the first intimation the blind man had of the meat's presence was the exclamation of his friend. But he said no more and went off with the meat, leaving his friend still wondering. And the advice a Mwila will give you is : " If a companion suddenly says, ' Here's an axe ! here's a hoe ! ' don't say, ' Whose is it ? ' but say, ' Yes, my friend, please hand me my axe.' " Or, as they put it : *Waangila adiinsha mbwakachita mofu* (" You seize the fleeting chance, just as the blind man did ").

The Ba-ila are adept in expressing things in a roundabout way. Sometimes in listening to their conversations, to our amazement we could not catch the drift of a sentence. The words were Ila, sure enough, but conveyed absolutely no sense to us. It was something probably they did not want us to understand.

Even as we are writing this, we hear a man some distance off shouting : *Menso menso kumbo o kwiwe !* (" Eyes, eyes, west and east "). He means to say that travellers are approaching.

2. RIDDLES

The time and place for asking riddles is the evening around the fires. The invariable formula is this : one says *Kako !* (" This ! ") *i.e.* Here is one for you ; and the reply is : *Kakeza* (" Let it come ! "). The name for riddle is *kalabi* (plural, *tulabi*), and to answer a riddle satisfactorily is *kulabukulula*. When one propounds a riddle the others make their guesses ; if incorrect, he simply repeats it. If they despair of getting the answer, they say : *twazhimina* (" we are lost "). He then tells them and propounds another. There are probably many hundreds of these riddles in circulation and new ones are constantly being made. Some people, even young lads, know a great many. Riddles are more than mere amusement : they serve to quicken the wits. We give a few examples that we have heard around the camp-fires at night.

The student of the language will not fail to notice that in the riddles, as in the proverbs, there are many words and phrases that baffle him. Here also we find unusual or archaic words, but there are also words that have no meaning and never, seemingly, had a meaning ; they are used simply to mystify. There are also plays on words introduced for the same purpose.

1. *Musune wa Kachikumbwa ngu shilwiyalomwi.*
   Kachikumbwa's ox is a one-horned beast.
   Answer : *Lukoma*—" A calabash dipper."
The point is the dipper's long stalk used as a handle.

2. *Kazuminina kalonga kwashala isale.*
   When the brook dried up the grass (on the bank) was left.
   Answer : *Ndinso*—" It is the eye."
The idea is that when the eye goes blind the eyebrows and
   eyelashes remain as before.

3. *Kafua ka Ntite kwina owatakasola.·*
   There is nobody who has not tasted the little bone of Ntite.
   Answer : *Ndukolo*—" the breast."
There is a play on the words *ka Ntite* (" of a little bird ") and
   Katiti (" the dugs ").

4. *Mb'uzhokela.*
   As you return !
   Answer : *Chilungamo*—" Threshold."
The idea is that whenever you return home you find the threshold.

5. *Uso ndamupa matimba takamana.*
   I give your father a small cupful of (a certain kind of) porridge
       and it does not end.
   Answer : *Tulo*—" Sleep."

6. *Umwenu mukadi kombe kafula bulele.*
   At your home there is a calf that grazes lying down.
   Answer : *Mwini*—" A hoe-handle."

7. *Umwenu mukadi okasubila ifu antumba.*
   In your house there is a little thing whose stomach is red
       outside.
   Answer : *Insua*—" A calabash churn."

8. *Mupepe wa Shikwidikwikwi tobonwa mainza.*
   The feather of Shikwidikwikwi (a bird) is not seen in the
       rainy season.
   Answer : *Kambizhi*—" A whirlwind."
The point is that the name Shikwidikwikwi is applied to the
   whirlwind, and whirlwinds are not seen during the rains.

9. *Kuunga balanda mwini taunga.*
   The things possessed may blow away, the owner does not.
   Answer : *Ndulu*—" An ant-heap."
The allusion is to the flying ants.

10. *Ukwa Leza ndachileta chitasakululwa.*
   I brought a thing from God that cannot be taken off like
       clothes.
   Answer : *Matwi*—" Ears."

11. *Munzhila ndayana chitaamba.*
    In the road I found something that does not speak.
    Answer : *Banyama*—" Animals."

12. *Bimbile uvhunikile a mai akwe.*
    A hawk that covers up its eggs !
    Answer : *Nduludi*—" It's a roof."

13. *Muzovu umina ch'amba mwifu.*
    An elephant that swallows something which speaks in its
        stomach.
    Answer : *Ing'anda*—" A house."

14. *Balumbu ninkuti kutena.*
    Foreigners that are covered all over.
    Answer : *Inyemo*—" Ground-nuts."

15. *Ukwa Leza ndakachileta chanda chitapapuka.*
    From God I brought a forked stick which does not split.
    Answer : *Chifunzhi*—" Shoulder."

16. *Owakafwa ngu mpampa, umudyezhina ngu mpampa.*
    He who dies is *Mpampa* and the heir is also *Mpampa*.
    Answer : *Ngongwa*—" A grub."

17. *Owakafwa ngu choye, umudyezhina ngu choye.*
    He who died is *Choye* and the heir is also *Choye*.
    Answer : *Mbwiya*—" It is a thorn."

18. *Ku mulonga twakwatana o Nkamba.*
    At the river I had a wrestle with Nkamba.
    Answer : *Mbutezhi*—" A slippery place."
    Kukamba means to clutch : the man who made the riddle was
    at the river one day and slipped in the mud ; falling, he
    clutched the ground. Putting it into the form of an enigma
    to puzzle his hearers, he makes the word *kamba* (" clutch ")
    into a proper name Nkamba, and says he had a wrestle
    with him.

19. *Baambana bami.*
    The chiefs are having a dispute.
    Answer : *Matende*—" The feet."

20. *Kakalo katazuminini.*
    A little spring that never dries up.
    Answer : *Ndinango dia umbwa*—" It's a dog's nose."

21. *Mukamwami owakeza kupukwa ndi aba ikadi.*
    The wife of a chief who came to have her hair dressed and
        became a resident.
    Answer : *Nditovu*—" It's a leaf."

Photo Rev. W. Chapman.

A GANG OF BA-ILA CARRIERS.

22. *Ndatenta isokwe mubalo washala.*
    I burnt the veld and the crooked stick remained.
    Answer : *Ninzhila*—" It's a road."

23. *Mung'anda ya muchembele mulatonkwa ishishi diomwi.*
    Into the house of the old man you can only push one firestick.
    Answer : *Ndinango*—" It's the nostril."
i.e. You can only push one finger at a time into the nostril.

24. *Twamupa, twamunanga.*
    We give it to him and then take it away.
    Answer : *Inkidi*—" A stamping-block," *i.e.* we put grain in
    and take it out as meal.

25. *Twakeenda oba ch'ambuka-ambuka.*
    We travelled with those who were constantly going off the
        road.
    Answer : *Mubwa*—" A dog."

26. *Obadi awa kutaanzha.*
    Those here do not salute.
    Answer : *Ninkuku*—" It is fowls."

27. *Kachea okachina tata.*
    It is a small thing that choked my father.
    Answer : *Tulo*—" Sleep."   Cf. No. 5.
The word for " sleep " is a diminutive.

28. *Kaka kalonga menzhi katola kwi ?*
    This little river, where does the water go to ?
    Answer : *Chibia chidi a mudilo*—" A pot on the fire."
The point is the evaporation of the water in the pot.

29. *Muzovu tanwi u mukalo.*
    The elephant does not drink from a spring.
    Answer : *Mbwato*—" It's a canoe."

30. *Twayaya munyama twadya bula, isalo twasowa.*
    We killed an animal, ate the inside and threw away the
        skin.
    Answer : *Fulwe*—" A tortoise."

31. *Ndayaya intite, ibanda diezula buloa.*
    I killed a little bird and the plain filled with blood.
    Answer : *Mudilo*—" Fire."

32. *Bula bwa shiluwe tabukala inzhi.*
    The intestine of a leopard is not to be sat upon by a fly.
    Answer : *Mudilo*—" Fire."

33. *Ndo wanshia, ndo wanshia.*
    My dear, you leave me !   My dear, you leave me !
    Answer : *Matende*—" Feet."

34. *Bachungwe bakala isamo diomwi.*
The fish-eagles that sit on one tree.
Answer : *Matwi*—" The ears."

35. *Umwesu mung'anda mukadi kaumbo katavhunukulwa.*
At our home there is a little receptacle that is not to be uncovered.
Answer : *Chilendi*—" A grave."

36. *Kachea kadindi kezwile bulengwa Leza.*
The hole is small that is full of God's creation.
Answer : *Maila*—" Grain."

37. *Machela ataandana.*
Bellows-spouts which do not separate.
Answer : *Izuba o mwezhi*—" The sun and moon."

38. *Mbwakalukankila.*
How he ran away !
Answer : *Kabwenga*—" A hyena."

39. *Ni kuluma tokusha.*
Although it bites you, you can't get rid of it.
Answer : *Mutwi*—" The head."

40. *Ku kuya ndachiyana, ku kuzhoka shichiyene.*
Going I found it, returning I found it not.
Answer : *Mume*—" The dew."

41. *Kulampa nku baanzhika insazhi Bambala.*
It is high that the Bambala hang up their pots of fat.
Answer : *Mangvhuma*—" Fruit of the palm."

42. *Kabwe ka lubanza tokakonzha kukapapula.*
A little stone in the courtyard which you cannot pull up with two hands.
Answer : *Mukofu*—" A scar."

43. *Bana ba Mala balamba chilambo chomwi.*
People of Mala who all whiten themselves in one way.
Answer : *Bachikwangala*—" White-breasted crows."

44. *Chakolela mushinze chiloba.*
The old thing endured the dark seven days.
Answer : *Inkidi*—" A stamping-block."

45. *Ndadima munda kutebula mwitashi.*
I cultivated a field and the harvest was in my hand.
Answer : *Masusu*—" The hair."

46. *Ulaamba zwanga chikutu udi umwini.*
The old dry thing talked tumultuously all by itself.
Answer : *Ndisamo*—" It's a tree."

47. *Ndawala mwitala.*
   Something I threw over to the other side of the river.
   Answer : *Menso*—" Eyes."

The following are examples of another kind of riddle,
in which the answer is given not in a word but in a phrase.

48. *Mbu bakaila.*
   Answer : *Obafwa tabazhoka.*
   Since they went away !   The dead do not return !

49. *Kwa lampa !*
   Answer : *Okwa Leza nkule !*
   It is far !   And it's a long way to God !

Finally we may notice a series of riddles that are more
than riddles.   The enigma propounded is the same all the
way through ; the answer takes different forms.   They are
a kind of catechism challenging the self-complacency of
men who think they know everything.   They seem like
a weak echo of some passages in the Book of Job—
" Knowest thou . . . ?   Canst thou . . . ? " [1]

> *Nudi mwelwe*—" You who are so clever ! "
> *Mu chivhuna cha mbwila tozuba mo !*
> " You can't hide away under a bean plant ! "
>
> *Nudi mwelwe*—" You who are so clever ! "
> *Ing'ombe ya kwenu divhwelene mukupa toiboni !*
> " When the milk of your cows is put together you can't tell
>   which is which ! "
>
> *Nudi mwelwe !*—" You who are so clever ! "
> *Ing'ombe sha kwenu disangana ing'ombe ya beni toizhiba !*
> " When your cow is mixed up with a stranger's herd you
>   can't distinguish it ! "
>
> *Nudi mwelwe !*—" You who are so clever ! "
> *Ansonga sha masumo tokala o.*
> " You can't sit on the point of a spear."
>
> *Nudi mwelwe !*—" You who are so clever ! "
> *Mwenzhi toanga mwavhu !*
> " You can't tie water in a lump ! "
>
> *Nudi mwelwe !*—" You who are so clever ! "
> *Menzhi ulaanga o musantu ?*
> " And can you tie water up in a bundle ? "

---

[1] We do not mean, of course, that they are copied from the Book of
Job.   They are indigenous sayings.

Nudi mwelwe !—" You who are so clever ! "
No mai a nkuku ulabona mudiango ?
" Can you make out the doorway of a fowl's egg ? "

Nudi mwelwe !—" You who are so clever ! "
No muntu umishi ulamubona ati wedia udimishi ?
" In the early days can you tell that a woman is pregnant ? "

Nudi mwelwe !—" You who are so clever ! "
Mishu ya nkuku wakebona ?
" Did you ever see a fowl's urine ? "

Noba mwelwe !—" You who have grown so clever ! "
*Sa mukaintu ulamwizhiba ati udimishi mulombwana na
    mukaintu ?*
" Can you tell whether the woman is pregnant of a male or
    female ? "

Noba mwelwe !—" You who have grown so clever ! "
Mai ulezhiba ati ledi iyi mukombwe na inseke ?
" And as for eggs, do you know whether this egg is a cock or
    a hen ? "

Noba mwelwe !—" You who have grown so clever ! "
Sa inzhila ulakeenzha nj'iela ?
" Can you follow up a road to where it ends ? "

Noba mwelwe !—" You who have grown so clever ! "
Sa lufu lwako ulaluzhiba ati uzona ndafwa ?
" As for your own death, do you know whether you will die
    to-morrow ? "

Noba mwelwe !—" You who have grown so clever ! "
Sa chingvhule ulachikwata ?
" Can you catch hold of a shadow ? "

Noba mwelwe !—" You who have grown so clever ! "
Sa chilonda chidi kunuma ulachitulula buti ?
" If you have an abscess on your back, can you lance it
    yourself ? "

Noba mwelwe !—" You who have grown so clever ! "
Mubiabe sa ulamubwezha mwifu ati abote ?
" Can you put an ugly person back into the womb to be
    reborn handsome ? "

3. CONUNDRUMS

Besides their ordinary folk-tales, which are dealt with
in the next chapter, the Ba-ila have stories which take
the form of conundrums or problems. We have only got

three examples of these.   Their likeness to familiar problems in our own tongue is evident, especially the third one, but they seem to be genuinely native productions and not borrowed from Europeans.[1]

1. A certain man had five children, four sons and a daughter. He died, leaving his widow and the five children. Some time afterwards the daughter was missing, and nobody could make out what had become of her.

The mother called her sons together and set them to finding their sister. They were remarkably gifted men.

The eldest, by reason of his wisdom, was able to see things at a very great distance. On casting his eyes around he discovered his sister fifty miles away in the clutches of a lion.

Consternation ! What was to be done ? The brothers went off.

One of them, who had the gift of stealing in unseen, made himself invisible and was able to rescue his sister from the lion's claws.

The lion on missing its prey went rampaging about, but the third brother killed it.

Then they took up the girl and carried her home. But she was dead. On reaching home they began to make preparations for the funeral, but the fourth son said, "Wait!" He went off into the forest, got some medicines, and restored her to life.

The mother was overjoyed, and taking a large piece of meat she gave it to her sons, saying : "Eat, my sons. I give it you in gratitude for your cleverness and faithfulness."

But the brothers said : "No, give it to only one of us—the one who did most in giving our sister back to you safe ! "

Here is the problem : To whom was she to give the meat ? To him who discovered the girl first at a great distance ; to him who rescued her from the lion ; to him who killed the lion ; or to him who restored her to life ? Each seems dependent upon the others. Who got the meat ?

Natives argue long and excitedly about this, but nobody has ever yet determined the question. It is said that once they took the problem to Lewanika and it was argued in the khotla at Lealui, but even he was baffled.

2. A man and his wife went to visit their friends. On their return homewards they were accompanied by their respective mothers. On the road, the four were set upon by all manner of horrible creatures—lions, snakes, leopards, etc. etc. They managed to elude them and got to a river.

---

[1] Since writing these down we have read two similar ones in *Congo Life and Folklore*, by Rev. J. H. Weeks, pp. 43, 122.

There they found a canoe, but to their horror it would only hold three people. Their enemies were pressing hard upon their trail. The river was full of crocodiles ; they couldn't hope to swim. Only three could escape. One must die ! Who was it to be ?

The man sacrificed his mother-in-law, you say. No ! His wife would not allow him. She would not desert her mother, nor he his : the elders would not forsake their children.

How did they get out of their difficulty ?

The native answer is that they all sat down on the river-bank and died together.

3. A man travelling with a leopard, a rat, a goat, and a basket of corn arrived at a river, and found that the only means of crossing was a very small canoe that would hold only himself and one other thing. He put the leopard into the canoe and started off : but as soon as his back was turned the rat commenced to eat the corn.

" This won't do," said he, " I shall have no corn left."

He went back and took the rat ; but the leopard, now left behind, began to eat the goat.

" This won't do," said he, " I shall have no goat left."

He put back again. But when he came to select his load, he was puzzled. Should he sacrifice the rat or the leopard ? No, they were his children, he could not part with them.

What, then, did he do ?

The native answer is that he stayed where he was.

CHAPTER XXVIII

*

FOLK-TALES

INTRODUCTION

A SAVAGE people is no more than a civilised people to be understood apart from its literature. The Ba-ila, like all the Bantu, have no written lore, it is true, but they have a considerable amount of oral lore ; and these fables and proverbs, myths and legends, handed down from generation to generation, all throw a most vivid light upon the moral and mental constitution of the people.

In this chapter we give, out of a larger collection, sixty-one examples of Ila tales, which were almost all written down by one of us from dictation, the only exceptions being those few, not more than six in all, which were written for us by intelligent natives.[1] Moreover, allowing for the translation, we have given them precisely as they were dictated or written, and the translation is as literal as possible consonant with smoothness and intelligibility. They might have been improved by altering the sequence of some sentences and pruning away some of the redundancies, but we did not wish so to retouch them as to obliterate the characteristics of the original.

We have to reconcile ourselves to the fact that for us, at least, it is impossible to do justice to these tales, and we doubt if the most skilful hand could reproduce in a translation the quaintness, the liveliness, and humour of the original. For one thing, fully to appreciate them one

[1] The originals of some of the tales will be found in the writer's *Ila Handbook* and *Ila Reader No. 2* ("The Adventures of Sulwe and his Friends").

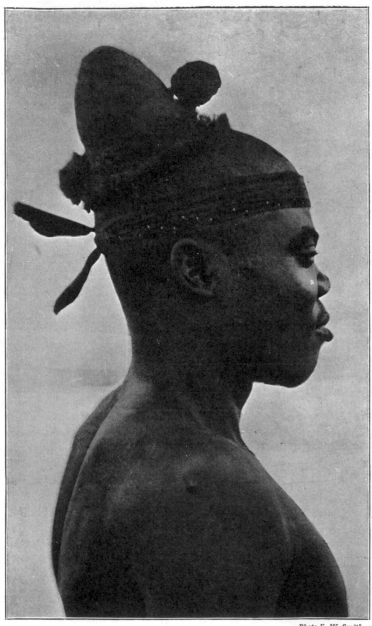

A MWILA : A GREAT TELLER OF TALES.

must be familiar, as only those who have always lived in the country can be familiar, with the characteristics of the animals spoken of ; and then they gradually lose flavour as they pass from the African's telling, first into writing and then into a foreign idiom. It would need a combination of phonograph and kinematograph to reproduce a tale as it is told. One listens to a clever story-teller, as was our old friend Mungalo, from whom we derived many of these tales. Speak of eloquence ! Here was no lip mumbling, but every muscle of face and body spoke, a swift gesture often supplying the place of a whole sentence. He would have made a fortune as a raconteur upon the English stage. The animals spoke each in its own tone : the deep rumbling voice of Momba, the ground hornbill, for example, con- trasting vividly with the piping accents of Sulwe, the hare. It was all good to listen to—impossible to put on paper. Ask him now to repeat the story slowly so that you may write it. You will, with patience, get the gist of it, but the unnaturalness of the circumstance disconcerts him, your repeated request for the repetition of a phrase, the absence of the encouragement of his friends, and, above all, the hampering slowness of your pen, all combine to kill the spirit of story-telling. Hence we have to be content with far less than the tales as they are told. And the tales need effort of imagination to place readers in the stead of the original listeners.

It is at evening around the fires that the tales are told, especially on dark nights, when the people cannot dance so comfortably. Many of the tales are known far and wide, others in lesser areas. But, however often the people hear them, they never seem weary of the repetition. They never say, " Oh, that's an old tale," or make sarcastic references to chestnuts, but enter into the spirit of the thing all the more for knowing all that is to come. They heard the tales first as children from their mothers or grandmothers, but nevertheless they will, with no trace of boredom, come in with their ejaculations just at the right points, take, it may be, a sentence out of the narrator's mouth, or even keep up a running echo of his words.

We have divided the tales into four parts. The first

contains etiological or explanatory myths. It is usual to
regard savages as uneducated people, and, as far as books
are concerned, they certainly are, but in the book of
Nature they are well read. From an early age they learn
to recognise the animals, to distinguish their footprints
and cries, to know their names, their habitats and customs.
And not only are they keen observers, they reflect on the
facts, and, comparing the facts one with another, they want
to know the reasons of things. They ask not so much, How?
as Why? Why are things as they are? Some of the
questions are serious enough; certain of them exercise the
minds of cultured men among ourselves. Why are monkeys
so like and yet so different from men? How is it that men
came to kill each other? What is the origin of the domestic
fire? Other questions are more puerile. Why has the
zebra alone of the *banyama* no horns? Why does the
honey-guide lead people to honey? Why are the leopard
and cheetah so much alike in appearance and so diverse
in character? The answers to such questions are embodied
in tales. If the explanations are naïve, they bear witness
to considerable powers of observation and reflection, of
imagination and humour.

Data for answering these questions are almost entirely
or quite absent. We could not ourselves give any rational
answer to some of them. Why has the zebra no horns?
Who can say? It is better to use the fact and construct
an amusing, and, in this instance, an instructive tale upon
it than simply not to ask the question and cease to take an
interest in the matter.

As for these explanations, it will be seen that none of
them is assigned to any natural cause, but all to personal
volition. And not always, indeed but rarely, to that of
higher powers. It seems that in the ancient time, when
things were still fluid, before animals and men had assumed
their final forms, it was possible for one creature to affect
another, favourably or adversely, by merely pronouncing
its destiny. Thus Mintengwe, the blackbird, dooms the
rest of the feathered tribe to persecution and death; and
tortoise confers on hare the dignity of pre-eminent wisdom.
Here, of course, we have the world-wide belief in the efficacy

of the spoken word, whether for curse or blessing. It is significant that much of the destiny of the animals concerned is the outcome of lying and cheating. Many of them get what they want by downright chicane. Thus, in the beginning, the hippopotamus wore horns and the rhinoceros tusks, and the reverse state of things, as we see it to-day, has come through the former's thievery. Sometimes, as in the case of the elephant and the wart-hog, an exchange of ornaments meant to be temporary is, by the treachery of one of the parties, made permanent. Sometimes a promise is made and not fulfilled ; and so the tailless squirrel came into possession of the fine bushy tail of the coney, who ever since has been so ashamed of himself that he lives in the obscurity of the rocks. Occasionally a plan is made to intoxicate invited guests for the purpose of robbing them of some coveted property ; it was in this way that the duiker got his handsome dress away from the oribi. And, once again, it is a common thing to get another person into trouble by leading people to believe that he and not yourself was the thief ; it was so that leopard and cheetah received their various destinies. In one case, it is not knavery but something like gratitude that settles the fate ; the lion is granted the kingship over the animal world because he helped the troubled tortoise by showing it how to dig a burrow.

But, whether it springs from good or evil, it is always a person that affects the destiny. This, one may say, is typical of the higher native thought, that explains things not by mere self-acting dynamism but by the activity of the will.

This assumes, of course, that the makers of these tales regarded these animals as persons capable of volition. We are not prepared to say that sophisticated listeners to these tales to-day all believe that animals act and speak like men, however eagerly they may receive the tales ; but most of the natives would, we believe, accept them as veridical. Perhaps some of them, if pressed hard, would turn round and say, as the little girl of our acquaintance once did, after a dramatical performance with her dolls and teddy bears: "we're only 'tending." But, however it may be with present-day retailers of the stories, we are confident that the tales arose in the stage of culture when the vital differences between men and animals were not yet recognised. In this respect it is significant that, grammatically, the animals with few exceptions are classed as persons. The great scholar, Dr. Bleek, in the days when Bantu folklore was just beginning to be studied, imagined that all animal tales were derived from the Hottentots and Bushmen, because, their languages being " sex-denoting," it was easy and natural for them to personify animals, while the Bantu, owing to the nature of their languages, could not. We know now that, without being " sex-denoting," these languages have a remarkable facility for personification. In Ila, as in all Bantu tongues, the first class of nouns contains personal substantives. Thus *chi-ntu* (" a thing "), of the seventh class, becomes *mu-ntu* (" a person ") by giving the root the personal prefix, *mu-*. In Suto the ordinary word for lion is *tau* ; in the tales it is *motau* (" Mr. Lion "). In Ila the names of animals mostly need no change of this kind, because they belong to the personal class. In form, such names as *kabwenga* (" hyena ") and *chibizi* (" zebra ") may appear to be neuter nouns of classes 6 and 7 respectively, but really they are of the first class, taking the plural prefix *ba-* and all the pronouns proper to those nouns ; that is to say, the animal is never referred to as " it " but always as " he." In the tales, if you did not know that Sulwe meant " hare," you would never dream it was not a person being spoken of. It was not unnatural for the makers of these tales to ascribe human characteristics to the lower animals, for they did not recognise any psychical difference between them and us.

We have thrown into a separate division the tales which narrate the adventures of Sulwe, the hare. He deserves a section to himself. He is the most popular of all the dramatis personae. In the minds of the Ba-ila he embodies all subtlety. He is skilful in practical jokes; he is cruel, he is cunning, he is false ; a Macchiavel, a Tartuffe, a downright rogue. He should be a despicable character, but the Ba-ila shake and roll about with laughter as they listen, for the hundredth time, to his adventures. Nor

can we resist joining in the laughter ; he is such a droll
creature that we forget his treacherous conduct.

Sulwe is only a small creature, but, with one exception,
all the animals are as clay in his hands.   He offers to nurse
Mrs. Lion's children and eats them one by one, meanwhile
heartlessly deceiving the mother into thinking them still
alive.   He wants to drink beer at a feast, and on being
told that no animal without horns may do so, he deliberately shapes himself horns of beeswax and mingles with
the company, only to flee when the horns melt in the heat of
the fire, though not before he has had his fill of beer.   He
entraps his fellows into all kinds of unpleasant situations.
And so he dances his merry way through life.   Only one
animal gets the better of him and that is Fulwe, the Tortoise.
In the expressive words of *Uncle Remus* about Brer
Tarrypin : " Honey, he tuck'n made a fool out'n 'im."
In the famous race between the two animals Fulwe wins,
not by patient running, but by cunningly hiding her family
in numbers along the course, so that whenever Sulwe halts
to jeer at his rival he hears a Tortoise ahead of him crying
to him to Come on ! until after days of running he gives
in exhausted, and the Tortoise, as fresh as ever, brings him
water from the river that was their goal.   And in the last
act of this wonderful drama, it is Fulwe who finally beats
Sulwe.   There is a drought, and the animals meet to dig
a well—all but Sulwe, who refuses to dig.   He comes at
night and cunningly manages to tie up the sentries one
after another ; then Fulwe offers to keep watch, has himself covered with birdlime, and when Sulwe brushes past
him in contempt he sticks fast, and the more he fights the
faster he sticks, and is ignominiously slain by his enraged
victims.

These two creatures, Sulwe and Fulwe, who, in the minds
of the Ba-ila, are rivals in cunning and far surpass the
other animals, are in many respects the very antithesis the
one of the other : the Tortoise is the slowest as the Hare
is the swiftest.   It is not difficult to understand why the
Hare should be regarded as he is.   He is extremely wary ;
as poachers and others in England know, it is most difficult
to entrap him.   He has the power, more than most animals,

of lying low and saying nothing. You may step over him in the veld and never know he is there. We were once pitching our tent in the bush—-standing with a number of men together, when from out, it seemed, beneath our feet there darted a hare. The incident caused immense excitement among our men, and that night, and for many nights afterwards, it was cited as an example of Sulwe's amazing wisdom. He had come, they declared, especially to study the white man and his ways, and having seen all, had gone off to tell the other animals. And, of course, this swiftness of foot which enables him so quickly to escape from his enemies, is another element in his reputation for cleverness. The wisdom of Fulwe, the Tortoise, is, on the other hand, founded on its power of shutting itself up tightly in its shell and the difficulty of killing it. So we have two types of cunning—the active and the passive ; the one which gains by nimbleness, the other by quiescence ; the one goes abroad to seek its victims, the other circumvents those who come to it. And in the estimation of the Ba-ila, the slow-moving, passive, undemonstrative kind of cunning is the one that wins in the long run.

In sketching these animals, not Sulwe and Fulwe only, but all the animals in these tales, the Ba-ila are sketching themselves. The virtues they esteem, the vices they condemn, the follies they ridicule—-all are here in the animals. It is a picture of Ba-ila drawn by Ba-ila, albeit unconsciously, and valuable accordingly. In the hero, Sulwe, we may find some at least of the characteristics that the African most admires. The tales show us that he esteems mind above physical strength, brain above brawn. The Elephant and the Lion are types of the latter, the Hare of the former, and Sulwe always wins ; if at last he is beaten it is only by superior cunning. In real life among the Bantu, it is not so much a Hector as an Odysseus that prevails ; even in those cases where, as with Moshesh and Chaka and Sebitwane, the chief is also a great warrior, he does more by subtlety than by the assegai. The greatest figure in Basuto history is not Moshesh but Mohlomi, the mystic and seer. The most powerful persons, because most feared, among the Ba-ila are the *munganga* and *musonzhi*, the doctor and diviner, who with much knowledge have also abundance of wit and cunning. Yes, the Ba-ila appreciate mind, but the type that appeals most to them is the Sulwe type or the Fulwe type : to get the better of one's neighbours without being found out—that is wisdom. We wonder in reading these tales that the great beasts should so readily be deceived ; could they not see through Sulwe's specious lying and clumsy stratagems ? Our wonder ceases when here, too, we recognise a picture of the people. Along certain lines the Ba-ila are the most credulous of men ; the greatest liar finds the readiest credence. We have only to think of the various " prophets " that arise with marvellous claims, and the way in which they jockey the people into parting with their goods, to realise that Sulwe is no overdrawn picture.

We have no intention of making an excursion into the fields of comparative folklore, but it is worth while, perhaps, just to point out in a paragraph that similar tales to these we give are told throughout Africa. Indeed it might be claimed that Africa is the home of animal tales. Was not the greatest fabulist of all an African ?—the famous Lokman to whom Mohammed inscribed the 31st Sura of the Koran, and whom the Greeks, not knowing his real name, called Aesop, *i.e.* Ethiops ? Be that as it may, we can claim the stories of *Uncle Remus* as African in origin ; they were taken by the slaves across to America. Brer Rabbit, Brer Tarrypin, and many others in that collection, are the same as our Sulwe and Fulwe and the rest. Not only are similar tales told by the Ba-ila to-day, but actually, allowing for certain changes of detail due to the different environment, the same tales. An excellent example is given on p. 377 : the tug-of-war between Hippo and Rhino is that in " Brer Tarrypin shows his Strength " in *Uncle Remus*. We have inserted notes at the foot of the tales, drawing attention to resemblances we have noticed between the Ba-ila tales and those from other peoples.

The persistence of the same incidents in tales coming from such widely separate African tribes is not to be accounted for by any hypothesis of borrowing, but seems

to point to the fact that before the Bantu migrated from
their original home in the north, they already possessed
these tales. If that is so, we are dealing with things not of
yesterday, but of two or three thousand years ago. That
would not, of course, apply to all the tales, many of them
may be quite modern. The day will come perhaps, when,
by comparing such collections of tales from different parts
of the field, we shall be able to get some idea which are
ancient.

The remaining sections of our collection contain respectively tales of people and animals, and tales of people—
mostly fools. These will speak for themselves and do
not require much by way of introduction.

Many of them have a special name given to them, *i.e.*
Kashimi. All the other tales were made, and are told, for
amusement, with no didactic purpose, but these have a
definite aim. They end with the words : *Inzho bamushima,*
which means, " And so they make a byword of him, put
him on record as an example not to be followed." A nagging woman, an ungrateful, cruel son, a querulous wife, a
man who hurts himself, a naughty child, silly women who
entrust their children to old hags, fools who do not understand—all are put on record as solemn or humorous warnings to the younger generation.

In these latter tales there is apparent a certain strait-
ness of fancy. By taking animals and not men as the usual
figures of the tales they are following instinctively a safer
path. Animals are a more fluid medium than men. In
dealing with men the fabulist encounters obstructions to
his imagination. In speaking of them men must not cease
to be men, otherwise hearers can always say they have
never known such beings. But in telling about animals
he has the advantage that they are comparatively unknown ; their forms and habits may be familiar enough,
but not their inward life, and a large part of their outward
life is also unknown. He has therefore a wide field, he can
keep up the names of the animals and certain well-known
habits, and all the rest he can fill in out of his own mind ;
they act as he might act if he were not so hampered by the
limitation of human power. To his mind those limitations

are not drawn so straitly as they are with ourselves. Without going beyond what he believes to be actual human experience, he can conceive the animals doing things which we should deem out of all reason, and from these he can glide into highly imaginative situations without too rude a shock to the credulity of his hearers. He lifts the curtain surrounding them and portrays his heroes doing things themselves would like to do but cannot. And the minds of the listeners are turned from the cramping actualities of life into the wider, freer, ideal world, and so find relief and refreshment.

To us there is a lack of coherence in many of the details, and explicit contradictions pull us up and spoil our pleasure, as when Fulwe, after being cooked and eaten, gives Sulwe his doom. But such things do not annoy the Ba-ila or detract from their enjoyment. For one thing Fulwe, though dead, lives in his race ; it is a mere accident that one individual dies ; it is the ideal Fulwe, not the Fulwe who merely breathes, but the Fulwe in the narrator's mind, and *he* is immortal.

If we cannot always appreciate the humour of these tales, we have to remember that ideas of humour vary according to race. Certainly to the Ba-ila they are full of humour ; they roll about and laugh themselves almost into hysterics when they hear the tales. What are the things that appeal thus to them ?

First of all, they find exquisite delight in the buffoonery. The rough, practical jokes of Sulwe, with his absurd dressing up, his slashing and chopping, his breaking of teeth, and all the rest of it, are distinctly humorous to them. And it must be said, too, that to them facility in deception is humorous. Sulwe owes his popularity very largely to his unveracity and his diabolical skill in deceiving those bulkier than himself. And as with ourselves, the element of incongruity in many of these situations appeals to their sense of humour. The incongruity between Hare and Elephant in point of size, makes them laugh when the little ties up the big. The mildness of the Hare and the ferocity of the Lion in actual life make it all the more amusing when Sulwe ties the Lion up and deceives him in other ways. One of the stories full of humour to them is that of the Hippo and Rhino. When one asks the other for his razor and he replies that he took it to shave his wife with, we have a very incongruous scene ; the idea of such huge, unwieldy creatures using a small delicate instrument such as a razor, and the fact that neither of them has much hair to speak of, and so needs no shaving—this is what constitutes the humour. Smart sayings, clever retorts, and cryptic utterances also appeal to their sense of humour. When, for example, Hare, carrying unknown to himself his mother in a bundle, and greeted the first time in a village, makes no answer, his companions, who know the secret, give cryptic replies which puzzle Sulwe ; he discovers the secret, and is ready with his reply when next he is greeted : " Cunning he has who cunning has," says he. That is all a very amusing incident to the Ba-ila. And they delight also in plays on words and the mistakes people make in misunderstanding words that are similar in pronunciation but different in meaning. General obtuseness of mind is also humorous to them. It is these things which give point to the stories of fools, of which we give a few examples.

It may be said in conclusion, that man's common human-heartedness is in these tales. Grief and joy are shown to touch the same chords in their breasts as in ours. How simply, yet how touchingly, are the fundamental human emotions described : the love of parents, the grief that accompanies bereavement, the joy in offspring—these, as well as the jealousy, the envy, the malice of our human nature find place here. Separated by deep gulfs as they are from ourselves in many things, yet across the abysses we can clasp hands in a common humanity.

PART I

ETIOLOGICAL OR EXPLANATORY TALES

1. *How the Mason-Wasp fetched Fire from God*

VULTURE, Fish-eagle, and Crow were without fire, for there was no fire on earth. So, needing fire, all the birds assembled together and asked : " Whence shall we find fire ? " Some of the birds said : " Perhaps from God." Thereupon Mason-Wasp volunteered, saying : " Who will go with me to God ? " Vulture answered and said : " We will go with you, I and Fish-eagle and Crow."

So on the morrow they took leave of all the other birds, saying : " We are going to see whether we can get fire from God." Then they flew off. After they had spent ten days on the road, there fell to earth some small bones—that was Vulture ; later, there also fell to earth some other small bones—that was Fish-eagle ; Mason-Wasp and Crow were left to go on alone. When the second ten days were ended, there fell other small bones to earth—that was Crow. Mason-Wasp was left to go on by himself. When the third ten days were over, he was going along, reposing upon the clouds. Nevertheless he never reached the summit of the sky.

As soon as God heard of it, He came to where Mason-Wasp was, and answering His question Mason-Wasp said : " No, Chief, I am not going anywhere particular, I have only come to beg some fire. All my companions have stopped short ; but, nevertheless, I have persevered in coming, for I had set my heart upon arriving to where the Chief is." Thereupon God answered him, saying : " Mason-Wasp, since you have reached Me, you shall be chief over all the birds and reptiles on earth. You, now, I give a blessing. You shall not have to beget children. When you desire a child, go and look into a grainstalk and you will find an insect whose name is Ngongwa. When you have found him, take and carry him into a house. When you arrive in the house, look out for the fireplace where men cook, and build there a dwelling for your child Ngongwa. When you have finished building, put him in and let him remain there. When many days have elapsed, just go and have a look at him ; and one day you will find he has changed and become just as you are yourself."

So it is to-day : Mason-Wasp builds a house, looking for the fireplace, just as he was commanded by God.

NOTE.—The Mason-Wasp, the Prometheus of the Ba-ila, with its indigo-blue wings, yellow abdomen, and black and orange legs, is a common object in Central Africa. It builds its cell of mud not only on the fireplaces, as the tale narrates, but also (and in this is a great nuisance) on walls, books, and pictures in one's dwelling. In the cell it lays its eggs, together with a caterpillar or grub, and seals them up ; then it builds other cells, until quite a large unsightly lump of clay is left on the wall. As the young grubs hatch out they eat the insects which have been benumbed, but not killed, by the sting of their parent. We have here an interesting example of how the observation of natives is correct up to a certain point ; but not taking into consideration, because they have not noticed, all the facts, the conclusion they draw is wrong. They suppose Ngongwa to metamorphose into a Mason-Wasp ; and this tale is to explain why it is so, as well as to account for the domestic fire.

2. *The Story of the Blue-Jay who married the Daughter of God*

Long ago Blue-Jay had a wife. After a time he went to God ; he went to seek the Daughter of God as his wife. God replied : " Since you ask for her, you must not take her to the earth, you must stay just here in the sky. Because, if you take her to the earth, she may not eat meat of Zebra or Gnu or Kudu ; of any large animal she may not eat. If you desire to carry her to earth, let her eat only of the smaller animals." Blue-Jay answered : " It is well, Chief."

So Blue-Jay was allowed to bring the Daughter of God to earth. Upon his arrival on earth he told these things to his earthly wife, saying : " I was told by God that His child may not eat of Zebra or Gnu or Kudu ; she may not eat of any large animal." These things he told his wife and mother ; when they heard them, his mother said : " It is well, my child." Nevertheless his wife was terribly jealous.

One day Blue-Jay went off hunting. He went and killed a Zebra and a young Duiker. When he returned to his first wife, he ordered her, saying : " You must on no account give my wife the meat of the Zebra. Let her eat only of the young Duiker." His wife replied : " It is well."

Another day while Blue-Jay was out walking, the old wife deceived her fellow, the Daughter of God, giving her zebra meat and saying : " Eat, it is young Duiker." But she was simply deceiving her. As soon as the Daughter of

God ate it, she died. Then Blue-Jay returned ; on his arrival he asked : " My wife ! What has she died of ? " The old wife replied : " I don't know."

Nevertheless God had seen her from the sky. Said He : " It is that one yonder who killed My child."

Thereupon Blue-Jay returned to the sky ; on arrival he went to tell the news, saying : " My wife is dead, Chief." God answered, saying : " You forgot the orders I gave you that My child must not eat of Zebra or Gnu or Kudu ; nevertheless, there on earth you went and gave her it. She ate and died." Then Blue-Jay replied : " It may be so, Chief." God answered : " Return."

When thirty days had passed, God gathered together a small cloud. Then He opened wide His mouth and thundered. After a time He descended and swept open the grave in which His child was buried ; He took her out and carried her to the sky. Nevertheless, Blue-Jay did not survive ; He took him away also. When He arrived midway He thrust him down to earth ; but he never arrived : only some small bones reached the ground. He died just there midway. To this very day this is what Blue-Jay does : when he flies he goes up into the air with a loud cry ; on the point of descending he dies.

NOTE.—This idea of Chikambwe's fate is still prevalent, so that any one in charge of a child will, on seeing the bird, distract the child's attention from it, lest by seeing or hearing it the child should become like it in dying a sudden death. Its feathers are made into a charm against a similar fate.

The tale illustrates, as we have seen, the Ba-ila conception of God (see p. 207). Blue-Jay, it is evident, is held responsible for the wrong-doing of his household.

3. How God first gave Men Grain and Fruits

Long ago when God caused men to descend to earth, He gave them grain, and said : " Take good care of the grain." On their arrival, they cultivated the grain and got a fine harvest. When they had gathered it, they put it into their temporary bins. Having put it into their temporary bins, they ate ; they ate bread, but (extravagant people) they ate during the day. Having eaten all day, they said: " This great quantity of meal will never get finished, whereas we are altogether satisfied." So as they were filled, they said : " Let us burn the grain." And they rose up with firebrands and burnt the grain. After they had burnt all the grain, famine came upon them. However, he alone who had come as their leader, did not burn his. Thereupon all the people flocked out of the village and went to gather fruit. And God gave them fruits, saying : " Here are fruits, you foolish people ; I gave you great quantities of grain, and when you had eaten of it you burnt the rest. Now, as you have burnt it, you will have to eat only *mantembe* and *mankolongwa* and *busala*." And so, truly, since He said that, to this day the people have found it so. To this day, people act in this manner. They destroy the grain, they waste it ; some brew beer, others follow their own inclinations. When the grain is finished, they have to go after *mankolongwa* and *mantembe* and *busala*. To this day they eat those roots.

4. *Why Men became Baboons*

Long ago Baboons were men ; their clan was the Bankontwe. In the years of long ago they were just as men are. They got their living on earth by stealing. After a time they said : " As we have become lazy, let us go into the veld." They went off to live in the veld. When they reached the veld they ate wild fruits. After a time they said : " We cannot live well on these fruits, and as for returning to the village we cannot return, so let us just steal from the fields." To this day, as soon as they see a man's field they send their servant to spy out the land. When he arrives, he looks round and climbs a tree ; if he finds that the owner is not there, he goes back to tell them and takes them some maize. On his arrival he says : " Here is some maize ; there are no people." Then they come. When they reach the field, they break off all the maize and steal. When they have finished stealing they go away. To look at their hands and feet they are human, all but the hair and overhanging forehead.

NOTE.—Similar tales from other parts of the world are mentioned by Tylor (*Primitive Culture*, vol. i. p. 376).

There is still a Bakontwe clan, the members of which are sometimes called baboons and thieves. On the other hand, baboons are often called *bankontwe*.

5. *The Explanation of the Origin of Murder*

A woman had a child. One day she went to work in the fields. When she was going to her work the child cried. When it stopped crying she suckled it, and when she had finished suckling it she laid it down in the shade. Then she went on hoeing. Once again the child cried, and a bird came —an Eagle—and sat upon it. It soothed the child with its wings. Then the child which was crying became silent. When she saw this the woman was greatly alarmed; said she: "Dear me! I am amazed; the Eagle is eating my child." When she went towards it the Eagle flew away, and she suckled her child. When she had done suckling it she put it upon her back. When she had finished hoeing, she left off work and returned to the village.

On her arrival there, she did not tell her husband the marvel she had seen but kept it to herself. Next morning, once again the woman went to work in the field with her child. The same thing happened; once again she laid the child to sleep in the shade. After a time the child cried. Then she beheld the Eagle come on to the child and quieten it. The woman was again amazed, and said: "What is that Eagle doing? It is sitting upon my child, but it neither bites nor scratches it—no, and then the child is quiet. Truly an astounding thing!" Once again the woman went to her child. When the Eagle saw her coming, it flew off and went to sit on a tree. The woman took her child and was greatly alarmed.

She returned to the village, and on her arrival told her husband about it, saying: "A great marvel!" Her husband answered, saying: "What about?" The woman said: "To-day is the second day I have seen the thing there where I hoe. This did I: I put my child to sleep in the shade, and as soon as it cried an Eagle came, and on its arrival stooped over its body and soothed it with its wings.

To-day is the second day that I have seen that bird act thus. Its name is Eagle." Thereupon the husband refused to believe, saying : " No, you are lying ; there never was such a thing." The wife said no more.

In the afternoon she took her hoe and went late to work in the field. On her arrival she laid her child in the shade. The child cried. Thereupon the woman thought : " Now I will go and call my husband, who disputed my word and said I lied." So the woman ran. When she arrived where her husband was, she said : " Come on ! It is you who disputed, saying there never was such a thing. Let us go and see now."

The man took his bow and three arrows. On his arrival the woman told him, saying : " Sit here, I will put the child to sleep in the shade yonder, and then, when you see the bird coming, hide yourself." The woman left the child and went away some distance, and the man hid himself there. Then the child cried very loudly. As he was watching, he saw the Eagle come and sit upon the child. Then the man was greatly alarmed, and charged his bow with two arrows that he might pierce the Eagle sitting on his child. Then he shot ; but at the moment of shooting the Eagle dodged, and both arrows pierced his child.

Now that is the explanation of the origin of murder. The Eagle was a kind person, nevertheless the father of the child wished to kill it. Then the Eagle cursed him, saying : " Now is kindness among men at an end ; because you killed your child, beginning with you and going on to all people, you shall kill each other." To this day people kill each other.

NOTE.—For a parallel to this story among the Lokele people of the Congo, see Sir H. H. Johnston, *Grenfell and the Congo*, vol. ii. pp. 819, 820.

6. *How the Ringdove came by its Ring*

Blackbird, Ringdove, and all the birds were met together. The Ringdove opened the conversation by addressing Blackbird, saying : " Here where we are met together, who is the most beautiful ? " All the birds answered : " Blackbird is the only beautiful one. How very black he is ! "

Then the Ringdove said to himself : " As for me, I am going
to ask for medicine that I may be like Blackbird." So
Ringdove made his petition, saying : " Blackbird, transform
me, so that we may be alike." Blackbird answered, saying :
" I will show you to-morrow. When we are all met together,
and Lapwing is there, and Kestrel and Eagle and Francolin
and Tomtit and Guinea-Fowl, when the birds of all species
are met together, I will show you the medicine." At that
Ringdove was very grateful, and said : " I shall be very
thankful to be like you."

On the morrow, all the birds were gathered together
feeding in the cool of the morning. Then Blackbird came
to where they were assembled, and said : " Ringdove, you
are wanting medicine ? " " Yes," he replied. Said Blackbird : " Come here." So Ringdove went. Blackbird put
his finger around Ringdove's neck, and so you see how
it is that Ringdove is like Blackbird in being black around
the neck. Thereupon all the birds were astounded. Another
bird said : " You shall give me medicine also." Blackbird
said : " What will you give me ? " All the birds answered :
" If only you will give us the medicine, you shall do to us
just whatever you please." Blackbird then told them :
" To-morrow I will give you all medicine, so that you may
become black."

On the morrow, Blackbird arose very early and went
into the forest, where he found some Guinea-Fowl eating
termites. " What are you eating ? " he asked. Guinea-
Fowl answered : " Termites." Thereupon Blackbird said :
" It is you who begged medicine from me, whereas you eat
earth and insects. Now, as that is what you eat, I will not
give you medicine. You, Guinea-Fowl, I will give you a
speckled coat so that you resemble a Leopard, and when a
Leopard finds you he will eat you—all because you do not
eat as I eat ; you always eat insects that live in the earth.
And you, Francolin, you shall be red about the mouth and
on the head, and you shall always eat the grain belonging
to other people, and then you shall always be trapped by
people and they shall trouble you. All the birds who begged
from me, I give them in the same manner, things good for
them or things not good for them."

Thereupon Ringdove, he about whose neck that finger had been encircled, he also was cursed and told : " And you also, Ringdove, you shall always eat the grain belonging to men, so that you may die. All the birds I condemn because they begged for medicines, saying : ' Let us be like Blackbird ' ; whereas in truth they do not at all resemble me, they do not act as I act nor eat as I eat. To be alike in the fashion of our bodies ! No, I refuse." So Ringdove has colour around the neck where Blackbird's finger encircled it. In that alone they are alike ; and as for the rest of the birds, they are in trouble, they are killed, they are ensnared, they are persecuted. Some are caught in traps. And all because they were cursed by Blackbird.

NOTE.—In *Uncle Remus* the speckled coat of the Guinea-Fowl is explained by a cow having sprinkled milk over its blue skin.

7. *How Ringdove got her Name—*
" *Giver-of-happiness-to-men-to-girls-not-so-much.*"

Ringdove and Grey Hornbill gave birth to children in the same house. Ringdove bore a beautiful child, a girl ; Hornbill also bore a female child, but it was ugly : so they nursed their children in the same house. One day Hornbill said to Ringdove : " Let us go and gather some food for our children." Said Ringdove : " Yes, let us go." So they went out, leaving the children in the house, and departed to gather food for their children. After going some distance, Hornbill said : " Let us separate." Ringdove said : " Yes, all right."

So they parted, Hornbill planning to go in one direction, and Ringdove going in another. Hornbill made haste and returned home, and finding the children alive and well she fed her child while Ringdove was still going gathering food. Now when Hornbill looked upon her child she saw that it was ugly, and when she looked at the child of Ringdove she saw that it was beautiful. So she took her child and went and threw it away in the veld. Coming back, she took Ringdove's child and went away with it into another country. When Ringdove returned home she found her child missing, and Hornbill's child missing, and Hornbill herself missing also.

Thereupon Ringdove was distressed, and began to weep for her child; then she went to Fish-eagle to have the matter divined. Fish-eagle said: "I am Fish-eagle, He-whose-business-cannot-be-brought-to-an-end! Did you give birth in the same house with Hornbill?" "Yes," answered Ringdove, "we gave birth in the same house." Said Fish-eagle: "As for your child, Ringdove, Hornbill has stolen her and thrown away her own child." Then Ringdove said: "Well, Fish-eagle, where has Hornbill taken my child to?" Said Fish-eagle: "To Mala; to-day she is married: she is the wife of a chief." Ringdove said to Fish-eagle: "Allow me to go to Mala to find my child." Said Fish-eagle: "Yes, go, and you will find your child, Ringdove."

When she reached Mala she found her child married to a chief. On her arrival she said: "Chief, this whom you have married is my child." The chief who had married Ringdove's daughter said: "No, my wife is the daughter of Hornbill." Then the chief killed Ringdove, whose daughter he had married. Thereupon that child of Ringdove said: "It is a good thing I am married as my mother is dead."

To this day Ringdove is Giver-of-happiness-to-men-to-girls-not-so-much. It is said, When Ringdove stretches out her wings you must say: "Make me happy, O *Chinakaduedue*, Giver-of-happiness-to-men-to-girls-not-so-much." The saying is, When Ringdove then flies off, it means that she blesses you.

NOTE.—This tale is meant to account for the belief in the Ringdove as a bird of good omen, the giver of happiness. When a person sees the bird spread out its wings in a certain way, he spits on the ground as an offering to the bird, and says: "*Chinakaduedue, Chisangidila-ku-balombe-ku-bashimbi-ndukubakuba nsangila*"—"You, Chinakaduedue, Giver-of-happiness-to-men-to-girls-not-so-much, make me happy." Then he says: *Yansangidila, ndikwete cholwe* —"It makes me happy (*or*, it spreads out its wings for me). I have got good fortune." The word in Ila "to be happy" is *kusangidilwa*, the root of which, *sanga*, is a widely-spread one, occurring in Nyanja, Lenje, Lala, Wisa, Senga, Kongo, Ganda, and Swahili, always with the same meaning. *Sangidila* would mean "spread out the wings on behalf of somebody," and that may be the idea in their mind, *i.e.* that in some way the spreading of the wings brings happiness. Or perhaps *sanga* may have had two meanings at some time, and then it was fancied that they must be connected and the story was invented to explain the connection. Be that as it may, the dove is associated with happiness among many peoples. It is for that reason, so we may suppose, that so often it has its place in marriage customs. Perhaps it is for some such reason that it has been so widely domesticated from antiquity and that it had a sacrosanct character among the Hebrews and other Semites. And it may be for the same reason that the Ba-ila so frequently have dovecotes in their villages.

The significant part of the name Chinaka*duedue* is probably onomatopoeic, cf. Hebrew, *tōr*, Latin, *turtur*.

8. *How Honey-guide came to have Authority over Honey*

Honey-guide and Capped Wheatear lived together in one place at first and ate out of one dish. Honey-guide was the elder, Wheatear the younger. They set their minds on going to hunt for honey, and it happened when they arrived in the vicinity of the honey that Honey-guide said : " Smile, Wheatear, when you see where the honey is." Wheatear smiled, but he did not see the honey ; when Honey-bird smiled he had seen it. That is what they did, and then they returned, leaving the honey behind. On their arrival at where they were staying, Wheatear quietly disappeared and went off to steal the honey.

Next morning Honey-guide said : " Let us go to our honey." There they found a bit of bare honeycomb mangled and thrown about, so he asked Wheatear about it, and Wheatear replied : " My brother, I have seen neither it nor him who has stolen the honey. Since we came out yesterday nobody has come back here to demolish the honey in this way." And once again Wheatear said to Honey-guide : " As for me, I could not eat any of this honey unless you had given it to me."

So then Honey-guide said no more, and they went out again looking for honey. Once more they found some honey. Honey-guide saw it before Wheatear did, and he tested Wheatear by saying : " Smile." Wheatear said : "I cannot see the honey, smile yourself, my brother." Honey-guide said : "No, child, smile." So Wheatear smiled and he saw the honey ; then Honey-guide asked him : " What do you see ? " Wheatear said : " It looks as if it might be flies fluttering before the eyes." Honey-guide said : " Haven't you seen it ? " But Wheatear was deceiving him, for he saw the honey all the time. When Honey-guide was about to smile, he saw the honey and said : " Let us cut down the tree to get it." Wheatear refused, saying : " No. As you said yesterday that I stole the honey, well, I am Wheatear ! Let us bring some bird-lime and set a trap beside the honey, then if it be I who steal the honey you will catch me." " Good business," replied Honey-guide.

They went off to get some bird-lime from the humans. Then when they arrived at their village, Honey-guide said : " We will come to-morrow to set the trap." But after a time Honey-guide quietly disappeared and went off to set the bird-lime at the honey. Said Wheatear to himself : " Let me go quietly and eat the honey," but the bird-lime was set already, although he did not notice it. When he thought of sitting down beside the honey, he sat on the bird-lime. Said he, " I will strike it with my wing," but he stuck to it. And when he struck with his tail he stuck to it. When he wanted to draw back his right wing, it was stuck fast. He tried to strike it with his breast but he stuck. When he attempted to bite it with his beak, he bit the bird-lime. Why, then he simply died for lack of breath.

Then Honey-guide appeared on the scene after he had looked for him at the village, and he found him already a dead man. Then he mocked him, saying : " Wheatear, smile ! " As he was dried up, he said that was the reward of thievery. " From to-day you will not steal any more. The chieftainship is mine over honey and to be extolled by people ! As for you, from to-day your portion shall be bird-lime already spread, and thus you will be killed by people."

Now since they separated there on account of thievery, Wheatear belongs to bird-lime and Honey-guide is still extolled. While he talked like this, Honey-guide was standing upon the corpse of Wheatear. They became distinct in other directions, while their cry remained the same, and to this day Wheatear's portion is bird-lime and to be entrapped by men.

9. *Why Honey-guide betrays the Bees to People*

Honey-guide went to look for a wife in Bee-town. On his arrival there he said : " I want a wife." The Bees gave him a wife, but after a time they took her away from him. When they took her away, Honey-guide said : " Since you refuse me my wife, I shall simply go and tell tales about you to the people who pass along the road."

Since he said that, to this day when he sees a person passing, he takes him and goes to show him the bees.

NOTE from Livingstone's *Missionary Travels*, p. 479.—" December 2, 1855. We remained near a small hill called Maundo, where we began to be frequently invited by the Honey-guide (*Cuculus indicator*). Wishing to ascertain the truth of the native assertion that this bird is a deceiver and by its call sometimes leads to a wild beast and not to honey, I inquired if any of my men had ever been led by this friendly bird to anything else than what its name implies. Only one of the 114 could say he had been led to an elephant instead of a hive, like myself with the black rhinoceros mentioned before. I am quite convinced that the majority of people who commit themselves to its guidance are led to honey and to it alone." The exceptions are numerous enough to earn for Solwe the name of liar. There is a Ba-ila clan of the Bana-Solwe, the members of which are nicknamed " the liars."

10. *How Squirrel robbed Coney of his Tail.*

Coney and Squirrel were brothers-in-law and always dwelt harmoniously together. But after some time Squirrel said : " Brother-in-law, let me have your tail to walk about with, I will return it." But Coney refused, saying : " No ; am I to remain tailless ? " Squirrel left off asking, but after some days he returned and said : " Truly, brother-in-law, you refused me your tail though I said I wanted simply to walk about with it and would bring it back." Then Coney consented and lent his tail to Squirrel, who said : " I will bring back your tail in eight days' time."

Then Squirrel went home. On his arrival there, his people said : " Wherever did you get that fine tail ? " Said he : " My brother-in-law gave it to me." They replied : " You are blest indeed ! You have got a fine tail."

When the eight days had passed, did Squirrel return the tail ? Not he ! Nine days passed, ten days were ended, and on the eleventh Coney followed his tail to Squirrel's place. On his arrival there he found him on the ground. " You have come ! " said he as soon as he saw him. Then Squirrel jumped up into a tree, climbed up and laughed heartily, saying : " What have you come after, brother-in-law ? " Coney had not a word to say. So he asked him a second time. And Coney answered then, saying : " As for me I am angry. You have simply deceived me. You did not bring back my tail." Thereupon Coney waxed very wroth. Squirrel laughed aloud and said : " As you are so angry, perhaps you will climb up into the tree and get your tail ! If you do not climb the tree you will never see your tail again."

Then Coney thought within his chest : " How am I to stay among all the other animals ? They have all got tails : I am the only one lacking a tail." Thereupon he went to a hill, and to this day he lives among the rocks.

11. *How Squirrel and Jackal became distinct*

Squirrel and Jackal were brothers-in-law ; they had married into one family. After a time Elephant said : " You, Squirrel and Jackal, come and work for me and I will give you a place in a chief's family, for you shall marry my daughters. At least he who is first to finish the work shall have the princeship."

Then they answered : " It is well." And they asked : " What work are we to do ? " Elephant said : " I will show you. But first you must forsake your old wives." So they forsook them.

Squirrel and Jackal went to Elephant. On their arrival he said : " As for you, Mr. Jackal, this is my daughter that I shall give you in marriage if you win. And, Mr. Squirrel, if *you* win, this is the one I shall give you."

So they went to work in the forests : Jackal was given his forest and Squirrel his. Elephant said : " Fell the trees, and the first to finish shall marry my daughter." Then they began to fell the trees. Squirrel felled two trees while Jackal felled one ; then Squirrel had three to Jackal's two.

When ten days had passed Squirrel had done his work, but Jackal's was too much for him. So they returned to Elephant; but all the time he had not been telling the truth but was simply lying.

Squirrel was given good fortune and told: "Nothing shall ever trouble you, you shall dwell up in a tree always, you shall live well all the years." Jackal was told: "As for you, you shall have but little joy in life. When you are going along the road in the vicinity of men, you will be caught in a trap, and men will trouble you as long as you live; they will spear you, and kill you, and eat you, and wear your skin."

NOTE.—The Ba-ila see some relationship or likeness between the squirrel and the jackal, seemingly because of the bushy tail each possesses; and this tale is meant to explain how they have become separated, so that the squirrel lives in trees practically immune from annoyance from men, while the poor jackal living on the ground is every one's chase.

12. *How Skunk came to be a Helper of Men*

Hare and Skunk went a-hunting. On the road Hare proposed a game of hide-and-seek, saying: "Skunk, hide yourself and I will hide myself; let us see how you can hide." Thereupon they hid themselves. After a time Hare got up and went outside to where Skunk was lying and deceived him by growling like a lion. Then Skunk cried out in fear, and Hare laughed and said: "What are you crying for? As for me I thought that perhaps you were brave, but now that you cry on being deceived, let us take a walk." So they went. On arriving yonder, Hare transformed himself, making himself like a leopard. Then Skunk shouted in alarm: "Mr. Hare!" He did not recognise Hare. He called again: "Mr. Hare!" Hare did not answer. At last Hare discovered himself and said: "What's the matter? Yonder where you began to shout did I hear you? Nevertheless, when you called me I answered. But as for you, you are a coward, you are like a hyena, you are like a chased cur, you poor infant!" Then Skunk said: "No, sir, I was afraid because I met a leopard, and I was alarmed because it was about to bite me." Then Hare was angry and said: "What was the matter with you that you could not hide ? '' Skunk said : " I don't know how." So Hare said : " You're Skunk. Your name is Mr. Turn-and-twist-about. I give you good fortune and you shall convey good fortune to men. And you will help them with some of your flesh and also with your body." And so to-day Skunk is helpful to them.

NOTE.—The name Salama-salama given to the Skunk indicates its manner of running, jumping from side to side, turning and twisting about, so that it is very difficult to catch or hit. From its being a difficult target to its enemies, the Ba-ila conceive it to be a valuable medicine in time of war. Some take its nose, others some of its hair, and put them in the *insengo*, medicine receptacles worn on the body. These are charms to ensure that the spears of the enemy will fail to reach the wearer : that, indeed, he will be as hard to hit as the Skunk. It is to this that the Hare refers when he says that some of the Skunk's flesh will be useful to men. He also refers to the fact that the Skunk's urine is used to perfume tobacco.

13. *Why Duiker has a fine Coat and parti-coloured Tail*

Duiker was the younger brother of Oribi, but one deceived the other. When Duiker looked at Oribi he found that Oribi was very handsome, that his body was white and his tail parti-coloured. After some days, Duiker went to pay a visit at Oribi's home.

On his arrival, Oribi said : " Good day, my brother ! " He replied : " Good day ! " " What have you come to look for ? " asked Oribi. " Nothing," said Duiker, " I have only come to see you. I said, the days are many since I saw my brother, so I will go to see him." Thereupon Oribi was glad. He took a cup of water and made an oblation, and after making the oblation he gave him a tuft on the head, saying : " This is my offering to you." Then he cooked food for him and Duiker ate. But in his heart Duiker was envying the body of Oribi and his parti-coloured tail. Then having finished eating, Duiker returned home and Oribi stayed behind. While he was on the road, Duiker thought : " How can I deceive him and take away yon body of his ? " Then he thought : " Let me brew some beer, and when I have brewed the beer I will call him to come and drink."

On arriving home, Duiker despatched his wives, saying :
" Brew some beer that I may entrap Oribi with it. Is my
body handsome ? "   The women said : " No, it is very
ugly.   You arc not fit to bear the name of Duiker because
your body is so very ugly ; you are red and your tail is
dark.   You ought to seize Oribi's body, which is white,
and also his parti-coloured tail."

Then the wives brewed the beer, and when it was ready
they sent the invitation : " Let Oribi and his wives come
and drink beer."   Then they arrived, and on arrival began
to drink beer.   At night when they spoke of returning,
Duiker said : " No, stay here and sleep, so that to-morrow
morning you can drink again."

Thereupon he gave them a house and they slept.   Then
Duiker said to his wives : " My dears, when they are asleep
to-night and undressed, take away their coats and parti-
coloured tails."   So indeed they slept, and while they were
asleep at night, Duiker and his wives arose and took away
the skins of the Oribi and his wives : the man robbed his
fellow-man and the women their fellows ; then they left
their home and went to hide.

As soon as it dawned, the Oribis found their white coats
and their parti-coloured tails—they found them missing ; they
found only those which had belonged to the Duikers.   They
dressed in them and tried to find where the others had
gone but did not succeed.   So after a time the Oribis got
very sad and said : " Now as our white coats have gone,
we must go into the open plain and live there.   When the
veldfire has swept over the plain we shall become Dwellers-
in-the-open."   Thereupon they dressed in the coats which
had been the Duikers' and went off to become Dwellers-in-
the-open.   Even to-day that is their name.

14. *How Elephant lost his Clothing*

Hare went to Elephant, and on his arrival said : " Uncle,
let us go to the river."   Elephant said : " What are we to
do ? "   Hare answered : " Only to play.   When we get
there let us dive into the water and sit at the bottom of
the river.   Only I, as I am a child, I will look outside.   Let

us stay a long time, and then in the late afternoon we will return." Thereupon Elephant said : " All right."

They dived into the river and went to sit under the water. They took off their clothes before going in and left them outside. After a time Hare said : " Uncle, I am going ; you stay and I will find you here. I am going to see the time outside : how far the sun has got. You must not rise to the surface ; simply sit still." Then Hare emerged ; on his arrival he took Elephant's clothing and carried it to the village. As soon as he reached the village he said : " Cook these clothes of Elephant's."

Afterwards he went back. He dived and found Elephant sitting where he left him. Said he : " It may be, my uncle, that you have been to the surface ? " He answered : " No, since you left me I have simply been sitting." Hare answered : " It is well, uncle ; let us stay on, the sun is still big." They stayed. After a time, Hare said : " I am going to see the sun." When he got out, Hare ran off to the village and said : " Cook some bread, we shall be back presently." When the sun reached the point where the shepherds are tired, Hare returned, dived, and found Elephant sitting in the same place. As he arrived, Elephant said : " How far has the sun got ? " " Uncle," he said, " it is when the shepherds are tired ; there is still a brief period and we shall go back." So they stayed on.

After a time, little Hare on another excursion found that the sun was weak, so he returned and told Elephant, saying : " Uncle, let us go now, the sun is setting." Then they came to the surface and emerged on to the bank. Little Hare put on his clothes. Elephant looked for his clothes but could not find them, so he asked : " Who has taken away my clothes ? " Then Hare answered : " I don't know, uncle. I haven't seen them myself ; when I came out on to the bank to have a look at the sun, I simply rose up for a moment and went back again." When Elephant heard Hare's words he was very sad and astonished, but although he searched a long time he did not find his clothes. Afterwards Hare said : " Uncle, we will come to look for them carefully, let us now go and eat at my village."

So they went off and arrived. Then Hare took one pot off the fire and dished up all the contents into a basin, brought as much bread as would suffice him, and gave it all to Elephant. As soon as he had finished eating, Hare asked him : " Have you finished eating, uncle ? " Said he : " Yes." " Well, it is you who were looking for your clothes, and it is these which you have eaten. You are really a fool. You eat your clothes without knowing it." Upon that Elephant was very sad. To this day Elephant's clothes are not to be seen outside ; as he ate them long ago, they are not seen outside, but are within.

NOTE.—This tale cannot be understood without knowing that " clothes " is a euphemism for testicles ; the tale is designed to explain why it is that those parts of the elephant are not visible.

In Bantu tales the elephant is very commonly the butt of the Hare's witticisms. We shall meet the two again later on. There is a Baganda tale (Sir H. H. Johnston, *The Uganda Protectorate*, pp. 711-13), in which the Hare says to the Elephant : " Mr. Elephant, I can't say I admire your dancing, there seems to be too much of you and the flesh on your buttocks goes flop, flop, flop. Let us cut off a few slices and then try. You will then dance as well as I do." The rest of the tale is occupied with the elephant's endeavours to regain his steaks. See also the Banyoro tale (*ibid.* pp. 604-5).

15. *Why the Elephant is distinct from the Wart-hog*

Wart-hog was Elephant's nephew. Once upon a time they went to the water. On their arrival, Elephant said : " Who is to drink first ? " Wart-hog : " I will." So Wart-hog went into the water. When he had finished drinking—Elephant all the while standing on the bank—he stirred up the water, and having done this, he said : " Now, uncle, come and drink." Elephant drank and drank.

When he had done drinking a leech bit him in the trunk. When he felt this, he said : " Take out this thing that is biting me." But the leech wouldn't come out. Then he began to hit his trunk on a tree ; but the leech wouldn't leave go. He went on bashing it, but the leech stuck on. Then his trunk began to bleed, and Elephant continued bashing it. By and by the trunk broke, but the leech wouldn't leave go. Then Elephant was amazed and said : " This insect won't come out of my trunk." Afterwards the trunk got rotten, but Elephant never ceased bashing it. After many days, Elephant died.

Wart-hog said : "My uncle is dead. Now as my uncle is dead I become the great one." Then he marvelled, saying : "Was it I who spoilt the water when I was the first to drink ? It was a leech that bit him, was it not ? " Thereupon they became distinct. Elephant took the big tusks ; Wart-hog took tusks like those of Elephant. Elephant went on growing, and Wart-hog diminishing. As for being alike, they are alike ; body and hair, Wart-hog and Elephant are the same. If you look at the tusks, both Wart-hog's and Elephant's are white. And the hair is alike and the body identical.

NOTE.—We do not know that it would occur to many people to trace these resemblances between the two animals, but they have struck the Ba-ila and this tale is meant to account for them. That a leech should cause the death of an elephant is no mere fancy, as will be seen from the following : " This same ponderous elephant positively trembles at the thought of a tiny leech. And no wonder, for many an elephant dies an awful death, from a leech sucking the inner membrane of his trunk until the monster tusker is maddened to death. . . . You can come across a huge clearing in the grass where the writhing giant has nearly beaten his own brains out, the agony being all centred in that finest and most delicate of all his organs, the marconigram trunk. . . . On Lake Mweru this is called the ' leech-doom,' and is the cause of that curious ceremony all elephants perform when they come across drinking water. This function is called the benediction (kupava) and the elephant passes a scared, wistful gaze over the sheet of water, at the same time waving his trunk like a mesmerist again and again over the solemn treacherous pond. But the trunk, as a matter of fact, is no mere magician's wand, but the supreme headquarters of Jumbo's cunning, and supplying him with not so much a sixth sense as a *sensorium commune*. Instead of ' praying ' a sort of grace-before-meat petition, as the native suggests, he is really wringing from the water its leech-secret."—D. Crawford, *Christian Express*, 1. 3. 10.

16. *Why the Wart-hog lives in a Burrow*

Once again there was deception between Wart-hog and Elephant. Elephant came to Wart-hog and on his arrival said : " Uncle, do you still keep up resentment against me ? " Wart-hog answered : " Yes, because one day you said you would destroy things for me, but you broke your

word, and so now we have no more to do with each other."
Said Elephant : " No, uncle, you must not be resentful."
Wart-hog said : " I don't want to fight again." Elephant
said : " No, I will not fight again.   I only came to admire
your tusks."   Thereupon Wart-hog said : " Here they are,
you may admire them."   And Elephant also said : " Here
are mine, you may admire them."   So they dressed up,
Wart-hog wearing Elephant's tusks and Elephant Wart-hog's.

After they had done this, Elephant said : " These
tusks, uncle, I am going to take home and I will bring them
back the day after to-morrow."   But he was simply deceiving him.   So Elephant went off.   On the way he said :
" I have cheated him — the fool.   He whose name is
Mufwafwi (' stumpy ') should he have great tusks, and
I the great one wear small tusks !   He shan't see these
again ! "   Thereupon, mumbling much against him, he
entered the *matondo* forest and went off a long way.

Wart-hog looked for the day of which Elephant spoke
when he said good-bye, saying, I will bring back your tusks,
but he did not see him.   So he followed him, and when he
came upon him said : " I want my tusks."   Elephant said :
" Really !   Why, you fool, I said, we make an exchange,
and now you are still talking about *your* tusks ! "   Then
Wart-hog said : " You are lying.   You said nothing about
making an exchange ; all you said was, let me walk with
them and I will bring them back.   Now to-day you have
turned round."   He said : " No."   And Wart-hog said :
" From to-day I am going to sleep in a burrow ; as for you,
you shall travel about the whole day and go far ; we shall
not be friends again because you have deceived me so."

Thereupon Wart-hog returned ; he considered the matter
and his considerations told him : " Go to Ant-bear.   See
that body of yours, in your bare condition you ought not
to sleep simply on the ground, you ought to be in a burrow."
So Wart-hog went to Ant-bear.   On his arrival, he said :
" Ant-bear, look after me well and I will give you a blessing."
Said he : " What sort of a blessing ? "   He answered :
" You shall not have to eat as your fellow-animals eat ;
but I will give you a blessing ; of grass you shall eat but
little, only to taste ; when you are sleeping then on to your

tongue shall come your food, which you will find while
lying down.''

To this day Ant-bear only eats little grass, but when he
puts out his tongue insects collect upon it, and all he has
to do is simply to draw in his tongue and eat. Ant-bear's
custom is to dig burrows, and Wart-hog enters one and
sleeps ; when he has had enough of one he looks out for
another. On his arrival he enters the burrow dug by Ant-
bear. To this day it is so.

17. *Why Bushbuck came to have a Red Coat*

One day Hare said : '' Bushbuck, let us go and pay
some calls.'' Bushbuck said : '' It is well.'' They went
off, and arriving at a village they stayed there and their
hosts gave them something to eat. After a time Hare
said : '' Bushbuck.'' Bushbuck replied : '' Yes ! '' '' Let
us go and steal a goat.'' They went off to another village,
and on arrival there found some goats. They stole one,
took it to their host's place and killed it. Having killed it,
Hare said : '' Bushbuck, bring a basin to put the blood in.''
So Bushbuck brought a basin and they put the blood into
it. When the basin was full, Hare placed it up on a shelf.
Then they cooked their meat and, having cooked, ate it.
And when they had done eating they went to sleep.

In the night Hare got up and aroused Bushbuck, saying :
'' Bushbuck ! '' Bushbuck replied : '' Speak ! '' Said he :
'' Let us go and make burrows, so that if the owners of the
goat we stole should chase us we can enter the burrows.''
So they went, arrived, and dug the burrows, Hare digging
his and Bushbuck his. They also pierced escape-holes by
which they might emerge, saying : '' Let us do this : as
soon as we enter those people will say, ' They are inside ' ;
whereas we are out at the escape-holes.'' So they worked
and that same night they finished. When they had finished,
Hare brought a big stone and threw it into Bushbuck's
burrow, so that Bushbuck, having once entered, should not
be able to get out and they would catch him.

So when their work was done, they returned to their
host's place. Before very long the day dawned and the

owners missed their goat. Then Hare arose, took down
the basin of blood and poured it all over Bushbuck's body.
Then the owners of the goat arrived, and on their arrival
said : " Who has stolen our goat ? " Hare answered :
" Look at our claws and bodies and you will see who has
blood on him, and that is he who ate your goat which you
have missed." So they said : " Bushbuck, you are the one
who has eaten our goat. See the blood on all your body ! "

Upon that Bushbuck and Hare ran off and went to
their burrows. On their arrival Bushbuck entered, but
upon entering he encountered the stone and the way was
blocked. All he could do was to crouch down and hide.
As for Master Hare, he went out at his escape-hole. So
the owners of the goat said : " Bring hoes and let us dig."
When they brought the hoes, some dug at Bushbuck's burrow,
others at Hare's. Those who dug at Bushbuck's caught
him ; but when the digging was finished at Hare's—to see
him, No !

When they caught hold of Bushbuck, he said : " As
you have caught me, do not kill me on the stone. Take me
to a clear space and kill me there, for it is there only I shall
die." So they took him into the flat. On arrival there,
he said : " Throw me up into the air. When I return to
earth, I shall simply be dead." So they threw him up into
the air. When they threw him, he at once ran off and
went away into the bush. The colour which he has is from
the blood of the goat which he and Hare stole. Only when
he got that colour from the blood which Hare spilt on him
did his name become Shichibangu, and since then he has
lived only in the bush. You will not find him in the flat ;
only in the bush now.

NOTE.—It is a favourite trick of the Hare to throw blame on to
his partners by smearing them with blood or with mud or something
else. In the Suto tale he smears mud on the Rabbit so that the
lion may think it is he who drank his water in the night. (Jacottet,
Basuto Lore, Part 2, p. 10). Mr. Jacottet gives references to similar
tricks played by the Hare in Subiya and Ronga tales. In a Lala
tale (Madan : *Lala-Lamba Handbook*, pp. 55-8) the Rabbit (*kalalu*)
plays the same trick on the March Hare (*Wachilulu ishilu*) ; he
kills a goat and puts the entrails on the neck of the Hare. Then
the people of the village find the Hare ; he escapes and gets into a
hole, whence he is dug out and killed.

18. *Why Jackals do not go in Herds*

Jackal and Weasel dwelt in a village together and Jackal married Weasel's daughter. One day Weasel went after honey. On his return home he brewed some beer, and when it was fermented he sent a message to Jackal, saying : " Let my son-in-law come and drink honey-beer." Thereupon he went with his children and women. On his arrival they gave him and his children and wives some honey-beer and they all drank. They drank all day, when it got dark they drank all night ; when it dawned they drank till noon, and when the sun began to show that it was about one o'clock, Jackal and his children were very drunk. He, when he set about emerging, ran like a madman ; he went off into the forest. Another came out and ran ; and another came out and ran also. They ran like that because they were drunk. They all ran off in different directions. In running, one went his way and another his. To-day Jackals do not go in a herd. If there are three together it means that one is a child ; they generally go two by two, he and his wife ; because of the way in which they were drunk long ago with honey-beer and separated in running away. To this day they do not go in herds, and if you see four together you may know that some are children ; as soon as they are grown they separate from the others.

19. *Why Zebra has no Horns*

All the animals were gathered together : Elephant and Wart-hog and Gnu and Zebra and Eland and Buffalo and Sable and Duiker and Reedbuck and Puku and Waterbuck and Roan and Lechwe and Oribi and Kudu—all the animals of different species were gathered together grazing.

After a while, the time came for going to select horns for themselves. All the animals said : " Let us choose horns." So all the animals ran, all of different species ran off to select horns. And they were all suited, whatever the animal was, great or small, all of different species were suited with horns.

Only Zebra remained behind.

After a time they said : " Zebra, they will make it impossible for you to select horns for yourself." As soon as he thought of this he ran off ; on reaching the place where the horns were being selected, he was simply sad to find no horn left, the others had finished them all. All he found there were a mane and long ears and stripes and a big mouth. Then his friends laughed at him, saying : " You, what has your eating done for you ! See, they have finished the horns, even the little children have got horns, and you— only colourings and a mane and ears and a drooping lip, that was what you had to take. See us all with horns, big and little ! " So his friends contemned him, saying : " You are a glutton, your eating has deprived you of horns."

Thereupon Zebra was very sad indeed as he was without horns. And so it is that as for eating and eating very much, to this day Zebra is a glutton. It seems that he surpasses all the other animals in eating. That is all.

20. *Why Leopard and Cheetah became distinct*

Leopard became distinct from Cheetah. Leopard bit the ox of a chief and after biting it, smeared the ox's blood upon Cheetah. Next morning when the people examined their cattle they found one missing, and they said : " Call Cheetah and his brother Leopard, so that we can ask them about the killing of the chief's ox."

On their arrival the people said : " Leopard ! " He answered : " What's the matter, chief ? " Said the chief : " One of the oxen is missing." Leopard said : " As for me, chief, I haven't seen it." And Cheetah said : " I also, chief, I haven't seen it." Presently Leopard answered again, saying : " Such being the case, you will find that whoever has blood on the mouth and hands is the one who saw your ox." Thereupon the chief looked at the mouth and hands of Leopard. As soon as he turned his eye upon Cheetah he saw the blood on his mouth and hands. So he sent that same brother of his, Leopard, to seize him, and he said : " Now, you, Leopard, shall be fierce towards men and animals. And you, Cheetah, you shall bite calves, so that the owners of the cattle shall kill you."

Now to this day, when Cheetah finds a calf he bites it. At the same time Leopard also still bites calves and men too. They did not become altogether distinct. Since they did not become distinct in their colourings, Leopard and Cheetah, if you say: " Run away, Cheetah," it will be a Leopard that runs. If you say: " Run away, Leopard," it is Cheetah that runs. Because they are similar in their markings.

NOTE.—The Cheetah or Chitah, or hunting leopard, has great resemblance to the leopard as regards the skin, but is not nearly so fierce an animal. This tale is supposed to account for the differences and likenesses.

21. *Tortoise, because of the way she and Fish-eagle deceived each other, does not eat Meat*

Tortoise and Fish-eagle made a covenant of friendship. Fish-eagle bore children but Tortoise had no children, and for that reason Fish-eagle laughed very much. One day, Fish-eagle said: " Oh, my friend, give me cunning ! " " What sort of cunning ? " Fish-eagle replied : " Cunning by which to withdraw one's head within, so that I also may not get into trouble. See my children, I leave them alone, and if a biting thing comes along to where I have left them, it will bite them, and all because they haven't cunning. And I have no cunning myself. That is why I ask you, and if you will give me that cunning I also will give you cunning."

Tortoise answered saying : " What sort of cunning ? "

Said she : " Why, to fly in the air ! You cannot fly now, no, you can't fly, all you can do is to crawl along the ground on your stomach, but, on the other hand, I fly. As for you, the only cunning you possess is to withdraw your head inside, that only you have ; so now let us exchange, you give me your wisdom of withdrawing the head within when I see a thing which kills ; and if you do that for me, I also will show you the cunning of flying."

Nevertheless Tortoise refused, and when she refused Fish-eagle stole Tortoise's axe, saying : " Let us see whether she will fly to fetch her axe."

Thereupon Fish-eagle took away Tortoise's axe. Tortoise sought for it carefully, and then she thought : " It is that friend of mine who has taken away my axe." After a time Tortoise considered the matter again in her chest, and said : " Let me kill an animal, and when I have killed the animal let me hide in the meat of its stomach, and Fish-eagle will be sure to come to the meat. As she has children, she will first, on her arrival at the meat, take off the stomach to carry it to her children, and then I shall find my axe."

Now thereupon Tortoise hid herself in the stomach of the meat and Fish-eagle came whirling round in the air ; as she looked down to earth she saw the meat red below, and said : " I have found meat." So she descended upon the meat, and on arrival took off the stomach in which Tortoise had hidden herself ; she took it to her children at the village on the tree-top.

When she came to her children she said : " Catch the meat, I am going back to where I found it to eat." So Fish-eagle returned to the meat. Her children set about eating the meat which their mother had brought. Just as they were about to eat they heard a hiss, and all the children were afraid. Then Tortoise came out of the meat and looked about for her axe ; looking about she found it, took it, and descended and returned to her village.

Then Fish-eagle returned to her village, and on reaching it found her children absent and called out : " My children, where have you gone ? " They answered : " We were afraid, in that meat which you brought us there was something that hissed, that is why we ran away afraid ; and we haven't eaten the meat." Then she was greatly astounded and said : " Tortoise came here. Who is it gave her cunning to get up here so high ? She has no wings." She asked again : " Where is my axe ? " The children said : " We haven't seen it."

Then she returned to Tortoise. On arriving she sat down and found that Tortoise had killed another animal, a Python. So on her arrival she said : " My friend, to-day we find peace ; I will not deceive you again. I will do this to you ; when you bite an animal I will come to be given of it by you, I will not again do you wrong."

To-day, yes, to-day, where Tortoise has meat, whether it is a Snake he kills, or whether it is a breast of meat he finds, the Fish-eagle also passes there, and on arrival Fish-eagle sits on top. Tortoise simply hisses, because he does not eat meat. Since the one deceived the other, Tortoise does not eat it : all he eats is rushes, it is Fish-eagle that eats meat.

22. *Why Rhinoceros and Hippopotamus became distinct*

Rhinoceros and Hippopotamus had a fight. Hippo had taken Rhino's razor : that is why they fought. Rhino said : " Who has taken my razor ? " Hippo answered : " I did. I wanted to shave my wife." Rhino said : " Bring it here." Hippo said : " I haven't seen it." Thereupon they fought. Afterwards Rhino said : " Let us separate. As for me I am going off to eat Euphorbia." And Hippo said : " And I to the water."

And so the saying to-day still is : Let us separate as did Rhino and Hippo.

Rhino and Hippo also once effected an exchange. Rhino had the tusks that Hippo has, and Hippo had Rhino's horns. It thus came about that they deceived each other a second time. First they fought about a razor and separated. Although that was the case, Hippo stole Rhino's tusks. He had said : " How can I deceive him and take his white tusks, and give him these black horns, which are not firm." So Hippo determined to invite him, saying : " Let Rhino come, and let us make peace, that the old quarrel may cease and we may love each other and dwell harmoniously, just as we used always to do."

So Rhino came ; when Hippo saw him coming he found how very white his tusks were. So on Rhino's arrival, Hippo said : " Brother, let us not fight again, let us now love each other very much and settle down comfortably."

It got dark, and as soon as it was night Hippo said : " Let us take off our horns and put them aside, we will wear them again in the morning." So they undressed and as it was night went to sleep. Hippo rose in the night and stole Rhino's white tusks and put down in their place his own black horns.   Then Hippo went into the water.

Next morning when Rhino wished to put on the tusks they did not fit, and he said : " These are not my tusks." When he looked where Hippo had been lying he found him gone,—and gone off with the tusks he had stolen.   So he went off to the Matondo forest, but the tusks he did not see again.

Then he shouted : " Hippo, you who have stolen my tusks, we are alike in body and in the thickness of our hide ; your hide shall be red and mine black because of your thievery.   You shall lodge in the water and it is at dusk that you shall come out to graze ; as for me I shall graze the whole day.   Neither of us shall ever be able to jump over a tree !   Because we are alike ; both of us have short legs and neither of us is greater than his fellow."

So, as it happened thus, they are alike in having short legs, but they are unlike in body ; that of the Hippo is red and that of Rhino is black.   Still, they are of one family.

23. *Why the Cracks in Tortoise's Shell*

Mr. Tortoise, who was married to Mrs. Tortoise, had in Vulture a friend who was assiduous in visiting him.   But, having no wings, Tortoise was unable to return the visits, and this displeased him.   One day he bethought himself of his cunning and said to his wife : " Wife ! "   Mrs. Tortoise answered : " Hallo, husband, what is it ? "   Said he : " Don't you see, wife, that we are becoming despicable in Vulture's eyes ? "   " How despicable ? "   " Despicable, because it *is* despicable for me not to visit Vulture.   He is always coming here, and I have never yet been to his house — and he my friend."   Mrs. Tortoise replied : " I don't see how Vulture should think us despicable unless we could fly as he does and yet did not pay him a visit."   But Mr. Tortoise persisted : " Nevertheless, wife, it *is* despicable." Said his wife : " Very well, then, sprout some wings and fly and visit your friend Vulture."   Mr Tortoise answered : " No, I shan't sprout any wings because I was not born that way." " Well," said Mrs. Tortoise, " what will you do ? " " I shall find a way," replied he. " Find it then," said Mrs Tortoise, " and let us see what you will do."

Later Tortoise said to his wife : " Come and tie me up in a parcel with a lump of tobacco, and when Vulture arrives give it to him and say it is tobacco, to buy grain for us." So Mrs. Tortoise took some palm leaf and made him into a parcel and put him down in the corner. At his usual time Vulture came to pay his visit, and said : " Where's your husband gone, Mrs. Tortoise ? " " My husband is gone some distance to visit some people, and he left hunger here ; we have not a bit of grain in the house." Vulture said : " You are in trouble indeed, not having any grain." Mrs. Tortoise replied : " We are in such trouble as human beings never knew." And she went on : " Vulture, at your place is there no grain to be bought ? " " Yes," said he, " any amount, Mrs. Tortoise." She brought the bundle and said : " My husband left this lump of tobacco thinking you would buy some grain with it for us and bring it here." Vulture took it willingly and returned to his home in the heights. As he was nearing his native town he was surprised to hear a voice saying : " Untie me, I am your friend Tortoise. I said I would pay a visit to you." But Vulture in his surprise let go his hold of the bundle and down crashed Tortoise—*pididi-pididi* ! He smashed up when he struck the earth and died. And so the friendship between Tortoise and Vulture was broken : and you can still see the cracks in Tortoise's shell.

24. *Why Hornbill has such a Big Beak and Tomtit a Small One*

Tomtit in the old days had a very large beak, and Hornbill, dying with envy for the beak, planned to rob him of it. One morning all the birds went out into the fields to seek for food, and Hornbill was there too, only he kept away from the crowd, as he was ashamed of being seen with such a tiny beak among birds who all had beaks so well-fitting. After a time Hornbill said to Tomtit : " Tomtit, bring your beak and let me try it on." So they exchanged—Hornbill taking Tomtit's big beak and Tomtit taking Hornbill's tiny one.   When the birds saw Hornbill they admired him and said : " Hornbill, that beak suits you fine ! "   Hornbill was very pleased and began crying : " It suits me fine ! It suits me fine ! It suits me fine, the great beak ! " [1]   Then Tomtit said to Hornbill : " Give me back my beak."   He replied : " No, I will never give it back as it suits me so well."   Then Tomtit began to cry : " *Katiti, katiti,* tiny, oh so tiny "—crying in that way and complaining about his tiny beak.   Hornbill went on wearing the big beak and crying : " It suits me fine ! It suits me fine ! "   And that is still his cry.   But Tomtit still goes complaining : " *Katiti ! Katiti !* Tiny, oh so tiny ! "   And people hearing his cry named him *Ntite, i.e.* Tiny.

PART II

THE ADVENTURES OF SULWE, THE HARE

I. *Why Hare had his Destiny foretold by Tortoise*

HARE went to borrow an axe from Tortoise with the intention of felling trees in the forest.   Tortoise handed him the axe and Hare went off to fell the trees.   But when he returned from the forest he did not restore the axe to Tortoise but kept it at his own place.   Then Tortoise said : " Hare, give me my axe."   Said Hare : " I will not give it you."   So Tortoise returned home and called his wife : " My wife ! "   Said she : " What's the matter ? "   Said he : " Cut me up into pieces and cook me in a big pot ; then when I am cooked boil some porridge also ; when you have finished boiling the porridge load yourself with it all and take it into the forest where Hare is felling trees.   On your arrival there put it on the ground where Hare will pass, and come back here."

Thereupon the wife of Tortoise cut him up into pieces and cooked him in a big pot, and she cooked also some porridge.   When she had finished cooking she loaded herself and took it into the forest where Hare was felling trees and put it down in Hare's tracks.   As Hare was

---

[1] This fits well with the tune, so to speak, of the Hornbill's cry.

returning from felling trees he found the porridge in his tracks where Mrs. Tortoise had put it and also the potful of meat. When he arrived and found this porridge and the potful of meat Hare was astounded, as it was in the midst of the forest; he stood and gazed and then he began to shout: " Who are you that has left the porridge and the potful of meat ? " There was no answer; he called and called, but there was not a voice in reply. Then he thought: " It is my wife who has brought it for me.".

So he began to eat the porridge and the potful of meat. When he had finished eating he took up his trees and went to his village. When he arrived at the village and was about to throw down the trees he heard a voice speaking: " Hare, give me my axe ! " Hare was amazed and said: " As I am the son of a stranger, these trees astonish me ! " He cut the trees up into pieces and threw them away. When he was about to sit on his stool, he heard the voice saying: " Hare, give me my axe ! " Hare said: " As I am Hare, this stool astonishes me ! " He took the stool and burnt it in the fire. Afterwards he thought of going to bed, and again he heard the voice saying: " Hare, give me my axe ! " He got up from the bed and burnt it, saying: " I am astonished ! " When he went outside he heard the voice saying: " Hare, my axe ! " And in the house he heard the voice saying: " Hare, give me my axe ! " Then he took fire, did Hare, and burnt the house. Said he: " As I am Hare, the house speaks ! "

Then Tortoise was amazed and said to himself: " Hare is a person of much cunning." Said Tortoise: " As you would not listen to my pleading, from to-day I put your destiny upon you; you shall not cease to deceive all the animals, you shall be a wise man. And in the end when you die you shall not have your skin stripped from you, you shall be like me in not being skinned; just as I am not skinned, you shall always have a tissue skin; I, He-who-refuses-to-be-surrounded, I say so."

He is not skinned in these days just as Tortoise is not skinned.

NOTE.—The voice haunting Hare seems like conscience; really, of course, it was Tortoise speaking from within Hare's stomach.

2. Hare makes Hippopotamus and Rhinoceros engage in a Tug-of-War

Now Hare set out upon an errand of mischief ; he went first to Rhinoceros and said : " These people have sworn to do so-and-so." Then he ran off to Hippopotamus, and when he arrived called : " You there ! " Hippopotamus answered : " Hallo ! " Said he : " Take hold of this rope and let us pull against each other." Then he ran off to Rhinoceros, and on arrival said : " Take hold of this rope and let us pull each other." Then Hare said : " I am going to return to the bank yonder."

So they began to pull each other, and Rhinoceros was so pulled that he came to put his foot in the water. Said he : " Stu-pendous ! " Then he in turn went back with a rush and Hippopotamus was pulled out upon the bank, and he also ejaculated : " Stu-pendous ! " Hippopotamus called out : " Hare ! Hare ! " Rhinoceros went on pulling and Hippopotamus went on pulling also. After a time Rhinoceros was exhausted and said : " I will go and see that man who is pulling me." And just then Hippopotamus put his head up out of the water and said : " Who is that pulling me ? " Said the other : " Why ! Shinakambeza, it's you pulling me ! " And Chipembele (the Rhino) answered : " It is I." " Why, who was it that tied you up, Chipembele ? " Then Rhinoceros answered : " It was Hare. Was it he who tied you up also, Hippopotamus ? " Said he : " Yes, it was he."

Now that is where the wisdom comes from, in that Rhinoceros comes to the water to drink although they had been at enmity, these two. Rhinoceros had said : " I will not tread in the river." Thus they became reconciled, and that is why Rhinoceros drinks water to-day. Rhinoceros and Hippopotamus, when they do not see each other in the flesh, Rhinoceros will drink water in the river where Hippo lives, and Hippopotamus comes out to go grazing where Rhinoceros has his home.

NOTE.—This is a well-known exploit of the artful Hare. The Babemba tell how he played the same trick upon the Elephant and Hippopotamus (*Journal of the African Society*, vol. iii. p. 68). Indeed it seems that these two animals are the usual figures in the story. See the same story from Calabar in *J.A.S.* vol. iv. p. 307. A Duala story almost identical with the latter is given by Herr Lederbogen in the *Transactions* of the Berlin Oriental Seminary. A Temne version is given by Miss Cronie in *Cunnie Rabbit* (reviewed in *J.A.S.* vol. iv. p. 251). In this it is the spider who challenges the Elephant and Hippopotamus. Mr. Monteil (see review of his *Contes Soudanais* in *J.A.S.* vol. vi. p. 65) also gives a version in which the Elephant takes the place of the Rhino. All the other versions treat the matter as a mere trial of strength, but the Mandinga begin by saying the Hare owed a slave apiece to the Elephant and Hippo ; he then got each to pull against the other on the plea that his captive was attached to the other end. It is the story of " Mr. Tarrypin shows his Strength " in *Uncle Remus*, where one end of Mrs. Meadow's bed-cord is given to Brer Bar.

These animals, like others, have their titles, their " praise-names," which are repeated by people on occasion. Thus Hippopotamus rejoices in the appellations : " Shinakambeza, Muzundazunda, Ingoma ya Batwa, Chiyayoka." And the Rhinoceros is called : " Chinyama chidya mulundongoma," *i.e.* " the great animal that eats the Euphorbia," and Chipembele.

3. *Hare deceives Lion and burns him to Death*

Hare called Lion, saying : " Uncle, stand over yonder, I am going into the ant-heap there." He went off into the ant-hill and then called out to Lion, saying : " Lion, make a fire there and surround the whole ant-hill with it, while I stay here." Lion made the fire ; the fire blazed up, and as soon as it came near him Hare got into a burrow. The whole ant-hill was on fire, while Master Hare had hidden himself in the burrow. When the fire on the ant-hill had burnt out, Master Hare came out of his retreat. He rolled about in the black ash of the grass, and went to show himself to Lion, saying : " Don't you see me, comrade, how that I am not burnt ? Don't you see this ash on me ? " Lion said : " You will give me some of that medicine, so that I may do the same."

So he plucked him some leaves and gave them to him. Then he looked for a large ant-heap with plenty of grass upon it, and Lion went to lie down in the midst of it. Then Hare surrounded the ant-hill on all sides with fire ; when the fire came near to Lion he called out in alarm. Hare answered him by saying : " You mustn't cry out because

of this fire, or you will be burnt." Then the fire got close
and Lion began to burn at his beard. Then the fire reached
his body and his hair began to burn. Then he got all afire
and died. When he had so perished, Master Hare ran off,
saying : " I have played a trick upon my elder." And he
went off to live elsewhere.

NOTE.—This tale reminds one of the tale in *Uncle Remus* about
the Hare and the Wolf. The Hare allured the Wolf to enter a hollow
tree to get the honey by telling him that fire would cause the honey
to " oozle out,"—" en mor'n dat, atter you git de honey all over you,
'taint no use ter try ter burn you up, kaze de honey will puzzuv
you." Of course the Wolf is burnt. The Hare had first led the
Wolf to believe that he himself had escaped easily from the same.
A tale, the motive of which is the same as this, is told by the
Balala (A. C. Madan, *Lala-Lamba Handbook*, pp. 49, 50) of the
Cock and the Wakansuwa (a night bird). There is a Nyanja story
of the Cock and the Swallow which is similar (A. Werner, *British
Central Africa*, p. 238). Also in a Suto tale (Jacottet, *Basuto Lore*,
p. 13) the Hare plays the same trick on the Hlolo rabbit.

4. *Hare plays a Trick upon the Dragon*

Hare and the she-Dragon were without fire, so Hare said :
" Dragon, as we have no fire, let us steal some from the
village." Dragon agreed and said : " All right, let us go."
And Dragon said to Hare : " How are we to steal the fire ? "
Hare answered : " Let us be cunning in our stealing."
Dragon said : " How cunning ? " Said Hare : " Come,
Dragon, let me tie some grass around your head." So
Dragon came to Hare and he tied a bunch of grass around
her head ; and Dragon asked him, saying : " How am I
to steal, now that you have tied a bunch of grass around
my head ? " Hare answered : " Go to the village and on
your arrival stick your head into the fire and the grass will
get ablaze ; then run off and come back here."

So Dragon went to the village of men, and on arrival
entered the village. When they saw her they said : " Here's
a Dragon." And all the people ran away in fear. Dragon
entered a house and found fire blazing ; she put in her
head tied round with grass and the grass on her head
caught fire. She ran off to return to Hare ; she ran
calling out : " Hare ! Hare ! " Hare answered, saying :

" Hallo ! " Said Dragon : " Here's the fire ! " Hare said : " Bring it here ! " So Dragon ran again. But Hare started running also and went on ahead. Then Dragon got on fire and died.

So when Dragon was dead, her child said : " As my mother has died from fire, I shall go and sleep in a hollow tree and in a burrow, I shall not again sit by a fire." Then he turned fierce and said : " I am truly Dragon. I am Lumanyendo. I am the one of the air ! " He got very fierce because of the fire which burnt his mother. He also got red about the neck. And the red wattles he has are the fire with which he was burnt long ago. It is Hare that made him fierce by killing him with fire. He has not again warmed himself at a fire. To this day Dragon frequently dies of fire, by being burnt in the hollow of a tree and in the burrows where he sleeps. It is Hare that established the death of Dragon by fire.

NOTE.—Whether there really is such a monster as Mulala we do not know, but certainly the description of it seems fabulous. It will, it is said, swallow as many as a hundred people in a day and as many cattle. It even flies through the air to reach its victims. Various places are pointed out as its habitat, and those places are carefully avoided by passers-by. Nobody can live within range of its depredations. In the imagination of the people it is a most terrific creature with its fire-darting eyes. " Dragon " seems to convey the idea of it.

5. *Hare makes himself Horns of Beeswax*

Hare and Ground Hornbill went off to a beer drink. It was said : " Nobody without horns is allowed to drink beer." So when Hare heard that he moulded beeswax on his head so that they might think he had horns. They went to the beer drink. On their arrival Hare went to sit near the fire while Hornbill stayed near the door. They gave them beer. Presently Hornbill said : " The beeswax is melting." The people said : " What does he say ? " Hare answered : " Hornbill is asking for the sediment of the beer." They gave him some. When Hornbill looked again at Hare, he saw the beeswax that he had moulded on his head beginning to run down, and he said : " The beeswax is melting." The people said : " What does Hornbill say ? " Hare answered : " He is asking for the lees." They gave him some and he drank. Presently Hare's beeswax melted ; and running Hare ran !—out of the house. That is how he deceived them.

6. *Hare plays a Trick on Ground Hornbill*

Hornbill and Hare left their homes and went off to pay a visit to some relations by marriage. When they left home, Hornbill had a lump of bread and Hare also had a lump of bread. As they were going along they found a stream of running water. Hare said : " Hornbill ! " Said Hornbill : " What do you say, Shanakanchiza ? " Hare said : " I spoke of this little river ; it cannot be crossed in the ordinary way. We must throw our bread into the river in order to cross all right." Hornbill gave his consent, and Hare, beginning, threw a lump of ants' nest, and Hornbill threw in his lump of bread. They crossed over. When they had crossed over Hare said : " The great discoverer has discovered his lump of bread ! " Hornbill said : " And what am I to eat ? " Hare answered, saying : " And you—you throw away your bread and then you say, ' What am I to eat ? ' " Hornbill took out his spear to buy Hare's lump of bread, and he gave it him. But although he ate, Hornbill was not satisfied.

Hare had coveted Hornbill's spear and thought, Let me trick him into selling his spear to me. So they arrived at Hare's relation by marriage, Hornbill and Chinkambaminwe.

NOTE.—Shanakanchiza and Chinkambaminwe are two of Hare's praise-names.

7. *Hare scares Hyena*

" Who are you ? " said Hyena.

" I am He-who-vomits-the-blood-of-his-victims. One family of Hyenas is wiped out. Now I am going to eat you and so start on the second."

Hyena ran off and got into a burrow. And to this day he sleeps in a burrow, does Hyena, and Hare in a bush.

8. *Hare causes Lion, who had stolen his Mother, to be stung to Death by Bees*

Lion stole Hare's mother in order to help a relation pay for a wife. Having stolen Hare's mother, he tied her up in a bundle of grass ; when he had done tying up the bundle he called Hare, Snake and Frog to carry it. So when those three, Hare, Snake and Frog, arrived, Lion said to them : " I called you, friends, to accompany me to my relations' place." So Hare and Snake and Frog consented. They said : " It is well, chief, let us go." Lion said : " Hare, carry the bundle." Hare carried it and they all went on their journey, Lion and Hare and Snake and Frog.

When they arrived at a village they entered, and the people greeted them. They greeted Lion, saying : " You are still in the land of the living ? " Lion answered : " We are." Said they : " What's the news ? " Said Lion : " Nothing particular, only that Hare is carrying a bundle that he knows nothing of." They greeted Hare and he simply answered : " Yes, we are still alive." Said they : " What's the news ? " Said he : " There is none." They greeted Snake, saying : " You are still alive ? " Snake answered : " We are still alive." Said they : " What's the news ? " Said he : " We went far, very far indeed, in order to swallow some little short people." They greeted Frog, saying : " Frog, you are still alive." Said he : " We are still alive." " What's the news ? " Said he : " One can swallow a softy without difficulty." All this puzzled Hare.

They left that village and went their way. On the road Hare stayed behind and untied the bundle and found his mother inside ; he took her out and tied up some bees in her stead. Again they arrived at a village, and the people greeted them in the same way, saying : " Lion, you are still alive ? " Said he : " We are still alive." " What's the news ? " Said he : " Nothing particular, only Hare is carrying a bundle that he knows nothing of." " Snake, you are still alive ? " Said he : " We are still alive." Said they : " What's the news ? " Said he : " We went far, very far indeed, in order to swallow some little short people."

" Frog, you are still alive ? "   Said he : " We are still alive."
" What's the news ? "   Said he :   " One can swallow a
softy without difficulty."   Said they :   " Hare, you are
still alive ? "   Said he :   " We are still alive."   " What's
the news ? "   Said he :   " Cunning he has who cunning
has."

They left that village and went on travelling to Lion's
relations' home ;   on arrival there they entered the house
and Lion put therein the bundle.   Hare went out with
Frog, leaving Snake and Lion in the house.   They shut the
door and Lion said to his relations, " Hare's mother is in
the bundle.   Untie it."   They untied it and all the house
was filled with bees.   Snake entered a burrow, but Lion
and his relations were killed by the bees ;   so they perished,
the whole lot of them.

9. *Hyena, incited thereto by Hare, wants to wear a Lion's Skin*

Hare said :   " I will wear Lion's skin."   When Hyena
saw Hare wearing Lion's skin, he said to Hare :   " Hare ! "
Hare answered :   " Hallo ! "   Said Hyena :   " Where did
you get that skin ? "   Said Hare :   " I got it by killing ;
go you and hunt and kill a Lion and you will get a skin
also."

Hyena agreed and went to hunt the Lions with a club.
He found the Lions did Hyena, but as he was throwing his
club the Lions chased him.   Hyena ran away and went
to Hare ;   and on reaching Hare said :   " Hare ! "   Hare
answered saying :   " Hallo ! "   Said Hyena :   " You deceived me and I shall kill you."   So Hare ran off, entered
a burrow, and stripped himself of the Lion's skin, and went
out at the escape-hole.   Hyena also entered the burrow, but
when he tried to get out found the Lions at the entrance.
He went back into the burrow and did not come out again
but died there in the burrow.   So it is said :   " A crow
doesn't find his Impande unsuitable to wear " (that is, a
man can wear his own armour but not another's).

NOTE.—An impande is the round white shell worn as an ornament, and the white-breasted crow is said to wear one.

10. *How Hare and Crocodile helped each other*

Hare was sitting in the bush by the side of a river and wanted a canoe. When he saw Crocodile travelling in a canoe Hare shouted out : " Take me in ! " So Crocodile brought the canoe to Hare.   Then Hare began to run down the canoe which Crocodile had brought to him ; said he : " It stinks horribly, vilely—awful ! " Then Crocodile said : " What do you say, Hare ? " Hare answered, saying : " No, chief, your canoe is very fine, it surpasses all other canoes." Again Hare was mumbling : " This canoe of a slave stinks horribly.   I have got myself into a mess by entering this canoe."   Again Crocodile said : " You, Hare, have got a lot to say, you are always talking about my canoe."   Hare said : " No, chief, I am very pleased indeed to enter the canoe of a chief."

Presently the canoe arrived at the bank.   Then Hare said : " Do you want some meat, Crocodile ? " Crocodile answered : " I want it very badly."   Then he said : " You must go and cover yourself up entirely with mud.   I am going to bring you some meat, and you must make yourself like a corpse."

So Crocodile wrapped himself up in mud, and Hare went off, going along calling out : " Is there nobody who wants meat ? " Now there was a Hyena near who heard and ran to Hare ; said he : " What do you say, Hare ? " Hare said : " My word !   There is meat yonder at the river, are you hungry ? " Hyena said : " I am very hungry indeed."

So they went off together.   When they arrived at the river, he said : " Now, Hyena, you must keep your eyes very wide open.   I left the meat here in this muddy place." Presently he said : " Hurrah !   There's the meat yonder." So Hyena took a spring and seized the meat, saying : " I am grateful, Hare."   Hare said : " You must not eat it here, take it yonder, and eat it in the deep water and wash the meat well."

Now Hyena did so ; he tugged and took the meat to the shallow water.   Then Hyena asked: " Is it here I am to eat ? " Hare said : " No, take it to deep water up to your neck." Then Hyena took it farther out, and Hare said : " Crocodile, seize him ; that slave wants very badly to eat." Then Crocodile arose and laid hold of Hyena with force, killed him, and drew him down below. Thereupon Hare went off and Hyena was at the bottom of the river.

NOTE.—Another version of this tale shows that the canoe that Hare was so contemptuous of was nothing but Crocodile's own body on which he was crossing the stream. No wonder he did not want Crocodile to hear his remarks in midstream. In this version, too, Hare opens the conversation by saying : " *Nvhuna olwa ku muma, ame ndakuvhuna olwa ku menzhi* : " Help me in my need on the bank and I will help you in yours in the water." That is now a proverb with something of the meaning of : " Do good to others that they may do good to you."

11. *Hare kills many Lions*

Hare once found some Lions eating meat, and when he found them he said : " Let me pick the fleas out of your tails." But he was deceiving them. They thought he was picking out fleas, whereas he was digging pits. When he had finished digging the pits, he buried their tails and rammed them down tight. When he had done ramming, he went into the forest and fetched a big drum ; he began beating it in order to deceive them. When the Lions heard the big drum they tried to flee, and he went on beating vigorously the big drum so that they should run away and leave the meat behind. Then again he said : " At the family of Hares is the place to take refuge." So the Lions broke away, leaving their tails, which he had rammed down so hard.

Later, Hare plucked the hair all out of his body, and came and met the Lions and asked them : " Haven't you seen those people who said they would eat me ? " The Lions answered saying : " We have not seen them who said they would eat you." And then the Lions said : " You are Hare who caused us to break our tails." Hare answered, saying : " No, I am not. Perhaps it is my namesake, Hare." Then Hare said to himself : " They will kill me, I had better trick them." So he called them, saying : " Come here and take down my axe for me." But underneath he had dug a game-pit. Then the Lions said : " Who was it that hung up the axe ? " Said he : " Come and take down the axe for me, I am too short." When Lion reached up to bring down the axe he fell into the game-pit. When he fell into the game-pit Hare took down his axe, jumped into the pit and cut Lion about and killed him. He called another. He also came, and in trying to take down the axe fell into the game-pit. He killed him. There came another, and he killed him. He finished them all. When he had done killing them, he went back to the meat ; on arriving at the meat he built a platform and dried the meat ; thereupon he built a village and became a chief.

12. *Hare deceives Jackal three times*

Hare and Jackal were going visiting and on the way found some grass. On finding the grass Hare said : " Comrade, this grass—when we are given ground-nuts there where we are going, fetch the grass so that we can roast the nuts with it."

When they arrived at their destination the people gave them nuts. When they gave them nuts, Hare said : " Comrade, go and bring yon grass that we left in the way, so that we may roast the nuts." During the time he was gone to fetch the grass, Hare ate the nuts they had been given. On Jackal's return he asked : " Where are the nuts that they gave us ? Here is the grass." Hare answered, saying : " The owners have eaten them."

Again they departed and went to the cattle-post. As they were going along in the way they found some pieces of calabash : and Hare said : " Comrade, when we are given milk you must come back for these bits of calabash so that we can use them to drink our milk." On their arrival they were given some thick milk ; on being given the milk, Hare said : " Comrade, bring those bits of calabash that we left in the way, let us drink our milk from them." While he was going Hare drank all the milk, only some he spilt on the ground. Then Jackal returned, bringing the bits of calabash, and said : " Here are the pieces of calabash, bring the milk and let us eat." Hare answered, saying : " I am greatly astonished, Comrade, because the milk they gave us they have taken it away again and eaten it. See here is where they were eating and spilt some of it." Jackal was grieved very much on account of his friend having deceived him twice. Jackal has no cunning.

On another occasion, Hare said : " Let us go and eat ground-nuts, Jackal." They went off and when they reached the nut field dug up the nuts. When they were drunk with them they slept ; Master Hare arose in the night and dug a deep hole and buried the tail of Jackal and rammed it down hard. When he had done ramming he aroused him, saying : " Get up, my dear, people are coming. They will kill us, let us be off." He himself ran, but his friend was unable to run, and the owners of the nuts found him. They killed Jackal. That is how his friend deceived him. Jackal has no cunning.

13. *Hare breaks all Lion's Teeth and so kills him*

Master Hare found Lion and said : " Let us go and play as my uncles the Elephants played." Lion answered, saying : " Let us go."

On their arrival Lion climbed a tree and Hare looked for a fairly large stone. Lion took that stone with him into the tree. When Lion was about to throw it from near by, Hare said : " No, go right away up there among the leaves, while I am still preparing myself here below." Hare plucked some leaves and chewed them. Lion let the stone go and Hare opened his mouth. When he saw it coming near him Hare jumped away and dodged so that it did not drop where he was. Just as it fell, Hare spat out the leaves on to the stone and asked Lion, saying : " Don't you see these little dirty things ? " [1] Lion agreed, saying : " Yes. And now I will open my mouth and you climb to the top of the tree with the stone."

Hare took it, and Lion below opened his mouth. Hare went right to the tip-top to let the stone go from there. Lion opened his mouth and when he saw the stone coming near he opened it very widely indeed. And as he opened

---

[1] The idea is, of course, that the stone went through his body.

his mouth in that manner the stone reached his teeth and all the teeth were smashed. And Lion died.

When Hare descended he said : " As for me I am astonished. How do these uncles of mine open their mouths ? I told him myself, saying : Open your mouth very widely. And he opened it only just a little. And so for that reason he has killed himself. Once again have I deceived these uncles of mine."

When he had done this, he ran and went away.

NOTE.—There is a Lala tale (A. C. Madan, *Lala-Lamba Handbook*, pp. 46, 47) called Kalulu ne Nkalamu which is similar. Instead of a tree, Hare tells Lion to climb a hill and roll down the stone. The Hare jumps aside and spits leaves upon it, seeing which the Lion thought the stone certainly went into Hare's stomach. Of course on trying to emulate Hare he meets with disaster ; not at once but next morning.

14. *Hare eats Lion's Children*

Mrs. Lion bore children, and after she had borne them Hare came to nurse them. Mrs. Lion went out to graze, and Hare ate one of the young Lions. He went about with a grain-mortar outside the village (that its impressions on the sand might resemble Elephant's footprints). When Mrs. Lion returned he deceived her by saying : " Some Elephants passed by and it is they who ate your child." He took out one of the children and went to suckle it at its mother. Afterwards Mrs. Lion went out to hunt, and on her return she found that Hare had eaten them all, every one.

Hare went travelling and he found some animals at their village that they had built, he found them playing. He deceived them, saying : " To-morrow I am going to bring my Dog, come and see it." He went back to tie Mrs. Lion up, and having tied her round the neck, he said : " Lion, I have found those who ate your children. I deceived them, saying : to-morrow I shall bring my Dog ; come and see it."

Next morning they went off ; Hare tied Mrs. Lion up with a rope around her neck and took her to that village, saying : " Let me take you to those who ate your children.

When I get there I shall say: See my Dog!—and then you shall kill them."

On his arrival, he said: "See my Dog!" All the animals admired it and said: "A fine Dog!" Presently he took the rope off her neck, and she ran and bit all the animals. When they were all bitten, they cut up the meat, and having cut up the meat they dried it, and when it was dry loaded themselves with it.

Hare loaded himself, so did Mrs. Lion, and they went off on their journey. On the way the carrying-stick of Mrs. Lion broke and Hare said: "Go and cut another." While she was away, Hare went off with all Mrs. Lion's meat. When Mrs. Lion came back she found the meat missing, and though she looked about she could not find Hare.

She went off to have the matter divined by Mr. Ant, and he said: "Go and look in the water and there you will see Hare." She went to the water; on arrival she looked and saw a shadow [1] in the water and the meat; she dived in and came up. Again she looked in the water and found the shadow, and again she dived into the water, but she was unable to see Hare. She went back to Mr. Ant, and he said: "Go and look in the tree on the river bank and you will see Hare." She went to look in the tree and found Hare. As soon as Hare saw her, he said: "Mrs. Lion, open your mouth, here is some bread." He put a stone into the bread, and when Mrs. Lion opened her mouth Hare threw it into her mouth. He destroyed all her teeth and then Hare ran off.

NOTE.—The eating of lioness's cubs by the Hare is a frequent incident in Bantu tales. In another version of the Ila tale, the cubs number ten and the Hare eats one each day, but every day, till the last, he deceives the mother by bringing out a cub ten times and taking it back. In a Suto tale (Jacottet, *op. cit.* p. 40) the Jackal deceives a Leopard in the same way. Mr. Jacottet quotes other references, and suggests that in the Suto tale the Jackal has been substituted for the Hare.

---

[1] It was, of course, Hare's shadow she saw and thought it was himself under the water, while really he was up in the tree. Another instance of the stupidity of the Lion tribe.

15. *Hare is outwitted by Mrs. Tortoise*

All the animals were dying of thirst, and they said : " Let us see who will be the first to reach the water." Now, Mrs. Tortoise had borne many children, and she went along burying them in the earth, and one child she buried by the side of the water.

Now all the animals said : " Let us run hard and go to the river and drink water."

They rose early and all ran, saying : " Let us see who will be the first to arrive."

So they ran and the Tortoises went on saying: "Forward, oh companions of Hare ! " Again they ran and again the tortoises said : " Forward, oh companions of Hare ! " The sun went down and they went on shouting : " One day has passed. Forward, oh companions of Hare ! "

Next day the animals were dead with fatigue, and the child of Mrs. Tortoise who was by the water-side shouted : " Forward, oh companions of Hare ! "

And Hare was done up and could not reach the water. And Mrs. Tortoise's child that was by the river-side brought them water in his mouth ; he came to spew it out for the animals. He said : " And it is you who started the dispute saying, We will outdo Tortoise in speed. And now what's the matter that you did not arrive ? You are youngsters. I am the great-one ; I reached the water. You are youngsters." Then he spat out the water for them which he had in his mouth. And they were unable to answer a word, but were simply ashamed.

NOTE.—Brer Rabbit in *Uncle Remus* is defeated in the same way by Brer Tarrypin. " He had a wife en th'ee chilluns, old Brer Tarrypin did, en dey wuz all de ve'y spin and image er de ole man. . ." On the day of the race : " ole Brer Tarrypin en his ole 'oman, en his th'ee chilluns dey got up 'fo' sun up and went ter de place. De ol 'oman she tuck 'er stan' nigh de fus' mile pos', she did, en de chilluns nigh de udders, up ter de las', en dar old Brer Tarrypin he tuck his stan'."

16. *How Hare deceives the Animals and drives them away from the Fruit*

Once in the season of the Imbula fruit all the animals of every species whatsoever were in the forest eating the fruit as ordained by God; only Jackal and Hare found none for them as the others gave them no room. This annoyed Jackal and Hare. Next day, being very hungry, Hare went to call Fish-eagle, saying: " Chungwe ! " The Fish-eagle answered: " Hallo, Sulwe! What is it ? " Said Hare : " You are able to fly, so come and sit on an Imbula tree where all the animals are eating. Then when I come to them I shall suggest to them that we call aloud to God and ask Him whose land this is, and do you reply : 'It belongs to Hare and Jackal.' Do you understand ? "

So Fish-eagle went and sat on the Imbula tree. It was early morning and there was a great crowd of animals wending their way to the Imbula forest. Hare and Jackal had made a compact. Hare had said : " Let us go at dawn and call to God. Those animals always cheat us so that we never get any Imbula." And Jackal had agreed, saying : " Splendid. We will get up very early." So they slept lightly, and when the first cock crowed they were on their feet going to the forest. When they got near they saw the great crowd of animals coming up, and as they were about to eat the fruit Jackal and Hare arrived. Hare said to them : " Now then, all of you. To-day you must not start eating yet." All the animals said to Hare : " Tell us what you have to say, Sulwe." Jackal and Hare replied : " What we have got to do is to call aloud to God in the sky, to ask whose land it is, so that we may hear what He says on the matter." The animals said : " We agree. That is good." Now Fish-eagle was sitting up in the tree and had been told by Hare : " When I shout, do not answer, but when Elephant shouts answer as I told you." So Hare shouted out first, and then Elephant shouted, and Fish-eagle made reply : " The land belongs to Jackal and Hare." Hearing this answer, all the animals were stricken with surprise and said : " What does God say ? " Elephant

answered : " He says the land belongs to Hare and Jackal."
So the animals said : " Elephant, ask again ; how can this
land belong to Jackal and Hare ? "   So Elephant shouted
again : " O God, to whom does the land belong ? "   And
Chungwe—whose voice they took to be God's—replied :
" It belongs to Hare and Jackal."   The animals yelled in
chorus : " How can it be theirs ? "   And Elephant asked
again : " O God, how can it belong to Hare and Jackal ? "
And Chungwe, whom they supposed to be God, replied : " It
does belong to them.   Leave off eating the fruit here in
this Imbula forest.   Only Jackal is to eat it ! "   So all the
animals made their departure crestfallen.   Since then they
have no longer eaten Imbula fruit ; which became the
property of Jackal and other soft-footed things like himself.
Hare has plenty of wisdom, but he himself does not
now eat Imbula.   Jackal became *Shimbula* ; that is his
name : " Eater of Imbula."   And this because of Hare's
deceiving them by sending Fish-eagle to the forest to
impersonate God.

17. *How Hare made a Fool of himself*

Hare and Crested Crane went out to dig up a certain root
named munkonyongo, and presently Hare left what he had
with Crested Crane while he went some distance off to dig
others.   While he was gone his companion ate Hare's roots.
On returning, Hare asked for his roots and Crested Crane
answered : " I have eaten them, my dear."   Hare then
claimed compensation, and was given the crest off Crane's
head.

Having received this, Hare went off to another district
and there met a man who had no head ornament.   He said
to the man : " You do not look well, oh man, without an
ornament on your head."   The man answered : " Lend
me your crest."   Hare handed it to him and he put it on.
He went off and on the road lost the crest and going back
to Hare said : " Sulwe, the crest is lost."   Hare said to
him : " No, don't say that.   How is it that you have thrown
away my crest ?   I got it from Crested Crane, my brother,
in return for my munkonyongo which he ate.   You must

give me compensation." So the man gave Hare a spear, who took it and went to another place.

There he found a man who was trying to skin an animal with his nails, and said to him : " You are in trouble having no spear." The man answered : " True, Sulwe, I am in trouble." Hare said : " Here's a spear, take it and skin your animal." The man took it and used it, but after finishing his work lost the spear. Presently Hare returned to him and said : " Where's the spear you were skinning with ? " Said he : " Since I finished skinning I haven't seen it." Hearing that, Hare said to the man : " You must give me something for the spear you have lost." The man gave him some lumps of meat, and after taking it, Hare went off to another place.

Here he found a man eating bread without a relish and said to him : " Here in this place what do you use as a relish with your food ? " The man replied : " Nothing. We only have bread." Said Hare : " Here's some meat." The man took and ate it and when he had done so Hare said to him : " Give me something for my meat you have eaten." The man paid Hare some meal.

Hare went off to another place carrying the meal, and there found a man making a supper off meat. Said Hare to him : " What are you eating ? " The man replied : " What am I supping ? Meat only." Said Hare : " Here's some meal ; eat." The man took it with thanks and ate it. Then Hare waxed indignant and said : " Give me back my meal which you have eaten." The man answered : " How can I do that ? I've eaten it." Hare said : " You must give me something then for the meal you have eaten. I got it from a man who was eating bread because he ate my meat, and the meat I got from a man skinning an animal with his nails who lost the spear I lent him ; and the spear I got from a man to whom I had given a crest ; the crest I got from Crested Crane, who had eaten my munkonyongo." The man gave Hare a new earthenware pot, unbaked.

So Hare went off to another place. On the way he came to a pool of water and took his pot from his shoulder to draw some water, but when he put it into water the pot dissolved and came to an end.

So Hare burst into tears and was much ashamed of himself. He could no longer go about extorting things from people now that his pot was dissolved. And so it is said : " Wisdom does not sleep in one head "—which is to say : Even a wise man is a fool sometimes.

18. *Hare's last Adventures and Death*

Elephant and Hare found some fruit called munjebele, and they found there also an old woman living in a tumble-down house. Lion passed by and found that old woman ; and she gathered some of the fruit as a welcoming gift, saying : " This is the food that I eat here." Lion asked, saying : " What is the name of that fruit ? " And she told him, saying : " Munjebele." Said she : " Go along saying it in the road and tell your friends, so that you may eat that which you found here."

But on the way Lion came to a slippery place and fell ; and on reaching his friends they asked him, saying : " What is the fruit which you ate there ? " He said : " I fell midway and have forgotten the name."

And so Elephant went there that he might ask the name. On Elephant's arrival at the old woman's she told him, saying : " That fruit is munjebele. Go along singing : Munjebele, munjebele. Don't forget." When he arrived at the same place where Lion fell, the Elephant fell also, and forgot the name of munjebele.

On his arrival Hare went off, and reaching that old woman he asked, saying : " What is the name of that fruit which they say they have forgotten ? " Said she : " Munjebele." And she gave him a bell. She tied the bell around his neck, saying : " When you are going to fall, call out : Munjebele ! munjebele ! " When he came there to the slippery place he fell, but called out : " Munjebele ! "

Hare arrived there where his friends were, and he plucked some of that munjebele fruit and ate. His friends inquired : " Do you know the name ? " Still going on eating, he said : " It is munjebele ; eat it without bother."

When he had done eating, Hare said : " Let us go to

water, I know where, and let us drink." When they had
done drinking they slept behind that pool.

It was said: "He who commits a nuisance will be
killed; this is the pool of other people." While they slept
in the night Hare had stomach-ache and went to relieve
himself near Elephant, so that they might say, Our uncles
the elephants have made the mess, and if anyone was to
be destroyed for it they would kill Elephant. So they
killed Elephant.

They said: "Who is to carry his head?" They said:
"Hare, of course!" So they took up their meat and
went off. Master Hare lagged behind, saying: "The
big head of Great-skull burdens me." Then he sang:
"He made a mess, that little one, and smeared it upon
Jumbo." He found Buffalo resting on ahead, and Buffalo
asked him, saying: "What are you going along singing
about, Hare?" Said he: "Nothing, my uncle. I was
singing: 'The big head burdens me, it needs Great-skull
to bear it himself.'" Buffalo called Hare, saying: "Let
us go on." Once again he put his burden down and
Buffalo passed on in front. And again he took up
his song, saying: "He made a mess, that little one, and
smeared it upon Jumbo."

Elephant caught hold of him, saying: "It is you who
told lies about the elder." Hare said: "Now as you
have taken me in this way, you must not hit me on the
rock, or I shall not die. Hit me yonder on the burrow of
Spring Hare; that is where I shall die." But the little
one was deceiving them. When they reached the burrow
and were about to hit him, he got into the burrow.

One of them put his arm into the burrow and caught
him by the leg, but he spoke in the burrow, saying: "It's
not me you are holding, it's a big root!" When he heard
that he who had hold of him let go, saying: "It seems
truly that I had hold of a root." So they brought a hoe
and began to dig, and the little one went out and came
along the road, with his hair braided and changed into a
human being. On his arrival he asked Elephant, saying:
"What are you digging here, uncle?" Said he: "We
are digging out Master Hare, he left us and got into the

burrow." Said he : " Bring the hoe and let me dig." He dug, and the hoe-handle came out. Said he : " What are we to hit the hoe upon ? If we hit it on a tree it will not be firm. Bring one of your legs and let us hit it on that."

He hit it a little, and dug, and again the handle came out. Said he : " Bring forward your head, uncle, let us hit it on that." He chopped him, he chopped him, and then went into the burrow.

Buffalo put in his arm and caught hold of him. And the little one sang his song—just this : " It is not me you have caught, you are holding a large root."

They said : " Let's go and divine the matter." They went off to get it divined by Mr. Ant. Mr. Ant said : " Now when you see him, simply get hold of him."

They came back. On arrival they dug. And the little one appeared in the road, coming along playing a hand-piano, and when he arrived he inquired, saying : " What are you digging ? " Said they : " We are digging-out that one who wounded our friend and killed him." Now they mistook him and so did not seize him : he took the hoe from them and dug. The handle came out and he said : "Buffalo, my uncle, bring your head, let us hit it on that." He wounded him just there, and got into the burrow. They caught hold of him and he sang his song : " It's not me you've caught, you are holding a big root."

Then they said : " He's too much for us. He has very great cunning. Let us leave him."

Later on, all the animals were collected together and they said : " Let us go and dig out the water-hole." When Hare heard that, he said : " I refuse to dig the water-hole. I have got my own water." When all the animals heard that, they said : " Hare, as you refuse to dig the water-hole, if we see you getting water out of our hole we shall kill you." When he heard that, Hare said : " No, as for me, I don't want to get water out of your hole."

Then all the animals went to dig out the water-hole. When they had done digging, Lion said : " Now it is necessary that one should watch, let it be Gnu." So Gnu stayed behind to guard the water-hole.

Then as he was looking out he saw Hare coming along to the hole ; so Gnu said : " Now though you have come here you shall not get water." He drove Hare away. As Hare was turning round Gnu saw the calabash of honey on his back, and said : " What's that ? " Hare answered : " In here there is mangwalozhi,[1] and if an adult is not tied up he cannot eat it." Gnu said : " Give me a taste." Hare gave him a taste. When he knew the niceness of it Gnu said to him : " Tie me ! " So he tied him up with strength and entered the hole and drew water. When he had done drawing, he went off, leaving Gnu tied up.

After a time all the animals came to drink and found Gnu tied up. Said they : " You big fellow, how did that little child tie you up ? " They unbound him. Then they left Lion, saying : " If you see him, bite him."

Later on Hare came back ; Lion got very fierce and said : " What do you want ? Yesterday you tied one person up." He got very fierce indeed, and drove him away. As Hare turned round Lion saw the calabash on his back and said : " What's that ? " Hare answered : " In here there is mangwalozhi, and if an adult is not tied up he may not eat it." Then Lion said : " Let me taste." Hare gave him some. Then he said : " Tie me up ! " So Hare tied him up and, after cutting off his tail, went off.

When the Elephants came down they said : " He has tied you up, you big fellow, you who are able to bite all the animals ! Why ? " Then Lion answered : " Because he has got cunning." Then they said : " We will leave Elephant." Elephant stayed behind and Hare came. Elephant drove him off, saying : " Leave me alone and go away." Then when he looked he saw the calabash, and said : " What have you got ? " Said he : " I have got some mangwalozhi, and unless an adult is tied up he may not eat it." Said he : " Let me taste." He gave him to taste, and Elephant said : " Tie me up ! " Then he tied

---

[1] *Mangwalozhi*, literally, " Things tied up with string." What they were we do not know. They must have been bewitchingly delicious to have enticed so easily Hare's enemies into offering themselves to be tied up, if only they might enjoy them. Evidently some ambrosia of Hare's own making. And we are led to suppose that, after all, his victims only had the preliminary taste.

him up, and threw him away over there and drew some water.

When he had done he went off. When the others came back they found Elephant already tied up, and said : " We cannot manage that person, he has got cunning."

Then Tortoise said : " I will stay behind at the hole and watch—I ! " Then they acted cunningly. They put bird-lime all over Tortoise's body and put him by the hole.

Presently he saw Hare coming ; then Tortoise said : " Let him come, that Hare, he shan't draw water." Then Hare arrived at the hole and said to himself : " It's that bad fellow they've left at the hole ! " Then Hare said : " I am going to draw water to-day." Hare went into the hole, and pushed past Tortoise, and his arm stuck fast. Then he kicked him with his feet, and they also stuck. Said he : " If I butt you with my head you will die." He butted him with his head and the head stuck fast. He struck him with his tail and that also stuck.

Then the big ones came, they seized Hare and killed him.

And that is the end of Hare's history.

NOTE.—The latter part of this tale is found among the Basuto (Jacottet : *op. cit.* p. 32), but there it is the Jackal that refuses to dig. The Rabbit keeps watch and is deceived again and again by the Jackal; then the Tortoise is set to watch and catches him. Mr. Jacottet says the story seems to be very popular in S. Africa and cites tales from the Basubia, Baronga, and Basumbwa in which Hare plays the part taken by the Jackal in the Suto story. He suggests that Hare is the original figure, and that Jackal is substituted probably through direct or indirect Hottentot influence.

Hare's end is to be compared with Uncle Remus's story of the wonderful tar-baby.

PART III

TALES OF PEOPLE AND ANIMALS

1. *The Man who called Lions to his aid*

A MAN lived in the forest with his wife and son. Some people were sent by their master, saying : " Go and hunt for some meat for me." During their hunting they found this woman in the forest, and she gave them some milk. Then they turned back, and on their return they said to their master: " There where we went we found a fine woman whom you, chief, ought to marry." Then the chief answered: " Go and bring her." They said: " We will go in the morning."

Next day they went their way for the purpose of finding that woman, and on their arrival they said to her: " You must take a journey." The woman did not refuse but said: " Let us go." She took her ceremonial axe. Then she went off, carrying her pot of fat.

Then the child began to call his father, saying: " Father, hunting, hunting game there in the forest ! " His father heard the calling and came back. Then the father put down his meat—Reedbuck—and asked his child, saying: " Who has taken away your mother ? " Said he: " Strangers." Thereupon his father went off, carrying his bow ; and the track that his wife had passed along was not lost. He found them and said: " Where are you taking my wife to ? " They said: " We were sent by the chief." Then he drove them off, killing one and cutting off the lips of the other. He who had his lips cut off, when he arrived at the chief's, said: " It is not possible to arrive there." The chief answered, saying: " You are fools." And he said also: " My men shall go."

Then he sounded his alarm bell, did the chief of the district, and it called the young men. Then they assembled at the chief's. Next morning they started to go to the woman. When they arrived the woman gave them milk. When they had drunk the milk, they inquired: " Where has your husband gone ? " She answered: " He has gone into the forest." Then they told the woman: " It is you we have come for, the chief wants you to be his wife."

Then the woman rose up, and that child began to look about and to call: " Father, where you are hunting game yonder ! " When his father heard it he came running, and on arrival said to the child: " Who are they ? " Said he: " The same that took her first." So on his arrival he said to the child: " Stay here, I am going to bring your mother."

He found those people had already arrived at their chief's. And he pressed on after them, and on arrival he sat down and the chief said : " Give that person some water." But the man refused to take water from a slave. Then the chief said : " As he refuses, let some good man take the water." And again he said : " Who will take water to that person ? " Then they said : " Bring out his wife." So they brought her out, gave her water, and said : " Take and carry it to your husband." She smiled and was pleased. And the man said : " Let us sit here under the tree until we return." So the woman sat down. Then the man said : " Kalundungoma, my wife ! " When it grew dark he asked his wife : " My wife, Kalundungoma, do you like being here ? " And the woman said : " I shall return home, I can't be a chief's wife." The man said : " Let us go." So that night when it was dark they made their escape.

When he arrived at his village he went off to summon the Lions, saying : Those people must not come back here again. When the Lions arrived they sat down in the road so that those people should not return. Those Lions numbered six.

Once again that chief sent his people, saying : " Go and fetch me my wife, the one whom I admired so." Then when the man saw the people sent by the chief—there were seventy of them—he sent the Lions, saying : " Do not spare them, eat them all, let them come to an end." On hearing that the Lions were glad and said : " We see meat ! "

Then they rushed upon them, scattered and finished them ; they spared one only. He returned to the chief and said : " By the ash ! oh chief, do not send people again : that man has summoned to his assistance sixty lions ! "

Then the chief abandoned his scheme, being afraid, and said : " All my people will be finished if I go on with it." So the man and his wife lived on happily.

2. *Kantanga and the Lions*

There was a Lion and a pregnant woman. Famine had entered the district. When the woman saw the Lions she

said : " Oh you Lions, what meat have you ? "   The lions
answered : " We have got Nabunga meat."   Then she
said : " Yes, you have meat, give me some."   And she
added : " I have a child in my womb, and if you will give
me meat, when the child is born I will give him to you ;
when the famine is over you shall fetch and eat him."
Then the Lions gave her meat, saying : " Take and eat and
live."   Then she accepted the meat, took it home, and ate.

The Lions waited as the days went by, and then set out ;
on their arrival they said : " Where is our meat ? "   The
woman answered : " He is over yonder—my child.   His
name is Kantanga ; go and call aloud : ' Kantanga ! ' "
They shouted : " Kantanga !   Your mother is calling you."
Then Kantanga, as he had ivory bracelets on his arms, took
them off and gave to his companions, one he gave a bracelet
and to another another.[1]   Then his friends said : " We
are all of us Kantanga ! "   The Lions called, saying :
" Youngster, Kantanga, come, your mother is calling you ! "

Not finding him the Lions went back in anger, and on
arriving at the mother they fiercely said : " We have not
seen your child."   Then she told them : " Hide there in
the nut-patch, conceal yourselves under the nut-bushes."
Then the woman called her child, saying : " Come here,
Kantanga, namesake of my father, go into the nut-patch
and bring me a pumpkin."   Now her child had a play-
spear in his hand, and he said to his companions : " I am
going to throw it yonder and spear the thing that is there."
Thereupon he threw his toy-spear into the nut-bushes, but
it was where a Lion was lying hiding, and he speared it
with his toy-spear.   Then the Lions ran away.   On arriving
where his mother was, she asked him : " Kantanga, where
is the pumpkin I sent you for ? "   Kantanga answered :
" Here it is."   When the woman saw the pumpkin she
was alarmed ; and she herself thought : " Now the Lions
will kill me when they return."

The Lions came back.   On their arrival they said :
" Give us our meat."   The woman answered : " Go to the

---

[1] Kantanga is on the alert, fearing some danger. He tries to minimise
it by making his friends as much like himself as possible—so that one may
be taken in mistake for himself.

water-hole, and when you get there, hide by diving into the water. When you are hid I will send him to fetch water, and just there you will catch him." Then she called her child, saying : " Kantanga, my child, I am thirsty, go and fetch me some water." Then she gave Kantanga the water-calabashes. When he came to a bush he called a Mason-Wasp, saying : " Mason-Wasp, go and fetch me water." The Mason-Wasp went and drew water for him. Then his mother was alarmed and said : " Where does he get this wisdom from ? "

After a time the Lions came out of the water and said : " That person is deceiving us. Her child that she said was coming to the water, what is he doing ? " Then they returned to the mother angrily, saying, let us eat the mother. On their arrival they said : " Our meat ! " The woman answered, saying : " My masters, do not kill me. Go and hide in the house."

Then the woman put the Lions in the house and hid them in big water-jars and covered them up. Then she called him : " Kantanga, Kantanga ! " On his arrival, he said : " What do you call me for ? " His mother said : "I called you, my child, to give me a pot out of the house." Then Kantanga answered : " This little old woman beats us very much, and now she has her friends in the house, and she wants them to catch me." He went in ; as he was uncovering a pot they seized him, took him away, and tied him up in a bundle of grass. On arrival in their district they seized him, and, washing out a pot, put him therein, and after pouring water into the pot they put it on the fire. They said : " Tell the child of So-and-so, who survived Mr. Hare's consumption of his brothers, to come and stir up the fire." They went off hunting.

Now when Kantanga felt the pot getting hot, he came out, and took from their child the fringed blanket he had on and clothed himself in it ; then he seized the lionet and put him into the pot. And then he himself sat down to stir up the fire.

Late in the afternoon they came back from where they had gone to hunt. On their arrival they inquired : " Is the meat cooked, child ? " He answered : " It is cooked."

Said they : " Bring it here." He took the pot off the fire and carried it to where they were. They proceeded to dish up, and when they had finished, they offered him a leg of the child, but he refused, saying : " No, dad, I don't eat cooked meat." When they had done eating, he escaped at dawn. In the morning the Lions looked about and called : " Where are you, orphan ? Come and give us water." They came to find all quiet in the place ; he had gone. Then they said : " That person cooked for us our own child, and as for him he won't return to his mother, but has gone to a foreign country." Indeed he had gone to another country, and had gone to live at Kapepe's place.

Thereupon the Lions swiftly made their way to his mother, and on arrival said : " Where has your child gone to ? He went and killed our child for us." Then his mother answered : " I haven't seen him, my brothers, and if you keep on coming here always you will get into trouble." Then the Lions were afraid, and said : " This saying is true. If we keep on coming here always we shall find trouble." That's all.

3. *The Woman who married a Fish*

There was a woman who had no husband, and she said : " I wish I had a man to marry me." Then they told her : " As you want a husband, cut some small sticks and weave a fish-trap. When you have finished weaving it, go to the river. When you arrive set your trap in the river. Then you will kill a barbel. When you have killed it, bring it to the village. Then look for a large water-jar, put it in and cover it up. When you uncover it you will find it has become a human being, and so you will get a husband." The woman went off to catch a barbel. When she saw that the people had gone out of the village she went to uncover the pot, and looking into it saw that the barbel had become a man. Said he: "Do not cook me; I am a man. And as you have no husband, marry me. And as for my food, I do not eat grain, I eat baboon's fruit. If you eat it also I shall go back to the water and you won't see me again." The woman agreed ; after a time she stole some of his fruit. When the man returned he examined his food and said : " My fruit is not all here. The woman has stolen some." Then he grew angry, saying : " As you have taken my food, I am going back into the water." Now next morning the woman took her hoe and left her husband in the village. When the woman came back from hoeing, on her arrival she uncovered the pot where her husband lived, and found that he had gone out of the pot. He said : " I am going back to my home as you ate my food." The woman said : " We will go together." When they arrived at the water the man went in. Said he : " I am going back. You, oh woman, will find other men." So he went alone into the water to his home. The woman watched and watched, but she never saw him again.

PART IV

TALES OF PEOPLE—MOSTLY FOOLS

1. *The Little Old Woman who changed into a Maiden*

THERE was a little old woman who lived away among the fields. Long ago when the people had cattle they sent their children, saying : " Take the cattle into the plain, let them graze, and build yourselves a house." So they built a village.

The people at that cattle-post were in the act of playing when that little old woman entered the house and stole out of Mbwalu's churn. Then when the cattle-post men returned and came to look about they found there that little old woman. In her malice that little old woman, after stealing out of the churn, put into it a whole lot of fleas. When they arrived the cattle-post men said : " Who has done this ? " Others said : " It's yon little old woman." When the little old woman heard that she came back, and on arrival said : " Mbwalu has married me." Mbwalu said : " I am still a youngster, I cannot marry." But the little old woman stuck to it, saying : " You have married me." Then Mbwalu said : " No, I will not marry you because you purposely stole out of my churn." Wherever Mbwalu sat the little old woman followed him, saying : " You have married me." Then his comrades laughed at Mbwalu, saying : " You fool ! If you cry about it, shall we not kill the little old woman ? " Then they went off to the fields, to the elders their fathers. And the same little old woman went also to the village. They inquired : " What is the matter ? " Mbwalu answered, saying : " I shall kill that little old woman who sticks to me." So when the sun went down, Mbwalu went into one of the huts and the little old woman followed him. Next day the elders said : " Just marry the little old woman as she keeps on at it." So afterwards Mbwalu consented, and he went off crying into one of the huts. At night, when it was about to dawn, she that had been a little old woman was found to have changed into a pretty maiden. And after it dawned all the village came in some alarm, saying : " Is not that the little old woman who cried after you ? " Mbwalu answered, saying : " It is she." His comrades were confounded then who had laughed at Mbwalu, saying : " You have married a little old woman."

2. *The Little Old Woman who killed a Child*

There was a little old woman who nursed a child. When the mother got up early to go to hoe, that little old woman said : " Bring your child and I will nurse it for you." The woman answered : " Take it and nurse it for me so that I can hoe easily." When the woman left off work, she called the little old woman, saying : " Little old woman, my child ! " The woman came quickly and said to the mother : " To-morrow you can bring your child again and I will nurse it for you."

The woman went back to her home and slept. Next morning she rose early and on arrival called : " Little old woman ! " The little old woman answered : " Hallo ! " When she arrived she gave her the child. On arrival at her village the little old woman passed through to where the melons were—she went to get a melon. After getting the melon, she throttled the child, killed it, and having killed it put it into a pot. The arms of the child, which she had cut off, she attached to the melon, and she also fastened on the head to the melon.

When the mother left off work she called, saying : " Little old woman ! " Said she " Hallo ! Come here, here is your child." The child's mother declined, saying : " Bring me here my child, I want to go." The little old woman refused, saying : " Come here." So the mother went to the little old woman. On arrival there she said : " Now sit down in there." Then the little old woman took a basin and went to dish up ; she put a leg into the dish and took it to the mother. The woman took and ate, and asked : " This meat, what is it ? " The little old woman answered : " It is young wart-hog. My husband killed it." Then she went back and fetched another leg. The mother did not refuse, but ate. When she had finished eating, she said : " Now bring my child, and let us go." Then the little old woman said : " Turn round, so that I can give you the child on your back." When the little old woman was putting it on the mother's back, the mother saw the melon fall down. The woman cried and said : " Little old woman, you have killed my child." Then the little old woman answered : " You ate my meat, we both ate it."

Then the woman went off weeping to the village. On her arrival at the village the people laughed at her, saying : " You are a fool to go and give your child to a little old woman, and now you see she has eaten your child." Then they began to weep.

3. *The Foolish Woman who killed her Child*

A foolish woman bore a child, and after birth the child was always crying and crying, and then the woman said : " What's the matter with this child of mine ? " The elder women told her : " That's how children cry." Now she, in the darkness of the night, wrung the child's neck, and said : " I have taken the thing out of my child's head that always made it cry." The elders asked her : " In taking it out what did you do to the child ? " She said : " It is sleeping," whereas really it was dead.

Next day her child was partly rotten, and the elders asked,

saying : " To-day your child that is not seen, where has it
gone to ? " The woman answered : " It's in the house,
asleep." The elders said : " Let us go and see it." That
was an exceedingly foolish woman. As soon as they arrived
she lifted the blanket from its face and said : " Here it is,
it's asleep." Then when the elders entered and came to
take the child, they said : " You are a fool ; you say your
child is asleep, don't you see that it is rotten-dead ? You
talk like that, but you killed it long ago." Thereupon the
woman went out of the house swiftly and threw herself
on the ground with grief. They said : " What do you
throw yourself down for ? Didn't you yourself kill your
child ? And now to-day you howl ! " Then they said :
" That girl is really a big fool ! "

4. *The Fool that hunted for his Axe*

He put his axe on his shoulder. Nevertheless when he
thought of his axe, he began to search for it ; beginning
early in the morning he sought it. One day went by, and
then his thoughts told him : " My axe is lost." He went
seeking it everywhere where he had been walking about.
All the time the axe was on his shoulder. When the people
saw him they said : " What is that person looking for ? "
He could not ask he was so busy searching. Next day one
asked him : " What are you looking for ? Yonder where
we were gathering fruit we saw you looking about."

Then he said : " I am in great trouble." One answered :
" What's troubling you ? " Said he : " My axe is lost."
One said : " Have you two axes ? " He said : " No, only
one." Then they said : " What about the one on your
shoulder, whose is that ? " He was greatly astonished
and said : " I *am* a fool."

And to this day it is put on record. When a person
looks for a thing he has got, they say : " You are like yon
man who looked for the axe that was on his shoulder."

5. *The Fool who chopped himself*

Some men went hunting. While they were going about
hunting the sun went down, and when it set they said :

" Let us build a shelter." So they built a shelter, and having done so went to gather firewood. When it was dark they went to sleep. As they were sleeping, in the night one man got up and made a fire. When he had done making the fire, he went back to sleep. Another was lying asleep on his back with his knees sticking up in the air ; he slept very soundly. After a time he woke up, and when he looked he saw his knees and was very much alarmed. Said he : " Oh dear ! oh dear ! that lion is going to bite me ! " Presently his thoughts said : " Take your axe, which you put near your head, and wound that lion before it bites you." So he reached out his hand towards the axe very carefully, on feeling about he found the axe, and then taking it in both hands he brought it down with all his force and chopped into his knee, and split it all to pieces. Then he set up a loud yell. One of his companions got up and asked him : " What's bitten you ? " He was astounded to see the axe fixed in his knee and he asked : " What have you done ? " Said he : " My thoughts are of foolishness. I saw the knee sticking up and I thought it was a lion, and now I have killed myself."

And to this day if a man hurts himself or wounds himself with an axe or a spear, they say : " In your foolishness you are like yon man who wounded himself with an axe in the knee."

6. *The Fool who lay down and slept in the Road*

A traveller was passing to another district. When he reached a certain village he inquired, saying : " Where does this road lead to ? " They answered : " It goes there to the village." " Is it there where my relations come from ? " The others answered : " Yes." " And is the road one only ? " They said : " No, there are two. You will go along some way, and when you reach the dividing of the road, take the one to the left ; turn aside, and take that one."

He went on and when he arrived at the dividing of the roads, he lay down and slept. As he was sleeping and sleeping, next day some people passed by and found him asleep, and they said : " Is this man dead or alive, or what's

the matter with him ? " Then they roused him and found
that on one side of him the termites had been building.
They asked him : " Why do you sleep in the road ? "
Said he : " I slept because they said : when you get to the
dividing of the road, take the one to the left, lie down, and
leave the one to the right." Then those wise people asked
him : " Which is the right and which is the left ? " He
answered, saying : " I do not know the roads." Then
they told him : " This is the one to the right and this the
one to the left." Then they said : " Come on, let us go."

When they reached the village, to the people, they said
to them : " This fool of a man whom you told the road,
when he got to the dividing of the roads lay down to sleep
as you said to him, when you reach the dividing of the
roads turn aside." Now to this day they do not forget
that man. Youngsters and children and adults say : " That
man was a fool." His fame went abroad in all the land :
" That person was truly a fool. A fool who was told, ' When
you reach the dividing of the roads turn aside (*pinuka*)
and take the left,' and when he reached there he lay down
(*pinuka*) and slept until the termites built on him. Foolishness indeed ! "

7. *The Fools who started Mourning when promised some Milk with their Bread*

On earth many, in the sky one only. Some men went to
visit. On their arrival the people cooked bread for them.
When they had done cooking the men ate, dipping it into
gravy ; and their host said : " Eat, travellers. When
you have done eating this you shall eat with milk." The
travellers ate, and when they had eaten they took their
spears and began to mourn by running up and down.
The people were astonished, and said : " What are these
travellers mourning for ? " So they called them and
asked : " What are you mourning for ? " They said :
" We are mourning because you said, when you have done
eating you will mourn." Then all were astonished and
said : " We said that when you have finished eating the
sop you can eat with milk. To eat with milk (*kandila*) is

not to mourn (*kudila*). We said we would give you milk in which to dip your bread."

NOTE : This tale, like the last, is founded on the likeness of words. They were told *mukandile,* " you will eat with milk," and they misunderstood it for *mukadile,* " you will mourn."

There are Italian tales with similar motives. A man, for example, tells his wife to prepare dinner for a friend and to be sure to have *broccoli strascinati* and *uovi spersi* as they are his favourite dishes. *Strascinare* is to drag anything along, but is technically used of broccoli chopped up and fried—the common Roman dish. *Spergere* is to scatter, but the word is used of eggs poached in broth, a favourite delicacy. The woman, taking the words literally, drags the broccoli all over the house and yard, and scatters the eggs all about the place instead of poaching them (*Roman Folklore,* pp. 366 sq.).

8. *The Fools who waited for Ground-nuts to fall from a Tree*

Two people were travelling, and midway along the road they found some nut-shells under a tree, and they sat down and watched, saying : " The nuts that were in these shells fell out of this tree." So they were sitting until the nuts should fall from the tree. After many days they were still sitting. Then some other people came along and said : " What are you doing here under the tree ? " " We are waiting for the ground-nuts to fall." Then they laughed at them and said : " You are fools. These are only shells left by people who ate the nuts." They laughed very much at them.

And to this day they are a byword. When a person does a thing that is not right they liken him to those people who watched for shells. They say to him : " You are like yon people who when they found shells under the tree waited for nuts to fall out of the tree." To this day it is a well-known thing which does not come to an end.

9. *How Two Men had a Dispute*

Two men started off, one with a dog and the other with a pot. When they got into the veld he who had the dog killed an animal. He with the pot said : " Let us cook and eat." When they had done cooking they ate. Then the dog got into the pot to lick it out, and when he wanted to withdraw his head he stuck fast. The owner of the pot said : " Friend, my pot will be broken. Your dog is stuck fast in my pot. Come and take him out." The owner of the dog said : " I cannot manage the dog." " Well, as you cannot manage the dog, let us cut off his head so that it may come out of the pot." Said he : " You, my friend, which is more valuable, the dog or the pot ? " Said he in answer : " My pot is the more valuable." Said he : " All right, cut away." So the owner of the pot took an axe and cut the dog's head off. When he had cut off his head, he took his pot and found it was not broken, so he brought water and washed out the blood. When he had done washing it, he brought some string, tied it, put it on his shoulder, and went off to the village. And the owner of the dog went also to the village.

When he arrived at the village, the owner of the dog found his child sick, and he thought : " Yon person who has the pot, his child took my brass bracelet." So he ran quickly and went where he was. On arrival he said : " My friend, give me my bracelet." They called the girl, but the bracelet refused to come off her arm, for it had been put on long ago while she was yet a child, and now she was grown into a maiden. Said he : " As it refuses to come off let us cut off the hand." Said he : " My friend, don't cut off the hand, let us rather give you another bracelet." That man said : " I don't want another, this is my bracelet." " Which is of more consequence, the bracelet or the hand of the child ? " That man refused, saying : " As for me it is my bracelet that I want." So the father of the child said : " Take an axe and cut off the hand." He cut it off and the bracelet came away. He took his bracelet, saying : " This is the hand of your child, join it up, and let us see how you will join it. You cut my dog's head off." He took the bracelet and went to divine for his child who was sick. When he reached the diviner, the oracle said : " Dig up some medicine and your child will recover." He came back and dug the medicine, gave it to her, and she recovered.

10. *The Scold who split her Mouth*

There was once a woman named Mukamunkomba and she was a scold, always finding fault with everybody. In particular she would never allow people to talk, but always stopped them. She was always the same, railing and nagging. Now in those old days she was nursing two of her daughter's children: they were young and were always disputing with each other, as is the way of children. The old woman so surpassed herself in nagging those children, her own grandchildren, that her mouth split. And so they have put her on record as a warning, and when they hear any one nagging they say: " Beware, you will split at the mouth as old Mukamunkomba did with her railing. If you have to find fault with any one, do it once only ; don't keep on at it."

11. *The Man and the Mushrooms*

There was once a great famine in the land and many people were dying with hunger. A certain woman found some mushrooms and filled her pot with them and water. The husband was looking on and noticed that the pot was quite full when it was put on the fire to boil. He went out, and on his return shortly after the woman took the pot off the fire and set it between his legs. Now the man said : " The pot is not full. Where are the rest ? " So he began to hint that she had helped herself to them in his absence. " I saw the pot full," said he, " now it is half empty." The woman said : " But, my husband, don't mushrooms shrink when cooked ? " But he wouldn't have it. " You're lying," he said. " Well," she went on, " if they haven't shrunk, where are they ? " " You have eaten them," said he. His wife replied : " No, my husband, I couldn't eat the food in your absence." But the man got very angry and said to her : " You are a bad woman. You stole the mushrooms while I was away." The woman denied, saying : " I did not steal. They shrank in the boiling," but he took a stick and beat her to death. Then he told the people that his wife had died of starvation. As he had no other wife, he had to fend for himself. One day he brought home some mushrooms and filled that same pot his dead wife had used. He sat there and watched it boil, and when he took it off the fire saw that the mushrooms had so shrunk that there was hardly anything left at the bottom of the pot—that pot which had been full to overflowing. The man was greatly startled. He began to tremble and cry: " Oh dear! oh dear! This pot which I filled with mushrooms and now they have shrunk away! I killed my wife without reason. She did not steal; the mushrooms did shrink as she said. Dear! oh dear! I am the child of a foreigner! "

Since that day they have put him on record as an example. Do not be in a hurry to accuse people of stealing.

12. *The Bogle and his Child*

(Told to frighten children.)

There was once a bogle named Shezhimwe who married a woman, and in course of time a baby was born to them. All the neighbours rejoiced with them, and the child flourished and grew big. Before it was weaned the mother left it one day in charge of Shezhimwe while she went to work in the field, and the bogle, when he found himself alone with his child and the mother far away, ate the child and made tracks. The mother left off work later in the day and returning home sought her child, and sought in vain. While she was wondering what had become of it, her husband, the bogle, suddenly reappeared, and she said to him: " Shezhimwe, bring the child for its food." The bogle began to be astonished, clapped his hands in amazement, and said: " What child do you mean? " The woman replied: " Why, to be sure, the same child I left with you when I went to work this morning." Said the bogle: " I laid him down on the bed. I wonder who could have eaten him? " They hunted all about, but no child could be found. They gave up the search at last and the mother had to reconcile herself to the fact that her child was lost. Some time later another child was born in that house, and all Mrs. Shezhimwe's friends rejoiced with her again.

But not many days after, while the woman was gone to the other side of the village, Shezhimwe, in whose charge she left the child, ate it in a moment and went out. Presently she came back, and not seeing her husband, called him loudly : " Shezhimwe ! Shezhimwe ! Bring the child to drink." The bogle made no reply, but soon came in as if nothing had happened, and said to her : " Was it you calling ? " " Yes," she answered, " bring the child I left with you, it's time for it to drink." Said Shezhimwe : " Why, I left the child only a moment ago, where can it have gone ? " Then the woman lost her temper and cried out : " No, that won't do. Just you produce my child. I would like to know how the children get lost that are left in your hands." Shezhimwe had no excuse to make ; he remained silent. They wept for the child, and afterwards the woman went to her own home and told her parents all about it. They comforted her and said : " Go back to your husband. The child will return to you : and when it is to be born come home here." So the woman went back to her husband the bogle. Later on, she made her escape and went home again. Shezhimwe, seeing that she had gone, followed her. They saluted him politely did his wife's people, and cooked food for him. When he had finished eating they seized and killed him. After killing him they·burnt him in the fire, and out of the fire there came a great whirlwind. That was really a bogle—and he is still alive and on the look-out for naughty children.

13. *Tale of an Expectant Mother's Fancies*

(Told as a warning to such women.)

There was once a woman in the family way who would not eat porridge and refused all food offered to her. One day she called her husband. " Yes, wife," said he, " what do you want ? " " I want some bird's eggs ; all this bread and other food I can't eat." The husband answered : " Very well, my wife, but to get eggs is not easy. Where can I get bird's eggs ? " Said she : " Go and hunt in the birds' nests and find some." So the husband consented to go searching for eggs, and came back with some, which the

woman ate—all of them. Next day the man and his son
went out again ; they saw two birds and a nest in a tree
and the man climbed up and got the eggs. Now in that
tree there was a snake, and though the man did not see it
the boy who was on the ground did, and seeing it called
out, " Father, there is a snake there, look out." The man
in his fright fell—and with him the basket of eggs, which,
fortunately, did not break. They returned home, and the
woman received the eggs and said " Thank you." The boy
said : " Mother ! "   " Well, child, what do you say ? "
" I say, do not eat all these eggs at once. It is a great
trouble to go climbing trees, and besides there are snakes.
Father was nearly bitten to-day." But the woman cooked
and ate all the eggs that evening, and in the morning
clamoured for more. So the husband went out again, this
time alone, for the boy stayed at home. After searching
for some time he found a nest with eggs in it, and climbing
the tree put them in his basket.   But hidden in a hole in that
tree was a *mulala* snake, and just as the man was descending
it bit him. The man fell and died in a few minutes.   It
was away in the forest and there was nobody to take the
news. After sunset when he did not come, the boy grew
anxious and said to his mother : " Mother, I believe father
is dead."   Then the woman began to recall her son's warning not to eat all the eggs at once, because of the trouble and
danger involved in getting them. In the morning they
went out to search and found him at the foot of the tree.
He was stone dead and stank horribly already. The woman
bereft of her husband died also.

14. *A Man and his Mother*

A man and his mother were once in great difficulty for
food, and were reduced to going about from village to
village begging. After a time they went to live on an
island in the river and there they were still worse off. They
did not know how to find food. At last the woman said to
her son : " Go and wander about among the villages, and
when you find an ox bring it here." The man went off,
and finding some cattle grazing he drove off one and brought

it to the river. Now the old woman had medicine, and when the man reached the river he called to her, saying: " Mother, strike the water ! " The mother took her medicine root and with it smote the water so that the man and ox passed over dry-shod and then the river flowed on. The man killed the ox, cut it up, and giving his mother a bit of a bone ate the rest with his wife. The mother made no fuss, but kept quiet. When the meat was finished he went to another place and stole an ox, but the herdsmen saw him and gave chase. He reached the river first with the ox and called to his mother as before : " Mother, strike the water ! " The woman smote the water ; the river divided allowing them to pass, and then joined up again. Once again the man killed and cut up the ox and threw his mother a bone. Now she said to him : " My son, you bring home an ox and eat all the meat with your wife and to me you give only a bone. I your mother see your doings ! " The man got angry and said to her : " That's the way with you old women, you are never grateful for what you are given." His mother said no more. Not long after the man went off to a place some distance away, where the news of his thievery had not reached, and there he found many cattle. He drove off two. The people saw him, raised an alarm, and chased him to the river. There he called his mother as before : " Mother, strike the river ! " But his mother answered : " I will not strike it because you wouldn't give me any meat." And the villagers coming up killed him.

15. *The Child who wanted to sleep in the Middle*

(Told to warn men against ignorant children.)

A man took his child with him hunting in the veld. There the boy set four traps by the side of a pool while his father looked for game. They were by themselves—those two, no third. The boy presently caught a guinea-fowl in one of his traps and went off to the shelter he and his father had built in the veld. He found there his father, who had returned unsuccessful, and was therefore glad to see the guinea-fowl brought by his son. The boy said : " Father ! "

The man replied : " What do you say, namesake of my father ? " " I say, cook this guinea-fowl and eat it alone ; I won't eat it, no, no. And to-night when we sleep put me in the middle." The father answered nothing : he thought the boy was only playing by talking about being put in the middle. When the fowl was cooked the man called the boy and said : " Namesake of my father, come and let us eat the guinea-fowl you killed, it's already cooked." But the boy said : " Eat it alone, father, as I told you before. But when we sleep put me in the middle, because I do not wish to sleep on the outside for fear of being bitten by some wild beast in the night." So the father ate the guinea-fowl by himself. Presently the boy said : " Father, have you done eating ? " " Yes, namesake of my father, I have done." Said the child : " As you have done eating, let us sleep." The father replied : " Right, namesake of my father, let us sleep." They went into the shelter and the man lay down first. Then his child asked him : " Where am I to lie, Dad ? " " Wherever you please, namesake of my father." " Where I like," said the child, " is in the middle." " How can I put you in the middle ? " replied the man, " I am only one person." But the child began to cry, sitting on the ground. Presently his father got up and tied a bundle of grass and laid it on one side of the bed, then took hold of the child's hand and said : " Come sleep here in the middle as you wished." The child lay down, but as he was falling asleep he touched the thing by his side and found it was not a person but only grass. He got up and began to cry. His father was fast asleep. Then the boy took his father's spear—it was an *iyonga*, with a blade, broad and long and sharp—a spear that a man takes to tackle a wart-hog. He sharpened it on a stone and then lifting it in two hands he brought the point down with all his strength upon his father's stomach, cutting him open. He did not think of his father dying, but he died. And the child died too : he died of fright.

Sed nos immensum spatiis confecimus aequor,
Et iam tempus equum fumantia solvere colla.

INDEX

Names of chiefs, i. 57 *sq.*
Foods and drinks, i. 149 *sqq.*
Parts of human body, i. 222 *sq.*
Diseases and remedies, i. 232 *sqq.*, 275 *sqq.*

Clans, etc., i. 310 *sqq.*
Communities, i. 313 *sqq.*
Tables of relationship, i. 323 *sqq.*
Games, ii. 246 *sqq.*

INDEX

423

Excrement, as medicine, i. 232, 240, 242 ; causes disease, i. 240 ; throwing a person upon, i. 371
Exposure of person, i. 82 ; deliberate, i. 416
Expression of emotions, i. 83
Expressions, rude, i. 377 *sq.*
Eyes, pupils of, i. 224 ; colour of, i. 60 ; hiding "life" in, i. 256
Eyesight, i. 89 *sq.* ; ideas of, i. 224

Faeces, an offence to mention, in mixed company, i. 377
False accusations and witness, i. 371
Family, i. 283 *sqq.*
Fashions, i. 102 *sq.*
Fatalism, ii. 62, 202, 322
Fauna, i. 11 *sq.*
Feathers, significance of, i. 104 *sqq.*
Fees, doctor's, i. 256, 275 ; diviner's, i. 266
Festivals, Feasts, annual (i-kubi, ma-), ii. 189, 193 ; funeral (i-dilwe, ma-), ii. 106, 174 *sq.* ; cattle, i. 131 *sq.* ; initiation, ii. 20, 25
Feticide, i. 418
Fibres, i. 184 *sqq.*
Fillet (mu-shini, mi-), worn by women, i. 101
Fines inflicted, i. 359
Fire, in cattle kraal, i. 129 ; made by friction, i. 142 *sq.*, ii. 30 ; how conveyed, i. 143 ; taboos, i. 142 *sq.*, 210 ; new, i. 235, ii. 27, 60, 62 ; funeral, ii. 96 *sq.*
Fireflies, ii. 226
Firstfruits, i. 139 *sq.*
Fish, names of, i. 151, 160 ; abundance of, i. 144, 159 *sq.* ; how cooked, i. 147 ; traps for, i. 161 *sq.* ; nets, i. 163, 186 ; poisons, i. 166 ; spear, making of, i. 213 *sq.*
Fish-eagle, tales of, ii. 370, 391
Fish-hooks, i. 160
Fishing, methods of, i. 159 *sqq.* ; rites before, i. 388 *sq.*
Flies, ii. 225
Flying-people, ii. 230
Foetus, formation of, i. 227 ; buried, i. 234 ; disease and, i. 234 *sq.*
Folk-tales, ii. 334 *sqq.*
Fontanelle, non-closing of, i. 243 ; heart-beating at, i. 226 ; medicine applied to, ii. 11
Foods, formalities connected with, i. 364 ; staple, i. 144 ; preserved, i. 148 ; list of, i. 149 *sqq.*
Footsteps, to trace, i. 260
Fowls, domestic, i. 134
Frazer, Sir J., i. 291, 292 *n.*, ii. 100
Friendship, covenants of, i. 295, 308

Frogs, ii. 228
Fruits, names of, i. 150
Funeral, description of, ii. 104 *sqq.*, 114 ; feasts, ii. 110 *sq.* ; oxen killed at, i. 130 ; when corpse is not recovered, ii. 116 ; of suicides, ii. 116 ; of a stranger, ii. 116

Game pits, i. 157 *sq.*
Games, ii. 232 *sq.* ; indavu, ii. 21 *sq.* ; mantombwa, ii. 36 *sqq.* ; mimic fight, i. 172 *sq.*
Genitalia, names for, i. 223 ; seat of vitality, i. 226 ; diseases of, i. 238 ; when not spoken of, i. 377 ; named in songs, i. 208, ii. 113 ; distension and enlargement of, ii. 5, 17, 20, 30 ; admired, ii. 45
Genius (Guardian Spirit), i. 54, ii. 156 *sqq.*, 165
Gestation, period of, ii. 7
Ghosts (mu-sangushi, ba-), where they go, ii. 119 ; underground, ii. 110 *n.*, 119 ; near graves and in houses, ii. 120 *sqq.* ; near doorways, ii. 122 ; in the matongo, ii. 123, 186 ; enter living persons, ii. 136 ; doings of, ii. 122, 132 ; speak through mediums, ii. 140 *sq.* ; in divination, i. 270 *sq.* ; act as witch-familiars, ii. 91, 95, 132 ; act as guardians, i. 388 ; come in dreams, ii. 134 *sq.* ; reveal medicines, i. 230, 253 ; disease caused by, ii. 235, 244 *sq.*, ii. 27 ; visible to animals, ii. 122 ; attitude towards, ii. 167 *sqq.* ; offerings to, ii. 123 ; various kinds of, ii. 132 ; vengeful (mutalu), i. 264 ; harmful, ii. 115, 168 ; driven off, i. 179, ii. 163 ; medicine to stupefy, i. 264 ; of elephants, i. 168 ; tale of, ii. 133. *See* Divinities
Gibbon, quoted, i. 22
Gibbons, A. St. H., explorations of, i. 54 ; his opinion of the Ba-ila, i. 54, 361
Gielgud, Mr., i. 54
Gift, taken with both hands, i. 364
Gingivitis, i. 66 *sqq.*
Girdle, woman's, i. 101 ; cutting the, ii. 60, 62
Goats, i. 134
God. *See* Leza
Grain, kinds of, i. 139 *sq.*, 149 ; provenance of, i. 139
Grain-bins, i. 138 *sq.* ; the shumbwa, i. 121
Grandchildren, i. 320 *sq.*, 339, 342
Grandparents, i. 320 ; my power over their persons and property, i. 339
Grass-fires, annual, i. 4, 11
Gratitude, ii. 315

* These technical Ila terms are verbs in the infinitive mood ; they may be found in the text without *ku* or *kw.* the sign of that mood ; thus, *badikila, inda.*

Language, the Ila, ii. 277 *sqq.*; closest
affinities of, i. 18; words in, express-
ing approval and disapproval, i. 343
Lathe, for ivory-turning, i. 180 *sqq.*
Lechwe, vast herds of, i. 12; hunting,
i. 155; skins of, as dress, i. 98
Leech, ii. 224; in tale, ii. 363 *sq.*
Legend of the Banampongo, i. 20; of
the old woman who sought God, ii.
197
Leglets, i. 101 *sq.*
Leopard, tale of, ii. 369
Leprosy, i. 232; medicine for, i. 277
Leselo, i. 34 *n.*, 45 (photo)
Levellers, ii. 316
Lewanika (Lobosi), chief of Barotsi,
supports Nyambo, i. 24; birth, ac-
cession, policy, and death of, i. 41;
raids the Ba-ila, i. 42 *sqq.*; frees
slaves, i. 411; sees the Lengongole,
ii. 129
Leza (the Supreme Being), ii. 197 *sqq.*;
name, i. 18; customs established by,
i. 345; his family and "death," ii.
102; son of, ii. 144 *sqq.*; causes
disease, i. 232, 245; death ascribed
to, i. 268, 357; gives medicine for
propagating the race, i. 258, ii. 102;
clan named from, i. 311; angry, ii.
145; prayers addressed to, i. 162,
ii. 1; offerings made to, i. 168; named
in oaths, i. 355; in songs, ii. 273; in
proverbs, ii. 322; in riddles, ii. 325
sq., 329 *sq.*; in children's sayings, i.
242; in myths and folk-tales, ii. 102,
ii. 345, 347 *sqq.*, 391
Life (bumi), associated with genitals, i.
226; hidden away, i. 256
"Life-token," i. 255 *sqq.*
Lightning, ii. 204 *sq.*, 220; medicine to
ward off, i. 261
Lions, habits of, i. 12; cattle killed by,
i. 14, 129, 158; hunted by natives,
i. 14, 158; name of, i. 289; men
turn into, ii. 124 *sqq.*; tales of, ii.
378, 382 *sq.*, 385, 387 *sq.*, 394, 398,
400
Litigiousness of Ba-ila, i. 360
Livingstone, Dr., at Linyanti, i. 38; his
account of the Mambari, i. 39; his
map of the Zambesi, i. 47; his servant, Mukubu, i. 29; impression left
by, on native mind, i. 47; his teaching, ii. 146; cited, i. 28 *n.*, 33;
quoted, i. 38 *sq.*, ii. 357
Load-carrying, i. 87
Lobengula, chief of the Matabele, i. 46,
140
Locusts, i. 143 *sq.*, ii. 225
Longo (Shianamwenda), Basala chief-
tainess and prophetess, i. 29, ii. 142

Loss of property, i. 393
Love-philtres, i. 249 *sq.*
Lubambo, ii. 67 *sq.*
Lubanda, conflict at, i. 23
Lubeta, description and occasions of,
i. 351 *sq.*, 387
Lubwe, village at, i. 109 *sq.*; list of
chiefs at, i. 57
Luck, i. 252, 262 *sq.*, ii. 219
Lucky-hand (chesha), i. 139
Lukono, i. 303, 390, 392
Luloa (blood-offering), i. 411, 417, ii.
187, 192, 211 *sq.*
Lulonga, Holub at, i. 50, 52
Lunacy, i. 239
Lunda country, i. 25; Munyama came
from, i. 26 *n.*
Lusasa (or chibinde), ii. 61 *sq.*
Lushinga, i. 231
Lutango, Barotsi leader, i. 41
Luvhumwe, i. 243, ii. 11
Lwando, i. 161, 169
Lwanga (sacred forked pole, "village
altar"), ii. 156, 172, 177; cooking at,
i. 262
Lwanzu (or Chanzu), ii. 137
Lwembe (blood-money, weregild), for
homicide, i. 359, 417, ii. 72; for
feticide, i. 418 *sq.*; for burning village,
i. 404
Lying, characteristic of Ba-ila, i. 378 *sq.*

Mabamba, warrior's belt, i. 106
Mabwabwa, ii. 120 (photo)
Macgregor, J. C., cited, i. 28 *n.*
Madan, A. C., cited, ii. 292, 296, 367,
379, 388
Madyanshima, ii. 55
Mafwele, list of chiefs at, i. 58
"Magic," "Magical," i. 222, 255, 346;
effect of beans, i. 205; why the words
are not used in later chapters, ii. 80
Makobo, isle of, i. 8
Makololo (Sebitwane's people), attack
Batonga, i. 28; kill Sezongo, i. 35 *sq.*;
attack Chimbulamukoa, i. 40; raid
Ba-ila, i. 40; exterminated, i. 41
Mala, district of, i. 54; chiefs at, i. 57
Malaria, i. 11, 234
Malumbe, a demigod, i. 57, ii. 182
Malweza, definition of, i. 347; instances
of, i. 420, 423, ii. 86 *sq.*
Mambari, slave traders, among the Ba-
ila, i. 36, 39; beads introduced by,
i. 106
Mampuba ("awe"), ii. 168
Manes' huts, i. 113. *See* Grave,
"temples"
Manimbwa, i. 36, 42
Mankoya, i. xxvii. 94; clans, i. 313
Mantembe, poisonous drink, i. 35

Mantimbwa, instrument, ii. 21 *sq.*, 262

Mantombwa, game of, ii. 36 *sqq.*

Marriage, discussed by clan, i. 297 ; ceremonies, ii. 54 *sqq.* ; of a widower and of a widow, ii. 60 *sq.* ; of chief's daughter and of a chief, ii. 63 ; of slave, i. 408 *sq.*, ii. 64 ; of widow to whom you have no right, i. 374 ; allowed between offspring of brother and sister respectively not between offspring of two sisters, i. 318 ; other restrictions, i. 293, ii. 41 ; happy, ii. 75 *n.* ; proverbs about, ii. 59, 320. *See* Sexual relations

Masamba, a charm, i. 261

Masansa, ii. 56, 58

Mashukulumbwe, name given by Barotsi to Ba-ila (= Bashikulompo), meaning of, i. xxv, 42

Mason-wasp, ii. 345 *sq.*

Massage, practised, i. 230 *sq.*

Masturbation, ii. 29, 74

Masunto, oxen killed at funeral, i. 130, ii. 110

Matabele, fight Sebitwane, i. 30 *sq.* ; massacred by Sezongo I., i. 35 ; raid the Ba-ila, i. 44 *sqq.* ; Ba-ila helpless against, i. 178

Matjokotjoko, Matabele name for Ba-ila, i. xxv

Matongo, deserted sites, ii. 123

Matushi, vilifications, i. 374 ; examples of, i. 375 *sq.*

Mbeza, Sebitwane at, i. 29 ; Barotsi defeated at, i. 44 ; Holub at, i. 50

Mbololo, last of Makololo chiefs, i. 41

Meal, how prepared, i. 146

Mealies (= maize), how grown, i. 137

Meals, times and description of, i. 145

Measles, i. 232

Meat, eaten, liking for, i. 144 *sq.* ; how cooked, i. 147

Medicine (mu-samo, mi-), meaning of word, i. 222 ; faith in, i. 228 *sq.*, 252 ; methods of administration, i. 230 *sq.* ; classification of, i. 229, 250 *sq.* ; lists of names of, i. 232 *sqq.*, 275 *sqq.* ; powers of, ii. 84 ; damage to another's, is buditazhi, i. 395 ; taboos attached to, i. 231, 255 ; curse attached to, i. 254 ; addressed, i. 249, 262, ii. 85, 93 ; offerings made to, i. 262 ; derived from trees, etc., i. 229 ; from skunk, ii. 360 ; from frogs, ii. 228 ; from excrement, i. 232, 240, 242 ; used in smelting iron, i. 203 *sq.*, 209, 278 ; in hunting, i. 167 *sq.*, 260, 262, 277 *sq.* ; in fishing, i. 161, 169, 279 ; in blacksmithing, i. 219 *sq.*, 278 ; in making butter, i. 277 ; in turning

ivory, i. 182 ; in agriculture, i. 277 ; in divination, i. 266, 269 *sq.* ; in initiation, ii. 21, 30 ; in rain-making, ii. 209 ; in war, i. 178 *sq.*, 263, 278 *sq.* ; for protecting and increasing cattle, i. 129, 253 ; for propagating the species (luzhalo), i. 258, ii. 102 ; for impotence, i. 227, 277 ; love-philtres, i. 249 *sq.* ; to induce conception, i. 228, 276, 280, ii. 2 ; to induce abortion, i. 250, 419 ; after abortion, ii. 6 ; for overdue menstruation, i. 277 ; for midwifery, i. 277 ; given to pregnant woman and husband, ii. 2, 5 ; during parturition, i. 277, ii. 7, 8 ; given to new-born child, ii. 10 *sq.* ; for bewitching, ii. 95 ; for avoiding and curing witchcraft, i. 253, 259 *sq.*, 275, 277 *sqq.*, 300 ; for general well-being, i. 259 ; good luck, i. 261, 263 ; insambwe, i. 395 ; for wealth, i. 381 ; for making rich and famous, i. 263 ; for use in court, i. 264 ; to soften and defend from enemies, i. 259 *sq.* ; to obviate result of ordeal, i. 356 ; poured into images, ii. 169 ; for rebellion, i. 263 ; to cause unhappiness, i. 264 ; to keep away thieves, i. 277 ; for snake-bites, i. 245 *sq.* ; for purification, i. 169 ; for hardening one's heart, i. 259 ; against lightning, i. 261 ; for protecting chief, i. 300 *sq.*, 307 ; for ensuring prosperity and popularity, i. 253, 260 *sq.* ; for protecting village, i. 301, ii. 178 ; for defending commune, i. 178, 254 ; for long life, i. 259 ; for hiding the "life," i. 256 ; for kulumbuzha, i. 257 ; for feeding on life-substance of others, i. 258 ; to draw life from trees, i. 258 ; for seeing ghost, ii. 122 ; for purging ghost, ii. 168 *sq.* ; for stupefying ghost, i. 264 ; for keeping off, driving off ghost, i. 179, ii. 168 ; for transforming dead into animals, etc., i. 264, 381, ii. 125, 130 ; for wiping out family, i. 264 ; for sudden death, i. 265 ; for resuscitation, i. 265, ii. 103 (lwende) ; for seeing itoshi, ii. 129 ; references to, in folk-tales, ii. 416

Mediums, ii. 140, 150, 188, 194. *See* Prophets

Meinhof, cited, ii. 282, 284, 286, 288

Menstruating women, taboo, i. 207 ; clouts of, used as remedy, i. 239 ; not to approach gun in house, i. 262 ; warnings against, i. 262 *sq.* ; drive away tsetse, ii. 27

Menstruation, medicine for overdue, i. 277 ; taboos, ii. 21, 26 *sq.*

Metals, ii. 222

THE END